In Reunion

SARA DOCAN-MORGAN

IN REUNION

*Transnational Korean Adoptees and the
Communication of Family*

TEMPLE UNIVERSITY PRESS
Philadelphia   •   Rome   •   Tokyo

TEMPLE UNIVERSITY PRESS
Philadelphia, Pennsylvania 19122
tupress.temple.edu

Library of Congress Cataloging-in-Publication Data

Names: Docan-Morgan, Sara Jane, author.
Title: In reunion : transnational Korean adoptees and the communication of
family / Sara Docan-Morgan.
Description: Philadelphia : Temple University Press, 2024. | Includes
bibliographical references and index. | Summary: "Over 200,000
transnational Korean adoptees live throughout the world today, and many
have searched for, and reunited with, birth family members. In this
book, Sara Docan-Morgan examines how Korean adoptees from the USA and
Denmark navigate reunions with their Korean birth families and attempt
to maintain these relationships over time"— Provided by publisher.
Identifiers: LCCN 2023013074 (print) | LCCN 2023013075 (ebook) | ISBN
9781439922828 (cloth) | ISBN 9781439922835 (paperback) | ISBN
9781439922842 (pdf)
Subjects: LCSH: Adoptees—Family relationships—Korea (South) |
Adoptees—Family relationships—Denmark. | Adoptees—Family
relationships—United States. | Family reunification—Korea
(South)—Psychological aspects. | Communication in families—Korea
(South) | Intercountry adoption—Korea (South) | Intercountry
adoption—Denmark. | Intercountry adoption—United States. | Interracial
adoption—Korea (South) | Interracial adoption—Denmark. | Interracial
adoption—United States. | Birthparents—Korea (South)—Identification.
Classification: LCC HV875.58.K6 D633 2024 (print) | LCC HV875.58.K6
(ebook) | DDC 362.734089/957—dc23/eng/20230907
LC record available at https://lccn.loc.gov/2023013074
LC ebook record available at https://lccn.loc.gov/2023013075

To Mom and Dad

And

사랑하는 나의 가족에게,
나를 잊지 않고 찾아 주셔서 고맙습니다.
있는 그대로의 나를 맞아준 가족을 항상 그리워
하며 가족의 모든 길을 응원하며 함께합니다.

Contents

Acknowledgments

I owe deep, heartfelt thanks to the adoptees whose reunion stories are featured in this book. Thank you for your trust, vulnerability, and insights. You taught me so much, as well as inspired me each time I sat down to write.

Thank you to Shaun Vigil and the team at Temple University Press for supporting this project from the beginning and offering encouragement and guidance at each step of the process.

I am honored to have artwork by Leah Nichols featured on my book cover. Thank you, Leah, for taking on this project and for using your talent to communicate the complexities and beauty of reunion.

I am grateful for the support of my department chair and friend, Dr. Linda Dickmeyer, and my colleagues in Communication Studies at the University of Wisconsin, La Crosse (UW-L). The College of Arts, Social Sciences, and Humanities at UW-L, and the University of Wisconsin System's Institute on Race and Ethnicity provided vital grants to support this work.

The late Dr. Kathleen Galvin provided mentorship during the early stages of this project, and her work ethic and kindness continue to influence me. Thanks also to Dr. Elizabeth Suter for her valuable contributions to critical family communication studies and to the study of adoption within the field of communication.

This book would not have been possible without the foundation laid by the Korean adoption scholars and activists cited throughout this book. I'm particularly thankful to have had the opportunity to work alongside fellow Korean adoptees and adoption scholars Elizabeth Raleigh and Kimberly McKee in helping to plan the International Symposium on Korean Adoption Studies in 2016, 2019, and 2023. I have sincere respect for Kim Park Nelson for being a pioneer in Korean adoption studies and for her vital role in establishing the Symposium. Special thanks to Nicole Sheppard, LPCC, for sharing her expertise and providing valuable feedback on the mental health recommendations in Chapter 7.

Throughout my undergraduate and graduate education, I had professors who challenged me while helping me to develop my strengths. They helped me to interrogate the present and the past and encouraged me to look both inward and outward. Thank you to Drs. Dale Gauthreaux, the late Glenda Sehested, Sandra Looney, Chris Segrin, Gerry Philipsen, and Ralina Joseph. Extra thanks to Dr. Valerie Manusov, my doctoral advisor, who encouraged and guided my adoption research from the beginning and whose compassion and graciousness never wavered.

Over the years, several trusted friends have helped me communicate with my Korean family. Sujin Son has met them on multiple occasions and translated countless (often long!) emails, both ways. I have valued her personal and scholarly investment in reunion, along with her endless kindness and insight, more than words can convey. Sincerest thanks also go to Mirim Kim, Soojin Yoo, and Jane Park. Their help has allowed me to build and maintain some of the most valued connections in my life.

During my time in La Crosse, I have been lucky to meet extraordinary people whose friendship helped sustain me through writing this book, whether we were going for walks, sharing a meal, texting, or grabbing coffee. I am forever grateful for Amanda Goodenough, Christine Hippert, Mahruq Khan, Kristin Koepke, Uttara Manohar, Kathy and Marty Passe, Alessandro Quartiroli, Erica Srinivasan, Sheyda Babakhani Teimouri, Jodi Vandenberg-Daves, and Jörg Vianden. Pavak, Puja, Arya, and Adiya Mehta became our in-town family. The funny, smart, and resilient members of my book club remind me that we are all just "walking each other home."[1] In Seoul, the close friendships of Lili Kim and Mee Joo Kim were beautiful gifts, and I am thankful that our connections have endured.

Each day, I give thanks for a network of close, longtime friends whose encouragement, intelligence, love, and humor have carried me through some of life's darkest seasons and who always make good times great: Elena Jackson Albarrán, Jessica Harvey, Taylor Hatcher, Rachel Knight, and McHale Newport-Berra. An extra shout-out to Laura Springhetti, who always shows up for me, no matter the time or the continent.

Special thanks to Shelley Hawthorne Smith, my star, who carries all of my stories. Thank you for always asking about the book (and everything else) and for the times you told me to get off the phone with you and go write.

I am thankful to have in-laws whom I adore. Nick and Carol Docan and Nicole Fanelli have embraced me warmly from the first time we met and have always made me feel like family.

My sisters, Stacey Lang and Amy Van Den Einde, have cheered me on at every step of my journey, since childhood. They have been constant sources of strength and understanding during times of deepest loss. Knowing that they are always on my team has been one of my life's greatest gifts. I am thankful that my sisters married wonderful people—Kim Lang and Scott Van Den Einde—and had the most hilarious, loving children who are now some of my favorite adults—my nephews Cole and Landon Lang, and Jordan, Dylan, Brandon, and Ryan Van Den Einde.

To me, Tony Docan-Morgan is home. I would not have started down the path toward reunion were it not for his steadfast love and reassurance. His encouragement and faith in me help me to be brave. His love for the family we have built makes me love him even more.

William, Hope, and Abe, your love and laughter bring me joy and healing each day. I am beyond grateful that I get to be your mom.

In Reunion

Introduction

On a chilly fall evening in 2001, I received a message from my Korean birth family for the first time. The message was relayed through a friendly social worker in Minnesota and left on my home answering machine.

"Hi Sara, this is Lynn from Lutheran Social Services in Minneapolis. We have some information from your birth family. Please call me back at xxx-xxx-xxxx."

I replayed the message twice more but remained confused. I had never even considered searching for my birth family, much less taken any steps to do so. I had believed what my adoptive parents had told me, the same thing the adoption agency had told them: I was found on the doorstep of a police station in Seoul with my name and birthdate pinned on my clothing. My Korean parents were unknown.

I played the message again, this time writing down the name and phone number on a scrap of paper.

I picked up the phone and dialed.

An answering machine message lasting less than ten seconds was the pivot point between Before and After. Before, I didn't spend time thinking about my family in Korea. I had visited Korea for two weeks in 1999 on an adoptee tour, but because I had been told throughout my life that there was no way to find my birth parents, I never asked for more information. After, I knew that they were there, that they wanted to be in contact with me, and I couldn't unknow it. Yet I needed six years before I was ready to open the door to a relationship with them. I had spent nearly every moment of my life turning away from Korea, accepting the unknowability of my personal and family history. I was fearful of what lay beyond the life and family I knew.

Looking back, I regret having taken so long to meet my Korean family; at the same time, I understand that hearing from them left me unsettled to the core. The ground beneath me had felt solid up to that point. I knew whose daughter I was: Tom and Sharon Morgan's youngest daughter—the Korean adopted one. I knew whose sister I was: Stacey and Amy Morgan's little sister. The thought of another family, with different people whose faces and stories I didn't know but who wanted to connect with me, was terrifying. I felt frozen by uncertainty and shock and also confused beyond words: I had always been told that there were no records linking me to my Korean family. How could they reach through space and time to contact me on an ordinary Wednesday?

Just as significant were my concerns about my adoptive family. Even though I knew they would always love and support me, I feared that meeting my Korean family would hurt them. Reuniting would expose and call into question a fundamental, tacit belief, one that had been cultivated over the past two decades: My adoptive family *was* my real family.

Paradoxes of Family: Transnational Korean Adoptees in Reunion

This book focuses on the birth family reunions—both the initial meetings and ongoing relationships—of transnational Korean adoptees. For many years, South Korea was the go-to country for Western parents wanting to adopt internationally. Indeed, South Korea has been viewed as the template for other countries hoping to develop a transnational adoption infrastructure (McKee, 2016). Since the Korean Armistice Agreement in 1953, over two hundred thousand Korean infants and children have been sent overseas for adoption. The great majority of these Koreans were adopted into homes in the United States, yet other countries, particularly in Europe, also received thousands of Korean adoptees. Nearly all adoptive parents in these receiving countries were White, and the racial majority (both by number and power) in these countries was, and remains, White.

Judith Modell (1997) has pointed out that *reunion* can refer to either the initial meeting between individuals or the sustained contact that happens after this initial meeting and occurs over time. The first moments between adoptees and birth families are often depicted in dramatic television shows in both the United States and Korea and in online videos. Most of us can picture it: The long-lost child—now an adult—returns to the arms of their blood relatives, embraced and lost in a sea of happy tears. All questions are answered, and everyone's wounds are healed in that instant. The End.

But reunions are much more than these made-for-TV moments and are often a beginning rather than an end. In fact, when reunions refer to ongoing contact over the long term, they call into question the very basic notions of family, adoption, and parenthood for many White middle-class Americans, adoptive parents in particular. These assumptions are (1) that an adoptive family should approximate a biogenetically related, nuclear family as closely as possible by being composed of two married parents and their child(ren), (2) that a child can have only one set of parents, and (3) that birth parents should remain invisible and relegated to the past (Modell, 1997). Birth family reunions and relationships negate the premises on which the nuclear adoptive family unit was built.

However, even in the absence of reunion, adoptees tend to receive regular, unsolicited inquiries about their family status and membership from people outside the family. These questions often make implicit comparisons between the adoptive family and the birth family. One common question is "Do you know your real parents?" (Baden, 2016; Docan-Morgan, 2010), referring to one's biogenetic, or birth, parents. The implications, of course, are that one's adoptive parents are not one's "real" parents and that adoptees should find their birth parents. And yet adoptive parents are the ones with whom an adopted person shares what communication scholar Leslie Baxter (2004) calls *chronotopic similarity*, "the stockpile of shared time-space experiences that a pair constructs through their joint interaction events over time" (p. 4). This chronotopic similarity is created in both mundane, everyday interactions and in sharing more significant life events, cultivating a shared history between people. Regardless of how emotionally close they feel with one another, an adoptee and their adoptive parents share a relational history—formed through communication—that often creates and reflects a sense of family.

In contrast, an adoptee and their birth parents share a biogenetic bond, usually in the absence of a shared history of interacting, especially from the perspective of the adoptee and especially at the time of the initial meeting; exceptions include adoptees relinquished at a later age who have memories of their birth family. Yet there are often decades between relinquishment and reunion, which creates a void of daily interactions and familiarity between an adoptee and their birth family. Reunions, then, may cast light on the emotional ties and relational history between the adoptee and their adoptive family, which an adoptee often does not share with their birth family, especially during first meetings. These incongruencies can be profoundly unsettling.

The paradoxes of reunion and family—shared history without blood relations, and blood relations without shared history—are a rich context for exploring larger questions: What does it mean to be "family"? How do people use communication to constitute family relationships? How are family relationships created, maintained, and negotiated over time? These are the broad questions that frame this book.

For clarity, I will refer to the first time an adoptee and birth family meet as *initial meetings*, *first meetings*, or *initial interactions*. I will refer to adoptees who are in contact with their birth family, even if that contact is intermittent, as being *in reunion*. This language acknowledges that there is often more to a reunion than the first meeting, and there is typically no clear end point to these relationships. Initial meetings and ongoing relationships between adoptees and their birth families have been studied by researchers focused on domestic, or in-country, adoptions, but there is much less research on transnational adoptees' reunions, which are complicated by differences in culture and language.

When writing and speaking about adoption across national borders, I employ the term *transnational*, rather than the more widely circulated modifier *inter*national, borrowing from the work of anthropologist Toby Alice Volkman (2005) and other adoption scholars, who note that the phenomena of this practice involve "ongoing, crisscrossing flows in multiple directions, in space that is both real and virtual" (p. 2). Perhaps the term *international* was more apt when movement was unidirectional: When adoptive parents were not required to travel to the country of the child's birth, when it was assumed that adoptees would fully assimilate to the receiving country and not return to their birth country, and when information wasn't so quickly and easily exchanged across space and time. Now, as most adoptive parents are required to spend time in their child's birth country, as adoptees return to their country of birth to visit or live, and as media and correspondence flow back and forth within seconds, the people and information involved in these transactions are in constant movement, in many directions. The term *transnational*, then, seems particularly appropriate when talking about Korean adoptees in reunion, who often must travel back and forth between countries and who often exchange messages with family members across national borders, whether they are in Korea, their adoptive country, or elsewhere.

Adoptees and the Search for Identity

Adoptive Identity

The research on domestic adoptees provides an important foundation for understanding adoptee development and the reasons underlying adoptees' desire to search and reunite. As adoptees grow up, they develop what psychology professor Harold Grotevant and colleagues (2000) refer to as *adoptive identity*, a subjective sense of what it means to be adopted. Adoptive identity involves one's thoughts about their adoption, relationships with their family, and the social world beyond the family. Naturally, one's adoptive identity affects, and is affected by, communication within one's family, as well as other social interactions. An adoptive family's stories, discussions, names, and rituals (Galvin, 2003) all impact how an adoptee views their family and their place in the family. For some adoptees, adoptive identity is a salient part of their self-concept, whereas other adoptees may not consider being adopted as an important part of who they are. Of course, the salience of adoptive identity, as well as other identities such as gender, cultural, racial, ethnic, and so on, may fluctuate over an adoptee's life span and depend on context (Grotevant et al., 2000). For example, an adopted person may find themselves thinking about their adoption and birth family more than usual as they approach life milestones such as having a child, confronting an inherited illness, or on their birthday.

For many adoptees, part of forming an adoptive identity is thinking about their birth family. Psychology professor Gretchen Wrobel and colleagues (2013) found that most adoptees are curious about their birth family at some point in their lives. As adoptees think about their birth families, they might notice a disjuncture between their questions and the information they possess. This "information gap" (Wrobel et al., 2013) leads some adoptees to seek further information about their birth families and origins through asking questions of their adoptive family; reading their adoption file, if available; attempting to gather information about birth family members; and, for some, searching and reuniting. Naturally, some information may be easier or harder to obtain, depending on the nature of the adoption.

In seeking information about their adoption and birth family, adoptees are attempting to construct the story of who they are (McAdams, 2008). Upon adoption, adoptees lose their daily relationship with their birth families, much of their personal and family history, and the comfort of finding physical similarities between themselves and their family members. In addition to these losses, transnational adoptees lose the language and culture of their birth country and the experience of being the racial and ethnic majority in their communities. And although these losses may never be regained fully, some adoptees may seek to fill in gaps by traveling to their birth country, conducting a birth search, and/or, if possible and desired, reuniting.

However, some adoptees choose, for varying reasons, not to search and/or reunite, and this choice is equally valid. Eleana Kim (2010) pointed out a dramatic shift in adoption practice and discourse in the past three decades: Previously, adoptees who searched for birth family members were stigmatized as being maladjusted, but now, adoptees who choose *not* to search for their biological origins are often viewed as being in denial. The paradigm of secrecy and silence surrounding adoption, where adoptive parents tried to hide or minimize their child's adoption, has shifted toward genetic or biological essentialism, which presumes that an adoptee's identity will be incomplete without a search for their origins (Patton-Imani, 2000). Matching and closed adoptions deny adoptees access to their family and history, but assigning preeminence to biogenetic relations and idealizing reunion carries risk as well. Although research suggests that adoptees who have reunited tend to be glad that they met biological family members (Campbell et al., 1991), reunions do not necessarily lead to healing or closure. Instead, reunions most often involve a reappraisal of one's identity, an adjustment of expectations of one's birth parent, and a redefinition of family relationships (Modell, 1997). Thus, although this project focuses on transnational adoptees in reunion, adoptees' choice to not search and/or reunite must be respected and the tendency to idealize reunion should be avoided.

Cultural Identity

The nature of transnational Korean adoption has created what psychology professor Richard Lee (2003) calls the transracial adoption paradox: "Adoptees are racial/ethnic minorities in society, but they are perceived and treated by others, and sometimes themselves, as if they are members of the majority culture (i.e., racially White and ethnically European) due to adoption into a White family" (p. 711). Professor of intercultural studies and comparative literature Tobias Hübinette (2007) captured the process by which this paradox occurs, writing,

> We may believe in an innate, coherent, independent and stable identity, but in reality it is imposed on our bodies and incorporated in our minds, governed by cultural traditions and social conventions and maintained and reproduced by the help of constant reenactment, recitation, and the reiteration of performatives. (p. 141)

Taken together, Lee's and Hübinette's words (among others) suggest that, over time, adoptees develop the cultural identities of their adoptive family and the country of their adoption. A Korean adoptee raised in the United States may identify much more comfortably and closely with White middle-class Americans than with nonadopted Korean Americans or Korean nationals due to being steeped in White culture at both the familial and cultural levels. Indeed, research has found that, due to their White American upbringing, some Korean adoptees have reported feeling uncomfortable, inadequate, or inauthentic when interacting with Koreans in their adoptive country and in Korea (Palmer, 2010; Park Nelson, 2016). Naturally, reunion may cause a sense of cultural unfamiliarity and alienation.

The study of intercultural communication—interactions among people from different cultures—has its roots in research aiming to improve the communication competencies of American international diplomats and businesspeople (Leeds-Hurwitz, 1990), but comparatively little research has been published on intercultural communication among family members. Existing intercultural communication research on families tends to focus on communication between immigrant parents whose cultural identities differ from those of their children (e.g., Kim et al., 2015; Tannenbaum, 2005) and communication in marriages between partners from different cultures (e.g., Moriizumi, 2011). However, Korean adoptees and their birth families embody and enact different cultural identities and speak different languages. These differences exist within the most intimate of biogenetic relationships: Mother-child, father-child, and sibling-sibling (G.O.A.'L., 2008). Although transnational adoptees can access information online about the process of *searching* for their birth families, they often must rely on personal contacts with other adoptees to learn what happens once contact is made and how other transnational adoptees in reunion have explored cultural identity and navigated cultural differences over time. Therefore, this book examines the stories of transnational Korean adoptees who have reunited and been in contact with their birth families for ten years or more.

Barriers to Transnational Adoptee Reunions

Transnational adoptees may experience bigger or more daunting information gaps than domestic adoptees, particularly when it comes to birth family information. Historically, transnational adoptions have been closed, meaning that little, if any, birth family information is provided to adoptive parents at the time of adoption. When an infant or child is abandoned, information about the birth family may be virtually impossible to obtain. Other times, social service agencies, orphanages, or other parties in the birth country may omit or hide information that would be otherwise available in order to make a child legally eligible for adoption. There is evidence for such practices in South Korea (Kim, 2010). Other times, information on adoptees' birth families has been lost or destroyed inadvertently through flood or fire or during moves. Adoptees have also reported that the outcome of a search can vary depending on which Korean adoption agency worker they speak with on a given day (Park Nelson, 2016), highlighting the maddening role of luck and timing in transnational adoptee birth search. Finally, birth mothers may decide to have their identity hidden to protect themselves or their families. Although South Korea is a wealthy and modern country, unmarried mothers face severe social scrutiny and discrimination. They are often ostracized by their family and friends, rejected by potential romantic partners, and/or forced out of jobs and school (Bae, 2018; Kim, 2016). It has been estimated that, although most Korean adoptees do not search for their birth families, only 8.3 percent of searchers found their relatives between 2000 and 2005 (Hong, 2006, cited in Park Nelson, 2016). Some adoptees must wait years after initiating a search before they gain legitimate information or reunite.

In some cases, deception, crime, and corruption are the means by which a child becomes available for international adoption. Evidence of these practices, which include kidnapping or buying children from birth parents and selling children to orphanages for profit, has been found in countries such as China, Vietnam, Cambodia, India, Guatemala, and the Marshall Islands (Brown & Roby, 2016; Custer, 2013; Roby & Matsumura, 2002; Schuster Institute, 2008–2014; Smolin, 2005). Legal scholar David Smolin (2005) has coined the term *child laundering* to describe the process by which these children, taken illegally from their birth parents, are processed through the intercountry adoption system and transformed into orphans and then adoptees. These practices, of course, create significant barriers for transnational adoptees hoping to find information and/or reunite.

Other barriers include the financial cost and emotional risks of reunion. Professor of ethnic studies Kim Park Nelson (2016) has pointed out that some Korean adoption agencies charge up to $400 for adoptee records. Adoptees who are prepared to travel to Korea for search and/or reunion incur the cost of passports, flights, and lodging, and most must use vacation time and/or lose pay for hours they would have otherwise worked. These costs come with no guarantee of connection or answers but instead the possibility of a second abandonment by the birth family. These personal stakes—financial cost and emotional risk—add to the structural and interpersonal barriers to reunion.

Yet transnational adoptees and their birth parents have continued to reunite, even amid a worldwide pandemic (Pietsch, 2020), and their interactions give rise to important questions about family and communication.

With the anticipation of increased access to DNA technology within sending countries, including Korea, reunions between transnational adoptees and birth families will become more common. Still, some adoptive parents impede transnational adoptee reunion, even if unintentionally. Scholars such as Kristi Brian (2012) and Sara Dorow (2006) have indicated that for some adoptive parents, part of the appeal of transnational adoption is the physical and legal distance placed between the adopted child and their birth parents. Adoptive parents in Dorow's study expressed their preference for not having to deal with the possibility of a birth parent wanting to reclaim a child or wanting to be a part of the child's life. When reunion is imminent, adoptive parents' responses have been found to vary. Even within the same family, one adoptive parent may have a positive reaction to their child's desire to reunite, whereas the other parent may have a strong negative reaction (Silverman et al., 1994). Even in today's comparatively open climate surrounding adoption, many adoptive parents remain steeped in the belief that the nuclear family should be preeminent and self-contained. Adoptive parents who do not cultivate regular family conversations about adoption and birth parents send an implicit message to adoptees that discourages search and reunion. As a result, some adoptees choose to forgo searching altogether to avoid threatening their relationship with their adoptive parents. Adoptive parents with children in reunion may express fear of losing their child to the birth parent (Powell & Afifi, 2005), implying that a child can have only one mother or one father. Therefore, an adoptee who chooses to reunite may be viewed as questioning or even violating the adoptive family and their relationship. This perspective centers on the adoptive parents, not the adopted person whose history and identity are at stake.

Because of the closed nature of most transnational adoptions, adoptive parents' responses to reunions of transnational adoptees have not been studied extensively. One exception is U.S. adoptions from the Republic of the Marshall Islands (RMI), which began in the early 1990s and were based on an expectation of openness due to Marshallese cultural norms. Professor of social work and legal scholar Jini Roby and colleagues (2005) researched adoptive parents of Marshallese children and found that most of these parents felt positively about remaining in contact with the birth family. However, the researchers pointed out that because adoption agencies stress the importance of openness in RMI adoptions, this positivity toward openness may not be representative of most transnational adoptive parents.

In addition, despite many adoptive parents' positivity toward their child's birth family, research suggests that these parents may struggle with reunion. Sociologist Leslie Wang and colleagues (2015) found that parents of transnational Chinese adoptees, including those who were highly supportive of, and even facilitated, their children's reunions, still struggled with "sharing" their children with the birth parents and "letting go" during the reunion experience. Still, little research has been published regarding transnational adoptees' and adoptive parents' communication surrounding reunions: What are their conversations before, during, and after reunion meetings? What messages from adoptive parents do adoptees find supportive and helpful versus those that are perceived as unsupportive and unhelpful? What do transnational adoptees recommend to adoptive parents with adopted children in reunion? Answers to these questions may help to equip adoptive families to enact support during reunion, particularly because much of the communicative responsibility—what I will refer to as *discursive burden* throughout the book—of reunion rests on the adopted person.

Approach and Tone

Throughout this chapter and the remainder of the book, I include brief personal stories as a way to connect with readers and the participants in my research. Although interviewees' words make up the primary data for this project, adding autoethnographic elements allows me to try to bridge the gap between social sciences and the humanities as well as to make my scholarship "more human, useful, emotional, and evocative" (Adams et al., 2015, p. 3). I believe, as Nash (2019) argues, that deep introspection and storytelling within scholarly writing hold both particular and universal value. At the same time, I respect the personal, political, and methodological choices underlying other adoptee scholars' and other adoptees' decisions to keep their adoption and/or reunion stories private. Korean adoptees are often burdened with the unreasonable expectation to share their adoption experiences with outsiders at any time (Docan-Morgan, 2010), to enact what professor of English Jenny Heijun Wills has referred to as "narrative availability," regarding their life stories (Crisp & Gustafson, 2022). Although I make some of my adoption narrative available in this project, in my daily life, I set boundaries around what to share, based on a variety of criteria such as the context, my fellow communicator(s), the topic, and my subjectivity in the moment (Petronio, 2002). In what follows, however, I hope that my personal stories exemplify wider themes about identity, family, and belonging and that they resonate with readers, adoptees and non-adoptees alike. Yet I do not claim to represent any other adoptee, researcher, or person. Including my own stories in these pages creates an uncomfortable vulnerability for me but also compels me to engage in reflexivity that strengthens my understanding of my role and my responsibilities as a researcher and as a human who advocates for social justice in personal and professional contexts.

I have written this book primarily for transnational adoptees who are at any stage of reunion, for people who want to know how best to support transnational adoptees in reunion, and for researchers and students of adoption studies, family communication, interpersonal communication, and other related disciplines. I draw on communication theory and terminology to illuminate the dynamics of communication at play throughout reunion. However, I aim to discuss adoptees' family relationships in ways that are accessible to a wide audience and useful to readers, whether their interests are personal, professional, and/or academic.

Adoption and Family *Communication*

Messages and Meanings

When I tell people that I am a professor of communication, I am often met with comments such as "Oh, I loved (or hated) public speaking in college!" And although the communication discipline has its roots in rhetoric and oratory, I find that people often equate the field solely with the practice of public speaking or the study of public discourse. This perception, though understandable, omits a wide range of communication topics, subfields, and methodological approaches. Yet what all communication scholars have in common is our interest in how humans use *messages* to create *meanings* (National Communication Association, n.d., italics added). As a researcher and teacher, I value the breadth of topics and methods within the field of communication, yet its wide scope requires me to clarify what studying communication means to me specifically.

As a scholar, I situate myself in the subdiscipline of interpersonal communication with a particular interest in family communication. Interpersonal communication has been described as "the way that humans negotiate meanings, identity, and relationships through person-to-person communication" (Braithwaite & Baxter, 2008, p. 4). This definition captures my belief that the fundamental elements of our humanness—meanings, identity, and relationships—are subjective and dynamic. People in any relationship attach meanings to the messages they exchange with one another, and these meanings may or may not align with those of their fellow communicators. Furthermore, the meaning one person attaches to a message, regardless of who deployed it, may be different today than it is tomorrow or years from now. The subjectivity and dynamism in communication, although fascinating (at least to me), compels a view of all relationships as complex, nuanced, and ever-changing.

And yet humans also crave patterns, predictability, and solutions to problems they perceive and experience in their relationships. I recently conducted a workshop for adoptive parents, talking with them about my research on Korean adoptees' communication with birth families and adoptive families. During the Q and A, one adoptive parent asked me, "What can we do to ensure our child grows up to be emotionally healthy?" I couldn't help but smile at the question and responded rhetorically, "Wouldn't all parents like to know the answer to that question! As a parent myself, I certainly would!" And then I answered to the best of my abilities, saying that, as a communication researcher, my expertise is not in the areas of emotional or mental health, although these are incredibly important matters within adoption.[1] I shared that, in my research, I have found that adoptees who felt that their adoption and birth family were ongoing, safe topics to discuss with their adoptive parents tended to describe their relationships with them as closer than those who said that their adoptive parents did not facilitate discussion about these topics. For many adoptive families, building trust and talking about adoption can be challenging. Yet, as Kathleen Galvin and colleagues (2019) pointed out, members of well-functioning families understand that effective family communication requires effort and the ability to adapt and forge connections. Messages and meanings are central to who we are and to our relationships; this fact seems obvious, and yet relationships—family relationships, in particular—are often far from simple or effortless.

As a researcher, my interest is in *messages* exchanged in adoptive and birth families and how these messages *create, change,* and *sustain* relationships. Reflecting a social constructionist approach, I believe that everyday interactions create social reality and family relationships (Leeds-Hurwitz, 2006). In other words, relationships, messages, and meanings are intertwined and inseparable.

Discursive Struggle and Discursive Burden

Leslie Baxter's (2011) relational dialectics theory (RDT) can be used to examine and understand the ongoing, contradictory messages that infuse adoptees' talk about their birth families and adoptive families. The core premise of RDT is that "meaning making is a process that emerges from the struggle of different, often competing, discourses" (Baxter & Braithwaite, 2010, p. 65). A *discourse* is an articulated worldview, and adoptees often articulate multiple, competing discourses when talking about family relationships. For example, Meagan, a participant in my research, expressed:

> I feel such an emotional connection with these people [birth family], yet I don't feel like I *look* like I'm *really* part of this family. You know, even though physically we all look alike. But then if you put a picture of my *family*, my adoptive family, you know, I *love* these people. These people are my family, yet I don't look like them. So it's like, how do you mix those two together to create that perfect family?

In this excerpt, Meagan invokes specific discourses, including "families are emotionally connected" and "families resemble one another physically." These discourses have been referred to as the *discourse of mutual care* and *the discourse of the "real family,"* respectively (Baxter & Braithwaite, 2010). In the context of adoption and reunion, these discourses can be viewed as contradictory or competing, as there tends to be an emotional connection with one family and physical resemblance or biogenetic ties with another. Together, these discourses demonstrate Meagan's attempt to make sense of how she can be "family" with her adoptive family despite their physical differences, yet not feel like a part of her birth family even with their physical similarities and emotional connection. Concurrent relationships with birth families and adoptive families draw attention to the most basic questions of family and relatedness. The ways that adoptees talk about reunion and adoption are complex and contradictory. These contradictions—also called *discursive struggles* or *tensions*—will manifest throughout this book.

In addition, I observe that much of the communicative responsibility of reunion falls on the shoulders of adoptees. They bear a *discursive burden* to "maintain their rightful—and sometimes tenuous—place within two families: the family they grew up knowing as their family, and the family whose blood and ethnic heritage they share" (Docan-Morgan, 2019, p. 95). Adoptees did not choose to be relinquished and adopted transnationally, and they often grow up facing racism (Docan-Morgan, 2011) and adoption-related microaggressions (Baden, 2016; Docan-Morgan, 2010). Yet adoptees bear the majority of the discursive burden, or communicative responsibility, surrounding reunion. Some of these discursive burdens include but are not limited to:

- Initiating search and reunion
- Reassuring adoptive parents of their commitment to the adoptive family despite search and reunion

- Accommodating to their birth family's Korean cultural expectations
- Expressing forgiveness to the birth family
- Narrating a positive life story to the birth family
- Learning some (or more) Korean language
- The emotion work (Hochschild, 1979) of masking unpleasant emotions (e.g., anger, discomfort) during reunion meetings
- Holding back questions or affection toward the birth family to protect adoptive parents' feelings
- Asking questions, often repeatedly, to learn about their life history and family's history without being overly intrusive
- Engaging in relational repair if there is conflict or misunderstanding with birth family members
- Protecting the feelings of other adoptees who have searched and not located birth families
- Maintaining contact with the birth family while apart

These discursive burdens combine with the emotions of reunion, which participants described as grief, happiness, sadness, anger, confusion, and more. In addition, reunion requires adult adoptees to plan and coordinate logistics, such as travel planning and budgeting for a trip, purchasing or making gifts for the birth family, navigating an unfamiliar city, and researching Korean culture, among others.

Although birth families and adoptive families also experience a discursive burden surrounding reunion, the adopted person is saddled with the responsibility for communicating in ways that create or preserve family relationships that have been viewed traditionally as mutually exclusive or competing. Even though many, though not all, contemporary adoptees have some degree of support from adoptive parents during search and reunion, the adopted person must navigate the waters of reunion alone when it comes to building a relationship with the birth family, negotiating how or whether a long-term relationship will unfold, deciding what to communicate to whom, and how to interpret and respond to birth family messages, all while maintaining a relationship with adoptive parents that is often expected to remain unchanged or even improved.

A deep interest in messages, relationships, and subjective meanings served as my starting point for my research on transnational Korean adoption, but it has taken me a long time, and much self-reflection, to understand what it means to research this topic as a scholar, a Korean adopted daughter and sister, a Korean American daughter and sister in reunion, and a Korean American woman.

Studying Korean Adoption as a Korean Adoptee:
A Research Journey

Finding my Footing

In this section, I engage in author reflexivity, the "inclusion of (re)positionings of the author's self in relation to or as embodied in the project" (Suter, 2016, p. 3). Reflexivity challenges the assumption that pure objectivity is possible and/or desirable and calls the researcher to be mindful of the ways in which their own identities, experiences, and biases might impact the research at every stage of the project (Tracy, 2020). In qualitative research, the *researcher is the research instrument*, and this acknowledgment "reflects the likelihood that the researcher's own subjectivity will come to bear on the research project and any subsequent reporting of findings" (Bourke, 2014, p. 2). I detail my research journey to hold my subjectivity to the light, enabling for readers an understanding and evaluation of my findings that are as informed as possible.

In addition, I share my journey to draw back the curtain on the long and often arduous process of developing a scholarly research agenda. It can often be easy or tempting to view published, respected researchers with a bit of awe. As a young researcher, I tended to assume that others' processes were almost effortless due to their preternatural intellect and insight. Of course, in comparison, I failed to measure up, and even moments of accomplishment were dimmed by a sense that I was somehow still not enough. This *imposter syndrome* is common among women of color in academia (Womble Edwards, 2019). Through the years, however, I have learned that struggle is the norm, not the exception, particularly in the earliest years of developing one's identity as a researcher. In the hopes that future scholars are among this book's readers, I lay out my struggles to demonstrate the work—intellectual and emotional— that goes into researching a topic of great personal significance.

When I began studying Korean adoption in my doctoral program in the early 2000s, I found myself needing to fuse interpersonal communication research with adoption studies research, a new and interdisciplinary field of study. At the time, there were very few communication scholars studying adoption and, as far as I knew, no adoption scholars focusing on communication. In addition, most published interpersonal and family communication studies relied on numbers: Large sample sizes, descriptive or inferential statistics, and generalizable results. In the first several decades of adoption research, published studies also tended to reflect a quantitative social scientific paradigm.

Many of the existing studies on adoption at that time seemed devoted to predicting *outcomes* of transracial adoption[2] (e.g., delinquency, academic performance, racial identity) to arrive at something resembling a verdict: Transracial adoption is good/recommended, or transracial adoption is bad/unrecommended. For example, one well-known book titled *The Case for Transracial Adoption* (Simon et al., 1994) examined adoptions of African American, Korean, and American Indian[3] children by White parents. Such books aimed to resolve the "transracial adoption debate"—a debate that, as long as White parents want to adopt non-White children, will never be resolved. Adoptive parents, not adoptees, tended to be the informants and audience for this research. As Kim Park Nelson (2016) writes,

> Adoptive parents and adoption workers, who have tended to favor the continuation or expansion of adoption, have long dominated adoption studies research and policy making as expert sources of adoption knowledge. Their authority was largely unquestioned and their biases seldom examined. (p. 290)

In early research, Korean adoption was often treated as an independent variable alongside other transracial adoptions; same-race adoptees or nonadopted children served as the control group. For example, Feigelman and Silverman (1984) examined the "long-term effects of transracial adoption" by comparing Korean, Colombian, and African American adoptees with White same-race adoptees on variables such as emotional adjustment, grades, and sibling conflict—measured by adoptive parents' perceptions. In these types of studies, adoptees were often being talked *about* but not talked *with* or listened to. Their voices were not invited into the conversation about transracial adoption.

As I gained a sense of the state of research on transnational Korean adoptees, the questions that persisted in my mind were more about interactions and relationships and less about outcomes. I felt uncomfortable with treating adoption—transracial, transnational, or otherwise—as a static variable that may or may not yield positive or desirable results that were embodied in adoptees like me. I wanted to know how Korean adoptees interacted within their families, given that notions of "family" are complex for adoptees, and that racial differences add to this complexity (Docan-Morgan, 2011). I also wanted to know how adoptees created or experienced a sense of family identity when they didn't share DNA (in the case of adoptive families) or didn't share language or culture (in the case of birth families).

Eventually, the work of communication scholar Kathleen Galvin (2006) provided an important lens for my research. She contended that families who do not conform to the biogenetic, nuclear model of family are *discourse-dependent*; they rely on communication with one another, and with those outside the family, to constitute themselves as a family. Galvin's work gave me an entry point for studying Korean adoption in a way that focused on messages and meanings, rather than variables and outcomes. Readers will see her fingerprints throughout this work.

Finally, I came to realize that I have always been interested in people's stories and in Korean adoptees' stories in particular. I devoured Jane Jeong Trenka's (2003) beautiful memoir, *The Language of Blood*, and watched, over and over, Deann Borshay Liem's (2000) autobiographical documentary, *First Person Plural*. These stories were some of the first opportunities I had had to see another Korean adoptee's story in a book or on the screen, but when I viewed them as a researcher, there was more: These narratives affirmed my sense that adoptees can display "positive outcomes" from an adoptive parent's point of view, yet still feel a sense of alienation and ambiguous loss, or feelings of grief over someone who is (likely) alive; in this case, their birth parents (Powell & Afifi, 2005). Growing up, Trenka excelled at academics and piano, but her adoptive parents could not acknowledge the loss she felt, nor would they cultivate her connection with Korea and her Korean family. Borshay Liem was popular with her classmates, a university cheerleader, and beloved by her adoptive family, and yet she was haunted by memories of her family and life in Korea. These autobiographical accounts were evidence to me that the "outcomes" of transnational adoption are only a very small part of the story and were more important to adoptive parents than to adoptees themselves.

My identity as a researcher had started to coalesce, although the process had been slow and sometimes isolating and painful. The path to being a strict quantitative social scientist, as I had been trained, was clear and well-worn, but it would not take me where I wanted to go. Instead, I took courses from prominent ethnographer of communication Professor Gerry Philipsen and spent time learning about qualitative interviewing and ethnography. These methods suited my primary goal to "understand how realities are produced and maintained through the everyday practices of people and families" (Braithwaite et al., 2018, p. 6) and enabled me to collect and try to understand the stories of Korean adoptees, centering their perspectives.

My primary aim remains to describe the particularities of my participants' relational experiences and their interpretations of these experiences. Although these narratives depict a range of reunion stories and perspectives, the interactions and relationships described in this book are neither exhaustive nor representative. In addition, I recognize that the meanings that adoptees ascribe to their interactions and relationships may differ from those of their adoptive parents and birth parents and that their own meanings may shift over time. Regardless, I believe that adoptees' experiences and perspectives are of paramount importance in studying adoption. Korean adoptees are placed at the intersection of adoptive families and birth families, adoptive culture and birth culture, and White and non-White families, and thus commonly experience a sense of belonging to and alienation from both families and cultures (Lee, 2003). In addition, adoptees are often infantilized in public discourse (Park Nelson, 2016). One important goal of my research, then, is to give space for adult adoptees' voices to be heard and validated.

Adoption, Critique, and Contradiction

As I was developing my identity as a qualitative researcher, I was also learning more about race relations in the United States and developing a critical understanding of the ways in which social and legal institutions, including the family and adoption, often serve to perpetuate hierarchies of domination that center and normalize White, middle-class, straight identities and persons. As a product of public American education in the 1980s and 1990s, and as a daughter of White American adoptive parents growing up in North Dakota and South Dakota, I had been taught, both implicitly and explicitly, to believe that racism was only manifest through overt, mean actions or words and that I should be proud to be an American. But reading and discussing works during my doctoral program such as Eduardo Bonilla-Silva's (2003) book, *Racism without Racists: Color-Blind Racism and the Persistence of Racial Inequality in America*, and Tom Nakayama and Robert Krizek's (1995) article "Whiteness: A Strategic Rhetoric," among many others, enabled me to see the many gaps in my understandings of race and racism. In addition, the more I read about Asian American history, in books such as Ronald Takaki's (1998) *Strangers from a Different Shore: A History of Asian Americans*, the more I realized how my own story fit in with the stories of other Asian American immigrants. The book *Outsiders Within: Writing on Transracial Adoption*, edited by transracial adoptees Jane Jeong Trenka, Julia Chinyere Oparah, and Sun Yung Shin (2006) was among the first works that drew my attention to the forces that had shaped my understanding of adoption, but it took me time to absorb the impact of this new knowledge.

Growing up, I heard and internalized messages from my adoptive family: They love me, and they had "chosen" me. These messages were consonant with cultural messages: Outsiders telling me how "lucky" I am to be adopted and rags-to-riches stories of adoption portrayed in movies such as 1982's *Annie*, a movie I adored. As a result, research that was critical of Korean adoption, especially by other Korean adoptees, challenged my assumptions about my adoption story and the rightness of my place within my adoptive family. This critical work created cognitive dissonance: How could I make sense of the problematics of transnational adoption alongside my loving, steadfast adoptive parents and sisters, whom I looked up to and adored? These things didn't add up. Critical adoption research called into question the way I had always been taught to view adoption: As a beautiful way for children in need to find loving families, and for loving families to be made complete.

And yet the facts remained then as they do now: Transnational adoption involves the systematic movement of children from less affluent to more affluent countries and, most often, the transfer of children of color to parents who are White. The process is legalized in the sending and receiving countries, but this legalization does not ensure that the children have been placed for adoption via legal means or that the birth mothers who "consented" to adoption did so freely and willingly. The image of the selfless birth mother who makes an "adoption plan" for her child has been curated by adoptive parents and adoption professionals who hope to decrease the pain of abandonment for adoptees (Yngvesson, 2002) and to create an adoption narrative that assuages the guilt adoptive parents may feel for benefiting from another parent's hardship.

In addition, transnational adoption strips adoptees of their birth families, their access to their culture, and their racial belonging. Upon adoption, Korean children are transplanted from a family and country where being Korean is normal and accepted to a family and country where being Korean is ambiguous and foreign, and where White middle-class identity is normalized and encouraged. As Tobias Hübinette (2005) points out, these adoptees "all too often internalise and develop self-loathing tendencies caused by their more or less complete white subjectivation" (p. 149).

Finally, transnational adoption is an economic transaction and a means of tacit political engagement between nations. Therefore, it is a power-laden transaction and institution, what Korean adoption scholars such as Kimberly McKee (2016) have called the *transnational adoption industrial complex.* Those who view transnational adoption solely through the lens of nuclear family formation, as I did for many years, tend to focus on the needs of adoptive parents and the wealth of the adoptive country. Such views miss larger ramifications of the practice, including but not limited to

- Family separation (Briggs, 2012)
- Child trafficking in the sending country (Smolin, 2005)
- Justification for lack of economic and/or social support for unwed mothers in the sending country (Bae, 2018)
- Adoptee lack of cultural identity (Hoffman & Peña, 2013)
- Adoptees feeling isolated due to racism (Docan-Morgan, 2011)

- Adoptees being separated from their culture (Palmer, 2010)
- Maintaining paternalistic, neocolonial relationships between sending and receiving countries (Oh, 2015)

As strange as it sounds, I lived as a Korean adoptee for many years knowing very little about Korean adoption. As someone who grew up feeling thankful for my adoption and the life and family I had, I found it difficult and painful to see my adoption—indeed, my family—as a by-product of a larger system that benefits wealthy countries and wealthy parents at the expense of poorer countries and poorer parents. The outrage I felt at sending and receiving countries for being complicit in maintaining an unjust system and the sadness I felt for adoptees like myself, who had been conditioned to see their adoption as an unequivocal blessing felt dissonant with the love I felt for, and from, my adoptive parents and sisters. I had to reconcile two of my identities—Korean adoptee and Korean adoption researcher—which until then hadn't seemed discordant. As a Korean adoptee with a loving family, I felt somehow disloyal in critiquing the practice of Korean adoption, and yet, as a researcher, I felt inauthentic and dishonest attempting to portray Korean adoption or Korean adoptees' experiences with neutrality or indifference.

It took me years to feel that I have enough space, emotionally and intellectually, to embody all of the contradictions inherent in being a Korean adoptee who studies and critiques transnational Korean adoption. I have learned to accept that adoption is an act of domination on individual, national, and international levels, *and* it is an institution that has resulted in genuine connection and family for many people. Even as I type these words, I have to draw in a deep breath because the contradictions feel so immense and so personal. But I am reminded of what has been called the *unfinalizability of interplay*, the notion that meaning making between competing discourses is never overcome but rather continually in flux (Suter & Seurer, 2018). This flux can create room for new, emergent meanings and meaning making.

Based on the inherent contradictions in transnational adoption, some adoptees, scholars, and activists have identified, or felt pressure to identify, as *proadoption* or *antiadoption*. But, inspired by fellow Korean adoptee and activist Kevin Haebeom Vollmers (Werman & Yuen, 2013) and the idea that one can create new meanings and identities, I choose to identify as *proadoptee*. I believe that adoptees have rights to information about their origins; that adoptees should have a prominent voice in decisions that impact them; and that when adoption is necessary, the process should be as transparent as possible. This position leads to the question that drives all of my research: What can be done to best support transnational adoptees?

At the same time, I support the rights of birth parents and birth mothers, in particular. Research suggests that birth mothers are often pressured to relinquish their children for adoption and would choose to parent their children if they had adequate support (Coleman & Garratt, 2016). In addition, birth mothers must also endure a combined stigma of invisibility and microaggressions related to their choice to not parent their child (Baden, 2016), both of which suggest that they are insignificant and deeply flawed as women. My hope is that the reunion stories shared in this book will draw attention to the emotional and relational tolls of transnational adoption for birth families, birth mothers especially.

In contrast to birth mothers, adoptive parents tend to be valorized in both public and private discourse, viewed as saving their transnationally adopted children from poverty and the misguided ways of their birth country. Although the work of many adoptees, both transnational and domestic, has opened up important conversations surrounding adoption and reunion, there is still work to do for adoptees to feel a full sense of empowerment and support in exploring their racial, ethnic, and adoptive identities and in pursuing family relationships they find meaningful, in their own ways and on their own timeline. My hope is that parents who have adopted transnationally will use this book to further open their minds and hearts to new and more expansive ways of communicating about adoption and family.

Goals and Contributions

My main goal in this book is to understand, examine, and illuminate the experiences of transnational Korean adoptees in reunion. I trace their stories, bringing particular attention to the messages they exchange with their families and the meanings they ascribe to their own and others' communicative behaviors. I describe their first meetings and the unfolding of these relationships over time. I note the ways in which their relationships with their birth families develop and are maintained alongside adoptive family relationships, and how both types of family relationships—birth and adoptive—cause us to question the static, unidimensional views of family and relationships that are often imposed on families and that family members sometimes impose on themselves.

Second and importantly, I draw special attention to the role of cultural and language differences in the development and maintenance of relationships between transnational adoptees and birth families. Culture impacts the way people see the world, their relationships, and themselves. Language differences pose a challenge to direct communication between adoptees and their birth families, but just as importantly, language imparts knowledge about culture itself, revealing assumptions that play a significant role in Korean family interactions. Although this book focuses on transnational Korean adoptees, I hope to provide insight that is helpful and useful to all transnational adoptees who reunite with their birth families. May these types of reunions become more common in the years to come.

Although my inability to speak Korean prevents me from interviewing and quoting Korean birth families directly, a third aim of this book is to bring their stories, told through adoptees, into the broader conversation surrounding transnational adoption. This move is significant, given that international adoption processes involve the creation of "legal orphans" (a.k.a. paper orphans, social orphans) who are, at least according to adoption agency paperwork, motherless. As Hosu Kim (2016) writes,

> The birth mothers' legal erasure is a critical step for the child to be considered adoptable by prospective adoptive parents; and, the erasure is sealed when a new birth certificate is issued to the adopted child, completing the transfer of legal custody to the adoptive parents. (p. 8)

Hosu Kim's (2016) research on Korean birth mothers and Sara Dorow's (1999) letters from Korean birth mothers to their children sent abroad for adoption have allowed some Korean birth mothers' stories to emerge from the shadows, yet published, empirical work about birth families' communication during reunion is scant. The stories contained in this book provide insight into these families' lives and history, making evident that the common narrative of a birth mother lovingly and consciously creating an "adoption plan" (Harrigan & Braithwaite, 2010) to relinquish her child is often a fabrication intended to assuage the guilt of adoptive parents and to comfort adoptees.

I acknowledge that the adoptive family and birth family messages contained in this book have been told from the perspective of adoptees and are thus necessarily subjective. But given that adoptive parents have often been centered and privileged in both adoption practice and adoption research, I am confident in the decision to amplify adoptee voices and viewpoints. My hope is that the future will bring forth more reunion stories told from birth families' perspectives, as I know there is still much to learn.

Listening to Korean Adoptees' Stories of Reunions and Family

In the autumn of 2010, after receiving approval from the institutional review board at my university, I began recruiting Korean adoptees for interviews about their reunions with their birth families. To begin, I posted an announcement on Facebook pages for Korean adoptees, including those of Korean adoptee local organizations, such as Minneapolis's AK Connection, New York City's Also-Known-As, Boston Korean Adoptees, and Korea Klubben (Denmark). I also e-mailed the leaders of these organizations, who then posted an announcement about the study on their organizations' websites, and I also forwarded an e-mail announcement to their member lists. Participants were required to be at least eighteen years old and to have reunited with at least one member of their birth family. I scheduled interviews with all eligible participants who responded to my materials between December 2010 and August 2011. In addition, one participant was recruited through snowball sampling upon hearing about my study from another interviewee.

In the recruitment announcement, I disclosed that I am a Korean adoptee and professor of communication studies. The former disclosure aimed at creating a sense of identification with prospective participants, knowing that a researcher's identity may impact individuals' willingness to participate in a study (Kristensen & Ravn, 2015). At the same time, I wanted participants to approach the interview with as much openness and candor as possible, without feeling as though I would impose my own experiences or expectations on them. An interview is a specific communicative event occurring within a specific context, and interviewees may anticipate that the interviewer is going to evaluate what they say (Baxter & Braithwaite, 2010). Therefore, on occasions when participants asked questions about my adoption experience or reunion, I shared only after their interview concluded.

The goal of qualitative research is understanding (Manning & Kunkel, 2014), not prediction or generalization. Therefore, I do not assume that the stories of participants in this study exhaust the range of Korean adoptee experiences of reunion, or that they represent the experiences of other adoptees. Rather, I aim to understand their experiences from their perspective. I operate with the assumption that their interpretations make sense, and I strive to understand their sensemaking processes. Ultimately, I believe that if we contextualize their words and experiences, we can understand the dynamics of reunion and family communication more deeply.

I describe my research procedures and analysis in detail to provide transparency that may lead to an informed evaluation of the study (Kuper et al., 2008). In all, I conducted interviews with eighteen transnational Korean adoptees, interviewing each for the first time in 2010–2011. Fourteen participants were adopted to the United States, and four were adopted to Denmark. Two interviews were conducted face-to-face, as I was able to be in the same location as the interviewee, whereas the remainder were conducted via Skype or

Zoom. All interviews were audio recorded; video interviews were also video recorded. Before the interview, each participant provided informed consent and basic demographic and family information. Table I.1 lists the participants with relevant information. Note: Some participants chose to use a pseudonym, whereas others chose to use their Korean name or the name given by their adoptive parents.

Interviews were semistructured and in-depth, with the goal of understanding "the informant's point of view on some phenomenon or experience in as richly detailed a manner as possible" (Baxter & Babbie, 2003, p. 339). Participants were asked questions about their adoptive family, their birth search, their initial reunion with their birth family, their adoptive family's role in the reunion, and their relationships with their adoptive family and birth family, both before and after the reunion. Questions were phrased in a conversational manner to create comfort and rapport with each participant. The interview questions can be found in the Appendix, although each interview included follow-up questions, clarification questions, and inquiries that were suited to each person's experiences.

With the help of two trained research assistants, this first set of interviews was transcribed verbatim. To most accurately portray participants' meanings, paralinguistic (e.g., vocal emphasis, increase in volume) and other relevant nonverbal features were included in the transcripts: Italics indicated vocal emphasis, and other relevant features (e.g., pauses, laughing, crying, sarcasm) were listed in parentheses. Readers will see these notations throughout the book.

In the summer of 2020, I e-mailed participants and asked them if they would be willing to participate in a second interview about their relationship with their birth family. All participants responded, with seventeen indicating that they would be willing to be interviewed again. Only one stated that she had lost touch with her Korean family and had nothing to add. Another participant had limited time and ended up sending written responses instead of doing an interview. The remaining second interviews, all of which were conducted through Zoom or another video meeting program, took place between August 2020 and February 2022. These programs both video-recorded the interviews and transcribed the audio; however, because the transcripts were program-generated, I reviewed them while listening to the audio recordings to ensure accuracy and add paralinguistic features.

For both sets of interviews, I engaged in phronetic analysis, which is aimed at producing "use-inspired, practical research that not only builds theory, but also provides guidance on social practice and action" (Tracy, 2020, p. 210). As Srivastava and Hopwood (2009) write, "The qualitative data analyst is constantly on the hunt for concepts and themes that, when taken together, will

TABLE I.1 ADOPTEE PARTICIPANT INFORMATION

Name or pseudonym	Gender	Age at time of first interview	Age at time of first meeting with birth family	Birth family members met during first reunion	Intact birth family (i.e., birth parents married one another)?	Adoptive family or other support persons present during first meeting	In contact with birth family at time of second interview (approx. 10 years later)?
Sylvia	F	28	28	Mother, father, aunt, cousins	Yes	Husband, mother, father, siblings	Yes
Catherine	F	21	10	Mother, father, older sisters, younger brother, grandmother, aunt, uncles, cousins	Yes	Mother, father, younger sister	Yes
Alexander	M	18	16	Mother, father, younger half-siblings, grandmother, aunt, uncle, cousins	No	Mother, father, sister	Yes
Eric	M	30	29	Father, older brother, mother, aunts, uncles, half-sister	No: married one another, then divorced	Girlfriend	Yes
Jorgen	M	37	27	Mother, grandmother, half-brothers, aunts, uncles, cousins	No: father deceased before first meeting	None	Yes
Sun Ok	F	28	27	Mother, father, grandmother, older sisters, younger brother	Yes	None	Yes
Mark	M	23	14	Mother, father, father's wife, younger half-brothers	No: married one another, then divorced	Mother, father, brother	No
Olivia	F	35	32	Mother, father, aunts, uncles, grandmother	No: married one another, then divorced	Best friend	No
Minsun	F	29	26	Mother, aunt	No	None	Yes

(continued)

TABLE I.1 ADOPTEE PARTICIPANT INFORMATION (continued)

Name or pseudonym	Gender	Age at time of first interview	Age at time of first meeting with birth family	Birth family members met during first reunion	Intact birth family (i.e., birth parents married one another)?	Adoptive family or other support persons present during first meeting	In contact with birth family at time of second interview (approx. 10 years later)?
Christine	F	20	9	Mother, father, older sisters, younger brother, grandmother	Yes	Mother, father	Yes
Ashley	F	25	18	Mother, father, younger brother, younger sister, grandparents, aunts, uncles, cousins	Yes	Mother, father, brother	Yes
Ji Kyoung	F	35	34	Mother, father, older sisters, one younger brother	Yes	Friend	Yes
Meagan	F	26	20	Father, older sisters, older brother	Yes; mother deceased before first meeting	Mother	Yes
Nikki	F	24	22	Mother, grandmother	No	Mother, father, sister	No
Hanne	F	38	36	Mother, half-brothers, half-sister, uncle	No	Sister	No
Isabel	F	31	18	Mother, father, older sisters	Yes	Mother	Yes
Mee Joo	F	29	21	Mother, father, older sisters, older brothers	Yes	None	Yes
Cat	F	35	35	Mother, mother's boyfriend, twin sister	Yes; father deceased before first meeting	Son, boyfriend, best friend	Yes

provide the best explanation of 'what's going on' in an inquiry" (p. 77). I began by reading the transcripts repeatedly until I had a sense of each person's reunion story, as well as an understanding of the data as a whole. From there, I approached the data with questions that were germane to particular topics, one at a time. For example, "What questions do participants have when meeting their birth families for the first time?" or "What cultural differences do participants mention in talking about their interactions with their birth families?" I then reread each interview, line by line, highlighting codes, or excerpts, that seemed relevant to the question at hand. In this step, it was also important for me to read and view these excerpts in the context of each participant's larger story to make sure I was being true to their words. After highlighting the relevant excerpts from each interviewee's transcript, I looked across all of the excerpts for themes: Common experiences, viewpoints, and/or interpretations. I also examined the data for negative cases (Tracy, 2020) and exceptions to the emerging themes, and tried to discern meaningful reasons for these exceptions. In qualitative research, this step is important, as it helps the researcher to avoid overlooking data that do not conform to the themes. I named each theme as it emerged, and then revisited the excerpts and transcripts to ensure that the name suited the theme and that interview excerpts reflected the meaning of the theme. At times, this called for a renaming of the theme or another analysis of the data. This iterative process is both common and necessary during qualitative research as meanings emerge and the researcher's understanding of the data deepen (Tracy, 2020).

My overall goal in analysis was to understand and describe participants' reunions, family relationships, and the meanings they ascribe to interactions with their birth families and adoptive families. This sounds like a fairly straightforward goal, yet I revisited the interview transcripts hundreds of times throughout this ongoing project, both to ensure my understanding and to make sure that I "get it right." In this case, "right" refers to what Cho and Trent (2006) have labeled *transactional validity*, "an interactive process between the researcher, the researched, and the collected data that is aimed at achieving a relatively higher level of accuracy and consensus by means of revisiting facts, feelings, experiences, and values or beliefs collected and interpreted" (p. 321). In my opinion, the most compelling qualitative research reads like a story, and yet this quasi-narrative form can sometimes obscure how challenging and nonlinear this type of research is. At each stage of the research process, I asked myself whether I was being true to participants' intended meanings. I view the time and disclosures of my participants as sacred; I never want to impose meanings in ways that privilege my own interpretations over their voices and perspectives. Therefore, I have attempted, over the years, to remain accountable to them. For example, I e-mailed the first draft of a research article that used these interview data to the participants of this study, asking them whether my interpretations rang true to their experiences and perspectives. This process is called member checking (Creswell, 2003). Later, I e-mailed participants copies of the published articles or book chapters that emerged from their interviews, and I invited their feedback. I also sent them their interview transcripts and e-mailed them follow-up questions when I needed clarification. In addition, I have presented this research at various conferences where Korean adoptees constituted the main audience. These public presentations provided me with valuable feedback and questions that influenced my thinking and my approach.

Although my early days of researching Korean adoption seem long ago, I continue to learn and be influenced by others' research, writings, and creative works. And so, despite the retrospective nature of my research narrative, I know that my understandings and processes will continue to unfold and grow. And regardless of the amount of time that has passed since I started conducting adoption research, I remain true to my commitment to studying Korean adoptees with an emphasis on praxis: How can research inform and improve communication and relationships? I hope that the following pages either contain some answers or open up new questions toward that end.

Description of Chapters

This book focuses on Korean adoptees' interactions with their birth family as well as their adoptive family surrounding reunion. To understand these interactions, which occur at a micro, or interpersonal, level, it is crucial to understand the broader historical, political, and social contexts surrounding Korean adoption and reunion. I owe a great debt to scholars who have described these contexts with keen observation and insight. A few who have been instrumental in shaping my understanding include but are not limited to Tobias Hübinette (2006; 2007), Eleana Kim (2010), Hosu Kim (2016), JaeRan Kim (*Harlow's Monkey*, 2006–2022; 2021), Kimberly McKee (2016; 2019), Arissa Oh (2015), Kim Park Nelson (2016), Soojin Pate (2014), and Elizabeth Raleigh (2018). In Chapter 1, I draw on their and others' work to describe the factors that have made reunions between transnational Korean adoptees and their birth families possible.[4] In doing so, I contextualize participants' reunion stories, attempting to catalyze thought about the critical implications of cultural practices, such as adoption and reunion, which are often framed as unequivocally positive.

Chapter 2 describes adoptees' first meetings with their birth families. This chapter aims to answer questions such as *What is it like for transnational Korean adoptees to meet blood relatives for the first time? What messages do these adoptees and birth family members want to share with one another? What commonalities emerge during first meetings?* These meetings were often fraught with expectations, emotions, questions, and disclosures. Participants described the questions they brought to these initial meetings as well as their thoughts and feelings. Although a few interviewees described instantaneous connection with their birth family, most mentioned challenges and/or unmet expectations, underscoring the complexity of communication during reunion and the importance of attenuating expectations.

One of the most important contributions of this book is its focus on the intercultural dynamics inherent in transnational adoptees' reunions. Participants talked about facing and navigating cultural differences, as is discussed in Chapter 3. Although cultural behaviors, such as "Wait to eat until the oldest person has started" or "Give and receive gifts with two hands," are easy to modify, these differences are often manifestations of much deeper cultural values and assumptions that are less easily articulated or understood. Confucian values of hierarchy, family loyalty, and the priority of the collective over the individual exert a strong influence on Korean culture (Mitu, 2015). In contrast, Western culture, especially American culture, is highly individualistic and values egalitarianism, even between parents and children. Unsurprisingly, these cultural characteristics and differences often manifest themselves powerfully in the context of family interactions. Reunions are a particularly unique context for cultural differences about family to be perceived and communicated, even when family members have just met.

Although culture and language are linked inextricably, I have treated the two separately for conceptual and practical clarity. Chapter 4 examines how Korean adoptees and birth families navigate language differences during reunion. As all participants spoke little, if any, Korean during their initial meetings, they described the challenges of language differences as well as the benefits and challenges of communicating through interpreters. Despite these language differences, participants also reflect on the power of nonverbal communication and the ability to forge meaningful connections without words.

In Chapter 5, the focus turns toward interactions with adoptive families surrounding the birth family and reunion. Participants talked about their adoptive family members' reactions to reunion as well as how family members' presence impacted meetings with birth family members. Participants spoke about feeling protective of their adoptive parents' feelings during reunion and also the importance of receiving support from their adoptive family before, during, and after reunion meetings.

Chapter 6 details another important contribution of this book: An examination of Korean adoptees' birth family relationships over time. A decade after the first set of interviews, participants spoke with me a second time. During these follow-up interviews, participants recalled interactions with their birth family members since the previous interview and articulated their thoughts on how these relationships had changed in the past decade. They also discussed the challenges to maintaining these relationships, how evolving technology helps them to maintain contact, and the insights they have gained from maintaining these relationships over time.

The book concludes with Chapter 7, a summary of my observations and recommendations for adoptees in reunion and the people who support them. Although there is no singular or magical formula for a "successful" reunion or birth family relationship, I describe the recommendations that participants themselves have offered for other adoptees and adoptive parents. My hope is that these recommendations can inform the work of those who support transnational adoptees, birth parents, and/or adoptive parents. Overall, the final chapter reflects my main goals as a researcher of adoption and family communication: To promote effective, ethical, and appropriate communication in family relationships and to support expansive, meaningful definitions of family.

Conclusion

The study of transnational Korean adoptees in reunion raises important questions for all people, regardless of whether or not they have a personal connection to adoption. These questions include *What does it mean to be family? How do people use communication to create and negotiate family relationships? What role do cultural and language differences play in the formation and maintenance of family relationships?* As family forms become increasingly diverse, more attention has been drawn to the role of communication—rather than traditional bonds of blood or marriage—in constituting family relationships (Galvin, 2006).

The stories of the transnational Korean adoptees in this book demonstrate the effort, flexibility, empathy, self-reflection, and time required to navigate long-term relationships with birth families. Adoptees are, in nearly all cases, managing relationships with their adoptive parents simultaneously. As I look across all of these conversations, two observations continue to strike me. First, although adoptees have zero responsibility for their relinquishment in their birth country and their adoption into a country where they are perceived as the racial minority, they bear the great majority of the discursive burden when it comes to maintaining family relationships in reunion. They often feel a responsibility to communicate in ways that make both families feel comfortable and loved, to adapt to Korean culture and language, and to maintain relationships with birth families across distance and over time. These discursive burdens exist in addition to the daily need to live and communicate as a racialized Asian body in adoptive countries where Whiteness is viewed as the norm and standard (Nakayama & Krizek, 1995; Nakayama & Martin, 1998).

Second, adoptees in reunion must contend with and accept contradictions in relationships and communication: They have received cultural messages that their birth parents are their "real" parents *and* messages that their adoptive parents are their "real" parents. They experience feelings of being both inside and outside of their birth families *and* their adoptive families. They understand that their birth family's culture is different from their own as transnational adoptees, but at times, they still find their birth family's behaviors puzzling or frustrating. They want to communicate with their birth families and adoptive families but at times need space from them. Transnational adoptees in reunion, then, must have the willingness to live with these contradictions and the understanding that they will likely remain unresolved and yet retain a sense of hope that these relationships are, or will be, mutually meaningful.

1

Links between Past, Present, and Future

Context for Understanding Communication in Reunion

Fall 2001

The first person I called after listening to the message from my adoption agency was my dad, my adoptive dad, who lived in South Dakota. I wanted to know how the adoption agency had gotten my number in California, where I was living at the time, and also if they had told him anything else.

He answered the phone as if he were expecting my call. Yes, he had given them my number.

"What should I do?" I asked. I was looking for guidance but perhaps equally hoping for permission to be curious, to ask questions, to engage with my birth family.

"I can't tell you what to do. It's your life," he said. I detected passive aggression in his words, but that wasn't his style. My dad was direct and rational, both to a fault. Before I had the chance to register my confusion or frustration, he added, "They said this would never happen. You're ours now!"

His words and tone were so uncharacteristic that the room around me seemed to tilt. Typical of men of his generation and status, my dad never expressed insecurity, and his parenting style had always been practical. He gifted us, his daughters, windshield wiper blades, luggage, and tool sets for Christmas and graduations. He told us that he loved us, but he was more comfortable expressing his love using other words: "I put gas in your car" or "Does that job come with health insurance?" At times, I had longed for clearer expressions of his care. This conversation was the first time I had heard him convey any sense of possessiveness over me or anyone else. I found it both reassuring and unsettling. I had been his daughter for twenty-five years, since I was four months old. Yet, one message from my family in Korea sparked fear that he would lose me. His reaction reaffirmed what I knew already: this topic—my birth family and my feelings or questions about them—was off limits.

Although I didn't realize it at the time, my dad's response to my birth family's outreach is illustrative of much more than his personality, our relationship, or the situation. Rather, his possessiveness is understandable given the way that adoption had been marketed to prospective adoptive parents of Korean children: As a way to give a needy child—with "parents unknown"— a home. At a time when the nuclear family was still considered sacred and ideal, an adoptee's full incorporation into an adoptive family necessitated a deliberate erasure of the biological family, a process that, unbeknownst to adoptive parents, was common practice in Korea. But, as I would learn later, this erasure was one-sided: It is much easier for adoptive parents to omit birth parents from a child's history than for birth parents to forget a child they lost.

At the time, I also wondered how it was possible that my Korean family could simply talk with someone at my Korean adoption agency and ask for me to be contacted, and then hours or days later, I could receive a phone call from my American adoption agency. The undoing of my life history seemed almost laughably simple. Years later, I would learn that my adoptive parents had sent photos of me as a toddler to my American adoption agency and that my Korean family had received them and kept them in an album for many years. I still don't know if my adoptive parents knew that the photos were circulated to my Korean family. Regardless, my Korean adoption agency always knew who my Korean family was, yet they allowed my American family and me to believe that I had been found on the doorstep of the police station and that my birth parents were unknown. Many adoptees I have spoken with share similar stories of falsified adoption records and learn the true story of their relinquishment only after reuniting. These stories often involve birth mothers either not willingly relinquishing their children for adoption or doing so only under great duress. Korean adoptee stories of reunion, mine included, reflect a broader history of war, gendered oppression, national poverty, and economic recovery.

Thus, to more fully understand Korean adoptee and birth family reunions, we must move backward in time, zoom out, and sweep our view back and forth between continents. Rather than focusing only on the communication that is happening in the moment—what was said, how it was interpreted and intended—we must attend to how historical, cultural, and political contexts influence interactions and our perceptions of these interactions. In turn, our interactions can shape, reinforce, and challenge dominant discourse in the present and future. Family messages are not exchanged in a vacuum; they reflect, reinforce, and challenge history, culture, and power, and they lay the groundwork for the future.

In this chapter, I contextualize the interactions between Korean adoptees and their birth families and adoptive families to help cultivate a nuanced understanding of the interactions described in this book. This approach aims to dispel the notion of the public-private binary, which cleaves a family's daily interactions from the wider context in which these interactions occur. Baxter (2011) argues that messages do not exist in isolation but rather are connected to meanings articulated in the past and anticipated in the future. These articulated meanings, or *utterances*, are circulated within the culture at large as well as in daily interactions. Messages about family can be found, for example, in fairy tales about princesses finding their birth mothers or children escaping evil stepmothers, and in online stories showing adoptees finding relatives through DNA-matching websites with emphasized quotes such as "We connected right away" (Scull, 2019, para. 52). These messages circulate at the cultural, or *distal*, level (Baxter, 2011). Such messages can also be found on the everyday, or *proximal*, level (Baxter, 2011), in questions to adoptees from their classmates like "Do you know your 'real' mom?" or in comments from family friends like "You're so lucky to be adopted by such wonderful parents." The messages exchanged during and about reunion are often unknowing responses to utterances from the past, what Baxter calls "already-spokens," and also in anticipation of what could be said in the future, the "not-yet-spokens" (Baxter, 2011). In this way, messages are always "in dialogue" with the past and the future.

Korean adoption scholars in various fields have written extensively about the historical, political, cultural, and social forces in both Korea and the United States that contributed to the practice of sending Korean children overseas for adoption. The most prominent factors include Cold War politics; the U.S. military occupation of Korea starting in 1945; the Korean War and Korea's subsequent devastation following the military armistice in 1953; institutional and socially sanctioned violence against women in Korea; idealization of a monoracial Korea; White nuclear family ideologies; the America-as-rescuer narrative; and American hierarchies of race. These intersecting events, histories, and cultures disrupt the myth that transnational adoption is a simple story of orphans in one country needing families and families in another country wanting to adopt abroad. This discussion is necessarily abbreviated, so I encourage those interested in further details to explore work by the Korean adoption scholars listed in the Introduction. Their work has been powerful in shaping knowledge about Korean transnational adoption that digs beneath the long-accepted narrative of foreign orphans saved by adoptive parents.

Transnational Korean Adoption and the Birth of an "Orphan"

American Military Occupation, War, and "GI Babies"

Although some scholars pinpoint 1953 as the starting point for Korea's practice of sending children abroad for adoption, Korean adoption scholar Soojin Pate (2014) pointed out that the neocolonial relationship between the United States and Korea was established in 1945 when the United States and Russia liberated Korea from Japanese control. At that time, the peninsula was divided at the 38th parallel, with Russia responsible for the north and the United States for the south. The U.S. military occupation of what became South Korea and the millions of dollars of aid that accompanied this occupation laid the groundwork for an ongoing relationship between the two countries, where the United States is viewed as the benefactor and South Korea, the grateful recipient. This characterization continues today, even though the military occupation of Korea is maintained in the interest of U.S. geopolitical control in Asia (Pate, 2014).

The neocolonial relationship between the two countries was solidified in the years following the military armistice in 1953 when the country now recognized as South Korea was left in a state of total destruction. An estimated three to four million Koreans were killed, creating an estimated two hundred thousand to three hundred thousand widows and one hundred thousand orphans (Kim, 2007; Oh, 2015; Pate, 2014). In addition, hundreds of thousands of children were lost, abandoned, and neglected (Kim, 2007), resulting in a drastic increase in the number of orphanages and homeless youth. Families who managed to stay together were impoverished, with effectively no social welfare or work options, as most factories and businesses had been destroyed. In other words, the traditional family structure, which included the support of extended family, was itself a casualty of the war.

One consequence of military occupation was the establishment of camptowns, or *kijich'on*, Korean villages located adjacent to military bases, where prostitution was prevalent (Kim, 2010). Although sex work was viewed with shame and scorn by the general public, the Korean government saw it as a necessary service to keep American soldiers satisfied and as a way to bring foreign money into the Korean economy (Shorrock, 2019). Many women, orphaned and/or widowed, had no other means to make money to feed their children or other family members. Women in desperate circumstances found themselves lured into sex work through false promises (Oh, 2015). Grace M. Cho (2021) characterized *kijich'on* workers, writing

> She is the dutiful daughter who works to support the very same family that shuns her, the serviceman's wife who becomes her family's hope for the future, the protective mother who hides her past from her children. (p. 4)

Naturally, one result of sex work near military bases was the birth of mixed-race Korean infants, known as GI babies. Although some American servicemen married the women they met in camptowns and brought them to the United States, many women were left behind to raise their mixed-race children, some of whom were the product of rape. The mothers were stigmatized as immoral, and their children bore a triple stigma of being mixed race, fatherless, and the assumed child of a prostitute (Oh, 2015). As Eleana Kim (2010) and others have pointed out, GI babies were viewed as a threat to the ideology of ethnic homogeneity advocated by then-president Syngman Rhee and also served as an unwanted symbol to North Korea that South Korea was catering to American imperialists. In their daily lives, these children were the target of taunts and violence from adults and children, and, because they did not have Korean fathers, they would experience difficulty getting an education, finding employment, or getting married (Oh, 2015). Rather than outlaw persecution and discrimination against mixed-race persons, the Korean government sought to remove them from Korea. Adoption by families abroad offered a convenient and profitable solution.

American missionaries, American servicemen, and nongovernmental organization (NGO) relief workers in Korea were instrumental in promoting the story that orphans in Korea needed rescue by White adoptive parents abroad, a discourse that was used to justify Korean adoption for many years. Hungry and/or homeless, full Korean (i.e., not mixed race) and mixed-race children came into close and regular contact with these groups who provided free food and clothing (Oh, 2015). In addition, national news publications in the United States ran stories featuring photos of Korean and mixed-race children in various states: Malnourished and sad-eyed, smiling upon receiving foreign aid, and alongside American soldiers who had adopted them either formally or informally (Briggs, 2003; Kim, 2010). Importantly, these children were framed as orphans, regardless of whether they had living Korean relatives (Kim, 2010). Upon seeing the plight of hungry Korean children and learning of the fates of GI babies, missionaries and servicemen shared stories with their families, friends, and communities back in America and asked for their financial support. These stories humanized the children and elicited sympathy among White Americans back home. American monetary donations, which cultivated a financial and emotional investment in Korean children, followed. Very quickly, informal support gave rise to sponsorship programs, where American families were asked to make a monthly donation to support an "orphan" in exchange for personalized letters and information (Kim, 2010). Feeling a connection to these needy orphans, American families soon began petitioning to adopt them formally, which provided a solution to the "GI Baby Problem" of mixed-race children in Korea (Oh, 2015).

In 1955, Harry and Bertha Holt's widely publicized adoption of eight GI babies "triggered what would become a tidal wave of intercountry adoptions" (Oh, 2015, p. 162). In cooperation with governments in the United States and Korea, Holt established an adoption program shortly thereafter, which made it possible and relatively easy for Americans to adopt Korean infants and children. These adoptions took place via proxy so that prospective adoptive parents were not required to travel to Korea to formalize the adoption; rather, Korean children were placed on chartered flights and delivered to waiting parents in American airports. Thus, these parents, most of whom believed they were performing an act of patriotism and Christianity by saving orphan children (Oh, 2015), were not required to experience Korea or to confront their child's preadoption life. In addition, they were not aware of the common corruption that led to the child being placed in their arms.

Orphanages, Orphans with Families, and the Business of Overseas Adoption

These GI babies made up only one segment of overseas adoptions, and by the 1960s, the supply of these babies was declining sharply. However, military occupation and war left tens of thousands of families unable to care for their children as overpopulation, poverty, and child abandonment continued to plague Korea during its postwar recovery. In the years preceding the war, there were fewer than one hundred orphanages in Korea; by 1955, there were approximately five hundred, housing approximately fifty-three thousand children, twice the number as before the war (Oh, 2015; Pate, 2014). By the mid-1960s, the majority of infants and children sent abroad for adoption were of full Korean parentage—the children of single mothers, divorcées, widows, poor families, or families with twins or children with disabilities. Because the Korean government made national security and rapid economic growth its main priorities, only a very small portion of the government's budget was allocated to social programs that might have helped these families raise their children (Kim, 2016). Many poor families placed their children in orphanages temporarily so they would have food and shelter, necessities beyond the families' means (Oh, 2015). If parents were asked for permission for their child to be sent abroad, some would refuse, although some mothers were asked repeatedly until they relented (e.g., Kim, 2016; Liem, 2000). Some mothers learned, only after it was too late, that their infant or child had been relinquished to an orphanage by a relative, in-law, neighbor, or husband. In other words, the common story of adoption, where a birth mother makes an "adoption plan" for her child, is a rhetorical device that frees the adoptee for full incorporation into the adoptive family and culture and liberates the adoptive parent from guilt, as they are the recipient of this gift child (Yngvesson, 2002).

Overseas adoption served multiple interests. It removed some of Korea's "excess" population—mixed-race children, children with disabilities, twins, children of unmarried or divorced women, and children from poor families—all of whom experienced social and institutional discrimination (Kim, 2016). It also fostered goodwill between Korea and the United States, giving the former military protection and aid in exchange for an anticommunist stronghold in Asia. In addition, it secured Americans' beliefs in their humanitarianism abroad and provided a supply of healthy infants for prospective adoptive parents. Importantly, however, overseas adoption was a lucrative business for Korea. Orphanages received foreign aid based on the number of children they housed, and adoption agencies in Korea collected ambiguous fees for their services. As a result, employees of these organizations were incentivized to separate children from their parents and promote overseas adoption, appealing to Korean parents' desires to give their children opportunities and education that they would not have in Korea. Over the decades, Korean adoption, which eventually expanded to other receiving countries, brought in an estimated fifteen to twenty million dollars per year to South Korea (Kim & Klug, 2019; Pate, 2014). Today, Korea is the tenth-wealthiest country in the world, and some speculate that its meteoric rise to status as a world superpower can be attributed in part to its transnational adoption program (Kim, 2010). These adoptions not only brought revenue into Korea; they also relieved the Korean government from having to expend resources on social programs to support poor families and single mothers, who became the primary source of healthy Korean infants for parents abroad. Today, Korean adoptees often return to Korea with their disposable income, bolstering the economy through the purchase of plane tickets, meals, tourism, and souvenirs.

Predictably, the profitability of overseas adoption led to corruption in some Korean orphanages. Agencies were found to overstate the number of children they housed (Oh, 2015) to receive more aid. Maternity homes often worked in conjunction with adoption agencies, providing support for unmarried pregnant women, who were often excommunicated by their families. The food, shelter, and medical care that these homes provided was contingent on the mothers' relinquishment of the baby to the agency upon birth (Kim, 2016). Desperate pregnant women and mothers fell prey to orphanage employees and their affiliates. These mothers, most of whom were already struggling to support their children, were vulnerable to appeals from adoption agency personnel who leveled arguments that their child would have no future in Korea and would be better off being raised abroad. As multiple Korean adoption scholars have pointed out, the paradigm had shifted from "finding homes for children" to "finding children for homes." These homes were outside of Korea.

Regardless of how an infant or child ended up being tracked for overseas adoption, and even though many had living relatives, all were ascribed the same label: Orphan. Although this term refers to a parentless child, most children sent abroad for adoption, particularly from the 1960s on, had at least one living parent (Park Nelson, 2016). For most GI babies, both parents were alive (Pate, 2014). Thus, orphanage and adoption agency workers had to discursively and legally transform a child into an orphan. For example, although an orphanage and Korean adoption agency might have known that a child was the fourth daughter of the Lee family, they would have had to transform the child into an orphan eligible for adoption, a "legal orphan."[1] This "orphan" status erases the child's identity before their arrival at the orphanage and in doing so obliterates the existence of the birth mother (Kim, 2009), creating a "clean break" that "separates the child from everything that constitutes her grounds for belonging as a child to *this* family and *this* nation, while establishing her transferability to *that* family and *that* nation" (Yngvesson, 2005, p. 26, italics original). After this "clean break," the child becomes a blank slate. As Soojin Pate (2014) articulates,

> Cutting national ties becomes necessary for the Korean orphan to be adoptable and to become an American citizen. In other words, killing off the Korean family (by conflating the lost or abandoned child with the orphaned child) inadvertently destabilizes the child's national affiliation to Korea, which is required for the Korean child to take on an alternative American national identity. (p. 78)

Unsurprisingly, upon meeting or searching for their birth families, many Korean adoptees learn that their adoption paperwork was falsified. This paperwork, which described the child to their prospective adoptive parents,[2] often stated that, as infants, they were found abandoned with a "paper slip" with their name and birth date attached to their clothing and that their parents were unknown (Kimmel, 2021). Consider the ramifications if such paperwork were to have provided accurate descriptions, such as the following, all of which are true stories of relinquishment:

- The infant's father gambled away the family's money and refused to work. While the infant's mother was out searching for a job, her relatives placed the infant for adoption. They refused to tell the mother where they had taken him. (Chu, 2012)
- The infant's mother is a widow with five children and not enough money to care for them. The mother agreed to give her youngest daughter up for adoption only after repeated appeals from an orphanage employee who argued that the daughter would have a better life if she were to be adopted. (Borshay Liem, 2000)
- The child's father is physically abusive to the mother. The father took the child while the mother was recovering from a recent beating and placed the child for adoption without the mother's consent. (Kim, 2016)

Such descriptions suggest that overseas adoption was, and is, not an inevitability. They also imply the culpability of the Korean government for not supporting poor families, single mothers, or survivors of intimate partner violence, which was largely accepted in Korean culture until recently (Han & Choi, 2021). They also challenge the discourse of choice, which suggests that birth mothers make an active, informed decision to release their children for adoption (i.e., an adoption plan). Although some women do choose to not parent their children, the institution of intercountry adoption "disproportionately works against the desires and abilities of birth mothers who do wish to parent their children, or would wish to do so if their material circumstances were different" (Kim, 2009, p. 868). In addition, the previous descriptions push back against the notion that birth families are both unknown and unknowable. Instead, such information was withheld, as it would have suggested that adoptees had families and a past, making them less malleable for cultural assimilation and full integration into a new nuclear family.

Transnational, Transracial Adoption
and the Nuclear Family Ideal

There are myriad, interrelated explanations for why White American and eventually European and Australian parents began adopting Asian children seven decades ago and why this practice has persisted over time and expanded to numerous other sending countries such as China. The marketing of GI babies during and after the Korean War elicited sympathy from Americans, who saw overseas adoption as a way to enact their Christian responsibility to protect the world from the threat of communism, to save Korea's children, and to take care of the children of American GIs. Arissa Oh (2015) has labeled this motivation, or set of values, as Christian Americanism. Feeling an increased draw toward domesticity and family life following WWII and then the Korean War, many American families saw the nuclear family as a haven and America as a protector of freedom. The American family's expansion to include Korean or mixed-race Korean children was a metaphor for the hopeful American expansion of democracy.

Before the Korean War, intercountry adoption was a novel concept to many Americans. For most of the twentieth century, a process of *matching* had dominated formal American adoption practice, whereby White parents sought to replicate the biological, nuclear family as closely as possible by adopting infants who were perceived to be similar to them in terms of physical characteristics such as hair color and eye color, as well as demographic characteristics such as religion and intelligence (Herman, 2012). By the 1950s, the nuclear family—two married, heterosexual parents and their offspring living together under one roof—was entrenched as an American ideal, and deviations from this family form were often unaccepted in White middle-class homes. Thus, young unmarried women who became pregnant were often sent to maternity homes to bring their babies to term, give birth, relinquish the infant for adoption, and return to their families as if nothing had happened (Fessler, 2006). The babies were received by adoptive parents, many of whom kept the adoption a secret. The practices of matching and secrecy were assumed to spare the adoptive parents from the stigma of infertility, to protect adoptees from learning that they weren't related biologically to the rest of the family, and to save birth mothers from the shame of tarnishing their reputations.

Secrecy and matching in adoption, however, were not sustainable practices, as cultural changes decreased the supply of healthy White infants for White adoptive parents. The work of activists involved with the civil rights movement and second-wave feminism gave rise to developments such as the Equal Pay

Act (1963), increased access to birth control (1965), and the legalization of abortion (1973), as well as other more ongoing changes, such as an increased acceptance of single motherhood and more women in the workforce. These changes made it increasingly difficult for prospective adoptive parents, mostly couples who were infertile and White, to find healthy White infants. At the same time, across the ocean, the Korean government was willing to reap the economic benefits of ridding the country of its "excess children." The convergence of these factors—a need for healthy, adoptable infants in one country and a perceived excess number in another—sustained the practice of overseas Korean adoption for decades beyond the Korean War.

Of the over 200,000 Koreans sent for adoption abroad, 150,000 were adopted into the United States, and a combined 50,000 were adopted into Europe, Canada, and Australia (Hübinette, 2004; Moon, 2015; Oh, 2015). A similar convergence of the preceding factors has been cited for the adoption of Korean children in European countries. Tobias Hübinette (2003) points to the nexus of Swedes' humanitarian desire to save children in developing nations, the decrease in adoptable Swedish children in the 1960s, and the bond created between Sweden and Korea as the driving forces behind Korean adoption into Sweden. Lene Myong and Nina Trige Andersen (2015) point to similar humanitarian motivations in Denmark. The number of transnational Korean adoptees in Sweden and Denmark has been estimated at around nine thousand per country, resulting in some of the highest transnational adoption rates per capita (Hübinette, 2003; Koo, 2019). Other receiving countries include Australia, Belgium, Canada, France, Germany, Luxembourg, Netherlands, Norway, Switzerland, and the United Kingdom. In nearly all cases, adoptees were raised by White parents. Further, it was assumed that Korean adoptees would assimilate to their adoptive country and that a "successful" adoption was reflected in factors such as adoptees' academic achievement, lack of deviant behavior, and reports of close relationships with adoptive parents (e.g., Simon & Altstein, 1996).

Despite the history of violence and exclusion targeting Asian immigrants and Asian Americans in the United States and presumptions of ethnic homogeneity in receiving countries such as Denmark (Koo, 2019), adoptive parents-to-be were eager to bring Korean children into their homes and raise them as members of their families for several reasons. Media coverage and marketing of Korean orphans and adoptees contributed to a public belief that Asian children were docile and eager to assimilate into their adoptive country. Many adoptive American parents sought to transform their adopted Korean children into "all-American" (i.e., culturally White and middle-class) boys and girls (Choy, 2013). Headlines such as "Korean Waif Becomes Real American Boy" from the *Los Angeles Times* in 1953 (cited by Kim, 2010) created and solidified this perception. For Korean adoptees, full integration and assimilation into a White family and, often, a White community required forsaking claims to a Korean identity in favor of a White American one (Park Nelson, 2016). Because GI babies were usually mixed-race Korean and White, they provided a gradual entry point for couples adopting transracially and paved the way for the adoption of full-Korean children in the 1960s and beyond.

Then and now, East Asian infants and children are perceived as occupying the middle of the so-called racial hierarchy, perceived by Whites as less desirable than White children but more desirable than African American children. Asians are viewed with a complicated desire, as exotic and foreign but also as "model minorities" who can easily conform to meet White middle-class expectations (Park Nelson, 2016; Tuan, 1998). Illustrating this point, sociologist Elizabeth Raleigh's (2018) ethnographic research on adoption agency workers revealed a tendency for White adoptive parents and adoption agency professionals to view adoptions of Asian children as "less transracial" than adoptions of African or African American children. In other words, many prospective White adoptive parents view Asian children as being closer to White than Black children, despite their claims of color blindness (Park Nelson, 2016). Such views, despite being racist and erroneous, helped establish and sustain transnational adoptions from Korea and, later, Vietnam and China.

Overseas adoptions from Korea also became a mainstay in family formation due to preferences for infants over older children. Couples who decided to adopt after experiencing infertility wished to approximate a nuclear family and to parent a child as closely after birth as possible. Faced with a shortage of healthy White infants to adopt, prospective adoptive parents turned to Korean adoption for infants. To some, an added benefit was the physical distance from the birth family. Recent research suggests that some adoptive parents choose overseas adoption specifically because they want a closed adoption and feel more comfortable with birth parents who are an ocean away (Raleigh, 2018). For these adoptive parents, birth parents are viewed as a potential threat to the nuclear adoptive family and the legitimacy of the adoptive parents. The presence, physical or emotional, of birth parents also suggests that an adoptee has a meaningful history that precedes their integration into the adoptive family (Myers, 2014). As anthropologist Elise Prébin (2013) writes,

> A common problem is that in most cases, transnational adoption is constructed by the law as a replacement of blood ties, so when the figure of the birth parent reappears, it disrupts the myth of adoption and seems to threaten identities. (p. 15)

Although the work of adoption and birth mother activists has resulted in an increased promotion of openness in adoption and adoption practices in recent decades, negative stereotypes about birth mothers persist both in popular and interpersonal discourse. For example, adoptive parents have expressed negative expectations that, if reunited, birth parents would ask the adoptee for money or "get in the way" of the child's development (Myers, 2014, p. 181). This depiction aligns with the finding that, during adoption agency information sessions for prospective adoptive parents, Korean birth mothers are depicted as "third world women" (Brian, 2012). Although many adoptive parents have embraced, or at least accepted, the shift toward openness, birth family reunions may be viewed as a threat to the adoptive parents' relationship with their adopted child.

Finally and importantly, the discourse of God and destiny have permeated the language of adoptive parents and adoption agencies for many years. Indeed, the Bible depicts all humans as being made children of God through belief in Jesus Christ: "He predestined us to adoption as sons through Jesus Christ to Himself, according to the kind intention of His will" (Ephesians 1:5[3]). This metaphor operates in tandem with the color-blind logic of adoptive parents and others who claim to "not see color" because "We are all God's children" (Kim, 2006, p. 158) as well as with adoption agencies like All God's Children International, "an orphan care ministry answering God's call to provide the love and care that every child deserves" (AGCI, n.d.). In addition, adoptive parents commonly deploy language that invokes God, fate, or destiny when talking about their choice to adopt and/or about their adopted children. In a study by Leslie Baxter and colleagues (2014), for example, one adoptive parent was quoted as saying,

> I am not a religious person. . . . But I can tell you this. I have no doubt in my heart and soul that EVERYTHING that happens to us in life is for a reason. . . . My daughter . . . was brought into my life for a reason. She is my miracle baby . . . she was meant to be my daughter. My mother's death left me with so much sorrow. But my daughter has given me back so much joy. . . . All this pain brought me so much more happiness. Things definitely happen for a reason. For this, I am grateful. (p. 262)

Echoing this sentiment, when asked to tell the story of their child's adoption, other adoptive parents have made statements such as "We were destined to be together" and "God put us together" (Krusiewicz & Wood, 2001, pp. 793–794). A verse from one well-circulated poem, titled "Legacy of an Adopted Child," conveys similar sentiments. Two verses read:

Once there were two women who never knew each other
One you do not remember, the other you call mother.

. . .

One gave you up, it was all that she could do
The other prayed for a child and was led straight to you.
Author unknown (American Adoptions, 2015)

The pervasive discourse of God and destiny suggests the intimacy of the bonds between adoptive parents and adoptees. For many adoptive parents, these beliefs and interpretations provide deep meaning and comfort. At the same time, the fate of the adoptive parent to receive a child is contingent on the fate of the birth mother to lose that same child. Fate seems like an implausible explanation for birth mothers, who are often highly constrained in their economic and social circumstances (Yngvesson, 2002). Regardless of any individual's views on God and destiny, such language helps shape the context in which adoptees must communicate about adoption, birth families, and reunion. If an adoptee has been told (by her adoptive family, her church, or both) that it was God's plan for her to be adopted, she may feel that talking about her birth parents or searching for them are acts of disloyalty, both to her adoptive parents and to God. In this way, the already-spoken discourse of God and destiny impact family communication.

Transnational Korean Adoptees:
Adults, Scholars, Activists

Between 1971 and 2004, the number of Korean infants and young children sent to the United States for adoption swelled to over two thousand annually, with the highest numbers sent in the mid-1980s (close to nine thousand per year in 1985 and 1986). Sweden has the highest number of Korean adoptees per capita of any receiving country (Hübinette, 2003). However, before the 1990s, the general public—including most adoptive parents—knew very little about Korean adoptees' racialized experiences and their perspectives on being raised by White families and, most often, transplanted into White communities. The model minority myth and the color-blind paradigm of race (e.g., "We don't see color") dominated the broader cultural discourse about race in the 1980s and much of the 1990s. Combined, these discourses allowed many White adoptive parents to focus on their children's successes, to overlook or deny racial differences and racism, and to encourage Korean adoptees to perform White cultural identities (Park Nelson, 2016). In addition, many adoptive parents believed that the best thing for their adopted children was to parent them the same way they would parent children born to them. Family differences and birth families, then, were often viewed as threats to the nuclear adoptive family, which aimed to be "just like any other family." However, in areas with a high concentration of Korean adoptees (e.g., Minnesota), the 1980s also gave rise to Korean culture camps organized by adoptive parents and practitioners, where adoptees could learn about Korean art, music, and food (McGinnis et al., 2009). Although these weeklong camps tended to provide positive exposure to Korean culture on a surface level, adoptees needed more extensive support to develop their identities (McGinnis et al., 2009). In addition, only a small proportion of adoptees grew up attending these camps due to distance, access, and lack of knowledge.

Regardless, many adoptees could not deny or turn away from their experiences with racism, isolation, or thoughts about their families in Korea. Before the Internet, most grew up feeling alone in their experiences, having no idea that there were tens of thousands of other transnational Korean adoptees, many having similar thoughts and experiences in their families and communities. However, in 1986, Swedish adoptees formed the first association for Korean adoptees, AKF (Adopterade Koreaners Förening). Later, other Korean adoptee organizations would follow.

A global turning point came in 1988 with the Western media coverage of the Summer Olympics in Seoul, which highlighted South Korea's rise as a modern, first-world country but also brought to light the sheer magnitude of Korea's overseas adoption program. Journalists from publications such as the *New York Times* pointed out the Korean government's financial motivations for supporting and sustaining the practice (Chira, 1988), suggesting that part of South Korea's miraculous postwar recovery could be attributed to transnational adoption (Oh, 2015). This media coverage transformed overseas Korean adoption from an accepted practice to a source of international shame for South Korea[4] and made the United States complicit in what was framed as an unnecessary, lucrative practice for the now-thriving country. This coverage also indicated to many Korean adoptees that they were not alone in their experience of being raised in White families and White communities.

The 1990s proved a fertile time for the growth of what is now known as the Korean adoptee community. Many adoptees were entering young adulthood and exploring their racial, ethnic, and adoptive identities at the same time that the first online communities were forming. Korean adoptee community took root based on the experience of "not fitting into dominant categories of race, family, and nation" (Kim, 2010, p. 85); the ability to network online and meet face-to-face at adoptee conferences; and a desire for recognition as part of the Korean diaspora by Koreans and overseas Koreans. In addition to connecting online, more Korean adoptees started local Korean adoptee organizations in places like Denmark, Minneapolis, and New York City. At the same time, Korean adoptees also began publishing essays, art, memoirs, and films with resonant themes such as intrusive questions from people outside the family, enduring racism within adoptive families, and longing for Korea and one's birth family (e.g., Borshay Liem, 2000; Cox, 1999; Rankin & Bishoff, 1997), disseminating awareness of a shared Korean adoptee experience. In 1999, the first Gathering of the First Generation of Korean Adoptees took place in Washington, D.C. In 2004, the International Korean Adoptee Association (IKAA) was established in Europe and then in the United States to unite Korean adoptee organizations from around the world and support large-scale events referred to as Gatherings. Since then, Gatherings, some local and some international, have taken place nearly every year.

Regardless of whether they attend Gatherings, transnational Korean adoptees can engage with one another online. For example, the Facebook group Korean American Adoptees has over seven thousand members; Korea Klubben, the Facebook group related to Denmark's Korean adoptee organization, has over eight hundred members; and the official page for IKAA has over three thousand members. These online spaces have provided meaningful, accessible ways for Korean adoptees to connect, share information, and find support (Babe, 2021). In 2006, JaeRan Kim, former social worker and current professor of social work, started the well-known and often-cited blog, *Harlow's Monkey*, which provides resources for transnational and transracial adoptees as well as informed, critical perspectives on adoption (Kim, 2006–2022). More recently, podcasts produced and hosted by Korean adoptees, such as Kaomi Lee's *Adapted* (Lee, 2016–present) and Hana Crisp's and Ryan Gustafson's *Adopted Feels* (Crisp & Gustafson, 2019–present), address myriad topics such as living in Korea as a Korean adoptee, the ethics of transnational Korean adoption, intersectional identities, and birth family reunion.

Of course, the Korean adoptee community is not monolithic, singular, or static. Some Korean adoptees advocate for transnational adoption and have adopted from Korea themselves, whereas others seek to end the practice. Many others would consider themselves apolitical when it comes to the issue of transnational adoption. Some adoptees may seek information or support from social media groups for a limited amount of time, whereas others find an ongoing sense of community among other adoptees, online and/or in person. Regardless of other characteristics or circumstances, however, Korean adoptees share an essential experience (Kim, 2010) of being born in Korea to one family and then flown to a different country to be raised by another family. Within this experience and community, common topics include adoption-related trauma, mental health as it relates to transnational adoption, not fitting in with Korean immigrants in their adoptive country, being mislabeled as Chinese or Japanese in their adoptive country, the experience of birth search in Korea, challenges with adoptive families and/or birth families, the particular experience of being in Korea as a Korean with limited knowledge of the culture and language, and/or parenting as a Korean adoptee. These topics are discussed both online and in formal and informal spaces at adoptee conferences and gatherings.

One key development of the past fifteen years is the rapid growth in Korean adoption studies. Korean adoptee and ethnic studies scholar Kim Park Nelson spearheaded the organization of the first Korean Adoption Studies Research Symposium as part of the 2007 IKAA Gathering in Seoul. The symposium has become a feature of each subsequent Gathering in Seoul (2010, 2013, 2016, 2019). Korean adoption studies have attracted scholars from a wide range of fields, including but not limited to anthropology, communication studies, English, ethnic studies, gender studies, psychology, social work, and sociology. Many, though certainly not all, Korean adoption studies researchers are adult adoptees themselves who bring insider knowledge to their research but who are also subject to spurious questions of perceived bias (McGinnis et al., 2019). Korean adoption scholars have disseminated their work in various ways, presenting to academic and nonacademic audiences in Asia, Europe, Australia, and North America. They publish and are cited in academic journal articles and often serve as expert sources for news outlets such as the *New York Times* and National Public Radio. Importantly, much of the research on transnational Korean adoption has shed light on "how race, gender, class, politics, oppression, and inequity operate within the industries of adoption and in the social fabrics of both our birth societies and our adopted ones" (Park Nelson, 2018, p. 273). In doing so, this research has contributed to the impactful and wide-reaching dialogue surrounding the ethics of transnational Korean adoption and transnational adoption more broadly.

Research in the field of Korean adoption studies has often complemented the ongoing work of Korean adoptee activists. For example, Boonyoung Han, Tobias Hübinette, and Jane Jeong Trenka worked with other Korean adoptees and nonadopted Korean activists to advocate for and bring about changes in Korean adoption laws, such as the 2012 amendment to the Special Adoption Law, which provided greater transparency for adoptees seeking information about their history, to normalize domestic adoption in Korea, and to provide more support for unwed Korean mothers who wish to parent their children (Choe, 2013; Lee, 2021). Artist Kimura Byol, who lived in Korea for thirteen years, helped fellow Korean adoptees navigate the search process and advocated for adoptees' rights to access their adoption records (Lee, 2021). Shannon Doona Bae, an anthropologist focusing on Korean adoption, has worked alongside single mothers in Korea to decrease the stigma surrounding single motherhood, build community, and advocate for stronger governmental support for unmarried women parenting their children (Hu, 2015). These are only a few of the Korean adoptee activists who have worked to effect change for those impacted by transnational Korean adoption and discriminatory practices and policies in South Korea.

Korean adoptee community, art (memoir, poetry, visual art, documentary), research, and activism have contributed to increased normalization of search and reunion for Korean adoptees, although most adoptees choose to not search or may initiate searches without pursuing them further after experiencing setbacks (Park Nelson, 2016). Kim Park Nelson (2016) cites an estimate indicating that between 2000 and 2005, 8.3 percent of Korean adoptees who searched found relatives. However, transnational Korean adoptees wanting to learn about birth search, what it's like to interact with Korean adoption agency personnel, or about the nuances of trying to communicate with Korean family members for the first time can only get this information from other adoptees who share these experiences. Consequently, many Korean adoptee organizations, at local, national, and international levels, host events and provide information on their websites about these topics, such as how to begin the birth search process and testimonies of Korean adoptees who have searched. Regardless of an adoptee's experience with or perspective on search and/or reunion—actively searching, waiting for information, searched with no success, in reunion with the birth family, estranged from the birth family, or not remotely interested in searching—they are likely to find other adoptees who can relate. Often, those who do locate their Korean families are unfamiliar with how the historical and cultural significance of reunion in Korea may shape how their family communicates with them.

Family Separation and Family Reunification in Korea

Korean adoptees who are able to reunite with their birth families may encounter family members, particularly older parents, who conceptualize reunion and family in a way that adoptees find unrecognizable and hard to understand. The fairly recent history of family separation and reunion in Korea provides some explanation.

Since the figurative drawing of the 38th parallel, Korea has been a land of divided families. In the north, worsening conditions, the communist foothold, and shifts in policies between 1945 and 1950 led many Koreans to depart for the south, which was permitted before the war (Foley, 2002). Many left immediate and extended family members behind, planning to reunite at a later time. The subsequent battles of the Korean War, however, led to another wave of family separations due to individuals fleeing to safety or being taken as prisoners of war (Foley, 2002). Importantly, as they moved to or fled from one part of the peninsula to another, most Koreans believed that their family separations—whether they were from siblings, children, parents, or extended family—would be temporary, lasting only until the war's end (Foley, 2002). Instead, for millions of Koreans, these separations became permanent.

Although family separation was a known consequence of the war within Korea, it did not receive international attention until 1983, when the Korean Broadcasting System (KBS) aired a telethon aimed at reuniting relatives. Although the telethon was scheduled for forty-five minutes, the response was so overwhelming that it lasted 138 days and 453 hours, reuniting 10,189 individual family members (Foley, 2002), most residing within South Korea. The upheaval of the war, the destruction in its aftermath, and the lack of technology and infrastructure at that time meant that, for example, a sister living in Seoul and a brother living in Gwangju—both in South Korea—would have no idea what had happened to the other and no means of finding this information (Shvedsky, 2020). Elise Prébin (2013) notes that this telethon, which is still remembered by older Koreans today, was a watershed moment in bringing attention to the pain Koreans experienced due to family separation. In subsequent years, as animosity between the two Koreas waned slightly, a limited number of brief meetings were allowed between residents of North Korea and their relatives in South Korea, which contributed to the national narrative of family separation and reunion (Prébin, 2013).

Family reunions, characterized by heartache and the hope for redemption, made for compelling television, and by the 1990s, family reunion shows became a mainstay of Korean programming. One very popular show, *Ach'im Madang* (*Morning Forum*), which premiered in 1995, featured a weekly segment, *Geu Sarami Pogosipta* ("I miss this person"), in which Korean adoptees searched for, and sometimes reunited with, their birth families. Hosu Kim (2016) and Elise Prébin have pointed out that the inclusion of transnational Korean adoptees within the broader category of "divided families," as described previously, implies that war and poverty are the main causes of transnational adoption, glossing over the reality that transnational adoption has served the nation as a "biopolitical apparatus for managing excess population" (Kim, 2016, p. 138).

Televised reunions between adoptees and their Korean mothers were produced and edited in a melodramatic, formulaic fashion that portrayed adoptees as returning to "the motherland," and their reunions with blood relatives (birth mothers, especially) as moments of forgiveness and redemption. The adoptee's indelible blood connection to their mother and their homeland is emphasized, and the mother's tears, apologies, and embrace redeem her as a mother who made sacrifices for her child (Kim, 2016). Camera operators for these reunions were trained to zoom in on the crying faces of the mother and adoptee, and members of the live audience were paid to react and cry during emotional moments of the show (Kim, 2016; Prébin, 2013). Stories of Korean adoptee reunification, which were conflated with other stories of family separation, pulled at the heartstrings of viewers who mourned the division of family and also of the Korean peninsula. These programs were instrumental in shaping Korean cultural discourse surrounding reunion, shaping expectations for viewers, and reinforcing the collective sense of a sentiment known as *han*, a deep sorrow and bitterness combined with hope and the ability to endure (Glionna, 2011).

The reunion stories on *Ach'im Madang*, while emotionally evocative, constrained family members' communication during reunion, as they relied on "the elaborate construction of a near-fictional narrative that leaves little space for spontaneous attitudes or discourses and proves to be weak in the face of everyday life's obligations and societal pressures in the meetings' aftermaths" (Prébin, 2013, p. 11). Hosu Kim (2016) corroborated this point. Serving as an interpreter for a Korean adoptee's televised reunion with her birth parents and sisters, she noted how the program's framing of the reunion as a happy ending for both the adoptee and her birth family stood in sharp contrast to the difficult, contentious interactions both parties endured in the show's aftermath. Similarly, Tobias Hübinette (2005) points out that the first film to feature the real-life story of a transnational Korean adoptee, *Susan Brink's Arirang* (1991), tells the story of an adoptee—and a nation—redeemed through reunion. Yet complexities and challenges after first meetings were omitted from these representations and likely contributed to some Koreans' incomplete understanding and idealization of what it means to be in reunion.

Implications for Adoptees' Communication with Birth Families and Adoptive Families

Adoptees Interested in Search and Reunion

The historical context surrounding transnational Korean adoption has cultivated an expectation that Korean adoptees should be grateful to be adopted.

The narrative of the Asian orphan being rescued by White adoptive parents and brought to the prosperous West has persisted even as transnational adoption has expanded to other sending countries. For example, Elizabeth Suter and Bert Ballard (2009) found that White adoptive parents of Chinese children receive comments from outsiders that disparage China and suggest that the adoptee is "lucky" to be adopted. And although adoption is viewed by most as a permanent way to form a family, the threat of adoption discontinuity[5] (Kim, 2021) can loom over an adoptee, either in their imagination or in the words of their adoptive parents. Adult Korean adoptee Laura Klunder recalled that when she would lash out at her adoptive parents during her high school years, her adoptive father would say, "I didn't sign up for this. Send her back" (Jones, 2015, para. 25).

When adoptees critique transnational adoption or insist on their rights to know or claim their origins, they have often been labeled ungrateful, unhappy, and, above all, angry (McKee, 2019). This trope, the "angry adoptee," has served as grounds for dismissing adoptee activism and perspectives and as a mechanism to silence adoptees who don't want to be labeled as one of "*those* adoptees." Although research has found that satisfaction with one's adoptive family is unrelated to one's desire to search (Müller & Perry, 2001), adoptees who decide to search and reunite have been, at times, stigmatized as maladjusted or looking for a "new" set of parents to replace the adoptive parents. Unsurprisingly, adoptees have expressed feelings of guilt for wanting to meet their birth parents (Docan-Morgan, 2022); some adoptees choose to forgo searching entirely to avoid judgment or scrutiny (Park Nelson, 2016). Adoptees, many of whom have received positive feedback for "fitting in" with their adoptive families and White communities, know intuitively that searching is an act that highlights difference. The already-spoken discourses of Korean adoption as saving orphans and the discourse of the nuclear family can make it challenging for adoptees to initiate search and to engage in conversations with adoptive parents about their birth parents and for adoptees to navigate interactions involving both sets of parents (Colaner et al., 2014; Docan-Morgan, 2022).

Birth Families

For some Korean birth parents, particularly older generations, reunions symbolize redemption and healing from both personal and collective trauma. This symbolism imbues reunion with deep meaning for many birth parents, one that adoptees may not fully understand or share. At the same time, events surrounding war, poverty, and family separation are traumatic, and because trauma can suppress or erase memory (van der Kolk, 1998), birth family members may be unable to answer questions that adoptees might be eager to discuss, or they may find it too painful to revisit the past and wish to focus on the present and move forward. Indeed, at times, family members avoid topics to protect themselves (Guerrero & Afifi, 1995). Reunion may trigger painful memories for birth mothers who experienced intimate partner violence or who relinquished their child against their will. Often, adoptees search and reunite with the goal of learning the story of their relinquishment, but they may be unaware of how reunion meetings and revisiting the past might impact birth parents.

Relatedly, the majority of recent transnational adoptions from Korea have been due to ostracization of and discrimination toward unwed mothers. This gendered oppression continues to affect Korean women today, as employers often discriminate against single women, and their parents may cast them out of the family (Babe, 2018; KUMFA, 2016). Although a birth mother may be genuinely happy to hear from a child who was sent abroad for adoption, she may also feel deep shame for the circumstances surrounding the child's birth. Further, such a birth mother may be constrained in her ability to meet or communicate with the adoptee, particularly if she has a current husband and children who do not fully know her past. A disapproving husband who learns about a child from a previous relationship may see it as grounds for divorce, which will likely have detrimental impacts on the birth mother's financial situation and future opportunities (Park & Raymo, 2013). Not only do communicators interact against the backdrop of the past; they also communicate with the future in mind. Birth mothers who know that there will be negative consequences to a reunion meeting are anticipating what husbands will say if the meeting is discovered. Reunions are always situated temporally, culturally, and relationally.

Finally, despite a drastic increase in the number of foreigners living in Korea over the past decades (Statistics Korea, n.d.) and the increase in interracial marriage, particularly for Korean men marrying non-Korean women (Park, 2011), many Korean birth parents have likely not had extensive contact with people from other countries and cultures, due to circumstance, education, and social class. Their lives may have been stories of survival that limit their capacity to know or understand non-Korean perspectives. Dominant ethnic nationalism, resulting from occupation and war, presumes that to be Korean, one must be of full Korean parentage, speak Korean, and behave in culturally appropriate ways (Kim, 2010). Of course, Korean adoptees, having been raised outside Korea, may find it challenging to encounter birth families who expect them to adapt seamlessly to Korean culture and learn the Korean language quickly and easily. This expectation, however, will need to be attenuated for mutually satisfying interactions to occur and for understanding to be built.

The point is not that adoptees should avoid reunion or asking difficult questions to protect birth parents or themselves but rather to suggest the importance of avoiding simple or one-dimensional explanations for birth parents' communication or noncommunication, particularly in times of conflict, discomfort, or confusion. As adoptees have expressed that the fear of rejection is a deterrent to search and reunion (Park Nelson, 2016), it may be helpful to reframe potentially hurtful birth family messages through a historical and cultural lens. Doing so may provide more space for interactions and relationships to develop beyond initial meetings.

Adoptive Families

As adoptees in the 1980s and 1990s began speaking about their challenges growing up in White families and communities, their sense of loss related to adoption, and engaging in activist work supporting adoptee and Korean birth mothers' rights to parent their children, they were often met with backlash in their adoptive countries. Some adoptive parents, who expected gratitude for "saving" their child from Korea, were unprepared to discuss issues such as adoption grief and trauma, racism, and the broader complexities of adoption, much less help their children navigate these issues (Docan-Morgan, 2010). In many ways, given how transnational adoption from Korea had been marketed as "rescuing" children, many early adoptive parents did not consider the losses their children suffered; instead, many likely assumed that the benefits of growing up in Western, middle-class families outweighed anything adoptees left behind. Some Korean adoptees have reported that their adoptive parents spoke negatively about Korea and their birth parents (Palmer, 2010; Park Nelson, 2016).

In addition, prevailing cultural discourse tends to frame adoption as an act of love, nothing more, which minimizes context, delegitimizes adoptees' needs and desires for information about their past, and erases the existence of the birth family (Myers, 2014). In a time when definitions of family are being expanded, adoption advocates tend to characterize adoptive families as an alternate family form, yet adoptive families often replicate the heteronormative, nuclear family.[6] Slogans promoted by adoption agencies such as "Adoption is the new pregnant" and "Pregnant on paper" (Raleigh, 2018) suggest that adoption is equivalent to giving birth and discursively erase the birth mother and the adoptee's history.

Still, with each passing decade since the 1970s (Herman, 2012), adoption activists, researchers, and practitioners have called for increased openness, mainly in domestic adoptions, as contact with birth families abroad has often been deemed impossible.[7] This openness, sometimes referred to as structural openness, has become a regular practice in domestic adoptions (McGinnis et al., 2009). Relatedly, adoptive parents have also been increasingly encouraged to honor their child's birth country and culture, a practice that Heather Jacobson (2008) has called "culture keeping." Most adoptive parents of young transnational adoptees today are required to travel to their children's birth country, and many believe that they should cultivate their children's cultural knowledge and pride in their birth culture. For example, White American parents of a transnational adoptee from China may take her to Chinese restaurants and celebrate the Lunar New Year. However, culture keeping has been critiqued for being a simple solution to a complex set of issues. As Jacobson writes,

> Culture keeping is posed as an instrument—perhaps *the* instrument— to heal this rift [between adoptee and their past], to address race, address difference, mitigate future family conflict (especially that which arises in adolescence), and work through family issues. Culture keeping is intended to allow for the acknowledgement of the child's specific and unique origins while doing so in a way that does not necessarily jeopardize the feeling of exclusive kinship adoptive parents crave. (p. 93)

Thus, although adoptive parents may be open to consuming food from their child's birth country or having decorations in their home that reflect their visits to the country, they may be less comfortable with their child pursuing search and reunion.

Yet for adoptees and nonadoptees, the "search for roots" is becoming increasingly normalized, and genetic information is becoming more accessible. *Twinsters*, a 2015 documentary distributed on Netflix, tells the story of transnational Korean adoptees Samantha Futerman and Anaïs Bordier, identical twins who were separated at birth but who find one another via Facebook (Futerman & Miyamoto, 2015). They eventually reunite and confirm their relationship through DNA testing. *Found*, a 2021 documentary that follows three Chinese transnational adoptees who find out that they are cousins using a DNA database and then travel to China and visit their orphanages and caretakers, was also distributed on Netflix (Lipitz, 2021). In both of these documentaries, the featured adoptees form close relationships and view their biological ties to one another as meaningful.

In addition, companies such as 23andMe (over twelve million users) and AncestryDNA (over fifteen million users) offer consumers the ability to send in a saliva sample and receive information on relatives, health predispositions, and ethnic ancestry. The availability and ease of DNA searches have led many transnational Korean adoptees to submit samples, especially those who think about their birth family (Cai et al., 2020). Transnational Korean adoptee, inventor, and entrepreneur Thomas Park Clement donated one million dollars to cover the costs of DNA testing for other Korean adoptees, and many have been successful in locating relatives using their services (23andMe, 2018, 2019, 2020). Organization 325Kamra.org provides free genetic testing kits to Korean adoptees and Korean birth families. These representations and technological developments not only provide information to adoptees interested in searching and reuniting; they also add to the cultural discourse surrounding transnational adoptees and birth families, bolstering the message and belief that transnational adoptees' search for their origins is possible, normal, and healthy and that biological ties can lead to meaningful relationships.

Conclusion

Transnational Korean adoption has a history spanning over seventy years and across four continents. This history is inseparable from how adoptees, birth parents, and adoptive parents communicate during reunion. The U.S. military occupation of Korea, the Korean War, Korea's economic recovery, family separation in Korea, and Korean cultural values are just a few of the factors contributing to the *already-spokens*, the message context that interplays with how Korean birth families communicate during reunion. Adoptive parents in Western countries communicate within and contribute to a context of *already-spokens* that suggest that adoption saves orphan children whose Korean parents could not care for them, the value of the nuclear family, and that their family was destined to be created through adoption. Adoptees have been steeped in contradictory discourse suggesting that they should be grateful to their adoptive parents, but that their birth parents are their "real" parents, creating a discursive burden to reassure their adoptive parents, to communicate effectively with their birth parents, but above all, to not express anger. As the next chapters will reveal, understanding these various discursive contexts provide a nuanced understanding of the messages exchanged during adoptees' reunions with their birth families.

2

Communicating Family with "Strangers"

Initial Reunion Meetings

July 2009

I stand outside Exit 3 of Hwarangdae station in Seoul, waiting to see a blood relative for the first time—my *jageun oppa*, the younger of my two older brothers.[1] At any moment, he will meet us here and walk us to his apartment to meet the rest of our immediate family. Tony, my husband, stands nearby, his solid presence a comfort. I take deep breaths. I cross and uncross my arms, feeling like the wait is both too long and also not long enough. Suddenly, our friend M, who will be interpreting for us, announces, "Oh, Sara, here is your brother!" I turn around and see a person who bears little resemblance to the somber-faced man I had seen in a photo. Instead, he looks, actually, a lot like me, so much so that it is startling. He is cheerful and quick to smile, fast and purposeful in his movements. We exchange a light hug, and he gestures for us to follow him. I study his brisk walk and thin arms from behind. I give Tony a nervous smile and remind myself to breathe.

After five minutes, we approach a tall beige apartment building, identical to the ones surrounding it. Several stories up, a window is open, and friendly faces smile and call out to us, waving. "Your sister, your mother," my *jageun oppa* says in his tentative English, pointing up to the window. I smile and wave back.

We step into the elevator and ride up in friendly, awkward silence to meet the rest of the family. I expect that we will walk down a hallway to my *jageun oppa's* apartment, but as soon as the elevator issues its "Ding!" and the doors part, my mother and sister rush toward me in a blur. I am swallowed in arms and tears and the sounds of wailing and sobbing. We walk down an outdoor hallway to the apartment, my mother, *eomeoni*, still crying. She slips off her delicate sandals at the door without missing a beat in either her steps or her sobs. My *eonni*, older sister, holds *eomeoni's* arm as if to keep her from collapsing, while wiping away her own tears with the back of her hand. My oldest brother, my *keun oppa*, stands nearby, eyes rimmed in red.

The emotional tone of my initial meeting shifted in less than one second. It was as if I had been sitting in a dark room and someone had thrown open a shade; the change felt sudden and blinding. As my mother and sister were overtaken by emotion, I felt as if I were watching myself from the outside. I observed that I should be feeling . . . more. More sadness, more joy, more recognition, more like the people around me. Shouldn't I, too, be crying? Before the reunion, I had told myself to avoid having unrealistic expectations of my birth family, but I hadn't considered my expectations of myself.

M y first meeting with my Korean family took place before I started researching reunions.[2] Since then, I have become a collector of transnational adoptee reunion stories, and not just the ones discussed in this book. Whether they are in others' research, memoirs, films, or online, stories of reunion speak to adoptees' longing for identity and connection as well as the complicated ways people negotiate family relationships through communication. Even though adoptees, myself included, consider themselves fortunate to have connected with their birth families, reunion requires courage. In bringing together people who share DNA but little else, reunions are bound to have moments of uncertainty, confusion, and discomfort.

Transnational adoptees and birth parents differ greatly in their languages, cultures, and life experiences. As a result, they may have different expectations and hopes for the relationship. After all, birth parents remember the child who was lost or relinquished for adoption and may feel a genuine love for them, whereas adoptees often use the word *strangers* to refer to their birth family during initial reunions. These first meetings between family/strangers create a communicative context that is unlike any other, giving participants no experiential reference point or social script for how to communicate. Yet initial meetings have high stakes for adoptees who hope to establish a relationship with their birth family that goes deeper than knowledge of shared genetic material. Although adoptees can approach reunion with low expectations, many hope to find a connection that is ongoing and meaningful. Hopes are high, but knowledge of how to proceed is low.

This chapter focuses on the initial face-to-face meetings between Korean adoptees and their birth families. I asked participants why they chose to reunite and had them walk me through the first time they met members of their Korean families. Due to the travel involved, initial reunions usually involved multiple meetings over the course of several days. Of the eighteen people in the study, sixteen traveled to Korea to meet their families, and two participants' Korean families flew to the United States for the reunion. Table I.1 displays relevant demographic, birth family, and reunion information about each participant.

Adoptees live with uncertainty (Powell & Afifi, 2005), but initial meetings are fraught with an extraordinary amount of uncertainty: About the birth family members themselves; about Korea and Korean culture; about oneself; about the past, present, and future of the relationship; and even about one's adoptive family's reaction to the reunion. At the same time, reunions occur against a backdrop of cultural and everyday discourse: Messages that describe how reunions and birth families "should" be. This discursive context paints an idealized picture of instant connection with one's "real" family, finding unmistakable similarities, and adoptees finally being able to answer the question "Who am I?" Although some adoptees were able to find similarities with their birth families, the idealized cultural discourse surrounding reunions generally tended to contradict participants' experiences and led to feelings of disillusionment or disappointment among adoptees who had high expectations. Regardless, participants and their birth families attempted to communicate in ways that helped them make sense of the past and that facilitated getting acquainted in the present.

Why Reunite?

Reflecting past research on domestic adoptees' reunions, participants' decisions to reunite were often a culmination of circumstances, adoptive family communication, and personal characteristics of the adoptee. The last point is important to emphasize, as several participants indicated that although they had decided to reunite with their birth family, they had a Korean sibling in their adoptive family who was decidedly not interested in search or reunion.[3] These cases suggest that, even within the same adoptive family, individual experiences and characteristics shape one's interest in their identity, origins, and birth family.

Contrary to the belief that adoptees search and reunite with their birth parents to replace their adoptive parents, adoptees in reunion tend to report their relationships with adoptive parents as close (Müller & Perry, 2001) and are not attempting to swap one set of parents for another. Rather, nearly all participants emphasized that their decision to reunite was primarily about their desire to learn more about *themselves*. In other words, adoptees reunite to develop their own *adoptive identity*, the subjective sense of who they are as an adopted person (Grotevant et al., 2000). This process, called *adoptive identity work*, involves adoptees communicating and thinking about what their adoption means to them, constructing a life story, and making sense of who they are in the context of their adoptive family, birth family, and larger social contexts (Colaner et al., 2014; Grotevant et al., 2000). For many adoptees, thinking about their birth family, searching, and reuniting are a part of adoptive identity work. Although early research suggested that search was a result of a personal deficiency or pathology on the part of the adoptee, more recent studies have found searching to be a common component of adoptive identity work. Participants' reasons for reuniting reflected this identity work; they were curious about the story behind their relinquishment, whether or not they resembled anyone in their families, and their family's life today. Of course, participants tended to cite multiple reasons for their decision to reunite.

"Why Not?"

When asked why they chose to reunite, many participants expressed some degree of ambivalence. Of these, most indicated that they were already in or planning to go to Korea, and search and reunion were almost an afterthought. The likelihood of a successful search was, and remains, relatively low, leading many adoptees to visit Korea without even attempting to search. Many interviewees, some along with their adoptive parents, had confirmed plans to go on adoptee tours to Korea, which are often sponsored by adoption agencies such as Holt International, or NGOs such as Global Overseas Adoptees' Link (G.O.A.'L). These tours routinely allow attendees to review their adoption files and/or conduct a search, asking participants whether or not they are interested in doing so on the application form. Such was the case for Sun Ok, who, when asked why she chose to reunite, responded,

Why not? I mean, I was given up basically because I wasn't a boy. My papers say financial reasons, but the long and short of it was that I wasn't a boy. They had already had two girls and for *me* (pause) I never had any harsh feelings about that. Just because it's like, you know, this is what I know. My life in America's what I know. It certainly hasn't been the easiest, but this is my quote-unquote normal . . . but it was more like a "Why not?" and I was starting to become more curious about who *I* was, not so much who my birth family was, so this trip meeting my family and all that stuff was about finding out who I was. Not so much about my family. But it was more like a why not, I've got nothing to lose.

Sun Ok's response of "Why not?" reflects some ambivalence, but her words also corroborate past research that suggests that adoptees reunite as part of their adoptive identity work. She makes a distinction between learning about her birth family and learning about herself, although, in the context of reunion, these objectives can be hard to separate.

Eric's words also reflect some ambivalence about reuniting. He was living in Korea in 2010 when he realized his stay was going to be cut short. He recalled his decision to search before leaving Korea, saying,

The way that it came about was me just finally getting off my butt and realizing that I was lucky to be in Korea to begin with. And that if it was a part of my past that I was trying to run away *from*, there was no real good reason to do that anymore. And it wasn't as if I was dealing with anxiety from being adopted or anything. It was just like simple disinterest before. But while I was over there, at the dentist's office, I just decided to call up my adoption agency and have them open the file. I went in that day to do the file review. That was a Monday. And then, three days later, on Thursday, we *met*. So (pause) that's it. I just decided to stop taking things for granted (laughs), I guess.

Although Eric's narrative suggests that finding one's birth family is a quick and easy process, for most adoptees, it is not. On the contrary, most searches are unsuccessful, and some adoptees wait years for birth family information to become available. Regardless, the preceding responses reveal that some adoptees approach search and reunion with complicated feelings or even indifference. They are, of course, uncertain what, or who, they will find, and whether or not their birth family members will want to meet with them if contacted. After they reunite, this uncertainty may decrease, but it takes time, often years, to learn how interactions and relationships will unfold and how their own communication contributes to this process.

For Others, Not Oneself

Adoptees are often the ones to initiate search and reunion, but birth parents or adoptive parents also may choose to begin the process. When an adoptee is a minor, adoptive parents become gatekeepers of information and initiators and guardians of the search and reunion process. Initially, all communication, whether with adoption agencies or birth parents, passes through them. Consequently, young adoptees, in particular, may base their decisions about birth family contact on what they perceive as their adoptive parents' wishes. Ashley's story demonstrates the role of adoptive parents in a young adoptee's relationship with birth family members. Her experience is unique in that her birth parents attempted to reclaim her when she was five years old. At that time, Ashley's adoptive parents received a letter from her birth parents, via their adoption agency, asking if they could have Ashley back. Ashley remembers having very little reaction to this news, saying,

> At the time I really didn't care 'cuz, you know, I already had a family and friends and stuff, so I was just like, "Oh, whatever," you know. I think it was hard for my parents to decide, like, what to do or how to tell me and they were, like, thinking about this for a long time, how to tell me, and when they told me, I was just kind of like, "Meh, okay."

Through the years, Ashley's mother encouraged her to correspond with her Korean family via letters, which Ashley wrote rather grudgingly. Then, when she and her brother, who was also adopted from Korea and close to her in age, graduated from high school, Ashley's parents planned a trip to Korea for their family. Part of their planning involved working with Ashley's adoption agency to set up a meeting with Ashley's birth family. When I asked her why she chose to reunite, she said,

> I still wasn't really interested in Korea or being adopted and stuff at that point; I was just graduating from high school. I think my adoptive parents really, like, wanted us to have that experience, so I was just like, "Oh, you know, it'll make them happy and I might as well. I'm kind of curious," but there was really no real desire at that point, just kind of curiosity and just kind of like, "Oh my adoptive parents think it would be really cool and they're doing all this work and stuff, and they really want us to have this experience so I'll just do it," you know?

Although all participants expressed that they were ultimately glad they reunited, the stories of adoptees like Ashley, in particular, raise the question of the role of adoptive parents in initiating search and encouraging reunion.

Although Ashley based much of her choice to reunite on her adoptive parents' desires, other participants based their decisions on what they perceived as their birth parents' wishes or emotions. Minsun had been preparing for an adult adoptee tour to Korea and was surprised when she was told, a week before her departure, that her birth mother wanted to meet her. Although she had marked "Yes" on the tour application question that asked whether the organization could search for her birth family, she had assumed that no information would be available, as that is what was indicated in her adoption paperwork. Many Korean adoptees, like Minsun, have discovered that their adoption paperwork, which indicated that the birth parents were "unknown," is incomplete at best or falsified at worst. She recalled her reaction upon receiving the news that her Korean mother wanted to meet her, saying,

So it was a surprise because I didn't know if I *also* wanted to meet her (laughs). So I felt actually I would let her down if I didn't show up, or I didn't realize that that was what I was supposed to experience, so I was not prepared at all.

Minsun referenced a general message that she was "supposed to" reunite, but the source of this message is unclear. Perhaps the mere presence of the question on the application implied a "right" choice. However, the fact that her birth mother had been located compelled Minsun to meet her, as she understood that many adoptees who search for birth families are unsuccessful. Minsun was not alone in considering the feelings of her birth parents when reuniting. Other interviewees, as described later, saw the reunion as an opportunity to relieve their Korean parents of the guilt surrounding their adoption and the uncertainty about what happened to them after relinquishment. In addition, Minsun's words underscore the fact that reunions occur through a series of incremental decisions. First, an adoptee or birth parent must decide to search. If contact is made, an adoptee or birth parent may or may not choose to meet in person. Then, after adoptees meet their birth families face to face, they often decide how much time to spend together. Finally, adoptees and their family members must negotiate whether they are going to make efforts to meet again. Because relationships are constituted in communication, they are always in the process of being created and maintained and are never final or complete.

In addition to Ashley, four participants reported that, as minors, their adoptive parents initiated the search and reunion process. All of these participants described their adoptive parents as being very proactive in discussing adoption and cultivating their children's pride in Korean culture through books, summer camps, and activities. These participants also varied in their interest in their reunion. In fact, some participants' adoptive parents seemed more invested in reunion than their children were. Christine, who was nine years old at the time of her initial meeting, was preparing to travel to Korea with a Korean dance group from her hometown in the United States when her adoptive mother initiated the search. She reflected,

> Now that I'm older, I think it was really important for my adoptive parents to meet my biological parents as well. There's a lot of comfort and a lot of security knowing that, you know, the people that your child was born from are a good family, and I think for my mom, my adoption and my sister's adoption is such a gift. And I think what *my* mom really wanted to do for *herself* was to thank my birth parents for giving *them* the opportunity to have a child. Without my birth parents' willingness, they wouldn't be able to have. So for me, because I *don't* remember ever really feeling a need to meet my birth parents when I was young, it wasn't like, "Oh my gosh, like, Mom, I *really* want to meet my birth parents right now. Like, we're going to Korea, like, let's totally meet my birth parents." I was *totally* open to the idea, but it wasn't something that I really felt the need to push upon my adoptive parents. I think what really happened was my mom just came to me and was like, "Would you like to meet your birth parents? Would you like me to do that for you?" And I said, "Yeah sure, why not? Like if you can, great." Cuz even at that young age, I think I knew that it was very difficult to find adopted children's birth parents. So I was kind of like, if we find them, awesome. If we don't, you know, whatever. Like, I'll be fine if we don't find them. But I'm really grateful that my mom did take that initiative to *do* it.

Christine used the same phrase as Sun Ok, "Why not?" when referring to her reason for reuniting. Interestingly, Christine's words also suggest that sometimes, adoptive parents feel a strong pull toward the birth family and may have their own motivations for supporting reunion.

Mark was fourteen years old when he and his adoptive family were planning to go to Korea with tour led by his adoption agency. Initially, he turned down the opportunity for his agency to conduct a search for his birth family, but he changed his mind as the trip drew nearer:

> At first I didn't, you know, the question came up, [my adoptive parents] asked, "Do you want [the adoption agency] to do a search?" and at the time I said, this was, you know, maybe like six months before.

I said, "No it's fine. I don't. It's not a big part of my life, it's not some-thing that I really want to *deal* with. It's not something that I feel like I need to deal with." And then it got a little bit closer and we started *meeting* with the rest of the families that were going along with us and I started to think, "Well, when am I ever going to go back to Korea? When would I have this chance again?" So I guess a few months before we left, I changed my mind and just told [the adoption agency] that I'd like them to do a search and they got back to me within a couple weeks that they had found my birth mother, and my birth mother had then contacted my birth father because they were still in, not *close*, but they still had contact info for each other.

Whereas Ashley mentioned not really being interested in being adopted or being Korean, Mark stated that he didn't want to "deal with" search and re-union when he was a teenager. Their word choices suggest that their adoptive identities were somewhat on the periphery of their daily lives at the time of reunion. Both participants were adolescents when they reunited, and their am-bivalence at the time may have been a reflection of their developmental stage. Although adopted adolescents are capable of abstract thinking about their adoptive family and birth family, they also vary widely in their interest in these topics (Brodzinsky, 2011). Adolescents are also in the throes of forming their own identity, which includes their adoptive identity but also strengths/ weaknesses, likes/dislikes, interests, sexuality, and more. At the time, their adop-tive identity, which is developed internally and through communication with others (Dunbar & Grotevant, 2004), seemed to be a small part of how they viewed themselves, rather than the main "organizing theme" of their identity (Kohler et al., 2002). They had thought about their adoption but were not pre-occupied with it. Open communication in the adoptive family, which Ashley, Minsun, Christine, and Mark described, is negatively related to adoption pre-occupation (viewing adoption as one's primary identity) and positively related to self-esteem (Colaner et al., 2018). Stated differently, these participants' am-bivalence about reunion during adolescence seems healthy and developmen-tally appropriate given the communicative openness in their adoptive fami-lies. Yet despite this ambivalence, all participants reported being thankful to have been in reunion.

A Natural Next Step

Several participants viewed search and reunion as inevitabilities given the on-going, open communication about adoption and their birth parents with their adoptive parents from a young age, and also because of their natural curiosity. Catherine recalled a strong and consistent desire to meet her birth family and reunited with them when she was ten years old. Through the years, her parents had "always" asked if she wanted to search for her birth family, so when she and her family were planning to travel to Korea with her local Korean dance group, searching was a given. It took one week for the agency to put her and her adoptive parents in touch with her birth family, whom they all met when they were in Korea.

Similar to Catherine, Nikki, who reunited with her birth mother and maternal grandmother when she was twenty-two, indicated that her birth mother had always been on her mind. She told the following story:

> I don't think *all* adoptees want to meet their parents, but it's kind of that continuum of adoption. I think that it's always changing, and it was a natural step for me because I think I've always expressed interest in my birth parents and, you know, had questions about it. And, you know, I wonder what they *look* like, I wonder what kinda medical concerns they have, I wonder what the situation was. And so those were always conversations that I've had ever since I was in elementary school. And my mom would tell me that when I was really young, I had a bunk bed. And I would have all my animals above on my bunk bed and I put food up there. And she didn't realize until it started smelling and molding and being really gross. And she went up there, and I guess when she asked me, "What is all this food doing up there?" I responded by saying, "It's for my birth mom. I'm saving it for her." So I don't know how old I was exactly but young enough that I can't remember the experience. I mean, I've always been a questioning person, wanting to know different things and so this was just another one of those things that I had questioned and wanted to know about.

Nikki's words reveal ongoing thoughts about her birth mother. Notably, this story has become a family narrative that has been told and retold by Nikki and her adoptive mother. Perhaps Nikki's questions and curiosity cultivated a communicative openness in her adoptive family, or perhaps her adoptive parents were open about adoption-related topics, and this allowed Nikki to express her curiosity. Regardless, this openness made search and reunion seem like natural processes in Nikki's development.

Grotevant et al. (2000) found that *adoptive identity* is formed through interactions with adoptive parents and, if possible and desired, with birth parents. Nikki's words construct her reunion as a natural outgrowth of her curiosity about her birth mother, which she had discussed with her adoptive parents over the years. As mentioned previously, participants who reunited as minors or teenagers reported having adoptive parents who were active in fostering a healthy adoptive identity by initiating and welcoming open conversations about adoption and birth parents (Horstman et al., 2016) and engaging the child in social contexts with other Koreans and adoptees. Perhaps not surprisingly, participants who described their adoptive parents as being proactive in cultivating communicative openness about adoption and birth parents grew up in a U.S. state that has many resources and opportunities for families with transnational Korean adoptees. In addition, these participants were adopted in the late 1980s to 1990s, when communicative openness was increasingly normalized.

Reactions to First Meetings: Expectations versus Reality

As my story illustrates, it is difficult, perhaps even impossible, to know what to expect during initial meetings. Regardless of whether participants had been anticipating their reunion for years or had only given it minimal thought, many seemed surprised at their reaction to meeting their birth family for the first time. Participants indicated that they had either heard or read about other Korean adoptees' reunion stories or had a media-based perception of what it would be like the first time they saw people who shared their DNA. Mee Joo was among several participants who noted a disjuncture between how they *thought* they would feel or act, and how they actually did feel or act when they first met their families. She stated,

> I thought I would cry, but I didn't cry at all. I just pictured myself like in this, like, I don't know, wailing drama scene because, I don't know, I'm Korean and I'm emotional and I watch dramas (laughs). But I didn't cry at all and I think I was just very shocked. It was a very surreal experience because everything had happened so quickly and I didn't know what to expect. And I think it's just one of those awkward situations where, you know, like there's a really awkward silence or something and someone tells a really bad joke or says something and all you can really do is smile at them, even though that's not really how you feel.

Not only do Mee Joo's words suggest a discrepancy between her expectations and what actually happened; she also points to a difference between the emotion she was expressing at the time and how she was actually feeling. Korean adoptee Elise Prébin (2013) recalled similar experiences, writing,

I realized that my birth family and I had experienced our first encounter in very different ways: My Korean relatives had presented a united attitude of knowing sadness as they spoke to and about me, whereas I was far more perplexed by our interaction and was simply smiling at them. They were meeting somebody they thought they knew, someone to whom their relationship was clearly defined, whereas I was meeting strangers for the first time. (p. 8)

Birth parents, many of whom have suffered as a result of war, violence, their child being relinquished or lost, poverty, cultural gender preference, and/or social alienation due to single motherhood, may have hoped for, or feared, this moment for decades. In addition, because popular Korean television programs tend to frame reunions as dramatic events where adoptees return to the proverbial homeland to be reunified with their Korean family members who have endured hardship (Prébin, 2013), birth families may have a cultural script for initial meetings that dictates high levels of emotional expressiveness.

Discrepancies, whether between inner feelings and outward expressions or between the birth family's experiences and one's own, are uncomfortable but understandable given the various subjectivities of the persons involved. Adoptees often have no recollection of their birth family, and many have not had regular contact with people who are culturally Korean. As a result, these participants describe what psychologists and others have called *masking*, presenting "affective displays that differ from the emotions they are really experiencing" (Davis, 1995, p. 660). Sociologist Arlie Hochschild's (1979) term *emotion work* captures the effort required to experience one emotion while displaying another. As she pointed out, individuals are often aware of *feeling rules* that govern what we are expected to feel and how we are expected to display those feelings in specific situations. Furthermore, feeling rules are often based on idealized expectations (Hochschild, 1979). If an ideal reunion is one that is full of poignant emotion and tears of happiness, adoptees may feel a need to mask their bewilderment, numbness, and/or any other unpleasant or unexpected emotion they are experiencing. Adoptees who fear rejection for a second time, once at birth and again after reunion (March, 1997) may feel a particularly strong compulsion to adhere to feeling rules and mask their emotions accordingly. In other words, adoptees may experience a discursive burden to communicate emotions that meet others' expectations.

Nikki referenced the influence of Hollywood fantasies on her expectations for her initial reunion, noting a clear difference between what she hoped her initial meeting with her birth mother would be and what she experienced in actuality. She recalled that her birth mother walked past her before their meeting, and neither woman recognized the other. She felt bad for not intuiting that the woman who walked by was her mother. She stated,

> But it made me feel kind of ashamed, like, *"Oh man* you should *know* that." Or there, you know, there should be that connection somehow. But I guess that's just, you know, that fantasy of Hollywood and how they portray every other adoption story. That *"Oh yes, I knew that person. And I totally felt that in the pit of my stomach."* And so it was disappointing that I *didn't* have that.

Ji Kyoung remembers the differences between her expectations and actual experiences as well, but she spoke of this discrepancy positively. Relatedly, she also recalled telling her young daughter about the reunion afterward. She stated,

> I always expected if I ever would go to Korea, I would feel like some kind of a big crazy feeling of blending in, in the street, pictured something like that and I had to remind myself about it all the time because I didn't; it was so natural. And then I drove up to that foster home in the cab and I saw my mom and I saw my sisters. I also maybe had expected maybe I should feel butterflies or excited. Of course I was excited but it was a very calm experience. My daughter asked me, "Did she run towards you and you run towards her with your arms open?" I'm like, "No, it was not like that." I just walked over to her and she looked at me and asked, "Ji Kyoung?" That's my name in Korean, and I was like, "Yeah," and then she hugged me and I hugged her and it was nice, warm and quiet, nothing dramatic. My sisters and I started like (sniffles) crying, but it was a very nice pace and nothing dramatic or stressful, but it felt really nice and good and that's like the closest I could describe it. I think if I had any fears about meeting my family, what if it would be really awkward or I would feel smothered if my mother tried to hug me or I wouldn't feel comfortable about physical contact, but [it was] nothing at all like that. It felt really nice.

Participants' words suggest expectations of a specific emotional response as well as an innate knowing or recognition of either the birth parent or the reunion experience, but such expectations are based on myths or the common cultural discourse that portrays reunions in idealistic, oversimplified ways. Indeed, Ji Kyoung's daughter's question of whether the reunited birth mother and returned adoptee ran toward one another with open arms evokes dramatic, cinematic imagery. However, such portrayals may cultivate unrealistic expectations for reunion and add an additional discursive burden to perform emotions in specific ways.

Overall, participants were often surprised by their emotions surrounding reunion. Sometimes, these emotions were before or after the actual meeting. Sun Ok remembered the days leading up to her departure for Korea, saying, "There were days where I would just start crying, and I don't cry; I'm not very good with emotions and things like that. I'm a very rational person, and I'd just start randomly crying." Then, when she met her birth mother, she described a very different emotional reaction:

> My birth mother basically got up and just started doing this (squeezes her own upper arm/shoulder, moving her hand up and down) started grabbing my arm, basically, and I think it was just to see if I was really real, if I was really there. And I'm kinda standing there, like, "Hello, stranger," like, I didn't cry. I just wasn't really sure what to do, so I just kinda let her stand there and sit here and do this to me (repeats gesture) and eventually she hugs me so I hug her back. Like, if somebody hugs you, that's what you do. But to me, I am hugging a complete stranger. But she has memories of me, seeing me as a baby. I don't have memories of her. (pause) So if you could really sum that up, let's just call that awkward (laughs).

Sun Ok's quotation corroborates findings by anthropologist Judith Modell (1997), who interviewed domestic adoptees and birth parents. She found that birth mothers tended to report that they felt emotional and overwhelmed and had a sense of instant attachment to the adoptee during first meetings, whereas adoptees tended to be more emotionally restrained and rational.

Whereas Sun Ok's expectations diverged from her experiences before and during the reunion, Cat was unprepared for how she would feel *after* the reunion. She met her Korean mother and twin sister in the United States and spent time with them over one weekend, before returning home and to work. She spoke of her post-reunion experience, saying,

> I just had two days off and then I went back to work and I had kind of a breakdown, a meltdown, cuz I didn't give myself, I didn't realize I needed to process more than just, "Oh well, nice vacation" and then go back to work. And so I took, like, three more days off. I went to work for two days and then I went to my HR and I said, "I can't stop crying. Like, I can't pretend to be happy." Cuz I'm in sales, and I'm having a hard time pretending, so I really just need to go home.

Cat's post-reunion narrative speaks to the emotion work required for some adoptees after reunion. She was expected to perform emotions appropriate to customer service interactions and mask the complicated feelings she was experiencing after having met her birth mother and twin sister for the first time. Both Sun Ok and Cat experienced reunion in ways that took them by surprise, even though both of them attempted to prepare for the reunion in advance. Reunion preparations can include many activities, some logistical and others informational: Planning travel itineraries, booking tickets and accommodations, buying or creating gifts for family members (which often includes researching or asking others what would constitute culturally appropriate gifts), coordinating meeting logistics with an adoption agency or tour personnel, deciding what to wear to the reunion (often a fraught decision for Korean adoptee women), and reading about Korean culture to avoid cultural faux pas. I list these activities, certain that I have inadvertently omitted some, to detail the labor involved for adoptees in preparing for reunion and to highlight the fact that emotional preparation (e.g., seeking counseling, reading about reunion, talking with other adoptees, etc.) may be difficult amid other more pressing logistics.

Still, despite even a high level of preparedness, individuals possess no clear way to predict how their reunion will go because, by their very nature, initial reunion meetings are unlike any other life event that the adoptee has experienced up to that time. Because all birth families are as different as each adoptee in terms of their communication behaviors, personalities, and family dynamics, there is a high degree of uncertainty surrounding the first meeting. Just a few of the questions that might be racing through an adoptee's mind, in addition to numerous logistical details, include:

- Before the meeting: How is this meeting going to go? What if it goes badly? What if we don't like each other?
- During the meeting: Am I acting in culturally appropriate ways? Am I feeling what I should be feeling? What are my birth parents thinking and feeling? What are my adoptive parents thinking and feeling? What questions should I be asking? What is being said in Korean that I don't understand?
- After the meeting: Is my perception of the meeting accurate? What was my birth family's perception of me? What should I have done differently? What happens now?

Although it may be challenging to predict how any single reunion will unfold, what is clear is that transnational adoptees need a variety of types of support throughout the initial reunion process, and they may not always be able to anticipate the amount or type of support that they will need. People in the adoptee's life may show support in various ways (Goldsmith et al., 2000). Support may be informational (e.g., telling an adoptee about their own or others' reunion experiences), instrumental (e.g., helping the adoptee to research gifts or pack), and/or emotional (e.g., being compassionate and responsive to the adoptee's feelings).

Communicating "Family" with Strangers

Defining Family

Before looking at participants' experiences during their first meetings with their birth families, we must examine what is meant and implied by the term *family*. Throughout my years of interviewing Korean adoptees about their reunions with birth families and their relationships with their adoptive families, one question always lies beneath the surface: What *is* a family? This question nags at adoptees and most anyone whose family deviates from the so-called norm because, at least in contemporary Western culture, *family* connotes blood relations *and* subjective, mutual feelings of closeness and/or familiarity. Many adoptees approaching reunion experience the stark contrast between the familiarity of their adoptive family, who do not share their DNA, and the unfamiliarity and literal foreignness of their birth family.

Definitions by family communication scholars help to shed light on why some adoptees feel as though members of their birth family are "strangers" and why adoptees such as Ashley felt ambivalent about her birth family because she "already had" a family, her adoptive family. Kathleen Galvin and colleagues (2019) have defined family as

> networks of people who share their lives over long periods of time bound by marriage, blood, or commitment, legal or otherwise, who consider themselves as family and who share a significant history and antici-pated future of functioning in a family relationship. (p. 8)

This definition, however, is grounded in the Western notion of social construc-tionism, that family relationships are created through communication. No-tably, this definition points to the importance of *time* ("long periods of time," "history," and "future") and *self-definition* ("consider themselves a family"), whereas the bonds between persons can be myriad. On the verge of reuniting with their birth families for the first time, most Korean adoptees lack memories of Korea and time with their birth parents, if they had any at all. Further, because we live "in a society where a person can only have one mother and one father, and the legal apparatus around adoption totally obliterates the legal relationship between biological parents and children" (Park Nelson, 2016, p. 160), adoptees can struggle with the idea of having two sets of parents, each equally "real" but in different ways. Despite genetic ties, the adoptee and their birth family start at ground zero if they want to create a sense of family. However, this is not to say that all adoptees do, want to, or should want to create family-like relationships with their birth family members. One participant, Olivia, referred to her reunion as a "happy moment in time" and did not continue contact with her birth family once she returned to the United States.

Birth family relationships, then, can be viewed as a type of "voluntary kin." Interestingly, Braithwaite et al. (2010) define voluntary kin as "persons perceived to be family, but who are not related by blood or law" (p. 390). Their communication, rather than ties of DNA or marriage or adoption, reflects and creates a subjective sense of family. Although Korean adoptees and birth family members are related by blood, their *relationship* as family members must be created and sustained through interaction. Due to the distance between adoptees and their Korean relatives—physical distance, time elapsed, cultural and language differences—the *enactment* of these relationships is voluntary. I draw attention to this point in an attempt to avoid a type of biological essentialism that presumes that adoptees (Korean or otherwise) *should* search and/or reunite, and, that once reunited, they *should* attempt to create and maintain family relationships with their birth relatives. At the same time, I also advocate for the rights of adoptees to know their birth family and to initiate and maintain relationships with them to the extent that is feasible, desirable, and meaningful for themselves and their birth family. Regardless of any adoptee's decision, which may change over time, their family relationships are constituted by messages and meanings exchanged.

A Constitutive View of Relationships and Communication

From a communication perspective, families are "constituted in interaction and talked into (and out of) being" (Galvin & Braithwaite, 2014, p. 97). The family relationship is not a preexisting or independent context wherein communication occurs; rather, communication *is* the relationship. As Baxter (2004) articulates, "Persons and relationships are not analytically separable from communication; instead, communication constitutes these phenomena" (p. 3). Messages, both verbal and nonverbal, are used to create, negotiate, enact, and sometimes, end relationships. For example, if someone asks a middle-class American adult, "Are you close with your parents?" This "close" relationship, or lack thereof, is likely created through messages, such as frequency of communication exchanges, expressions of affection and support, validating listening behaviors, and talking about personal or meaningful topics.[4] An absence of these types of communication would likely cause the relationship to be deemed "not close," although certainly not meaningless or unimportant. This view differs from the Confucian view of family, in which biological lineage is paramount.

Although most participants had exchanged letters or e-mails with their birth families or talked with them via Skype before their face-to-face meeting, only Ashley had had ongoing communicative exchanges in the intervening years between her adoption and her first reunion, and these exchanges were sporadic, reflecting a somewhat open adoption arrangement. The creation of a relationship that *feels* like family takes an ongoing exchange of messages over time. Yet media representations and everyday discourse in which birth parents are referred to as "real" parents tend to frame blood relations as a near-mystical tie between individuals, one that creates an instantaneous sense of connection. As Elise Prébin wrote of televised reunions on *Ach'im Madang: Ku sarami bogosip'ta (Morning talk show: I miss this person)*,

> The program's strong emphasis on "real kinship" based on blood necessitates the elaborate construction of a near-fictional narrative that leaves little space for spontaneous attitudes or discourses, and proves to be weak in the face of everyday life's obligations and societal pressures in the meetings' aftermaths. (Prébin, 2013, p. 11)

In addition, everyday discourse, such as when adoptees are asked whether they have met their "real" parents (i.e., their birth parents) (Baden, 2016; Docan-Morgan, 2010), reifies biological essentialism. The essentialist discourse that "real kinship" can be found only through biogenetic relations and that it will be felt instantly can create unrealistic expectations for adoptees and birth families in reunion. In reality, first meetings and the emotions surrounding them tend to be complicated, and if people want to create relationships with one another, space must be made for reactions and messages that do not follow the made-for-TV formula. In addition, adoptees and birth families must, in some ways, work to construct novel forms of family that depart from nuclear models. As Deanne Borshay Liem (2000) reflected after visiting her Korean birth family with her adoptive parents,

> I wanna be close to my Korean mother and to my Korean family and um, I'm wondering whether the only way that I can actually be clos-

er to my Korean mother is to finally admit that she's not my mother anymore really (voice breaks). The only way for me to be closer to her is to acknowledge that, that she hasn't been my mother for over thirty years and that my other mother has been my mother for, in a way, my real mother, and if I somehow can acknowledge that she hasn't been my mother for all those years that maybe I can then (pause) begin to get closer to her and build a relationship with her, that I haven't had before. (45:55–47:05)

These words reflect how letting go of expectations for a specific type of family relationship can create space to build a closer relationship, but it can be challenging for adoptees and birth parents to build relationships outside the representations they have consumed and the relationships they have enacted previously. A Korean woman likely knows how to "mother" according to Korean culture, but she may not know how to build a relationship as a *birth* mother to a returned adult child adopted abroad. A Korean adoptee may know how to act as a child (including as an adult child) in their adoptive country but not as a child of a Korean mother. For their relationship to be established and built, communication must be adapted and expectations must be attenuated. One of the most important things my *jageun oppa* said to me during one of our first meetings was, "I told our mother that she cannot expect you to act like a Korean daughter, because you were not raised here." This acknowledgment felt like grace, and it gave me room to relax into our time together.

Communication and Family Boundaries

One way to think about communication in families is through what Kathleen Galvin (2006) called boundary management, a term for communication that demarcates who is, and who is not, a member of one's family. Galvin contends that all families, particularly those who deviate from the nuclear, biogenetically related family[5] (i.e., two married, heterosexual parents with their biological offspring, living together), are discourse-dependent; that is, they rely on communication to constitute themselves as a family. This communication occurs among members of the family through internal boundary management strategies, and with people outside the family through external boundary management strategies. These strategies give family members an "authentic, committed, and substantive feel of family" (Galvin, 2006, p. 8).

Internal boundary management strategies include discussing, narrating, ritualizing, and naming and are particularly relevant to how adoptees and their birth families communicate with one another. Because adoptees tend to have questions about the birth family and because birth family reunions tend to be highly ritualized (Prébin, 2013), reunion participants tend to *discuss* the family, provide *narratives* or stories about the birth family and their history, and engage in family *rituals*. They also use *naming* to signify relationships, whether through how they address certain family members or through how they refer to family members when talking about them. These communicative acts may begin to set a foundation for family relationships, although the negotiation of these relationships is neither seamless nor linear.

Discussions during Initial Meetings: Questions and Messages

The Big Question: Why?

I approached most interviews in a chronological fashion, asking participants what, if any, questions they had for their birth parents going into their first reunion, and if there were any messages they wanted to convey to their birth families. Perhaps not surprisingly, many participants indicated that the main question they had was *why* they were relinquished for adoption, or the circumstances that led to their adoption. This question addresses the adoptee's identity but also how they fit within the birth family. In line with previous research, many interviewees perceived their life stories to be incomplete because they didn't know about their preadoption lives. As Hanne stated,

> I've always had a life with a missing link, you can say. Because when I came to Denmark, I was one and a half years old. And of course, I had a report. I had been in foster care, but I didn't know what had happened before that, before I came to [the adoption agency]. I wanted to know the background story. That was *very* important for me.

Adoptees and adoption scholars have noted that adoptees' life stories are often told beginning from the time they were adopted rather than when they were born. As graphic novelist and Korean adoptee activist Lisa Wool-Rim Sjöblom (2019) writes, "It's no wonder we adoptees forget that we were ever born. We're taught that our existence began the day we met our new families. . . . Many of us actually believe that our lives started with a flight" (p. 13). Scholars have found that life story coherence, "an individual's ability to create and maintain an integrated and cohesive self-narrative" (Baerger & McAdams, 1999, p. 88), is correlated with mental well-being. Understandably, adoptees want to know the story of how their lives began and why they ended up being sent abroad for adoption.

Although most participants approached their reunions wondering why they had been placed for adoption, there were exceptions. Olivia stated that she didn't have any specific questions for her birth family and that she didn't want to hear "any excuses" for her relinquishment and adoption because she had had a "good life." She elaborated, saying,

> At the end of the *day*, whatever the, the reason is, I mean, I guess you can go back and ask them, you know, *why*? And why not try harder? I mean all those questions you can ask. I try not to ask those questions because there's no real answers for them . . . whatever the situation was, it happened for a reason.

Sun Ok also didn't have specific questions about her family history and her relinquishment when she went into her first meeting. She said she had "no expectations" but then felt pressure to ask questions. She recalled,

> I mean, I really went in there with no expectations, positive or negative. . . . One of the girls in our [tour] group had started a blog and she had listed like *twenty questions* she had wanted to ask her family. I looked at that and I was just like, "Holy *crap*, am I supposed to have all these questions to ask my family? Because I don't." I'm like, "What am I going to do? Like, I need to come up with questions or something."

One can see how the expectation that there were correct or necessary questions for birth parents created stress and an additional discursive burden. After her first meeting with her Korean mother, Sun Ok recalled debriefing with the director of the tour group, who advised her to ask more specific and personal questions the next time she met with her birth family, which was several days later. These questions were about topics such as the family's health background, her birth mother's pregnancy, and the decision to relinquish Sun Ok for adoption. At first, Sun Ok resisted, but eventually, she relented, letting the translator ask her birth mother some of these questions. When her Korean mother responded that she did not know the answers to the questions or did not remember, Sun Ok was not bothered at all. She stated,

> They weren't my questions. They were somebody else's questions who thought that they were important or they would be important to me later on in life. . . . So for me it's like if I don't ask now, maybe I can ask later; if I don't ask later, then whatever. It's not a big deal.

Although most participants expressed that they wanted to know the reasons for their relinquishment, Olivia's and Sun Ok's perspectives demonstrate that people who attempt to support adoptees during reunion (e.g., adoption tour leaders, interpreters, etc.) would do well to treat every adoptee and every meeting as unique, and not exert pressure on adoptees to enact particular scripts during reunion.

Searching for Similarities

Many participants approached reunions wanting to know whether or not they resembled any members of their Korean family physically. In line with previous research (March, 2000), because participants had lived their entire lives devoid of any biogenetic connection, they found great meaning and comfort in similarities with their birth family. Those who were unable to find similarities expressed disappointment. One of the first things Meagan wanted to tell me about her reunion was the following:

> I have short and wide thumbs (laughs). And they're very, sort of unlike, you know, anyone else in my family's or anything. Anyway, I always wondered where they came from. And wondered if my birth family had these thumbs, like if it was a hereditary thing. And so I asked them, or my translator translated it. And (laughs) my brother gets all excited and shows me his thumbs and they're exactly the same and it was just. It sounds really, you know, kind of funny because it's such a little thing but it meant so much to me.

When I asked Cat if she had any questions or anything she wanted to tell her birth mother and her identical twin when meeting them, she responded, saying,

> I told [my *eomma*] that when I was young, I used to wonder what she looked like and did I look like her and then, you know, it was just odd because I have curly hair and nobody could understand why I had really curly hair and then when I met her, my *eomma*, that was a question I asked her. I said, "I have curly hair, where does that come from?" And she said, "Your twin has curly hair, I have curly hair, and your father had curly hair." And so I thought that was funny, but I really, I was so overwhelmed and the whole thing kind of felt surreal, that I really didn't have a lot, and I remember kind of wanting break times *a lot* and wanting to just go, go sit down and be alone, but then I felt

bad you know, and when I would *be* away from them, I missed them or I felt bad.

Cat's words point out that although reunions can provide some answers, they can also bring about mixed or conflicting emotions and desires. Similarly, Eric was overjoyed at meeting his older brother and seeing their resemblances for the first time. Yet when his brother wanted to go out and spend the night together after their first meeting, Eric declined, telling me, "I must say, we really did bond instantly; I was just exhausted. Like there's only so much you can take in a day." Cat and Eric were among many participants who expressed the struggle between wanting to connect with their birth families and needing some separation and time away from them to manage emotions and recharge.

Other participants perceived similarities in their interests or occupations and those of their birth family. They found these similarities meaningful, as they offered a way to make sense of parts of their own identities. After meeting his birth mother and birth father separately during the same trip to Korea, Alexander reflected,

> The reason I liked architecture and art and like graphic design and stuff is because my father is an artist. So, it was very surprising how much of me is a part of them at the same time, even if we didn't know each other. . . . So I'm thinking that I was gonna go into graphic design school and I told my father and he was glad that he had passed on something, I'm thinking, to me. Besides physical appearances.

Similarly, Minsun, a documentary filmmaker, observed similarities between her occupation and those of her birth parents:

> Suddenly I was the child of a clothes designer and a very fine architect, you know? Maybe my artistic visions came from *somewhere*! That had to be shocking for me to realize that, okay, it's not only *me* who wants to be creative all the time.

The importance of adoptees finding similarities, whether physical or occupational, whether imagined or genuine, should not be understated. As Brodzinsky and Pinderhughes (2002) wrote, "The inability to look into the faces of their adoptive parents and siblings and see reflections of themselves—something that is typically taken for granted in biological families—is often experienced as disconcerting" (p. 291). In fact, physical resemblance has been found to be an important marker of family identity, suggested by the practice of matching in the early days of legal adoption. More recently, Suter et al. (2008) found that lesbian couples chose their sperm donor based on similarity in physical characteristics and, sometimes, even the interests and hobbies of the nonbiological mother to create a cohesive family identity. Such findings affirm the importance of physical resemblance in families and further validate adoptees' desires to find such similarities during reunion. Family similarities allow individuals to see themselves as a part of something larger and to make sense of their place in the family and in the social world.

In contrast to those who found common physical or occupational similarities with their birth families, some participants noticed an absence of such resemblances. Nikki stated,

> It was also disappointing because looking at her, I couldn't see myself in her. I couldn't see myself in my birth grandmother either, really. So it was just frustrating to have that thought and I was thinking, "Oh, I'm gonna look like her." Some part of me. And the first thing that she said to me, but then it was translated, was that I was short. And I am about five foot two . . . and I *think* she's five foot seven, five foot six or something. So she's just *a lot* taller than I am. So that was kind of also, you know, thinking back, "Oh this should be like a wonderful moment," and you think about these beautiful stories or whatever. Then my story goes, you know, "Oh, you're short."

Nikki continued describing the physical differences between herself and her mother within the context of South Korea, where idealization of thin body types has resulted in some of the highest rates of disordered eating and body dissatisfaction in all of East Asia (Jung & Forbes, 2007; Noh et al., 2018). She recalled,

> She was very tall, very thin. So she was probably only like 110 pounds and five foot seven. She was just stick rail thin. And that was the thing. I'm not a large person, and going to Korea, I just felt that I was, you know, *above* average in weight because everyone was just so teeny-tiny there and thin around my age grouping that I would see in town. So I just kind of looked like the fat, ugly daughter (laughs). Which I *knew* I wasn't, but I just felt like that almost. Seeing my birth mother and how she just had poise and presence.

Nikki contrasts her reunion meeting with the "wonderful" stories of others' reunions. The preexisting cultural discourse set an expectation that was ultimately unmet. In addition, her lack of similarity to her tall, thin mother and to Korean women more generally impacted how Nikki saw herself as a woman and as her mother's relative.

Although Sun Ok expressed that she didn't have any specific questions for her Korean family before their first meeting, her words reveal some disillusionment that she didn't bear more physical similarity to them, making them feel even more like "strangers." She stated,

> I didn't have any connection because we're *strangers*. And even after *seeing* a picture of (laughs) my birth family in 2006, I looked at it, and I'm like, I *still* don't look like anybody! Like, that was the funny-slash-ironic-slash-*what the heck* kind of thing, cuz I was like, "All my life I don't look like anybody," and as I went through high school and understanding the concept of family and what it meant in terms of being biologically related and *seeing* similarities in brothers and sisters, and then finally getting to see what *my* family looks like and being like, "Really, I still don't look like anybody?" Like, it was just, you just had to laugh at it, and I know that in some ways I did look like my second sister, we both had similar cheekbones and I had triangle eyebrows just like my *father* . . . I just had no connection to them because they're *strangers*, because they've not been in my life, and at that point in time, I still felt like I didn't look like them. Like, to be honest, when I first met my birth mother (pause) you could've pulled just any Asian woman off the street and I would've thought that would've been my birth mother.

Adoptees who found differences rather than similarities with their birth family experienced what has been referred to as a *personal-relational identity gap*, wherein one's self-concept or self-image does not align with one's relationship (Colaner et al., 2014); in other words, how these participants saw themselves contrasted with their membership in the birth family. Similar to the domestic adoptees in the same study by Colaner and colleagues, participants "struggled to define how they viewed these birth parents as influential to their identity" (p. 485). The lack of similarities can be particularly disorienting for adoptees who have longed to ground themselves in their identity as a member of their Korean family because there is no visual evidence of their membership in their adoptive family.

Participants who do not find similarities initially, however, may find them later. Years after her initial reunion, Ji Kyoung and her teenage daughter were diagnosed with attention-deficit/hyperactivity disorder (ADHD), which made her wonder whether anyone in her birth family had the same disorder. When she asked her Korean sister, she learned that her father, siblings, and nephews either had been diagnosed with ADHD or had diagnosed themselves informally. Ji Kyoung's reaction to this revelation was a mixture of incredulity, relief, and realization. She recalled,

> I was like, *what?* Why, why haven't you told me before? You could've told me ten years ago when I met you the first time, and I have struggled and suffered for so many years! . . . And then, all of a sudden, I could understand also why I feel so relaxed when I'm with them, because the way they function and also the way they think are similar to mine, or actually the same. I always felt like I had bad conscience when I'm with my own [adoptive] family, because I'm not, I just *always* feel wrong or odd, but I could just, the first time, every time I saw [my birth family], feel like I was okay! I wasn't "wrong" (makes air quotes gesture) in their eyes, because also I could see that they were just like me and now it's even more hysterical to think that they all are officially or unofficially diagnosed with ADHD.

Ji Kyoung's story illustrates that if initial meetings are the start of a long-term relationship with birth families, similarities may emerge over time in ways one might never expect. Ji Kyoung was not aware of her ADHD until years after her initial reunion, but her diagnosis led her to ask her birth family whether or not the disorder ran in the family, which it did. As a result, her diagnosis provided her with a new point of connection with her Korean family and a new understanding of herself.

From Strangers to Acquaintances: Getting to Know One Another

Participants also viewed first meetings as an opportunity to get to know their birth family. They were curious about their current lives and wanted to know what their daily routines were, asking basic questions about families, hobbies, and jobs. To move past being strangers, participants often began discussions at the level of "small talk."

Communication scholars such as Mark Knapp and Anita Vangelisti (2005) have developed models of relationship development that suggest that, as relationships become closer, disclosures become more personal. Although Knapp and Vangelisti's model has been most typically applied to romantic relationships and friendships and has been critiqued for its linear implications (Mongeau & Henningsen, 2008), the idea that communication is required for interlocutors to progress from strangers to acquaintances is inarguable. Further, the communication involved in this process tends to be rule-governed. In Western contexts, the rule is that initial disclosures between strangers are to be constrained to topics that are perceived as safe and surface-level, such as occupation, education, and hobbies.

However, adoptees and birth families may be sharing deeply personal, emotional information during their first meetings, which runs counter to the communicative rules or scripts for most Westerners' initial meetings between strangers. As Christine, who met her birth family when she was a child, articulated before her first meeting, "They are strangers who love me." At the time, Christine found this concept comforting, but the dynamic of birth parents who feel as though they are meeting a long-lost, beloved child, and an adoptee who feels as though they are meeting a stranger whose language and culture they do not share can create uneasiness for many adoptees.

The documentary film *Resilience* by Tammy Chu (2012) follows the intertwined stories of Korean adoptee Brent Beesley and his birth mother, Myung-ja, as they reunite and attempt to build a relationship. Sitting in Myung-ja's home among members of his birth family, Brent narrates, "Besides the language barrier, we were basically on a clean slate. We were starting from square one. As strangers. It was kind of awkward" (31:03). Juxtapose his words with his birth mother's: "I didn't get to see him grow up, and that breaks my heart. At least from now on, I want to take good care of him" (33:14). For decades, Myung-ja had been longing to meet Brent, who was in his thirties at the time of their first meeting, as she had never consented to his relinquishment as an infant. Minutes later in the film, she is shown holding a bite of *japchae*, Korean glass noodles and vegetables, in her bare fingertips in front of Brent's mouth and saying, "*Ahh ahh,*" as she tries to coax him into opening his mouth. She laughs and tells him in Korean, "Open wide. That's how we do it here" (32:44). Brent, who is unfamiliar with both the food and being hand-fed as an adult, winces and attempts to dodge his mother's hand, asking, "What is it?" before relenting. In under two minutes, the film highlights the multiple perspectives at play during this meeting, contrasting the parental love and care that Myung-ja wishes to provide with the unfamiliarity Brent experiences as an adoptee who only knows her as a stranger who loves him. Like Brent, it was common for participants to employ the word "awkward" in describing their first meetings with their birth parents.

Birth Family Messages: Apologies, Love, and Gratitude

Whereas participants seemed to approach reunions with questions, birth parents seemed to approach the initial meetings with messages that they wanted to convey to the adoptee and/or the adoptive parents. These messages, which were often relayed through interpreters, were composed mainly of *apologies*, *expressions of love*, and *gratitude toward the adoptive parents*.

Apologies

Often, the first message that birth parents wanted to convey to adoptees was that they were sorry for their child's relinquishment. Sylvia's description of her first meeting with her birth parents, which took place at the airport in the U.S. city where she lived, captures the intense emotions that can accompany apologies. She recalled,

> And my birth father was the first one that I met and he just, like, grabbed me. And like, his hug felt kind of tentative. Like, he would kinda tighten and loosen and tighten and loosen. And, he was crying too, so I don't know if that was just that. Or if it was just (pause), it was just a little, like, inconsistent, like that. Like he just wasn't sure, like, how tightly he could hold me, kind of. So he, like, grabbed my face and talked to me. And you know, from what I can understand, he would say "I'm sorry, I'm sorry, I'm sorry" (laughs). [He] just apologized and was crying. And I was crying. And (pause), and then, well at that time, my birth mom was hugging my aunt and meeting [my husband] and the kids. And he just was holding me for so long. But then she hugged me and apologized a lot and cried. They kept apologizing and telling me that they loved me. You know, that was most of what they could say in English.

Sylvia's birth parents learned two English expressions for their initial meeting, one of apology and one of love. These interconnected sentiments seem to capture the most important messages that birth parents wanted to convey to adoptees.

Sun Ok describes her initial meetings with her birth parents, indicating that they apologized profusely and also expressed gratitude toward her adoptive parents.

> Mostly the messages I wanted to convey were mostly in response to what they would say, the biggest one being them apologizing. Like eventually when I met my father also, all he did was apologize, my birth mother it was all she did, and my biggest thing was, No, I'm *fine*! Not

a big deal! Yeah, once in a while, this whole identity thing kind of sucks (laughs), like you're just like, I don't fit here, I don't fit there, and you're just lost, but everybody has their own identity crisis. And *everybody* goes through it and we all just do it in different ways at different times. So the biggest thing I was trying to convey to them as a response was I'm happy, I'm healthy (pause), don't feel bad, don't regret anything, it's *okay*, I'm here now . . . I know it was important for my adoptive mother to convey to my birth mother that, you know, she was a good mother and that, at the end of it, my birth mother wanted to convey her gratitude. So yeah, that was conveyed in there also, but mostly it was a response of "*I'm okay.*" Like there is (pause) more or less, nothing wrong with me, I mean I think we all have problems, our own problems, but more or less, I'm okay. I've got good parents, and I've had a good life, I continue to have a good life and I'm *happy* with where I am and who I am. And being in Korea and stuff made it that much *better*, that reassurance that it's okay, everything's fine, you made a decision and life moves on.

Like most participants, Sun Ok expressed an acceptance of her birth family's apologies and attempted to absolve them from feeling guilty. At the same time, her words suggest personal challenges with identity and belonging, which she and other participants experienced and which manifested in mental health struggles. However, Sun Ok and others attempted to minimize these difficulties because they did not want to compound their birth parents' feelings of guilt or shame. Thus, adoptees often felt compelled to exonerate their birth parents, an additional discursive burden.

Expressions of Love

Several participants indicated that their birth parents said "I love you" either in Korean or in English during their initial meetings. This direct verbal expression is notable, given Korean parents' tendency to express warmth and love to their children indirectly and nonverbally rather than explicitly (Choi et al., 2013). Two plausible explanations are that the birth parents are attempting to communicatively accommodate (Soliz & Colaner, 2018) to adoptees' culture and language, and/or that they felt the need to express their love directly, given that the adoptee was relinquished from the family.

Gratitude toward the Adoptive Parents

Either directly or indirectly, birth parents also used initial meetings to express gratitude toward participants' adoptive parents for taking care of their child. Meagan said,

My [adoptive] mom met them all. And they were so sweet to her. They just kept saying thank you, you know. And they were like, "Thank you for adopting her, thank you for giving her such a good life. We can tell that she's well-taken care of and that she's a great person." And they just kept thanking her over and over again. And my mom kept thanking them and saying, "No, thank you for giving her to me," you know. And it was just. It was ama—(stops mid-word). It was incredible. I don't even know, you know, how to describe it in words.

Although Eric met his Korean family without his adoptive parents present, his birth father emphasized his gratitude to them and advised Eric to be a good son to them.

Like he was, you know they're still very Confucian over there in the older generation and that's what he kept saying over and over is that we owe your American parents everything. . . . He just kept stressing over and over, you know, "Take care of your parents. You need to, you know, show them respect and spend time with them while they're still around."

Birth parents' gratitude toward adoptive parents reflects the assumption that, by raising the adoptee, the adoptive parents took on the birth parents' duty or responsibility. This sense of gratitude or indebtedness is connected to birth parents' feelings of shame, even though there were often significant barriers preventing them from raising their child. Such messages, while understandable, reflect and reify the narrative of Western adoptive parents "saving" Korean children. Birth parents took personal responsibility for the child's relinquishment, even though governmental, legal, cultural, and institutional forces strongly encouraged adoption. Adoptive parents, in turn, were the recipients of gratitude and recognition, even though they had more material and social resources to draw from as parents and even though they benefited from raising the child as a member of their family. Participants also reported that their adoptive parents expressed gratitude toward the birth family for letting them raise the adoptee, which implies and exaggerates the birth parents' agency in the adoptees' relinquishment and placement in a particular family. This exchange of messages, while likely meaningful, obscures the larger systems of inequality that have assigned certain parents as givers and others as receivers, and which commodify the adoptee as a gift (Yngvesson, 2002).

Birth Families Narrating the Past

During initial meetings, as most participants sought information on the reasons they were placed for adoption, birth parents shared narratives of their past and did their best to provide explanations for the adoptee's relinquishment. These narratives often manifested themes of poverty and illness in the decades following the Korean War, as well as Korean cultural values regarding gender. Isabel relayed the story her Korean mother told her during their first meeting:

> I learned that my mother, after she had me, went into a deep depression. She actually ended up having a hysterectomy. And what *really* gets me is that they said that she went back to go get me after four months . . . she just kind of regretted this decision, I guess. I was kind of surprised to learn that I was the youngest, I was always thinking maybe [I was] the oldest child, but I learned that I was the youngest of three. And basically they were just very poor at that time. They lived with a lot of family members, they had a *cart*, my older sister was sleeping under that. So it was very difficult at that time. When she went to go back to get me at four months, they had told her that I'd already been adopted out.

Cat corresponded with her twin sister before meeting her face-to-face and learned, via e-mail, the story surrounding her relinquishment. Cat described it, saying,

> She told me the whole story about how we were separated. She said that when our mother was pregnant and gave birth to *twins*, she lived with our father's sister. And she said, "You will not, you can't keep two. I won't feed two babies," so they kept the eldest baby and had *me* taken away. And I guess it was my aunt; she took me out of my mom's arms or *something* like that and they didn't get to name me, so they were really upset about that and then took me to the adoption agency. And then they needed a name, so my aunt just reversed *her* name. And so her name was Jung Hee[6] and so the adoption agency named me Hee Jung. And then when my father passed away of lung cancer . . . I guess his last words were that he wanted to *find* the other twin. And it's just, I was like reading this stuff and I can't believe, this is *intense*, you know? Just what, you know, but yeah (laughs, tearing up).

Several female adoptees indicated that their gender was the reason for their relinquishment. As Catherine was ten years old at the time of her initial meeting, her adoptive parents asked her birth parents questions through an interpreter.

> And I think my [adoptive] parents kind of asked why I was given up. And my birth parents won't really talk about it. They'll just say it was a hard time. And the translator kinda steps in and says, "Well, it's really, like, tradition. You're supposed to have a son." And so I mean everything else is kind of implied. You were given up because you weren't a boy. So they kept trying and they finally had a son, yay! (sarcastic tone)

Catherine's birth parents kept her younger brother, and he was raised with their family in Korea. Ji Kyoung, who had five older Korean sisters and a younger brother, remembered having a negative reaction to the narrative of her relinquishment due to gender. She stated that she was surprised by her own reaction, saying,

> I will say I've also always felt okay with being adopted. I met some people who feel really bitter about it, but I never felt bitter. I kind of always thought if someone chose to adopt her own child away, there has to be a really good *reason* so I don't hold any anger against my [birth] mother or anything like that. But when I sat there and I heard the story, which actually surprised me a lot, I didn't know it was inside of me and I heard how they told about the whole procedure and life back then, I (pause) suddenly was overcome by this feeling like, how could you do it? How could you? And now I cry (starts crying, tearing up) every time I think about it, but I was like, "How could you do that to me? How could you give me away you, you BASTARDS?" And I never *ever* felt like that, I never, and I don't feel like I'm someone who *lies* about or denies my feelings but it *really* surprised me. Of course I didn't *say* that to them but I could just feel it.

Catherine, Ji Kyoung, and other participants grew up in a time and in countries where the practice of parents relinquishing a child due to gender preferences is unthinkable. Therefore, their negative reactions to the stories of their relinquishment are understandable. Yet they also sensed that it was unacceptable to critique their birth parents' decisions and kept their strong reactions to themselves.

Answers . . . and More Questions

Although birth families were reported to have shared information regarding the circumstances leading up to participants' relinquishment, participants were often left with questions remaining. For example, Hanne learned that her Korean mother had been the "house teacher" for a wealthy family and became pregnant by the father of the family. Because Hanne's birth father could not divorce his wife and because single mothers and their children were, and are, stigmatized and discriminated against in South Korea (Babe, 2018; Bae, 2018), Hanne was relinquished. Still, she left the initial meeting with questions about her mother's life. She stated,

> She didn't *describe* her life in what do you call it, a chronological way. She wrote things about her life, you know, "When I was twenty-five" and now, and "When I was thirty-one," and "When I was married." And so it was like a puzzle in a way. I had to put it together myself. And still to this day, I have some missing years in her life. I don't know what happened, um, from the age of about thirty years old and up to about midforties. She hasn't described that period of her life. That's also why I think that, I *know* she has had a very rough life. Things didn't work out. Things didn't go the way she wanted it to go.

Eric, who was relinquished for adoption at the age of three, felt disappointed that his birth father was unable to answer his questions. He stated,

> It was so interesting because one of the whole reasons that I wanted to have this reunion of course was to like fill in all these blanks from my childhood. And find out what it was like to be *in this family*. And my father really couldn't fill in much (laughs). He didn't really re-member very much at all about when we were young. . . . I asked him for even just *one* story about when we were babies or what I was like as a baby. He couldn't remember. Which was incredibly disap-pointing I have to say (laughs). Like, our Western perception that, you know, it's like every baby is *documented* with such scrutiny. And, you know, I think about the babies born today. And, like, how many thousands more pictures there are of them than (laughs) anyone else in recorded history, you know. And so that was really *sobering*. I mean, there are no pictures of me or anything like that from that time period.

Mee Joo's perspective was unique in that she had worked for years with an adoptee organization in Korea, leading a first trip to Korea for adoptees. She reflected on her own experiences, saying,

> I think a lot of us [adoptees] tend to view birth family search as kind of like a closure or like the end of something because we've thought so long about birth family search and that we've been working ourselves up to even doing one and then we finally find them and that's gonna like kind of be this closure or this answer, it's gonna give us this solution to these problems or these questions that we didn't even know we had, et cetera. But really it's just the beginning of this really long road, depending on what your relationship's gonna be like with your birth family and we don't realize that because we're so concerned with just the beginning part of the journey. And once people, if they're able to reunite, it only leads to more questions and that's the thing is that you have all these questions. Even if you get them answered all it does is create (laughs) more questions and so I think that that was one of those challenges for me to realize that, yeah, okay, so you answered this about me but I just had, like, ten new questions based on that one thing you just said, because this doesn't make sense or then what happens. And so that's part of the challenge is also being able to navigate through this whole arena that I had never even anticipated because I had never allowed myself to think beyond if I had actually found them. You know, I was so concerned with if I didn't find them, how was I going to react. I never thought about reunion and what would happen after I met them because I never thought I would meet them and so *that* alone just created a lot more gray in my mind, I guess.

Isabel told me that she had a "gut feeling" that her birth mom was alive before her search and reunion. She spoke of her reason for searching and then her sentiment afterward, saying, "At least I wanted to know [whether she was alive] so I could move on with my life then and not have all those questions (pause). But even after them you still have questions, so (laughs)." Yngvesson (2005) has observed that the process of identity work for returning adoptees is complex and never-ending, writing that "moments of clarity are typically just that— mere moments in a process of self-constitution that is ongoing, painful, and turbulent, challenging any sense of a stable ground of belonging" (p. 41). Participants' words reflect this sentiment so clearly, and the knowledge they gained from their initial meetings often seemed incomplete, at best.

Adoptee Narratives: I'm Okay

As birth families shared narratives of the past, many participants felt that it was important to provide them with a positive narrative of their own lives post-adoption and to absolve them of guilt for their relinquishment. One can see this in Sun Ok's earlier description of her initial moments with her birth family, and also in Mark's retelling of the first time he met his birth father:

> I was also really, really nervous before, just in the minutes before, and then he came in and we hugged, and while we were still hugging each other, his first words were "I'm so sorry. I'm so sorry" and I was really, I didn't know what to say at first and I remember saying as we looked at each other, I said, "Well I'm so thankful" and at the time that's, you know, how I felt and how I still feel, that things worked out pretty serendipitously for me. But that was pretty much the only words he spoke of English (laughs) for about the next half hour.

Olivia was planning to go to Korea with her best friend, whose brother was stationed in Korea, when, a month before their departure, she received word from her adoption agency that her Korean family was trying to contact her. When I asked her why she decided to meet them, she emphasized her desire to reassure her birth family that she was doing well. She said,

> I think it was more for *them*. A lot of people asked me, just because from talking to other Korean adoptees and then also my friends who are *not* adoptees, they're very curious to know how I feel . . . I get this question a lot, you know, "One day are you gonna try to *find* your birth family?" And *my* answer, from day one, was no, because I feel like if anything, they should look for me. . . . And I said one day if they decide to find me, I will meet them. And, you know, I guess I have to keep my own promise! (laughs) But it was fun. And then after the idea was sinking in, I realized it'd be interesting. Just thinking, you know, who I got my dimples from. Do I look like my mom and dad? You know, am I short, am I tall, you know, compared to my family? And then the other thing was just to give them a peace of mind that I'm doing well. I'm alive. I'm doing well. I'm very happy. So it was mostly curiosity on my end, but I think emotionally I did it for them.

Olivia's expression that she reunited "for" her birth family to give them a peace of mind reflects a discursive burden. She felt a responsibility to communicate that she was doing well in order to ease their emotional pain. Similarly, adoptees in a study by Powell and Afifi (2005) viewed reunion as an opportunity to reduce their birth mothers' guilt and loss. Participants in their study, which included some domestic adoptees and some Korean adoptees, tended to focus on the positive parts of their lives after adoption, downplaying or omitting turbulent times. A number of adoptees I spoke with mentioned struggles related to mental health, such as depression, eating disorders, suicidal ideations, and/or questions of self-worth, and one spoke of sexual abuse by her adoptive father. Yet, during initial meetings, they all affirmed the adoption narrative that they assumed their birth families hoped to hear: That they were educated and had a good family. A main reason for doing so was to assuage their birth parents' guilt.

Rituals

Baxter and Braithwaite (2006) have defined a family ritual as a "voluntary, recurring, patterned communication event whose jointly enacted performance by family members pays homage to what they regard as sacred, thereby producing and reproducing a family's identity and its web of social relations" (pp. 262–263). Initial reunions allow for insight on Wolin and Bennett's (1984) conceptualization of family celebrations, which are "those holidays and occasions that are widely practiced throughout the culture and are special in the minds of the family" (p. 404).

Adoptee-birth family reunions have become a culturally recognized ritual in Korea. In addition to the large number of overseas Korean adoptees who return to Korea to search for and reunite with their birth families, the Korean media depicts Korean adoptees frequently, often dramatizing their stories of search and reunion. Elise Prébin (2013) found that reunions on the television show *Ach'im Madang* were highly ritualized, often to evoke emotion from audience members and to help create a collective memory that is sentimental and sympathetic toward transnational adoption and family separation. Her ethnographic study revealed that birth family reunions involve the rituals of time together, sharing a meal, and visiting family members' graves. Interviewees in my study also recalled spending time together, eating together, visiting family members' graves, engaging in symbolic family activities, and exchanging gifts.

Sharing Meals

All participants spoke of eating lunch or dinner with their birth families, and for some, it was their first time eating Korean food. Whether eating at a restaurant or in a relative's home, it was common for participants to report that their birth mother or another older female relative such as an aunt fed them hand to mouth. Sometimes, this feeding was due to participants' inexperience eating Korean food, as in Mark's case. He recalled his birth mother feeding him, saying,

> We went out to a barbecue place which was my first time having Korean barbecue and so she, you know, showed me how to cook the meat and wrap it and how to eat it and yeah, she was, you know, doting on me and (laughs) feeding me these lettuce wraps of meat the whole time.

Given that Mark was only fourteen at the time of this meeting, he seemed to enjoy and not mind this ritual. Cat, however, was thirty-eight at the time of her first meeting, and her son was nineteen. She remembered her initial reaction to being fed, saying,

> We went to dinner and it was funny because my *eomma* kept trying to feed me (laughs), *spoon* feed me *and* my son. And the adoption agency warned me that "She's probably going to want to feed you, like spoon feed you," and I told her, "I don't like being fed to" (laughs). But I let her and, you know, I had never tasted Korean food before, so that was cool cuz I *loved* it.

When Korean adoptees eat food from their birth country, this act can serve as a way for them to connect with their ethnic heritage (Bergquist, 2006). For some adoptees, time spent with birth families is linked intricately with eating Korean meals together. Consequently, eating Korean food outside of Korea is more than an act of ethnic identity expression; it becomes a conduit for connecting with memories of family in Korea.

Exchanging Gifts

Participants also brought gifts for their Korean families and received gifts from them. Kimberly McKee (2019) has pointed out that gift exchanges between Korean adoptees and their birth families can require a great deal of emotional and financial investment. Many adoptees will research what to gift their birth families, and birth families will often save money to spend on the adoptee during their times together. She writes,

> Gifts are the only visible way to attempt to mitigate the losses adoption causes between adoptee and birth family. This results in the most

banal items carrying the weight of decades of uncertainty—uncertainty of reunion and what might be. (p. 149)

In an effort to offer a meaningful gift, participants often gave their families photo albums with pictures of their childhood, current activities, and families in their adoptive country. Sun Ok perceived that it was important to her adoptive mother that her Korean family see pictures of her childhood. She said,

> One big thing that showed [my adoptive mom] was supportive in an *indirect* way was that she wanted to put a picture book together, a photo album, *for* my birth mother. And I think that was supportive, but I also think it was a, I wanna prove myself. I wanna say thank you but I also wanna prove myself, I wanna prove my worth, that not only am I thankful that your birth mother gave you up as an ultimate sacrifice, but just that, you know, hopefully she can see that you've *had* a good life and that you've been raised well.

Sun Ok described how her adoptive mother wanted to put the photo book together but did not have time, so it became an additional stressor for Sun Ok to prepare it. Yet she did so because she knew it was important to her adoptive mom. Interestingly, from Sun Ok's perspective, the photo album functioned as both a symbol of the adoptive mom's devotion to the daughter and the daughter's devotion to the adoptive mom. She described in detail how she created the photo album "from scratch" and how she was disappointed at her birth mother's lack of outward emotional response to it. She recalled, "I remember her not reacting to it at all and me being a little bit hurt about that." It is, of course, possible that Sun Ok misinterpreted her birth mother's reaction to the photo book. What appeared as a nonreaction could have been an attempt to mask an array of feelings—grief at the years lost, shame for relinquishing her child—due to culture, age, and/or personality. Narratives from Korean birth mothers that describe loss and shame (e.g., Dorow, 1999) suggest that Sun Ok's birth mother was likely experiencing many emotions, even though they weren't expressed in a way that Sun Ok could recognize.

Sometimes gift exchanges were clearly marked by cultural differences, such as when female participants were gifted bra and underwear sets by their birth family. These gifts were given during initial reunions and were opened in the presence of family members including brothers and brothers-in-law, adding to participants' awkward feelings. Olivia's family celebrated her birthday while she was in Korea, giving her multiple gifts, including bra sets. She recalled her

American best friend helping her navigate the situation when she opened the gift, saying,

> I looked at [my friend] and my face was blushing, and I'm like, "Dude! What do you think this is about?" And she's like, "Oh you know how she missed that whole teenage era with you? That's probably what it is." And I was like, "You know, you're right. Probably." And I didn't understand the gift at all, so I'm like, "Oh, thank you." And to say I liked it I hugged it and so that's how they knew I liked it. . . . I hugged it and so my mom knew that I liked it.

Olivia's friend's interpretation likely wasn't accurate, as gifts of bras and underwear tend to be viewed as nice, practical gifts by Koreans and are therefore common among family members. Such gifts, however, were surprising to participants, who tended to see them as overly intimate, especially from family members whom they'd only met recently, and especially in the presence of men. And yet Olivia felt the discursive burden to express that she liked the gift, despite her confusion and discomfort.

But not all gift exchanges were challenging. Alexander recalled going shopping with his Korean mom and buying identical rings. He showed me the ring on his finger and then stated,

> The way I perceive it is that even though we're so far apart, I'm thinking as long as I wear this ring, I am connected physically with my mom. The ring is a symbol for the hole that has been sealed shut over my heart, that I feel that I am spiritually connected with my mom and that we share a lot of things in common. That my past is part of her whole entire life.

Alexander imbued the rings with deep meaning because he knew that his mother had the same one, and they bought them together. The rings thus became signifiers of shared memory and their relationship. Minsun also received a gift of jewelry from her birth mother, a necklace with the word "Mommy" on a medallion. She indicated that she called her birth mother "Mommy" because of the word on the necklace. These gifts of jewelry are examples of what communication researchers such as Walid Afifi and Michelle L. Johnson (2005) have called "tie signs." Although tie signs can have various meanings, the most common function is to express intimacy between the people in the relationship. Alexander's and Minsun's gifts symbolized this intimacy and were a tangible symbol of their relationship.

Visits to Gravesites

Several participants told me about their visits to family gravesites, where they performed specific cultural rituals (*jesa*) to honor the dead, such as offering their favorite drink and fruit and performing specific bows. Typically, Koreans travel to gravesites on the two major holidays in Korea, *Chuseok* (fall harvest celebration) and *Seollal* (Lunar New Year), but the adoptees' return to Korea marked a special occasion where visits to grandparents' and parents' graves were warranted on nonholidays. Meagan spoke of her first experience, saying,

> We went to my birth mother's grave. It's like a forty-five-minute drive or something. My birth father came to pick us up and he also brought one of my aunts and two cousins. They came with us and then my sisters, my niece, and my brother. I don't know if you know, but they have like a traditional bow that they do for, like, honoring the dead. So we get out there and they lay down a tarp after we found her gravestone. . . . They brought fruit and this little can of coffee because she loved coffee, but she could never drink it because they didn't have a lot of money. And so we kind of, like, threw fruit around the grave and just sort of, you know, honor the dead and honor her. And then, my *brother* knelt down and showed us how to, showed me how to *bow*. And so you, like, kneel down and then you take your hands and then you bow down like that (demonstrates). And you do it twice. . . . And then afterwards, they let me have a moment to just, you know, sit there, and I was able to just touch her gravestone and feel all the writing on it (starts to cry).

Before meeting her birth family, Meagan had found out that her birth mother had died three days after giving birth to her. Before receiving this news, Meagan had a sense of hope that she and her mother would have a "strong connection," so visiting her mother's grave was particularly meaningful. She and her siblings have visited their mother's grave together on each of Meagan's subsequent visits, and doing so has become one of Meagan's favorite rituals with her birth family.

Eric was able to visit his maternal and paternal grandparents' gravesites as part of Chuseok rituals, an experience he described as "very powerful." This experience also enabled him to see himself as part of a Korean lineage. He recalled, "They took me to my maternal grandmother's gravesite and pointed to the place where my name will be listed when I die." Although most younger Americans do not make regular visits to their relatives' cemeteries, visits to gravesites and the enactment of ancestral rituals were clearly meaningful rituals for participants and helped them to feel more connected to their Korean families.

Symbolic Family Activities

Finally, participants talked about various rituals that had cultural and personal significance. For example, Christine, who was nine years old when she met her birth family, rode on her birth mother's back (piggyback-style) during their first meeting because this practice is traditional for Korean mothers and their babies. Cat's birth mother and twin sister, who traveled from Korea to the United States, brought her a *hanbok*, a Korean traditional dress, and took photos of her wearing it, even though most Korean adults only wear *hanbok* on special occasions such as weddings.

Participants also reported their Korean parents wanting to sleep with them, as co-sleeping (parents and children sleeping together) is also common practice for Korean mothers and young children and has been for centuries (Chung & An, 2014). Isabel recalled falling asleep in her birth mother's arms during her first reunion. She said,

> When I spent time with them on that weekend, you know, I was eighteen at that time, so a little bit older, but the first night she came with me into bed and basically held me like a little baby and told me all these things in Korean. I can't imagine probably everything she had wanted to tell me and [she] just had me fall asleep in her arms, and that was kind of surreal. It was, "Alright, this is where I was supposed to be" (laughs a little).

Older Koreans, in particular, may find it natural to sleep together on the floor, due to the arrangement of traditional Korean homes, which were heated through the floor. Chung and An (2014) explained that for older generations, the warm floor became the center of domestic life and "bed-sharing and room-sharing was comparatively much easier since the whole floor, instead of just the bed, could be used for sleeping" (para. 12). Today, although many Koreans have beds, couches, and chairs, many still find it comfortable to sit and sleep on the floor. And birth mothers may have wanted to sleep with their children because they were not able to do so at all, or for as long as they would have liked, prior to the child being separated. Jorgen also told me about co-sleeping with his birth family during his first visit. Although Jorgen had described his mother as very "stone-faced" when they met initially, her emotions were revealed during the night while Jorgen was sleeping. He recalled,

We actually went on a *mini* trip to some kind of family resort and then I had one of the most, I don't know, heartwarming experiences I have ever had. It was until that point my mother never cried and I was wondering why because I think every other member I had met of my family they would cry or at least be very close to tearing up. But then I woke up one night (laughs) in the middle of the *night* and then it was my mother. She was leaning over me and we all slept in the same room, my *mother* on one side and my aunt on the other side, so it was, like, packed in this cocoon. But then I woke up in the middle of the night and it was my mother; she was *crying* and the reason I woke up was because her tears, they were falling on my face. Then I found out, oh okay, that it was because she had just held it back all this time. So it was *amazing* to meet her. It was, like, *even* more amazing than meeting all the rest of my family because I felt very close to her just because of that connection between mother and child.

Jorgen's mother's expression of emotion while sleeping together contributed to a sense of connection that Jorgen had been hoping for. In addition, these symbolic family rituals seemed to allow birth parents to travel back in time to recapture moments with their children that they had assumed were lost.

Naming

Naming—how individuals address one another and refer to one another—reflects and sustains relationships. Previous research in communication has found that naming practices are intentional and meaningful and that they implicate identities and relationships (Philipsen & Huspek, 1985). In a clear example, adoptive parents change their adopted child's name to reflect the adoptive family identity and the adoptive country while sometimes keeping or adapting the child's birth culture name to retain a connection to the child's origins (Suter, 2012). In terms of family identity, names are used outside the family to label one another to outsiders (e.g., "This is my mom") and within the family when addressing another family member (e.g., "Hi Mom"). The use of names helps to create a sense of family identity. For example, communication researcher Jody Koenig Kellas and colleagues (2008) found that adult children's use labels for their stepparents in various ways—formal (e.g., "my dad's wife"), familiar (e.g., "my stepmom" or using their first name), familial (e.g., "my mom")—to signify solidarity or separateness or to protect their parents' feelings. Similarly, interviewees talked about using names in purposeful ways to distinguish between their adoptive and birth families.

During initial meetings, despite not speaking Korean, participants most commonly addressed birth parents using Korean language labels, such as *eomma* for mom (엄마) and *appa* for dad (아빠), and siblings, whose labels reflect their own gender, their sibling's gender, and their age relative to the sibling. However, a few participants used English or Danish terms. One example was Olivia, who spent time with members of her extended family and ended up reverting to English. Because Korean terms of address for extended family members are contingent on the addressee's gender, whether they are on the maternal or paternal side, whether they are related through marriage, and their age relative to the birth parent, these terms can be quite confusing for non-Korean speakers. She recalled,

> I would call my mom *eomma*, and then *appa* (dad) and then *gomo* (paternal aunt). And then I forgot uncle, so they pointed to themselves. And my mom was like "*eomma*," and I said, "mom." And then so they were like, "mom." So towards the end I was just calling them mom, dad, uncle, and aunt (laughs). In English (laughs). Yeah, and then the older aunt, I'd say "Auntie One," and "Auntie Two" (laughs). . . . Cuz I had a hard time remembering the Korean words. I mean, I wrote it down but then it was just like, "Forget it" (laughs). So I called them Mom, Dad, Auntie One and Auntie Two, and Uncle, and they responded. That's who they are.

Understandably, participants who met many relatives found it challenging to remember their relationships and their appropriate familial labels. Sometimes, participants avoided using terms of address because they either did not feel comfortable using Korean terms or they felt self-conscious using any term in the presence of their adoptive parent. As Nikki recalled, "I think I tried to skip around that so that I didn't offend anyone. Cuz I mean my [adoptive] mom was there, and this, this birth woman (laughs), you know, as crude as that sounds." Perhaps because Nikki's birth mother did not seem particularly warm during the reunion or after, Nikki felt a distance from her, evidenced by the reference to her as a "birth woman" in this quotation.

When talking about their Korean families to others, participants stated that they most commonly used the descriptor "birth" or "biological" to label them. It was also common to use "Korean" as a descriptor for birth family members, as in "my Korean mother." In contrast, most interviewees spoke of referring to their adoptive parents as simply "mom" or "dad" with no preceding descriptor. These labels reflect and affirm the family relationship they had established with their adoptive parents, over years of communication. Such labels also provided clarity to those who did not understand Korean terms. As Eric explained,

> When I'm talking to American friends, I can't really call them my *abeo-ji* (Korean word for father) or *hyeong-nim* (older brother to a male) because they would have no idea what I'm talking about, so I'll say my Korean father or my Korean brother.

Supporting the idea that naming practices reflect and affirm relationships, participants spoke of the rationale behind their naming choices. Most prominent was the sentiment that naming practices were symbolic of how participants felt about their two families. As Catherine said,

> In my head, "mom" means more to me than "*eomma*." Like, just in the context we've grown up in . . . who I would consider my real mother, if you're going to play that card, it would obviously be my adoptive mom. And to me, "mom" is a lot more intimate than "*eomma*." Because I mean, it's what you grow up with, I think.

Because Catherine grew up steeped in American discourse, "mom" carried an emotional weight that "*eomma*" did not. Eric echoed these sentiments, saying,

> I would never want either [my birth parents or adoptive parents] to think that I'm not substantiating their own existence with their own title you know? Because I think it is different. It's like, yeah *abeoji* means "father," but there's a huge difference between saying that and "dad" you know? My dad will always be my American dad.

Interestingly, although Catherine and Eric described a similar rationale behind their naming practices, Catherine described her relationships with her adoptive mom as very close, whereas Eric described his relationship with his adoptive dad as positive but not particularly close. Thus, although terms of address may indicate relative closeness, they may also indicate a relationship that is marked by time and shared history.

Regardless of labels, however, participants tended to resist the descriptor "real" to refer to either family. Christine stated,

> When I'm referring to them to other people, I call them my birth parents. My birth mom, my birth dad, or my biological mom, my biologi-

cal father, you know. And I never let people call my birth parents my real parents. I don't. I will go out of my way to stop people from speaking and correct them. Because it really is important to me that people understand that your adoptive parents are your real parents. And your biological parents or your birth parents are also your real parents. You can't use that word to differentiate between the two, because it's just not possible. You know, the definition of parent is so broad, I think. So it's just not fair to give that kind of significance to one or the other.

In this statement, Christine legitimizes both sets of parents. Some participants, however, used labels to reflect closeness and also to protect the feelings of their adoptive parents or as a symbol of their loyalty to them. Meagan reflected on her use of terms, saying,

I always struggle with this. I called them by their titles, not by their names. So I called my brother *oppa* [older brother to a female] and I called my birth father *appa*. But when I talk about them to, you know, my friends or family here, I guess it depends on the context I'm talking about, but I will always say birth or biological father. I'm not always quite the same way with my siblings. Like I will say "my brother." Or "my sisters." Or my brother in Korea or my sisters in Korea. But for some reason I guess with my [birth] father and I think it's because we're not as close, that I just feel like, I don't know, maybe it's also a sense of protection for my dad, for my adoptive dad, that I do say birth father. I don't know. . . . To their faces I would call them by their title. . . . But it's weird. I do, I feel a sense of betrayal even if my parents—even if my adoptive parents aren't there or aren't even a part of the conversation. But I feel like in a sense I'm betraying them when I say "my mother" or "my father." You know? . . . There has to be that distinguished, um, boundary between. Otherwise I feel guilty.

Reflecting the discourse of loyalty and gratitude expected of Korean adoptees (McKee, 2019) and the discourse of "exclusive belonging" to one set of parents (Yngvesson, 2005), participants like Meagan spoke of complicated feelings when it came to naming practices and a discursive burden to express their loyalty to adoptive parents. These established discourses of gratitude and belonging place adoptees in a difficult position. Although some participants spoke of using names for clarity and to avoid confusion between sets of parents, often, names were used to build, reflect, and maintain family relationships.

Communicating with Birth Siblings

Reunion research has tended to focus on adoptees' meetings with their birth parents, with a greater emphasis on birth mothers than birth fathers, perhaps because females tend to search more often than males (Müller & Perry, 2001) and also due to the physical connection between mother and child. However, past research on reunions and relationships with birth siblings suggests that they tend to be easier to manage than reunions with birth parents (Trinder et al., 2004). This finding rang true for many of the adoptees I interviewed. Some participants expressed a greater investment in their relationships with their birth siblings than with their birth parents even before the first meeting. Eric, for example, wanted to meet his brother before he met either of his birth parents. He explained,

> The reason I wanted to meet my brother was, number one, because he is so close in age to me. And number two, because he wasn't *complicit* in my adoption. And he lost a brother the same way that *I* did. With no explanation whatsoever. And in a lot of ways, it was probably a lot more shocking for him because he remembers me from when we were really young. You know, he was almost four when I left, and I was almost three. And so I just, I really wanted to talk with somebody who had as little say in it as I did.

Most often, participants such as Eric met and felt a bond with older siblings. Due to the birth families' poverty and/or preference for sons, many participants were the youngest sibling in their birth families, especially if their parents remained married. Confucianism still exerts influence on Korean culture, and older Korean siblings have both authority over and responsibility for younger siblings (Sung & Lee, 2013). Consequently, older siblings were reported to take care of participants and show them kindness during their time together. For example, Catherine, age ten at her first reunion, recalled a special memory involving her older Korean sisters. While her adoptive parents were in another room talking with her birth parents, she and her older sisters were able to spend time together in another room. Given that she was the oldest sibling in her adoptive family, being the youngest sister in her birth family felt like a novelty. She recounted,

> Something that really stood out to me, I still remember. My sisters, one of them gave me a necklace, and one of them gave me two barrettes. . . . Like I was sitting in like a little vanity, and my four sisters

were standing over me, like brushing my hair and like putting it up in the barrettes. And I just remember thinking, "This is what I've always wanted." . . . I just remember, like, they put the barrettes in my hair and I was just *so* excited that like *I had older sisters*!

Other participants discussed how, because the siblings were closer to their own age, they found it easier to relate to them than to their birth parents. Given that younger generations of Koreans tend to be less conservative than older generations (Eun, 2007), they were able to find similarities fairly easily. Hanne recalled meeting her half-siblings, the children of her birth father, saying,

We were just talking about, "How are you doing, what kind of life do you have, are you married, do you have children, what do you do in your daily life? How is your work life," and things like that. So you know it was just, you know, like meeting new friends, new people, if you were at a dinner or in a restaurant, you know. . . . They are not *that* much older than me, and they live in South Korea, so of course they are very, you know, they live a very *western* European life. And my father's family is a rich family and they have a very good education and very good jobs, and things like that so they kind of live the same life as I live.

Such similarities helped to make meetings with birth siblings more comfortable than meetings with birth parents. Past studies have also found the importance of perceived similarity in forging ongoing relationships and feelings of closeness with birth siblings after initial meetings (O'Neill et al., 2016; Ottaway, 2012).

Relationships with birth siblings may also have been easier for participants to conceptualize and enact than relationships with birth parents because people are expected to have only one "set" of parents but may have multiple siblings. Trinder and colleagues (2004) suggest that many people have an "additive" approach to siblings, that it is common to have multiple siblings and types of siblings (e.g., stepsiblings, half-siblings). However, the nuclear family formation, which adoption often aims to replicate, allows for only one mother and one father. Sylvia, who grew up with adoptive brothers and no sisters in her adoptive family, talked about finding her birth sister and contrasted this relationship with the one with her birth parents. Her response reflects this additive approach:

She's still kinda the relationship I care about the most. I never had a sister, so she's kinda filling a hole. Whereas I *have* parents. So (pause), you know, I wanted to know [my birth parents] and I'm glad to know them, but she's kinda what I've always missed. Having a sister.

However, some participants were not allowed to meet their siblings, their younger half-siblings, in particular. Such participants learned that after they had been sent abroad for adoption, their birth mothers had married someone other than their birth father and had children with the new husband. Due to the cultural stigma surrounding pregnancy out of wedlock, divorce, and child relinquishment, some mothers never told their current husbands and younger children that they had had a child who was relinquished for adoption.

Conclusion

Korean adoptees' first meetings with their birth families bring together strangers with different vantage points in the relationship, different cultures and languages, and personal histories that overlap very little. Many factors contribute to the communication that occurs during these meetings and that help to shape whether or not these meetings lead to future, ongoing contact. The *distal already-spokens* of culture (Baxter, 2011) refer to the messages that circulate in one's culture before the reunion. Such messages are often taken as assumptions and tend to paint birth family reunions as joyous, emotional events that result in healing for all parties and a newfound sense of connection and self-knowledge for the adopted person. In actual experience, however, reunions have happy *moments* but are often beginnings rather than endings and provide openings more than any sense of closure.

Reunions also occur within the context of what Baxter has termed *proximal already-spokens*, everyday messages about reunions and birth families. These messages are often contradictory: They suggest that birth families are an adoptee's "real" family while at the same time oversimplifying or erasing the birth family's personhood; they affirm the legitimacy and goodwill of one's adoptive parents while also presuming that the adoptive family is somehow deficient. This discursive context—one that tends to create idealistic expectations on one hand and dehumanize birth parents, especially birth mothers, on the other—complicates adoptees' and birth families' communication with one another.

Although all participants indicated that they were glad that they had chosen to reunite, initial reunions were fraught with mixed emotions and unmet expectations, particularly for adoptees who chose to reunite as adults. The discursive burden was woven throughout their stories. Particularly notable is how participants were positioned or felt an obligation to forgive, or exonerate, their birth parents for having relinquished them and how some participants indicated that they chose to reunite *for* their birth parents or their adoptive parents. As birth parents apologized and/or shared their family narratives, adoptees communicated that they were "okay" and, often, that they had a good life, a good family, and a good education. Yet when speaking with me, they spoke commonly of personal struggles with their adoption, their racial and cultural identities, their relationships with members of their adoptive families, and their complicated feelings toward their birth families. These topics were often glossed over during meetings with birth parents, usually with the goal of not making them "feel bad." In this way, participants took on the discursive burden of communicating the "happy ending" narrative of adoption and not compounding their birth parents' guilt. This position is complicated. In one way, it demonstrates adoptees' compassion for their birth families and empathy for the lack of agency they had due to poverty and/or gender as well as the privileges they have gained being raised abroad. In another way, it can be seen as another example of the communicative contortion that adoptees are often required to perform to make those around them comfortable. Whether in their adoptive country or their birth country, Korean adoptees are expected, or perceive that they are expected, to communicate gratitude for their adoption and to forgive the country and people who sent them away.

Simultaneously, participants were trying to obtain information about their birth family's past and present circumstances, to adapt to Korean culture and their perceptions of their birth parents' expectations, and to navigate language differences, all of which add further discursive burden. In addition, as will be discussed later, those who were accompanied by their adoptive parents also had to manage the presence and feelings of two sets of parents with different roles and stakes. Initial meetings with birth families require a great deal of emotional, cognitive, and communicative resources from transnational adoptees, who feel a significant discursive burden of communicating in ways that make those around them feel comfortable. Those who had multiple subsequent meetings over the years tended to describe more comfort and less emotional intensity over time, although misunderstandings and conflict were common. During these first interviews, Jorgen, who had been in reunion ten years at the time, suggested to me the importance of talking with adoptees who had been in reunion for years. His words indicate the dynamic nature of reunion relationships.

You have a lot of feelings and thoughts first when you meet but then *years* later, you will look at it in an entirely different light. You will be happy about everything that happened, but you will (pause, trails off).

It's very different, the way you think about it and the process you have gone through in analyzing. I think it was like a honeymoon in the first few years actually. It was, like, a honeymoon and we all had some kind of pretense. We all tried to, like, be on our best behavior and then after some years we actually began to *know* more and more. . . . We began to know more about the *real* me, the real you, like, how are you really. I think both me and my family began to be more *sure* about each other. It's like, "Okay, I'm not going anywhere and you're not going anywhere, so I can be honest and, you know, it's okay to disagree with me more and really show who I am with the good and the bad and not approve of everything." But it takes awhile. That actually takes awhile. It's very difficult to get to the point where you can say, like *convey*, the message "I *like* you" and whatever, "I even *love* you but I don't really like this and this," "This is not what I want," so that takes time. And I think I have come *somewhat* to that point with my family, that we can be honest with each other and I know they don't like everything about *me* and I don't like everything about them and it's okay. You don't have to pretend everything is good. . . . In the beginning, it was like all the time we had a mask, because we just wanted to show the other how we really wanted this.

Adoptees who are anticipating or have had an initial meeting may find comfort in knowing that these meetings are often only a starting point and that relationships and communication with birth families may change over time.

3

Korean Birth Parents, Westernized Adoptees

Navigating the Terrain of Cultural
Differences during Reunion

Winter 2017

I have asked my *eonni* to teach me to cook her *doenjang jjigae*, soybean paste stew. Hers is the best I have eaten. Balanced between spicy and savory, it is the perfect companion to a bowl of rice. I want to learn how to make this dish, but more than that, I want to have this memory: Living in Korea and learning how to cook Korean food from my *eonni*.

I wait as she pulls ingredients out of her refrigerator: Zucchini, garlic, tofu. She takes a ceramic coffee mug from a shelf, points to an invisible line on it, fills it with water, and pours it into a pot. I try to estimate: Maybe a cup and a half? She repeats the process: Same mug, water again, and perhaps the same invisible line? Maybe? I am lost already. I slice the zucchini into thick rounds, my single contribution, while she removes jars from her cabinets, and tells me the names of their contents, which I repeat and then forget immediately. She adds ingredients in various-sized pinches or spoonfuls, without hesitating. Her amounts are based on personal preference and intuition, not anything that could be measured or weighed. Before long, the pot bubbles on the stove, releasing aromas of warm garlic and sharp *doenjang* throughout the apartment. *Eonni* gives the stew a quick stir, removes the wooden spoon she has been using, and taps it a few times on the top of her hand, leaving several drops on the padded flesh between her index finger and thumb. She licks the sample, considers the flavors, and reaches into her cabinet for an unlabeled jar. She adds a small pinch, repeats her tasting, and appears satisfied.

By now, I have realized that I will not learn how to cook my *eonni's doenjang jjigae*, not because the ingredients or process are complicated or because she hasn't tried to teach me, but because Korean food is part of who she is in a way that it can never be for me. She has been cooking for herself since she was fifteen years old, and, like most Korean home cooks, she uses no recipes; instead, she relies on muscle memory and her senses of sight, taste, and smell—movements and perceptions that I never developed, will never develop in my lifetime. She can let me into the kitchen, but she can never impart her knowledge and palate from five decades of eating and cooking Korean food using ingredients that I never had in my own cabinets until I was in my thirties—*gochugaru, guk ganjang, mu,* and so many more. Although I can cook and eat Korean food, I will always think of it as just that—Korean food. For my *eonni* and millions of other Koreans, it is just food. Korean is assumed, a reflex. This reflex is how I have come to think of culture—as assumed, a default way of thinking, evaluating, communicating, behaving, and feeling, not just about food but about everything. Because I grew up with my adoptive family in the United States, my default is not Korean but White American, middle-class. As a transnational adoptee, cooking Korean food and trying to understand and enact Korean culture, in big and small ways, will always require varying amounts of effort for me. Yet I continue to try, creating and salvaging connections with my birth culture and birth family, sometimes one bite at a time.

I slide my spoon into my warm rice, take a small amount, and then dip into the steaming bowl of *jjigae*, letting the broth settle among the white grains. I slurp carefully, trying to not burn my lips but not wanting to let another moment pass without eating my *eonni's* food. She turns her gaze toward me. "*Mas-iss-eo?*" she asks. Is it delicious? I smile and nod because the *jjigae* is delicious, perfect. *Eonni,* who has endured so much, smiles back, her face full of light. I love making her happy even more than I love her food.

I will never be able to replicate my *eonni's sohn mat,* translated literally as her "hand taste," the specific flavors of her food and the love she puts into her cooking. But for now, we can share a table and a meal, two Korean sisters, content to be together, forgetting for a moment all that was lost.

When the concept of culture is discussed within transnational adoption circles, it is often reduced to consumables like food, art, or books, or activities related to historical traditions, such as playing folk instruments or performing dances.[1] White adoptive mothers, particularly in the past two decades, have been known for attempting to cultivate their children's ethnic identity through the purchase of clothing, picture books, dolls, or home decorations, or enrolling the children in classes based on their child's birth culture (Jacobson, 2008). Although this type of cultural engagement tends to be advocated by private adoption agencies, it might also be viewed as a form of cultural tourism, "the selective appropriation and consumption of renovated cultural symbols, artifacts, and cultural events as a means of constructing identity" (Quiroz, 2012, p. 528). Through cultural tourism, adoptive parents, most of whom lack interpersonal connections with their child's birth culture, are attempting to cultivate cultural identity and pride. However, on its own, cultural tourism will not impart adoptees with a nuanced or useful understanding of culture or intercultural relationships. Traditional decorations and music classes based on the birth culture, for example, may be enjoyable, but they tell very little about the lives of people in the birth country today.

Culture involves a set of assumptions about the world and relationships, dictating the way people act and communicate. When an infant or child is adopted transnationally, they lose the ability to see the world and relationships from the perspective of their birth culture. As my story at the beginning of this chapter demonstrates, a transnational adoptee can, of course, eat the food of their birth country, but unless they exert effort, they will not view food from their birth country as the norm and standard, nor will they know about its history and origins. To a transnational Korean adoptee raised in the United States, the word *breakfast* will first call to mind foods such as cereal, toast, or eggs, not rice and soup. Adoptees raised in Western countries will typically default to the assumption that a "good" relationship involves mutual respect among equal individuals, not hierarchy and adherence to roles based on age and gender. These deeper dimensions of culture, particularly assumptions about people and relationships, can be the most challenging to navigate during reunion. Rather than it feeling like a homecoming to their proverbial motherland and long-lost family, reunion can underscore transnational adoptees' rupture from Korea, their differences from their birth families, and their Western cultural identity.

In examining the role of culture in Korean adoptees' relationships with their birth families, I draw on key characteristics of *culture*[2] posed by intercultural communication scholars Judith Martin and Thomas Nakayama (2022), who observe that culture is learned, involves patterns of behavior and attitudes, and is shared by a group of people. Martin and Nakayama also point out that communication is the process by which culture is reinforced, negotiated, shaped, and challenged. Transnational Korean adoptees grow up learning the culture of their adoptive country virtually every moment of every day, through the examples and everyday interactions with their adoptive family and others, media messages, education, and social institutions. They learn *behaviors*, how to act in different contexts (e.g., call your older sister by her first name but not your teacher), and *attitudes*, what is good and likable versus what is not (e.g., it is good to be talkative and outgoing but bad to be shy). Underneath these behaviors and attitudes are cultural *values*, which tend to be overt and articulable (Schein, 1984). In the United States, these might include individualism and freedom. In Denmark, they might include equality and social justice (Nelson & Shavitt, 2002). These values, however, rest on invisible, taken-for-granted *assumptions* about the nature of human relationships; the nature of human activity; the nature of human nature itself; the nature of reality, time, and space; and about humans' relationship to the environment (Schein, 1984; Weaver, 1986). These assumptions may be so deeply embedded that people can have difficulty articulating them, and if they are articulated, they are viewed as undebatable. The distinction among cultural behaviors, values, and assumptions is an important one because although it may be possible for transnational Korean adoptees to learn and enact culturally appropriate behaviors, some of their values and assumptions are likely to differ from those of their Korean family. More importantly, intercultural misunderstandings or conflicts can evoke strong feelings of confusion, anger, and sadness, particularly because they suggest that one person is questioning or not respecting the other person's deeply held values and assumptions.

In examining participants' experiences with cultural differences, three things became most evident. First, there are ontological differences in how Korean birth parents and adoptees view family relationships. In most cases, culture dictates how individuals would answer questions such as "What does it mean to be a parent?" (or child, older sibling, etc.) or "What does it mean to be in a family?" These questions are often not examined, because they operate as assumptions and are taken for granted. However, appropriate behaviors in a family are predicated on the answers to these questions. Second and relatedly, cultural differences in communication are experienced as most challenging when they seem to contradict these fundamental assumptions about the nature of humans in relationships. The examples and stories that follow will illustrate these points. Third, as I listened to participants' stories of cultural differences with their birth families, I was struck by their *flexibility* in trying to accommodate, or adapt to, their birth families' communication, their *mindfulness* in trying to understand their own cultural identities, and their attempts to *empathize* with their birth families. Despite their discomfort, participants discussed ongoing attempts to adjust their own communication to accommodate

Korean culture and their Korean families. At the same time, there were moments when participants had to create boundaries and not accommodate, demonstrating their strength and conviction. In these emotionally laden, uncertain, intercultural exchanges, participants showed a great amount of awareness toward themselves and others, as well as resilience.

Transnational Korean Adoptees, in between Cultures and Families

As discussed in Chapter 1, for the first several decades of transnational Korean adoption, most adoptive parents raised their children in a climate of cultural assimilation, erasing or minimizing their Korean identities to help them "fit in" with their White communities and families. Tobias Hübinette (2007) has argued that Korean adoptees "have usually been subjected to self-identification as white after having grown up with a white family and living in wholly white surroundings" (p. 143). Transnational Korean adoptees themselves have reported a strong desire to "blend in" with their families and communities (Docan-Morgan, 2011), and cultural assimilation was typically the means by which they attempted to accomplish this goal, particularly throughout childhood. Furthermore, Korean adoptees have reported that they grew up receiving explicit messages from adoptive parents and friends that they didn't "see race" or that one should strive to be color-blind (Park Nelson, 2016). Such messages imply that the adoptee's race, their Koreanness or Asianness, is something that ought to be overlooked or ignored because it was inconsequential or undesirable.

Adoptees' experiences with racism (Docan-Morgan, 2011) and racial microaggressions (Baden, 2016) may create additional shame, particularly when adoptive parents fail to acknowledge the significance of race and racism. And although Korean adoptees have reported deidentifying with Whiteness as they grow into young adulthood and beyond (McGinnis et al., 2009), by the time this shift occurs, they have, in all likelihood, fully assimilated into dominant White culture and developed a "comprehensive understanding of White social and racial rules" (Park Nelson, 2016, p. 144). In addition, Korean adoptees have reported that identifying as non-White (e.g., Korean American, Asian American, person of color) can create friction with White adoptive parents who are reluctant to acknowledge their race privilege and/or to discuss adoptees' experiences with racism. As Eleana Kim (2010) points out, "Unlike second-generation ethnic Americans for whom cultural awakening or interest is often grounds for strengthening family ties and belonging, for transracial adoptees this assertion may instead be grounds for greater individuation and differentiation from the adoptive family" (p. 121). Thus, there are relational incentives for adoptees to perform White culture.

As discussed in the introduction, transnational Korean adoptees live with the *transracial adoption paradox*, which refers to the fact that Korean adoptees are racial/ethnic minorities in their adoptive country but are often perceived and treated by others, and sometimes themselves, as if they are White (Lee, 2003). Yet another paradox surfaces when Korean adoptees interact with non-adopted Koreans, whether in their adoptive country or in Korea: They appear to be racial/ethnic insiders and may be expected to act accordingly, but their primary cultural identity is that of their adoptive country. A Korean adoptee raised in Denmark may stand out as a racial minority growing up, but she is likely to speak Danish and English, understand unspoken rules governing Danish culture, and hold values similar to the Danish people surrounding her. In Korean cultural contexts, however, this adoptee displays the same racial characteristics of those around her but may feel fraudulent (Park Nelson, 2016) for her lack of familiarity with the Korean language, food, customs, and values. Maggie Jones (2015), a reporter for the *New York Times*, described how Korean adoptees who have moved back to Korea may experience a cultural alienation that is different from the racial alienation they experience in their adoptive countries:

> For many adoptees, those cultural divides—coupled with the fact that they can't speak the language, a frustrating and often heart-wrenching obstacle in their own birth country—solidifies the feeling that they hover in between: Not fully American, not fully Korean. Instead, they live in a third space: Asian, Western, white, adopted, other. (para. 60)

This experience of liminality, being in Korea and realizing that one doesn't belong fully, can be particularly troubling for adoptees who hope to fit in or "find themselves" in Korea. Adoptees may feel estranged from Korean culture while in Korea, but this feeling may be even more pronounced for adoptees in reunion. Indeed, experiences of cultural differences from one's birth family may lead adoptees to feel alienated, disappointed, and deeply hurt.

Adoptees who have high hopes or expectations for their reunion and their relationship with their birth families can be surprised or discouraged if they lack knowledge about Korean culture and/or the challenges of close intercultural relationships. Even those who have had some exposure to Korean culture often lack a deep understanding of Korean family relationships. Transnational adoptees may have experiences that are similar to those of *kyo'po*, children of

Korean immigrants who were raised outside of Korea. Both groups may be fully assimilated into the dominant culture in which they were raised and are likely to experience cultural differences with their Korean parents (Ahn et al., 2008). However, unlike transnational Korean adoptees, *kyo'po* grow up in the same household as their Korean immigrant parents, which provides them with the lived experience of being a son or daughter to Koreans and thus knowing the expected roles for Korean family relationships, even if they choose to deviate from expectations. *Kyo'po* are also likely to have visited relatives in Korea while growing up, which can also foster a sense of belonging within a family and within Korean culture. Unlike adoptees who reunite, *kyo'po* are not navigating cultural differences while forming a parental relationship virtually from scratch. Although *kyo'po* and transnational Korean adoptees may both, at times, develop the "double consciousness" (Du Bois, 1897) of seeing one's own race and culture from the perspective of the White majority, children of Korean immigrants are able, to varying extent, to associate their Koreanness with people and experiences (e.g., family relationships, food, language spoken at home). In contrast, transnational Korean adoptees have few, if any, personal reference points for what it means to be Korean.

Often, when people discuss ethnicity, race, and culture, they use these words somewhat interchangeably. Although these categories are socially constructed, they are often used to categorize and confer power or legitimacy to certain groups, and to mark other groups and individuals as different or abnormal. Many Korean adoptees, particularly those adopted before the 1990s, have talked about being "raised White." Here, *White* is referring to a set of cultural practices, such as language, food, and other daily habits, in addition to social contexts, latent values, and assumptions. Korean adoptees have also mentioned "feeling White," particularly when interacting with nonadopted Koreans, whether in their adoptive country or in Korea, because, as transnational adoptees, they do not understand or enact the cultural behaviors, shared experiences, and values that many people associate with Koreanness. Such adoptees are deploying the term *White* to describe the cultural knowledge that comes from being raised by White parents, contrasting it with the cultural knowledge that they would have had if they were raised by Korean parents.

Usually, "the experiences and communication patterns of Whites, or people perceived as White, are taken as the norm from which Others are marked" (Nakayama & Krizek, 1995, p. 293), but when adoptees interact with nonadopted Koreans, including their birth family, their White upbringing tends to evoke feelings of Otherness. For example, a Korean adoptee in Kim Park Nelson's (2016) research stated that she "feels very not White" when with her adoptive family, but that she feels "really White" (p. 143) around people who are culturally Korean. Here again, the terms *White* or *not White* are used to mark self-identification based on social context, but regardless, her words reference a sense of being perpetually on the outside or in between.

Transnational adoptee trips to Korea have been labeled as trips to the "Motherland" or "Homeland." These sentimental terms may be appealing to Korean adoptees who have been raised in countries where race is often (incorrectly) conflated with nationality. In the United States, White people are assumed to be American; those who are non-White are assumed to be foreigners. Trips "home" to Korea suggest the prospect of cultural and racial belonging not experienced in the adoptive country. In a study of Korean adoptees traveling to Korea, Ponting (2022) found that before the trip, all participants "idealized Korea as a place of belonging with answers to their identity affiliations" (p. 7). Yet, for many,

> any fantasies that adoptees may have harbored about their ability to be Korean or to be fully accepted in their homeland were easily disrupted by their encounters with the dominant ethnic nationalism that equates Koreanness with cultural, linguistic, and ethnic homogeneity based in shared blood and the myth of a five thousand year old history. (Kim, 2010, p. 186)

Adoptees in reunion experience cultural differences on a personal, intimate level—through interactions with their birth families. In some ways, the tenuous nature of these family relationships can make cultural differences seem more pronounced or significant. In fact, adoptees sometimes interpret these differences to mean that they don't belong in their birth families.

Intercultural Communication in Families

When Christine was fifteen years old, she met with her family in Korea for the third time. Although she had traveled to Seoul for a trip with her Korean dance group, she was able to visit her birth family's home for the first time. Her adoptive mom and a Korean foreign exchange student who had been living with them in the United States accompanied her. One highlight of their time together was a celebration Christine's Korean family threw for her birthday. "I remember that visit was really special because they kind of jam-packed every birthday I ever missed," she told me. There were "hundreds" of different dishes and a special birthday cake that included *tteok*, Korean rice cake. "It was, like, layered and tiered with different colored *tteok* and it was very good and I remember getting sick cuz I ate so much." At one point, however, differences between Christine and her birth family emerged. In her first interview, she recalled,

> My older brother was slightly overweight at the time and I just remember my birth family poking some jokes at him. Not, like, very meanly but, you know, just kind of like (pause), I didn't really know how to take it. Cuz I didn't know if culturally it was acceptable, but for me, it was just kinda like, "Oh, I wouldn't wanna poke fun at his weight," like, in front of people. And I know this cuz my exchange student told me what they were saying to him. And so it was just interesting because I mean, I know they're my family, but they're not like *my* family. They're not like the way *I* was raised. So just to know that my family is not, does not reflect who *I* have become. It was kind of even more *shocking* to realize, like, "Oh you have no influence by these people at *all* in your life except your genes." So it's definitely weird to see *your* family not acting like your family. Being like, "Oh jeez, that's not how I ever turned out." That's not *how* I was raised to be, you know. So yeah, definitely very interesting (speaking very quietly).

In reunion, family members from two cultures are attempting to find shared meaning. Often, the most vivid and challenging moments are those when communicators perceive an incompatibility of meanings. In Christine's story, her Korean family was attributing a very different meaning to their jokes about her brother's weight than Christine was. Parental teasing about children's weight is common in Korea (Bang et al., 2012; Ra et al., 2020), where high value is placed on conforming to idealized slender body types. Whereas Christine's family likely saw their teasing as fun and possibly even helpful, she saw it as inappropriate and potentially hurtful to her brother. This difference in perceived meaning had deep implications, as Christine notes a stark contrast between herself and her adoptive family versus her Korean family. As adoptees in reunion are often hungry to find even the most basic similarities to their birth families, moments of clear differences can be very unsettling, even if these differences can be attributed to culture. However, it is important to avoid the assumption that any culture is homogenous and that all members of any culture share the same characteristics equally (Leeds-Hurwitz, 2010). In addition, cultures change over time (Martin et al., 2002). Still, transnational Korean adoptees and their Korean birth families have different cultural identities, situated senses of self that are shaped by cultural experiences and social locations (Sorrells, 2016), and these identities impact their communication with one another.

Birth families and adoptees in reunion find themselves in a wholly unique communicative context. In nearly all cases, adoptees are meeting a biogenetically related parent for the first time in their memory. This blood connection, which is novel to the adoptee and has deep cultural significance for Korean nationals (Prébin, 2010), imbues their interactions with significance. In addition, the rarity of reunion meetings adds a sense of urgency for adoptees and birth families to make the most of their time together. Although interviewees expressed a desire to "get to know" their birth families through questions about occupation, hobbies, and interests, reunion meetings carry much more weight than the making of a new friend or acquaintance. This dynamic can motivate adoptees to attempt to communicate effectively and appropriately, but it can also make them feel hypervigilant of their own communication and their birth family's reactions. Understandably, then, they may feel that the stakes are high with each interaction.

Adding extra complexity, some Korean birth parents may be limited in their abilities to take non-Korean cultural perspectives, particularly if they have not spent extended time outside of Korea or with non-Koreans. As critical communication scholar Kathryn Sorrells (2016) notes,

> People from the dominant cultural group in a society are often unaware that the norms, values, practices, and institutes of the society are, in fact, deeply shaped by and infused with a particular cultural orientation and that these patterns of shared meaning have been normalized as "just the way things are" or "the way things should be." (p. 13)

The value of ethnic homogeneity that led the Korean government to expunge mixed-race babies from Korea in the 1950s and early 1960s also cultivated a sense of national superiority and insularity (Han, 2007). As a result, many Koreans who grew up in Korea, older Koreans especially, may have difficulty communicating effectively with those who do not share Korean cultural identity, values, and assumptions. This includes children with whom they are reuniting. In contrast, although Korean adoptees have been raised as cultural insiders given their familiarity with White social norms and behaviors, they have also been racialized and marked as "other" throughout their lives. Perhaps this insider-outsider identity explains why participants expressed a general willingness to accommodate to what they perceived as their birth family's cultural expectations, even when it was difficult. Korean adoptees are often masters at attempting to fit in with their social environment.

Cultural Differences with Birth Family

I remember [my adoptive dad] on the way over [to Korea], he was
reading a book called *Culture Shock Korea* and *The Culture Shock
Guide*. I remember, like, peeking over his shoulder, and he was more
into it than I was, you know. He would point things out to me like,
"Oh, you know, you're not supposed to touch your food before your
elders do at a Korean meal." I'm like, "Oh, hmm." Actually I don't
remember if he pointed it out to me or if I just, like, looked at that
over his shoulder, but I remember that it did come in handy when I met
my aunts and uncles . . . I waited until my birth grandfather [started
eating] and they were like, "Oh he's so Korean. He knows well."

—MARK

In this interview excerpt, Mark's behavior of waiting to start eating until his
grandfather had begun is a fairly simple behavior, but it has deep significance,
representing respect for one's elders and their role in the family. This behavior
led to Mark's Korean family evaluating him as "so Korean," a high compli-
ment in this context. Other adoptees, however, were unfamiliar with Korean
cultural expectations. Cat described how she didn't know that her behaviors
such as drinking, smoking, and not eating seafood and meat would be perceived as very offensive during her first trip to Korea. However, these behaviors
led her birth mother to force Cat to watch everyone finish eating before she
could start, give her the "silent treatment," and kick her out of the house; in
addition, Cat's twin sister "attacked" her verbally. These strong negative reactions were due to assumptions that Cat was being disrespectful and should have
known better, despite a complete lack of exposure to Korean culture while growing up. Of course, individuals' responses to perceived cultural differences and
missteps can vary dramatically. Cat's birth family's strong and punitive responses were an anomaly and may reflect particular family patterns and dynamics
more than Korean culture itself. Regardless, their responses made Cat fearful
of offending them again. Although she wanted desperately to repair her relationship with her birth family, her words expressed contrast and contradiction. She wrote to me, expressing the following:

There is a part of me that will always yearn for this blood tie—and
sometimes it feels like I'm begging them to talk to me, forgive me, love
me. And then there's the other part of me that desperately wants my
birth family to accept me for who I am, a person who was orphaned as
a newborn, raised in America, abused, given birth to a child I'd die for,
and have developed ways to not only cope but grow in an ever-changing world. I struggle with this dichotomy, selfish vs selfless. In America,

there is a social awareness about being transparent and authentic, and in Korea, it's about tradition and an unsaid authority to your elders.

Cat identifies a tension between her desire to be loved for "who she is," including the many ways she has persevered through life challenges and changes, versus her willingness to do anything (e.g., beg, forgive) for a connection with her birth family. She continued later, "As much as I want my birth family's acceptance, I cannot force myself to be submissive enough." Her words suggest that, despite a strong desire for a relationship, there may be—and perhaps should be—limits to what adoptees are willing to do to maintain communication with their birth families.

As Cat's and other participants' words illustrate, relationships—family relationships, especially—are embedded deeply in cultural values and assumptions. A contrast between dominant American cultural assumptions and traditional Korean cultural assumptions provides insight into why transnational Korean adoptees may experience cultural differences as challenging when interacting with their birth families. Dominant (i.e., White, middle-class) American culture tends to assume that people are uniquely endowed and discrete, and each person should make their own choices and not simply fulfill social roles (Philipsen, 1992). People *have* family relationships, but their identities can be viewed separately from these relationships. In dominant American culture, there is not a pervasive sense of obligation to live one's life for one's family. Independence is valorized; dependence is looked upon with derision. Individuality is praised; conformity is scorned. In contrast, most Koreans tend to assume that people cannot be understood apart from the social categories (age, gender, occupation, marital status) to which they belong because relationships are inherently hierarchical (Park & Cho, 1995). Conformity to expectations and roles based on age and gender is viewed as a sign of social awareness; those who do not conform tend to be seen as clueless, strange, or obnoxious.

An American may be surprised when, shortly after an initial introduction, a person who grew up in Korea may ask them, "How old are you?" because American culture tends to be horizontal, emphasizing equality regardless of age (Triandis & Gelfand, 1998). Americans tend to be taught that asking an adult their age is rude, particularly if the recipient of the question is perceived to be a woman. However, Koreans raised in Korea learn from an early age to interact with others based on hierarchical relationships rooted in age, reflecting characteristics of a vertical culture; therefore, knowing the age of one's fellow interlocutor is essential for effective and appropriate communication. In another example, in the United States, it is customary to address one's siblings by their first name. However, in Korea, there are specific terms to be used for addressing one's siblings based on the speaker's gender and age and their sibling's gender and relative age. For example, a younger female is to address her older sister as *eonni* (언니) and her older brother as *oppa* (오빠). A younger male is to address his older sister as *nuna* (누나) and his older brother as *hyeong* (형). These terms can also be used to address close friends according to their age. Calling one's older sibling by their first name would indicate disrespect, akin to an English speaker calling a parent by their first name. There is only one word for younger sibling, *dongsaeng* (동생), and it is not dependent on the speaker's or addressee's gender. The Korean language, then, both reflects and reinforces hierarchical relationships based on age and gender, but there are no equivalent terms in English. Instead, English speakers call siblings by their first names, which are reflections of their individual identity, a deep cultural assumption.

Mee Joo shared a story from her first meeting that illustrates cultural differences in assumptions about personhood. As many Koreans believe that certain personality characteristics are associated with blood type and that certain blood types are preferable over others (Chu, 2017), Mee Joo's Korean family asked her about her blood type the first time they met. This conversation resulted in confusion. She recalled,

> One of the big things that I remember from that night is that they wanted to know what blood type I was, because they wanted to know which parent I took after. And I was trying to explain to them that I didn't know what my blood type is and that people in the U.S. don't know their blood type; it's not a big deal. But they thought that I didn't understand the question so they went around the table and everybody said what blood type they were (laughs) and I was still trying to explain to them, "No, I don't know my blood type. People in the U.S. don't know their blood type," and they were trying to get me to understand, "Well, your adoptive mom in the States, what's her blood type?" and I was saying she doesn't know either and it was just (laughs) really frustrating for me to try and convey that it wasn't that I didn't understand the question; it was that it was hard for them to understand that Western people don't know that kind of a thing offhand.

This interaction illustrates further that cultural differences can be so deep that communicators can have difficulty even identifying the cause of confusion or misunderstanding. Of course, these deep assumptions affect communication, relationships, and even perceptions of love. As Eric stated,

The way Koreans work, if they had their way, you'd completely lose yourself, you know? You just would be folded back into that same hierarchical structure that they lived by. And they, they would call that *love*. And it is. But it's a very different love than we know, and it comes with a lot of frustrations too.

Given contrasts in cultural assumptions about people, communication, and family relationships, birth parents and adoptees in reunion may have differing expectations about what constitutes effective and appropriate family communication. In the following section, I discuss the cultural differences that participants described experiencing during their interactions with their birth families. I note the messages exchanged, the meanings the participants ascribed to them, and, where relevant, the impacts on relationships. Regardless of their individual experiences, all participants were able to discuss the role that cultural differences played during their reunion, and all disclosed their own attempts to understand their family's behavior through the lens of Korean culture.

Family Roles and Expectations: Birth Parents Acting like Parents

Cultural differences manifested fairly early in interactions between Korean birth family members and adoptees in reunion. These differences did not necessarily result in conflict, but participants often expressed a hypervigilance of their own communication (both verbal and nonverbal) to avoid intercultural misunderstandings or offenses. When cultural differences in communication did arise, participants recalled attempting, where possible, to adapt to their birth family's communication. Still, at times, these differences tended to cause feelings of hurt, confusion, and discomfort, particularly as they related to family roles and expectations.

Questions, Advice, and "Helping"

Participants noticed that their birth parents were quick to ask what seemed like personal questions and to offer their advice and opinions, particularly on topics related to romantic relationships. Birth parents and extended family members (e.g., aunts, grandmothers) routinely asked questions that stood out to participants as overly personal given that they had just met. Mee Joo recalled meeting her birth family for the first time while she was still in college, saying,

When they first met me, they said I think some very stereotypical things to me in terms of like, "Are you gonna get married? When are you gonna get married? You should marry a Korean man; you should really marry, like, a doctor or a lawyer or a teacher. Marry a teacher, that's, like, a good one." And I found out that that's one of the, you know, most respected professions to marry into in Korea. And, yeah, you know, things that they would say or do . . . it's this whole notion of being treated like a Korean because that's the only way they know how to treat you but not necessarily the way that Westerners are used to being treated.

Mee Joo's words display knowledge of cultural differences between herself and her Korean family as well as an awareness of her family's limited knowledge and ability for communicating in alternate ways. Historically and even today, people who are culturally Korean tend to place greater value on marriage and traditional gender roles than those who were raised in Western cultures, although younger generations tend to place lower value on both (Eun, 2007). Given the increased status (social and probable economic) that marriage confers on single people in Korea, birth parents often wish for their children, especially daughters, to marry, regardless of whether they grew up abroad or in Korea. Yet participants were unaccustomed to people whom they had just met—even if they were biogenetic relatives—asking questions and offering advice on this topic.

Elise Prébin (2013) recounted how her relationship with her Korean birth family changed as her marital, economic, and professional status changed over her years in reunion. She described how, when she came to Korea initially, as a single woman, her family took care of her by providing a place to stay and paying for her food/drinks while eating out. At that time, they also expressed their interest in her romantic prospects and advised her to marry within one to two years. Then, after her marriage, members of her birth family seemed to assume that she and her husband were an independent household and treated them with increased separation and independence. She described this change, writing, "My new status of fully adult daughter permits eased [*sic*] familial contacts and real exchanges on the maternal side, but also diminishing material dependence on the paternal side" (p. 149). In other words, through their actions, her Korean family expressed the cultural assumption that marriage provides women with legitimacy and independence from the natal family.

Other participants stated that their parents advised them to be a good son or daughter to their adoptive parents and to study hard in school. Eric described his birth father's advice as "very Confucian," recalling,

He just kept stressing over and over, you know, "Take care of your parents. You need to, you know, show them respect and spend time with them while they're still around." He was not afraid at all about giving advice, even, you know, *minutes* after we met (laughs).

As an American man in his late twenties when he met his birth family, Eric was not accustomed to receiving advice so early in a relationship, and yet he understood that his father's actions were situated in Korean culture and more specifically in Korean family relationships. Participants often attributed their birth parents' behavior to Korean culture, and, in many ways, cultural differences provided a means for adoptees to reframe behavior that they found challenging or puzzling.

However, sometimes attributing birth family behaviors to culture was only helpful to a certain extent. Sylvia had the unique experience of having her initial reunion in the U.S. city where she lived. For several days, her Korean parents stayed with her and her husband and children in their home. During this time, Sylvia hoped that her mother would sit down, relax, and have meaningful conversations (at least when an interpreter was present), whereas her birth mother wanted to spend time cleaning the kitchen and cooking meals. Sylvia reflected on this time, saying,

> I'm a professionally trained chef, so I always have control (laughs) of, like, my kitchen. And I *like* being in control there. And so I feel like even if I screw up something, I'm still in control and that it was as a result of something that *I did*. And so being *pushed* out of my kitchen, I felt like I had lost complete control over everything.

When I asked Sylvia how this interaction impacted her sense of connection with her birth parents, she stated,

> That's interesting, because (pause) once I started to realize that this is how they treat (pause) their *daughter*. You know, I knew that they were treating me like their daughter. And so, in a lot of ways that helped, but it also made me feel more American because we're so different.

Like Eric, Sylvia made a conscious effort to try to understand her birth parents' behavior in terms of Korean culture and family relationships while trying to forge a connection with them. She explained,

> It was hard because I really wanted to know what they were feeling and it might just be really embarrassing of me, I wanted them to be honest about what kind of emotions they were going through. They just

always wanted to tell me that they were happy. And I knew, well, there has to be more than that. This has to be difficult. Whether it's seeing my [adoptive] family or whatever. You know, there has to be more than just, "Oh, we're so happy" (laughs).

Sylvia's words reflect a cultural orientation that has been referred to as *low context*, which refers to a preference for direct, unambiguous communication (Hall, 1976; Kim et al., 1998). This style is more reflective of American culture than of Korean culture, which has been described as *high context*, where communicators are expected to infer meaning from indirect messages and situational cues. Regardless, Sylvia's reunion, which started joyously, required her to exert a great deal of cognitive, emotional, and communicative effort. Sylvia attempted to understand, empathize, and communicate with her birth parents, despite her own unfamiliarity with Korean culture and language. She also attempted to reflect on her own cultural identity as an American. In addition, she was required to undertake *emotion work* (Hochschild, 1979) in trying to suppress her feelings of frustration and discomfort to make her Korean parents comfortable and to ease the initiation of their relationship. All of these communicative acts reflect the discursive burden Sylvia felt at the time. After discussing these cultural differences, she said that during her birth parents' visit, she didn't get to see her adoptive mother very much and really missed "feeling normal" with her adoptive parents. To Sylvia, American culture and her adoptive parents felt normal because they were familiar and required little to no conscious effort, particularly because she described her relationship with both of her adoptive parents as "really close." In contrast, her interactions with her birth parents required navigating language and cultural differences in addition to the logistics and physical toll of "chasing around" her large city doing sightseeing during their visit. Add these efforts to Sylvia's hopes of learning more about her birth family's history and her goal of trying to engage in meaningful discussions with them, and her desire for more feelings of normalcy or comfort during her reunion is understandable.

"When Are You Moving to Korea?"

Participants also described messages from their birth families that encouraged them to move to Korea and be reintegrated into the family. Such hopes seemed to overlook the fact that adoptees have established lives and primary relationships outside of Korea. Ashley, who lived in Korea for a year after college, described messages from her birth family that encouraged her to return to Korea permanently and build a life there. She recalled,

I think, like, they wanted me to go to med school at Yonsei[3] or something, but I was like (sighs) I don't know Korean that well (laughs) and I kind of want to go in the U.S. They're always like, "Oh aren't you going to come live here for*ever*?" It's like, no, like, all my family and friends are back in the U.S., you know. I have family and friends [in Korea] now, but I mean that's my *life* that's in the U.S. My birth aunt, the one that speaks English, is like, "When are you going to move *here*?" And, "Aren't you going to come back for Chuseok[4] every year?" And they always expect me to kind of go there but never really make an effort to come this way . . . I think my birth father told my birth aunt that he's gonna get me back for good *someday* (laughs). . . . When they bought their new house, they had a room for me, like, waiting there, so stuff like that. I think they're hoping I move back forever, but yeah, I kind of made it clear to them that, you know, this is my home, so.

Ashley's birth parents had tried to reclaim her from her American adoptive parents when Ashley was young, so their hopes that she might return to Korea as an adult and be a part of the family permanently are unsurprising. Her words reflect her birth family's persistence in these unsuccessful attempts. Notably, Ashley's parents' continued efforts to reclaim her may have resulted from a misunderstanding of the nature of adoption. During the years of Korea's recovery and rapid industrialization, some struggling families placed their children in informal adoptions with people they knew in the hopes that their family situation would improve and they could take their child back, or they took them to an orphanage for a temporary stay (Prébin, 2013). Orphanages provided food, shelter, and basic education, all of which were out of reach for many poor families. Regardless, Ashley's birth family either did not understand or did not accept the permanence of her adoption and her American identity and life. Other participants also recalled that their Korean families encouraged them to move back to Korea. Eric spoke of how his family would like him to live in Korea, but his career as an actor in his adoptive country brings him a lot of joy; were he to live in Korea, his main employment option would be, like, many transnational adoptees, to teach English, which he did not want to do.

The Man of the House: Respect for the Birth Father

South Korea is among the wealthiest countries in the world and is known for its technology, cosmetics, and popular culture (e.g., K-pop, K-dramas). These modern exports, however, may obscure the continued impact of traditional Confucian values on public and private life. Confucianism, a philosophy credited to Chinese philosopher Confucius (551–479 B.C.E.), undergirds Korean family life and relationships. According to Park and Cho (1995), "Confucianism is not a formal religious institution in Korea but rather a code of latent ethics and values that has profoundly influenced the society for nearly two millennia" (p. 119). Confucianism emphasizes adherence to family roles, with appropriate respect and obedience accorded to family members based on relative age and gender, with fathers placed at the top of the hierarchy, above wives and certainly above children. As Park and Cho describe,

> The central familial relationship is not between husband and wife, but rather that between parent and child, especially father and son. Moreover, the relationships between family members are not horizontal—that is, based on mutual love and equality—but vertical filial piety characterized by benevolence, authority, and obedience. Authority rests with the (male) head of household, and differences in status exist among the other family members. (p. 124)

Confucianism dictates that children should respect their parents, especially their fathers, and this respect is demonstrated through obedience. In contrast, Westerners tend to emphasize equality in relationships, particularly among adults, including adult children. From this perspective, effective parenting is often viewed as a balance of rules and expectations with flexibility and open discussions, referred to as an authoritative parenting style (Aunola et al., 1999; Lee et al., 2006). When birth parents express rigid expectations or displeasure, adoptees may react strongly because of cultural differences and the lack of relational history with the parent. Perhaps because Korean fathers are accustomed to their authority being unquestioned, participants reported more difficulties with birth fathers than with birth mothers.

During the year that Ashley lived in Korea, she had a conflict with her birth father based on his perception that she was not communicating an appropriate amount of respect for him. She described the dynamics, saying,

> I sent him a text message, but he stopped talking to me for *six months* because, you know, I'm his child and a female and younger and to be speaking to him in that kind of, like, equalized way, which is okay in America; you know, when you're over twenty, people are pretty much adults, but you know in Korea they have the hierarchy and that's like a huge dig on his pride, I think. So we were both kind of like "*Grrrrrr*," both stubborn. We just didn't want to, I was like, "There's nothing wrong with what I said and he needs to just, you know, *suck* it up" and he was just kind of like, "You shouldn't talk to me like that, you know,

I'm above you" or whatever, so. That was, I think, the big difference, like the hard thing, the hierarchy thing was hard to get used to.

In this excerpt, Ashley describes how her lack of deference toward her birth father was met with severe resistance and then silence for six months, which is notable given that Ashley was only living in Korea for one year. She and her father differed in their values and assumptions about how parents and adult children are supposed to relate to one another, and despite her understanding of the intercultural dynamics of their exchanges, she refused to accommodate and had to face the consequences of her decision.

Eric also described situations where demonstrating respect for his birth father was paramount, but luckily, his older brother, his *hyeong*, was a willing accomplice in defying their father's expectations covertly. For his first meeting, Eric wanted to meet his older brother before he met his birth father, but his birth father would not have accepted such an arrangement. To avoid conflict, Eric and his brother arranged to meet first, just the two of them, and the next day, when Eric met his father for the first time, he and his brother had to pretend that they were meeting for the first time as well. He narrated,

> As you may know about Korean culture, it's like there's *so* many ways to step on people's toes. And so what my brother didn't want to have happen was for my father to be insulted that I met him first. And so we went into that meeting with my father under the guise that we had talked on the phone yesterday but that we hadn't met. So I was supposed to pretend to meet him for the first time as well (laughs). . . . Yep, very clearly, like, laid out, we *cannot* tell him. He'll be crushed.

Eric articulated that reuniting with his older brother was his highest priority in initiating his reunion because they were close in age and had memories of one another. Yet because Eric and his brother knew the importance of demonstrating unparalleled respect for their father, they found a way to both accommodate to cultural expectations and navigate the reunion according to Eric's wishes.

Ji Kyoung and her boyfriend also had to engage in some calculated efforts to not offend her birth father while in Korea during one of her visits. Because she and her boyfriend were unmarried, her birth parents would not allow them to stay together in their home. But when her parents inadvertently found out that Ji Kyoung was pregnant, they allowed the couple to stay together with them. Still, her birth father expressed the importance of Ji Kyoung's boyfriend showing him proper respect. Shortly after learning of Ji Kyoung's pregnancy, her younger brother and brother-in-law questioned the boyfriend, asking him what his intentions were and if he was going to marry Ji Kyoung. She described his response, saying,

> He was a bit baffled and didn't really know what to say, so they just kept nagging him for a long time, and then I think that he eventually said, "Yes, of course I'm gonna marry her" because that would kind of leave him in peace.

However, this peace did not last long. Shortly thereafter, the couple was expected to participate in a ceremony to honor Ji Kyoung's parents and receive their blessing. She said,

> [My boyfriend] was taken into the living room where my parents would sit on a couch and then him and I were instructed to actually stand in front of my parents doing the traditional Korean bow where you just go all the way down on the floor and do that several times and they would kind of bless us as a couple. And so it was like a ceremony, and he was invited to pour wine to my father who was sitting now at the table, and would question him, kind of thing. . . . The first question he asked was, "Who is the most important person to you, Ji Kyoung or [name of Ji Kyoung's daughter]?" . . . And I can't remember, if he said me or my daughter; either way it was the correct answer so my father's like, "Ahhh!" (happy sound) and then they took a drink. And then he said, "Who is the most important person in this family?" And then he was super confused if he should say me or [my birth father]. And then my brother walked behind my father's back and was pointing to his head (laughs) and my boyfriend said, "Oh, you!" and then my father was happy. "Yeah!" (imitating a cheer) and then they were drinking and so that happened, everything, within a very few hours from the first time my boyfriend met them.

Ji Kyoung recalled this story with humor, at one point saying with a bit of resignation, "What can you do." She was willing to adapt to Korean culture while with her birth family because she knew that these rituals and displays of respect were important to them. Perhaps because she was in her mid-thirties when she first reunited or perhaps because she felt an extremely strong connection with her birth family (likely both), the cultural differences and the adjustments she had to make did not feel consequential to her.

Christine, who met her birth family for the first time when she was nine years old, told me that she still experienced uncertainty about how to demonstrate respect for her birth father. During a visit in 2016, when she was twenty-five, a friend who was interpreting for her and whom Christine described as "very Korean" told her that she should feed her birth parents at dinner. Christine described the situation, which was heightened by the presence of her adoptive parents as well, saying,

> I'm like, that's very intimate, you know, as an American, like, to feed this into someone's mouth and I'm doing it to my birth father and my birth father won't even look me in the eye. Because he's, like, shamed, but also my friend who's Korean is like, "You should do that because he's the eldest here. He's your father, you're showing respect to him." So much pressure, you know what I mean? Like, Oh god, did I f--- up because I didn't do that beforehand? . . . Like, I have somebody whispering to my ear, "Just pay attention to the *cultural* norms," and at the same time I'm trying to emotionally process and protect everybody else in the space at the same time. It was so much.

Christine's words reveal the myriad thoughts that may be going through an adoptee's mind during reunion. Not only do adoptees bear the discursive burden of trying to enact appropriate behaviors in an unfamiliar culture; they are also dealing with the emotional weight of being with birth family members *and* trying to make others comfortable in an almost inherently uncomfortable situation. The presence of adoptive parents can add to the discomfort while also being a source of familiarity. Christine's expression that "It was so much" is perhaps part of the reason participants often reported feeling emotionally exhausted after reunion meetings.

Warm versus Cold

Some participants mentioned that their birth parents did not seem emotionally expressive—either happy or sad—or warm during their first meeting. For example, Jorgen described his mother as "stone faced" when he met her initially, and Nikki noted how her mother "never smiled" during their time together. Research has found that Americans tend to smile about 50 percent more than people in East Asian countries (Talhelm et al., 2019) and that Danes tend to interpret smiles as signs of friendliness (Chudnovskaya & O'Hara, 2022), suggesting that culture might be an explanation for differences in facial expressions and interpretations of these expressions.

During her first conversation with her birth mother, Sun Ok described how her mother did not engage verbally or nonverbally, saying,

> All in all, it was about five hours of me having to carry the conversation. She didn't have any questions for me because she had read about me in the letter . . . I had to keep asking questions. She had nothing to ask me. I even asked her, "Do you have anything to ask me? Do you wanna say anything?" "No." (shrugs, imitating her birth mother)

The differences that these participants experienced may have been due to personality or birth parents' emotional state, but culture may also provide an explanation. Confucianism places value on silence, "thrift on words," and being emotionally reserved in one's behavior (Kim, 2003; Lim & Choi, 1996), which may provide a cultural explanation for behaviors that seemed unexpressive or unengaged in the eyes of participants. In contrast, conversational competence in White, middle-class Western contexts tends to emphasize behaviors such as demonstrating attentiveness through asking questions of the other person and reciprocal disclosure—taking turns sharing personal information with the other (Spitzberg & Adams, n.d.). When Sun Ok's Korean mother did not engage in these behaviors, Sun Ok evaluated the conversation as being awkward.

Public discourse surrounding reunion may also have impacted participants' expectations of their birth parents' communication. In media representations of reunion, birth mothers, especially, tend to be sorrowful and/or joyful. Participants found a lack of expressiveness from birth mothers difficult to interpret, and, in this unfamiliar context, they attributed this stoicism to disinterest or unenthusiasm.

Adoptees Accommodating Their Communication

Communication accommodation theory (CAT) helps to explain how adoptees managed cultural differences between themselves and their birth families and why they chose to do (or not do) so. This theory, advanced and articulated by psychologist Howard Giles and associates (Giles & Powesland, 1975; Zhang & Giles, 2017), posits that communicators have an array of verbal and nonverbal codes that they can modify based on the identity of their fellow interlocutor. Particularly when interacting with someone whose social identities differ from one's own, a person can adapt their communication to be similar to, or different from, their partner's; these phenomena are referred to as convergence and divergence, respectively. Convergence and divergence can operate at varying levels of consciousness and can be observed in various communicative codes, including volume, accent, interruptions, speech rate, posture, and more. For example, one might notice that adolescents who spend time together may, over time, start to speak with the same vocabulary and speech patterns, as well as dress in a similar style; these are examples of convergence.

A communicator is more likely to converge with someone when the other person is perceived as having more relative power in a situation. In contrast, communicators may choose to diverge in order to exert control in a relationship (DiVerniero, 2013). Frequently, interviewees chose to converge with their family's communication by altering their appearance to be accepted or by allowing their families to touch them in ways that did not necessarily feel normal or comfortable to them. Participants talked about not wanting to "offend" their families, and for some, there was a pervasive sense that cultural missteps could lead to the end of their relationship.

Quiet, Cute, and Thin: Korean Expectations for Western Women

Nearly all women participants mentioned Korean standards for beauty and body type as a cultural difference that impacted their reunion interactions. Some participants described their own hypervigilance about their appearance before the reunion, recalling how they selected their outfit carefully and made sure their hair was done neatly. Participants also expressed awareness about their appearance and demeanor during the meetings. Meagan, for example, described,

> I'm really loud, and so I was very aware going into meeting them each time, you know, to sort of hold back a little bit or pull back. Like my [adoptive] mom was like, "I've never seen you this quiet before," because I didn't know what to say. And I like to use my hands a lot when I talk, and so I felt pressure to conform to cultural standards. And you know, definitely dressing appropriately. I didn't want them to think that I was like some *hussy* so, you know, I tried to make sure that like my hair was pulled back, you know, or it was at least done—not in some messy bun like it is right now or that I wasn't wearing *too* much makeup and that I was *covered*. I, you know, just wanted to make sure that I wasn't going to offend them in any way.

Although Meagan described her birth family as very loving and welcoming, she also described a sense of being watched, which made her highly cognizant of the impression she was creating. She continued, saying,

I felt like everyone's eyes were on me, and watching to see what my next move is. You know, in the broader sense I understand that because I'm this (laughs) new [person] . . . I felt like, you know, like I was in a fishbowl almost, with everybody looking at me, waiting to see the next move, waiting to see what I was going to do, waiting to see. And then I, of course, then felt that pressure. Cuz I was like, "Oh my gosh, I have to be perfect. I can't slip up in front of these people." And I also want to make a really good impression, you know, I want them to like me and so. It was almost, not a show, but yeah, I felt like I was just on display for people to *watch* and see what was gonna happen next.

Meagan expressed a sense of surveillance by her birth family and also self-surveillance, and an ensuing pressure to be "perfect." Her reference to her birth family as "these people" implies a sense of distance, perhaps created by her fear that they might judge her. Before and during her first reunion meeting, she was converging her communication (verbal and nonverbal), including her appearance, based on metaperception. In other words, she was attempting to perceive her birth family's perceptions of her. She draws on standards for Korean femininity that include being quiet or reserved, dressing and using makeup conservatively, and styling hair neatly, all of which seemed to require effort and vigilance on her part. From a communication perspective, Meagan is engaging in impression management, attempting to present herself, verbally and nonverbally, in a way that her birth family would find acceptable so that she is able to escalate their relationship. These behaviors are communicative and reflect an additional discursive burden for adoptee women.

Importantly, Meagan and other women experienced a specific type of pressure related to their intersectional identities of ethnicity (Korean), culture (American or western European), and gender (women). Research has found that Asian American women have reported lower evaluations of their own appearance compared with White American women, and one explanation is that they fit neither the tall, slender Westernized beauty ideal nor the petite, "cute" Korean beauty ideal (Frederick et al., 2016). In addition, participants have been assimilated into Western culture, with their beliefs often being based on idealized images of White women and Orientalist tropes that stereotype Asian women as being passive, quiet, and hyperfeminine. In a study of Korean American and Vietnamese American[5] young women, Pyke and Johnson (2003) found that participants tended to conceptualize White femininity as confident and independent, in contrast to Asian femininity, which is conceived as compliant and submissive. Similar to the participants in Pyke and Johnson's study, the Korean adoptee women who shared these stories with me made a distinction between what they perceived as their authentic selves and the version they presented to their Asian families. Nikki described the effort she took in preparing her outfit for her first meeting, saying,

> I wore a different outfit (laughs) coming in the taxi because I didn't want to get it wet and ruined. And then I thought I was supposed to, like, dress up and be all cute and wear a dress. Which isn't me. But I ran around the whole time thinking about what I was gonna wear and I tried buying stuff before I got there.

Later in the interview, Nikki described how, because her mother was tall and thin, and because Korean women tend to be, in her words, "teeny tiny," she felt like the "fat, ugly daughter" when with her birth mother. The fear of judgment and rejection is common for adoptees in reunion, and this fear drove participants' efforts to appear and act in ways that they perceived to be appropriate for Korean women in a Korean context.

Other women recalled feeling constrained in their behavior rather than their appearance. Cat, who was thirty-eight at the time of her first meeting, recalled that when she tried to order a beer at lunch with her birth mother, her birth mother forbade it, saying, "No drinking in the daytime." Cat also shared that during her initial reunion she had to create a "code word" with the American adoption agency worker to indicate that she wanted to excuse herself to smoke a cigarette because her birth mother would find it disrespectful if Cat left to go outside to smoke. Cat actually had tried to smoke less before their first meeting because her twin sister, whom she Skyped with before the meeting, had encouraged her to quit. However, she told me with a laugh that the stress of the reunion made her want to smoke more. The constraints on Cat's behavior led to feelings of scrutiny and pressure, and, quite naturally, she wanted relief.

In addition to policing their own behavior and appearance for reunion meetings, participants also recounted direct messages from their birth family about their bodies. These comments usually came from parents or extended family members (usually older females) and addressed participants' physical features such as the "dark" color of a participant's skin, their height, their weight, a tattoo, or their hair length or color. These comments seemed to bother some women more than others. Specifically, the Danish women I interviewed seemed less bothered by these comments than the American participants. For example, Ji Kyoung has five older birth sisters and described how, during her second visit to her family, they wanted to take her to a clinic to get Botox injections to her face. She described what happened, saying,

They kept wanting to take me to a clinic. I'm like, "Nah, I don't know, I'm fine." I didn't want to go to a clinic. And they just kept at it and kept pushing and I didn't understand the signals, what they were trying to say so, at last they say, "You need Botox." Like, "What? I don't think so, where do you think?" They're like, "Oh yes. There, there, there, there, there." (imitates them pointing at different places on her face) Okay, forget I asked, I don't wanna know! So they are more just like, "Why doesn't Ji Kyoung want to do more for herself and her presentation and try to look nice? Like, why?"

This emphasis on Ji Kyoung's appearance has been consistent over the past decade. She says that when they video call her, the first thing they do is comment on her weight or if her face looks "fat." Ji Kyoung attributed these comments to Korean culture, and did not seem bothered by them, even though she said that in Denmark where she was raised, one would "never" make such comments to another person. When I observed to Ji Kyoung that the American women in my research seem more bothered by appearance criticism than the Danish women, she explained,

Danish people, they like to think about themselves as those down-to-earth, grounded people, natural and more free-minded, free thinking and so, "Yeah, they can say to me, I am fat, but hey, that's who I am," like. That's very Danish, I think.

Similarly, Hanne, also from Denmark, said that her Korean mother was "very focused" on her skin during their one reunion meeting and suggested that Hanne have some moles on her face removed. Hanne, however, said, "I didn't give it much notice actually. I just thought it was funny." Like Ji Kyoung, she stated that when it comes to physical appearance, people tend to be more "laid back" in Denmark than in Korea or the United States.

American women participants tended to find their birth family's appearance-related comments very hurtful. These types of messages and their negative impacts have been noted by other transnational Korean adoptees as well (e.g., G.O.A.'L., 2008). For example, Catherine met her birth family for the first time when she was ten, in 2000, and visited Korea four times over the following five years. With the support of her adoptive parents, she had also devoted herself to intense Korean language study after her first meeting. By 2006, she no longer needed an interpreter, which had been her goal in studying Korean, but it also made her responsible for interpreting between her adoptive parents and her birth parents. She recounted a visit to her birth parents' house when she was sixteen, where the difficulties of translating across languages and cultures and two sets of parents became too much, especially when her birth father criticized her weight. She recalled,

> There was, you know, like *two* families, like, "What are they saying, what are they saying? Tell me right now." And like, it was so much to just *process*, to think. . . . But there was a point in time when [my birth father] just kept going, like, "Why are you so fat? Why are you so fat? Like, you need to lose weight. Like, go with your mom right now. We're gonna go buy you some diet juice" (imitating birth father's tone). And [my birth mother] grabbed my hand and starts leading me away and then my adoptive parents are like, *"Where are they taking you? What are you doing?"* You know, and I'm just like freaking out in my head. . . . And I guess, you know, *because* this is a family that, like, *gave* you up, you're really sensitive to what they think of you. But there were a lot of times that my birth father would tell me that I was overweight. And I mean, that's, like, *really* typical Korean parent. Like, if you're not ninety pounds you're overweight. For a *teenage girl* who's hearing this from, you know, the people who gave her up, like, it hit me really, really hard.

Catherine's experience with her father, whom she described as "very, *very* traditional," illuminates many challenges. She was interpreting between her two sets of parents and was also being told that she was "fat" by her birth father while her adoptive parents, who didn't speak Korean, looked on in confusion. Most Westerners would deem it hurtful for a father to tell his teenage daughter that she is overweight and even more hurtful to force her to go to the store to buy weight-loss products. Catherine provides insight in pointing out that her father's communication is "very typical" of Korean parents, and yet, this knowledge did not diminish the hurtful impact of his words, particularly because of her sensitivity to her birth family's opinion. Thus, although Korean cultural knowledge was helpful to Catherine in understanding her father's behavior, knowledge is different from emotion, and emotions often don't comply with reason, especially during heightened interactions. Several adoptees in the G.O.A.'L. (2008) collection recounted similar interactions with their birth families and the hurtful impact of such messages.

Catherine's birth father's words and actions can be further situated within Korean culture and history. South Korea's emphasis on physical "perfection," which is signified by a slender body type first and foremost, can be traced to various factors. Among them are collectivist tendencies to fit in with the group, fierce social competition driven by a desire for status and a survival mentality, media saturation, and an unabashed consumer capitalist culture (Epstein & Joo, 2012; Lee, 2018). Given this context, Koreans' family communication often both contributes to and reflects thin ideals and conforming to widely accepted standards. In addition, Catherine's birth father's behavior, while troubling to most Westerners, reflects several cultural assumptions about family and personhood. In a traditional Korean family, a father's role and opinion are sacrosanct, and because daughters' and fathers' identities are interdependent and inseparable, fathers can share their opinions freely and dictate their children's behavior; in other words, the assumption is that fathers know best. In contrast, White, middle-class American culture tends to view people as individuals and assumes that one of parents' main tasks is to help their children to develop "healthy" self-esteem and confidence. Note that even this assumption reflects an individualistic tendency because the child's "self" is thought to exist independently from the family, and the parent's responsibility is to send positive messages to develop this self. In both cultures, communication reflects and reinforces cultural assumptions about personhood and family relationships.

"We're One": Touch and Korean Family

Interpersonal communication scholars have noted that touch (also known as *haptics*) can vary in *frequency* (how often one is touched), *duration* (how long the touch lasts), *intensity* (how strong the touch is), and *location* (where on the body a touch occurs) (Burgoon et al., 2016). Each of these dimensions of touch provides an avenue for differences during intercultural encounters, and most participants described cultural differences with their birth families when it came to touch. For example, some participants recalled that their birth parents touched them often (frequency) and for long periods (duration). During her first interview, Catherine described the difficulty she experienced when being touched by older women in her Korean family:

> Another cultural difference when I was, like, ten and I'm just like, "Whoa, what are you doing? Like, Please stop. Stop touching me." You know Korean *ajummas*, or, like, middle-aged women and grandmothers have no sense of space. And they'll just keep petting you. Like grabbing your hand and petting you. I'm just kinda like, "Whoa, this is like. I have too many senses right now! Like the smells and the food and you're touching me" (laughs).

Over the years, Catherine spent an extensive amount of time in Korea and learned a great deal about Korean culture. Ten years after our first interview, she discussed touch again, this time describing it based on her knowledge of Korean culture and grounding her understanding in the maturity she has gained over the years. She explained,

> But, like, touch, it's such a different thing in Korea. And, like, family, the way that you touch your family, because there's, like, the stroking with the grandmother just like, stroking your arm. And I think as I'm older now, I see older Koreans do it with their kids, I kinda get it or just the mentality of, like, "We're family, we're one," like, "You came out of me" kind of feel, but it's just *so* not American style that it's *always* a little bit uncomfortable for me, and it always has been. I think, like, I remember as a kid when I was ten, me being really uncomfortable and then my [adoptive] sister being really uncomfortable, but just through the years, just even as a grown adult, I feel like there's this Korean, like, "You're healthy," like, "I'm gonna touch you and like physically see," and it's *so* not my style and I'll do it (small laugh). It's just like one of those things.

Despite her discomfort from a young age, Catherine accommodated her birth family's touch behavior. She also indicated that growing up has added to her understanding of touch within the Korean context. Her observation that touch behaviors are reflective of Korean assumptions about personhood seems accurate. Koreans tend to be more group-oriented (i.e., collectivistic) than Americans, and this orientation is reflected in language as well. For example, whereas English speakers use singular possessives to refer to their family and family members (e.g., "my family," "my sister," "my mother"), Korean speakers use the plural possessive *uri* (우리, our) when referring to family or family members (e.g., "our family," "our sister," "our mother").

Other participants noticed that their birth families touched them with great intensity, a common example being female family members holding their hands tightly. Nikki told me that during her first (and only) meeting with her birth mother, her birth mother held her hand so tightly that Nikki's hand was throbbing.

In addition, several participants told me about cultural differences in touch based on where on their bodies they were touched. Meagan described an encounter with her aunt just shortly after meeting her, saying,

> One thing culturally that was very strange, when I met my aunt. . . . So we were walking in the subway and I was in front of her, and she goes and like smacks my butt, like the side. And I was like, "What is

this?" you know? Because in America you don't just do that. And my interpreter said, "Oh, that's how she's commenting that you have big hips like all the women in your family." So then there were *those* things where *I* thought, "Oh, you wouldn't see that a lot," you know? Like with actions. But I was, you know, more concerned with my appearance.

Mee Joo also recalled being touched in an intimate way after her family had gifted her a bra that was too small and a discussion about her body ensued in front of the entire family. She recounted,

> We're in the middle of the living room, so, like, my brother-in-laws are around, my brothers are around, it's quite odd, and my oldest sister reaches out and she grabs my left breast (laughs) and she's just like jiggling it in her hand and I was like, "Wow this is just, I'm not really sure what to do." (laughs) It's a little bit odd. And so then they had this conversation about my breasts in the middle of the living room and yeah, it was odd. And then a couple years later when I saw my sister, I went to her house and it was just one of the summers that I came to visit and she opens the door, I go in, I sit down and one of the first things she does is reach over and jiggle my breasts (laughs) and I was just like, "Wow I guess this is just some kind of ritual between us in which I'm just sitting here and you're touching me a lot."

Meagan's use of the word "strange" and Mee Joo's use of the word "odd" reveal their discomfort or unfamiliarity with the touch they experienced. However, neither woman stopped the touch or expressed their discomfort. Rather, they accommodated to their birth family's communication.

Most empirical literature on Korean culture describes it as *high context* (a tendency to express thoughts and feelings indirectly with great concern for the other person's public self) (Kim et al., 1998) and touch avoidant (a tendency to maintain clear physical boundaries when interacting with others) (McDaniel & Andersen, 1998). However, past intercultural communication research tended to be conducted in the context of organizational or professional settings, not intimate family settings, wherein the communication "rules" are different. Brown and Winter (2019) challenged the idea that Koreans are touch avoidant, arguing instead that Koreans engage in frequent and varied physical contact with one another, but that status and setting influence touch behaviors. Perhaps this finding explains why women interviewees talked more frequently about being touched than men, and most often these touches came from older women in their birth family. Catherine's observation that older Koreans assume "We're family, we're one" helps to explain why older Koreans might initiate prolonged, intense, and intimate touch with adoptees during reunion. At the same time, touch behaviors can present dilemmas for adoptees who feel profoundly uncomfortable with being touched or being touched by people they do not know well. Although the adoptees I spoke with seemed to not have difficulty accommodating their birth family's touch behavior, it is important to emphasize that accommodation is not solely the responsibility—or communicative burden—of adoptees and that their personal boundaries should be validated and respected.

Korean Mothers, Constrained in the Past and Present

As discussed in Chapter 2, adoptees who enter into reunion often do so with the hope of understanding the circumstances that led to their adoption and of initiating a relationship with their birth family. However, cultural differences in assumptions and values can pose challenges that make it difficult for adoptees to accept the reasons for their relinquishment while at the same time making it risky for birth mothers to be a part of their lives in the present.

Stories of Relinquishment

Many participants told me that upon reuniting, they learned that their adoption paperwork had been falsified. The records that their adoptive parents had received with their referral indicated that they had been abandoned in a public space, with their name and birth date pinned to their clothing and their birth parents listed as unknown. In talking with their birth families, however, participants learned the true reasons that they were relinquished: Poverty, infidelity, their parents not being married, and, often, a combination of these.

Another common reason for relinquishment was the traditional Korean preference for sons over daughters (Park & Cho, 1995). Several participants reunited with parents who were married and learned that they had older sisters and a younger brother, which suggests that the parents relinquished the adoptee because she was a girl and then kept the younger brother because he was a boy. Given that gender equality and feminism have longer histories in the United States and Denmark than in Korea, some participants found it difficult, at least initially, to accept that gender was a sufficient reason for their relinquishment. Ji Kyoung, who reunited with her birth parents, five older sisters, and younger brother, told me that although she had never felt angry or "bitter" about her adoption before her reunion, she became overcome with emotion during a conversation with her birth parents, recalling,

Maybe I was just critical in my questions to them, so my father got *really* angry, but he's very dramatic so he's like, "Okay Korea was a lot different from where you come from. We were very poor. You can't imagine what it was like, so please *respect that*, okay?" And I was like, "Yeah, okay I respect that. Try to understand that that's why I have to ask all these questions." And my mother is very calm also, so she was like, "Okay that's fine." So that's, like, what I remember the most from the meeting that I actually got caught by that feeling, like, "How could you *do* it to me?"

Although an adoptee may understand their family's history and Korean culture abstractly, they may feel more personally impacted and emotional during reunion meetings when they come face-to-face with family members. After all, Ji Kyoung was meeting six full siblings who grew up with their parents, without her. The fact that she could have been part of this full family but wasn't, due to her sex at birth, was difficult to absorb and accept.

Similarly, Catherine, who reunited with her four older sisters and younger brother when she was ten, described to me how her understanding of her adoption changed over time. As a child, she was focused on the opportunities that her adoption afforded her, accepting the narrative of adoption as a happy ending for a child in need. However, as a teenager, she began to realize that she was relinquished because she was a girl. She described this realization, saying,

I never saw that kind of dark side of it, and I started to see that more. And I think maybe that also influenced how I went into the birth family meetings without even me realizing it. Like, "Well, why was I given up? Am I not good enough? How can they judge? They don't even *know* me, you know?" And so I did take it very personally.

A number of interviewees told me that, as they have gotten older and learned more about transnational Korean adoption, they have become more critical of the practice and, specifically, the relative lack of power for Korean women compared with Korean men. Participants spoke of gaining an understanding of the historical and political context shaping transnational Korean adoption, such as the desire of the South Korean government to expunge mixed-race babies and children to maintain racial homogeneity after the Korean War (Kim, 2016), and how the Korean government has used transnational adoption as a form of social welfare instead of strengthening programs to support single mothers in Korea, even today (Kim, 2010; Kim, 2016). Thus, reunions were not only a turning point for some adoptees in understanding their own identities; they were also a catalyst for understanding the history and sociopolitics of transnational Korean adoption. They were thus able to see their lives and their Korean families' lives as pieces of a larger story of Korean history and culture. Often, the larger story included the ways in which Korean women—especially single and/or poor mothers—have lacked power and choice.

Present-Day Secrets

Due to the continued stigma surrounding Korean women who have children out of wedlock, some participants described how their birth mothers had to meet them secretly, without their current family (husbands and children, participants' half-siblings) knowing. To attend reunion meetings, these mothers had to lie to their current husbands and children about where they were going or where they had been, or tell them that the adoptee was a family friend. A number of participants indicated that they did not know the extent to which their family was "out" as a birth family, even to extended family members. For example, in her first interview, Catherine said that she hoped that she would be invited to her older sisters' weddings, but she didn't know if she would be, because perhaps other people in the extended family did not know about her existence, and she did not know if she was a shameful secret that her family was keeping. After her first meeting, Cat posted a picture on Facebook and tagged her twin sister but was quickly reprimanded when her sister told her, "You don't understand Korean culture. What our mother did could be considered criminal." Cat removed the picture, and shortly thereafter, the conflict was resolved. She had apologized profusely, recalling,

> I felt so sad that I didn't talk to [my sister] for a couple of days, because I thought I had *dishonored* her, dishonored my *mother*, and she went on Facebook and deleted a bunch of friends she didn't know and then posted a picture of me hugging my *eomma*, our *eomma*, so I thought that was really sweet because she felt bad that I felt bad.

In an example of multiple types of secrecy, maintained over many years, Mark's Korean mother had to tell her husband that she was going shopping with a friend when she was attending their reunion meetings. Later, when her husband found a photo of Mark, she told him it was a photo of a family friend. Mark had been surprised at this information at the time, but he said that it gave him perspective on his mother's life and how much she had suffered as a Korean woman. In addition, Mark had met his two half-brothers during his first reunion in 2002, and when he moved to Korea in 2009 for several years and saw them occasionally, he had assumed that they knew that he was their older half-brother. In 2016, after his birth mother had divorced her husband, he found out otherwise when she told him it was difficult for her to meet up with him. He explained,

> The reason she told me it was hard was that she didn't want her sons, my half-brothers, to find out that I was their brother. And I didn't know. I was like, "What do you mean they don't know?" Like, I had been, like, talking to them as if they were my younger brothers, and they would call me *hyeong*.[6] I assumed that they knew, but it turned out that they were just calling me *hyeong*, like friend *hyeong*, like "older friend" *hyeong*, because my mom had told them that I was a family friend. So this *whole time*, (calculating the numbers) since, like 2009, when I first moved there, so, like, for seven years, I had thought they knew they were related to me, and only then did I find out that they had no idea that I was actually (small laugh) their older brother. . . . Or they did, and . . . maybe they figured things out or really wanted to bring it up. I don't know what they knew. And just knowing that it's, you know, it's hard for children of single mothers and knowing that my mom did tell me that, yeah, [my half-brothers] have a hard time because of that. I really didn't want to push anything or sort of, you know, impose myself upon my mom anymore (small laugh). So I just, yeah. I haven't talked to her for some years now.

Mark expressed a lot of acceptance for his mother and her constraints, especially after learning a fuller history of why he was relinquished. In 2018, his half-sister on his father's side asked their birth father to explain, and she told Mark the story: His birth parents were married, but his maternal grandfather did not like Mark's father because he was a poet and might not "amount to anything." The paternal grandfather was unhappy that Mark's mother had gotten pregnant and was going to force her to have an abortion. However, Mark's birth father went to the paternal grandfather and said,

> Let's make a deal. I will divorce your daughter, as long as you promise not to abort our child. And my grandfather agreed to that, but what he didn't tell him was that, yes, I'll let her give birth to him, but then we're going to send him away to the States.

Upon learning this history and how his mother's life had been dictated by the choices of two men, Mark was struck by his mother's lack of agency in her own life. Learning more about his own family history, coupled with learning the stories of other adoptees with similar histories, helped him to understand transnational Korean adoption in a sociopolitical context and also gave him great empathy for his mother. Perhaps unexpectedly, this empathy made him more reluctant to initiate contact with her. He reflected on the impact of learning more of his mother's story, saying,

> In terms of my personal relationship, you know, I think it just made me even more hesitant to really reach out to my birth mom, just maybe understanding for the first time just how *much* of a shock [the reunion] was. Obviously I knew it was a shock, but then to know the full circumstances, and to know how little control she had over what happened, you know, it made me realize just what a shock, and, in a way, me showing up to her was another uncontrollable thing, right? It's another thing that she has no control or agency over . . . God, if I'm in her position it's just like another thing, and it's, like, not necessarily a wonderful thing, although it is. You know, she clearly felt like it was a meaningful thing that I came back. Um, gosh, it's just like one more thing to deal with, it's another step on this whole rollercoaster of this whole journey for her, that is meaningful but at the same time, perhaps, like, an imposition, which is the same way that probably a lot of us adoptees feel as well, like, when you reunite.

At first glance, Mark's experience is somewhat ironic: Understanding his mother more led to a greater desire to give her space and to distance himself from her. At the same time, his words reflect a deep empathy for her situation and a selflessness in letting his mother live her life without what he perceived as his uninvited presence.

Minsun, however, spoke of the pain of being kept a secret. Although her birth mother had told her own extended family about Minsun's birth and their reunion, she had not told Minsun's birth father, her new husband, or her second daughter, Minsun's half-sister. In 2001, when I asked her whether there were any specific messages her birth mother wanted to convey to her, she said,

> [My birth mother] really wanted to stress the fact that she cannot talk about me yet to her present family. She really wants to tell, but she has a daughter. She is four years younger than me. And I think she wants her to be married before anything happens. Because if my birth mother gets rejected from her family, it will affect her daughter and their relationship and maybe their financial status. Because my birth mother will be abandoned from her present family if she tells about me.

After her first meeting, when Minsun would call her birth mother on the phone, her birth mother would sometimes hang up on her because of the presence of her current husband and daughter. Minsun expressed that she had "learned to live with that rejection" and instead kept in touch with her aunt, her mother's younger sister. In 2021, when I spoke to Minsun again, she told me that her birth mother's death in 2018 had strengthened her resolve to meet her half-sister and also to find her birth father. However, her late mother's siblings had told her that they did not want her to do so, which she found frustrating and hurtful.

In 2009, Nikki met her birth mother, who, since relinquishing Nikki, had married and had two children, Nikki's half-siblings. Since that meeting, Nikki has e-mailed her birth mother semiregularly, asking questions and providing updates, all through a social worker at her Korean adoption agency. In 2015, her birth mother refused Nikki's requests for recent pictures of her half-siblings and her birth mother's personal e-mail address. Now Nikki contacts her birth mother only one or two times per year. The agency social worker relays the messages back and forth, and the responses from Nikki's mother, if any, are typically very brief and cursory. Even though Nikki tries to understand her mother's constraints, she finds it hurtful that her mother keeps her at a distance. She explained,

> I try to remind myself when I'm doing it, that it's okay not to get a response and I should be okay with that and expect that (small laugh). I don't know if, like, a hundred percent I've, like, emotionally convinced myself that it's okay (small laugh). Because I think I would *like* more, I don't know. I don't really have other Korean adoptees who are in a similar position to me. So I don't have anything to compare it to, which is probably better (small laugh), because then I would probably say, "Oh, I wish I had that," or maybe it would be a reminder to me that, oh, I have it better than others. Yeah, I guess I'm secretly hoping that one day she'll kind of realize and want to, I don't know, *share* a little bit more about herself, but that probably won't happen (small laugh). That's just my fantasy.

She elaborated more, talking about her husband's reaction to her outreach to her birth mother, saying,

> I think he, you know, just on the fallout side, he doesn't like to see me *emotionally* get upset about it. And I think doesn't always understand and kinda just tells me more bluntly, like, "Why do you do that to your-

self? You know, like, you have your family here." . . . I guess I just hope
that one day she'll want to know more about me so I put it out there
and I don't know, I guess I just keep protecting myself and I'm saying,
it's okay that I don't get a response because that's what I expect and I
don't get too hopeful.

Nikki's efforts to maintain a relationship with her birth mother require deep
emotion work (Hochschild, 1979) as she attempts to lower her expectations
in order to minimize feeling hurt. At the same time, Nikki continues to try to
sustain a connection with her birth mother because she holds onto hope that
their relationship will change.

Conclusion

Participants shared with me a range of experiences regarding cultural differences when interacting with their birth families. Although some differences
were fairly easy to accommodate, others made adoptees feel as though they
couldn't be themselves or that they were being scrutinized, not necessarily because of the birth family's communication but because they so wanted to make
a good impression that would lead to a continued relationship. During reunion,
the stakes can seem high; adoptees may feel that if they fail to create a positive
impression or don't act in culturally appropriate ways, their birth family may
abandon them again.

At the time of reunion, adoptees have spent years becoming cultural insiders in their adoptive country. Often, due to shame, they may have minimized
their Korean identity and claimed labels such as "Twinkie" or "banana"—
Asian on the outside but White on the inside (Palmer, 2010). Although participants reported finding similarities with their birth families, cultural differences often highlighted their affiliation with their adoptive country and their
adoptive families, highlighting a distance from Korean culture and their Korean families.

Over years in reunion, some participants came to accept parts of Korean
culture and integrate them into their own individual identities. Catherine reflected on how, over the twenty years she has been in reunion, she has come
to see her cultural identity as a hybrid. She said,

I honestly feel like I'm this weird combination of being really Korean
and really American. Because obviously, I *think* like an American, I've
been *raised* like an American, like, I will argue with someone older than
me if I think they're *wrong* and that's very American (small laugh). Or,

like, I'll be quick to say something if I don't think it's right *but*, like, *age* is like a big deal, and I'll like, wanna be thoughtful about how I do things if someone's older than me or younger than me.

As someone who speaks Korean and who has, from a young age, spent extended amounts of time in Korea with her Korean family, Catherine claims a cultural identity that straddles multiple categories. She describes both resisting *and* upholding the age hierarchy that she has experienced as part of Korean culture. Her description of her cultural identity as a "weird mix" suggests what she perceives as a contradiction: "Really" Korean versus "really" American. And yet, over time, she has come to accept that these two identities can coexist.

In most ways, the responsibility of accommodating one's communication rested on participants more than on the birth parents, creating a discursive burden. Perhaps due to hardships or lack of resources and privileges (e.g., education, travel, intercultural exposure), most Korean birth parents seemed to be constrained in their ability to adapt their communication to accommodate participants. Or, perhaps because most of the meetings took place in Korea, adoptees were expected to adapt. Many birth parents, perhaps due to the primacy of blood ties in Korea, treated participants in ways that reflected traditional family roles and hierarchy. In contrast, participants viewed relationships from a social constructionist perspective, assuming that positive interactions would strengthen the relationship and negative interactions would damage it. The experiences highlighted in this chapter circle back to fundamental questions of what it means to be Korean and what it means to be in a family. These questions, difficult to answer individually, became even more challenging as they were braided together during moments of cultural confusion or difference.

Yet when interacting with their Korean families, adoptees reported communicating with an impressive level of intercultural communication competence. Individuals with such competence tend to be highly motivated, to possess knowledge about themselves and their interlocutors, to be nonjudgmental and empathetic, and to be adaptable in their behavior (Martin & Nakayama, 2022). Due to their desire to connect with their birth family, participants were highly motivated, and many recalled efforts to understand their family's communication in the context of history and culture. They also described adapting their own behavior, whether trying to alter their appearance or demeanor, tolerating touch that felt uncomfortable, or listening to unsolicited advice. Many participants spoke of how time and age contributed to increased empathy with their birth family and a more nuanced perspective on Korean culture, which helped them to be more flexible in their expectations and interactions.

4

(Not) Speaking Korean

Learning to Communicate with Family across Languages

Fall 2017

I walked into my first Korean language class on my forty-first birthday. Gana-da Korean School was housed in a nondescript office building in the wealthy and multicultural Yongsan district of Seoul. The school, and others like it, attract people who have flexible time for language study and who can afford the tuition of 230,000 won (approximately $200) per month. My classmates were two Japanese women who had relocated to Korea recently with their husbands who worked for Uniqlo clothing brand. We met for an hour and fifty minutes, two times a week. Our *sunsaengnim*, teacher, was a young woman in her twenties. She was, thankfully, quick to smile and laugh with us at our mutilated pronunciations and wrong vocabulary before offering her patient corrections. We formed a camaraderie based on our shared attempts at communication, a patchwork of tiny squares—Korean, English, facial expressions and gestures, laughter, and, occasionally, Google Translate.

Having spent much of my life in formal education settings as a student and a teacher, I was somewhat surprised to be a very average Korean language student, at best. I scribbled (indeed, my hangul looked like a toddler's) my homework right before class and passed most quizzes by very small margins. I was a Korean adoptee cliché, trying to learn Korean in Korea and struggling to do so. My difficulties can be attributed partly to the fact that I was squeezing language study in the spare time allotted between my university teaching job and parenting three young children. But also, a creeping feeling of defeat accompanied me in all of my efforts. The more I progressed in my Korean over the next six months, the more I was able to see the vast distance between my level of language competence and the level of Korean I would need in order to communicate with my Korean family with any level of ease and comfort. I came to realize that even if I did well in class, I would remain far away from being able to express the nuanced and nonlinear thoughts I have when I'm with my Korean family. Although I had dreamed of learning Korean for decades, the endeavor now felt almost pointless. Still, I continued to attend until we left Korea the following summer.

Several weeks into the class, we were practicing simple conversations. *Sun-saeng-nim* asked each student the same question and we were to respond individually. It was my turn:

"*Sara, ga-jok-eun nu-gu imni-kka?*"[1] *she asked.* Sara, who is in your family?

This question stumps me in English. How could I even begin to answer it in Korean? What is the translation for, "Well, I was sent from Korea to the United States for adoption when I was four months old, so I have a White American mom who died when I was twenty-six and a dad, who died five years later. I have two older, American sisters who are not adopted, as well as my brothers-in-law and nephews. I adore all of them. I've also met my family in Korea, which includes my mother, an older sister, two older brothers, and a niece and nephew, as well as a bunch of aunts and uncles and cousins that I can never quite keep straight. I am thankful for every moment I can spend with them. My birth father died before I met him. Did I mention that I also have a husband and three children?"

After some stumbling, I managed a stilted and simplified response: "*Ibyangin imnida. Du myeong miguk eonni gwa han myeong hanguk eonni gwa du hanguk oppa imnida.*" I am an adoptee. I have two American older sisters, one Korean older sister, and two Korean older brothers.

Weeks later, it was my turn again. *Sun-saeng-nim* looked at me with another question that was intended to be simple.

"*Sara, wae hangugeoreul gongbu hamnikka?*" Sara, why are you studying Korean?

This one was much easier to answer:

"*Gajok gwa iyagi hago sip-eoyo.*" I want to talk to my family.

In some ways, my experience studying Korean was a success: Over time, I was able to understand more of my birth family's conversations and tell them, in Korean, what we had been doing since we last saw them. I could ask them simple questions about what we were doing or what was happening at the moment. I was able to tell taxi drivers whether to go right, left, or straight and where I wanted them to take me, even though they often corrected my pronunciation or grammar.

In other ways, my efforts to "learn Korean"—whatever that means, as if it were a task that had an endpoint—could be viewed as a waste. Koreans we encountered in public praised my White American husband for his excellent Korean when he counted to three or said hello. The same people furrowed their brows in confusion at me when I spoke full sentences in Korean, even on the rare occasion when I knew my vocabulary and syntax were correct. I invested a lot of time and money for a language I almost never use, now that we have moved back to the United States. I still rely on Google Translate to check my understandings of my Korean family's texts, as I have forgotten most of what I learned. I know that the next time we go to Korea, I will understand a much smaller fraction of what I understood when we left, and the amount I will be able to communicate to others, including my family, will be even smaller.

Yet, I also know that through facial expressions, hugs, tears, laughter, and food, I will feel my brothers' and sister's care for me. I can only hope that the same is true for them. We will never share the same language, and I will never be able to convey to them the depth or complexity of what I feel for them. I am not sure that I can even articulate it in English. So, what we have is enough. It must be.

This chapter explores how adoptees in reunion navigate language differences. Participants ranged in their efforts to learn Korean to communicate with their birth family, with some choosing to not study the language in any formal way, and others spending extended amounts of time in Korea studying the language and undertaking formal, long-term study in their adoptive country. Taken together, participants' words both emphasize and deemphasize the importance of adoptees studying Korean to communicate with their birth families. In other words, their discourses about language reveal contradiction. Participants described the significance of being able to communicate directly with their birth families in Korean while also reiterating the usefulness of translation apps combined with nonverbal communication and piecemeal usage of Korean and English. They also spoke of issues related to language interpretation, of unavoidable awkward or challenging moments due to language differences, and the links between Korean language and Korean identity.

Learning (or Not Learning) Korean

I will never again have such a personal reason for learning any other language, and so we have a unique relationship, Korean and I. I fight with it every step of the way. If English is my mother tongue, Korean is a difficult and distant birth parent that enacts every bit of the rejection and ambivalence an adoptee might fear. From day to day, I love it—its vibrant kennings, its profound etymologies—and then hate it as it spits my best efforts at my face. It nourishes and teaches me, then coyly demands fealty in return. It tells me I will never measure up to its expectations, then reminds me merely trying is a virtue.

—SPENCER LEE LENFIELD, TRANSNATIONAL
KOREAN ADOPTEE LIVING IN KOREA,
"KOREAN AS A SECOND LANGUAGE," 2018

Transnational Korean adoptees who attempt to learn Korean often grapple with the difficulties, contradictions, and personal stakes that Spencer Lee Lenfield describes. As adoptees' "native" language, Korean holds symbolic value as a reclamation of one's ethnic identity. For adoptees in reunion, however, learning Korean carries even more weight, suggesting the possibility of direct, meaningful communication with one's birth family.

All participants spoke either no Korean or very few Korean words or phrases (e.g., hello, thank you) at the time of their first meeting with their birth families. And although nearly all participants had attempted to learn Korean over their years in reunion, most remained reliant on translation apps at the time of our second interview, ten years later. Overall, adoptees spoke of the challenge of learning Korean in the midst of other life priorities and demands, and the difficulty of retaining Korean when not forced to speak it in their daily lives. Interviewees also noted that they found Korean difficult, which is not surprising. Indeed, the Foreign Service Institute of the U.S. Department of State has categorized Korean as a Category IV language (the highest level), which reflects its designation as being a "Super-hard language," one that is "exceptionally difficult for native English speakers"; it would require an average of 2,200 class hours to achieve professional working proficiency (Foreign Service Institute, n.d.). In addition, and as the epigraph implies, the Korean language carries emotional weight for many Korean adoptees.

Inferring participants' Korean language proficiency during interviews was challenging, especially because participants learned Korean in various places and contexts and because my Korean language skills are very limited. Therefore, I asked participants, when relevant, to categorize their Korean language proficiency based on the following simple categories and definitions:

- **Basic Knowledge:** This is an elementary level equivalent to 101 or 102 college courses. Knowledge of vocabulary words, ability to speak simple phrases or sentences, have some difficulty understanding native speakers, elementary reading and writing skills.
- **Conversant:** An intermediate level where the speaker is able to handle a variety of uncomplicated, basic, and communicative tasks and social situations. Can talk simply about their self and family members. Can ask and answer questions and participate in simple conversations on topics beyond the most immediate needs. Reading and writing skills may or may not be at the same level.
- **Proficient:** The word, proficient, means a well-advanced skill level. In terms of language, the "proficient" label can refer to someone who is very skilled in the use of a language but who uses the language less easily and at a less-advanced level than a native or fluent speaker.
- **Fluent:** A high level of language proficiency, in this instance we are referring to proficiency of a foreign language or another learned language. At the fluent level, a speaker will have fluid speech as opposed to halting use. Generally, a person who is fluent in a foreign language will show mastery in the following areas:
  - Read: The ability to read and understand texts written in the language.
  - Write: The ability to formulate written texts in the language.
  - Comprehend: The ability to follow and understand speech in the language.
  - Speak: The ability to produce speech in the language and be understood by its speakers. (Cameron School of Business, n.d.)

Participants who spoke proficient or fluent Korean at the time of our second interview had spent considerable time in Korea and/or had taken Korean language classes or worked with tutors in their adoptive country. Needless to say, these participants had dedicated many hours to this task but still felt as though they had more to learn. Mee Joo, who started learning Korean in college and lived in Korea and worked in a Korean office for over a decade said, "I don't think I can say I've stopped learning Korean. I think it's just always a work in progress." Around the time of our second interview, Mee Joo worked with a Korean tutor who assessed Mee Joo's Korean language level as fluent. Catherine, who had had extensive and varied experiences with Korean language education, also expressed that language proficiency is never fixed or final. She started going to Korean school on Saturdays when she was three years old, began weekly sessions with a Korean language tutor at age ten, spent seven weeks in Seoul with her tutor at age eleven, went to immersive Korean language camps through high school, and continued her study of Korean in college. She also visited Korea frequently as she was growing up. Although she expressed that it's a "grace" that when she returns to Korea, she can communicate with her Korean family fairly easily, she also expressed that she had lost "a lot" of proficiency since college and relies on translation apps when necessary. During her most recent visit to Korea, she asked a Korean friend to accompany her to a family dinner to serve as an interpreter so that Catherine could express deeper, emotional messages, which she referred to as the "hard stuff." Further, she is unfamiliar with Korean medical terminology, which has made it challenging to understand her family's conversations about her birth father's health conditions. As the two participants who spoke the most Korean in this study, Mee Joo and Catherine emphasized both the meaningfulness of learning Korean for them *and* the idea that their abilities are ever changing and limited. This finding was striking, as it suggests that the more language a person learns, the more they realize all that remains to be learned.

Other participants spoke less Korean than Mee Joo and Catherine but had taken courses at universities in their home countries and in Korea for a month or several months. They indicated that they were able to have very simple conversations in Korean. Jorgen spoke of his efforts to learn Korean over the span of the two decades he has been in reunion, saying,

> Right from the beginning, I actually learned a few words in Korean. And then I also did some different language courses where I live. But I never got past a very basic level, where it's like, I don't know, that would be like a six-months-old child, maybe one-year-old child, whatever they can say (laughs). It's very basic. So I could express very basic emotions and needs. So I could communicate, but just on this very basic level. And that's not enough to have a conversation or express any opinions, but it's enough to say I'm cold or warm or I need to drink. I want to go there, I want this. So that's the level I reached and I thought Korean was difficult. It's very easy to learn the alphabet and reading and pronouncing it. But for me it was very difficult to get to the next level. Either that or I just never put enough time into it. And the last part is true actually because I did live in Korea for six months. And what I did was I spent most of my time actually hanging out with other adoptees, which is very normal.

In most instances, the factor that made the difference in participants' ability to speak Korean was immersion in Korean-speaking contexts and daily practice. Those who had regular, long-term exposure to Korean speakers, by living in Korea and through college classes, were more likely to express comfort and ease in speaking Korean with their families. However, as Jorgen expressed, adoptees can live in Korea without having to learn the language because their social circles can be composed of other transnational Korean adoptees who are visiting or living in Korea, who tend to speak English at a native or proficient level. In addition, English has become increasingly common in Korea, particularly in urban areas[2] where adoptees tend to visit and/or live. Mark lived in Seoul for seven years and stated, "I still can barely, barely hold a conversation. It's still just like survival Korean." He elaborated on his reasons for not studying the language, explaining,

> Like, the practical reason, sure, is because I was busy and freelancing, and I didn't really feel like I could take time off to take a class and the cost of working, and, you know, I didn't have any savings. So that was kind of my rationale for not sort of really hunkering down and spending a lot of time trying to learn Korean. But then, of course, there's a part of me that's like, well, maybe that's just like my excuse, my rationalization for avoidance.

Mark's words reveal the emotional layers associated with Korean adoptees learning Korean. And although he speculates that the busyness of life and work may be an "excuse" for not learning Korean, for most people, the daily obligations of career and relationships leave very little room for intensive language study, even when living in Korea. In addition, research suggests that Koreans may have unrealistic and high expectations for Korean adoptees' acquisition of the Korean language. Research by Christina Higgins and Kim Stoker (2011) revealed that it's common for Koreans to assume, wrongly, that Korean adoptees possess an innate ability to learn the Korean language. Sun Ok, who had been living in Korea for about a year and studying Korean through an intensive university program at the time of our second interview, described the difficulty of learning Korean, even when living in Korea. As someone who works in the field of language and interpretation, she wondered whether or not her birth family understood her efforts and the challenge of learning Korean as an adoptee, saying,

> And so I almost wonder if they look at me and it's like, "Is she just not studying hard enough?" I think that's one thing I wonder is, Do they really understand how hard it is to learn this language? And, you know, even if I'm in Korea, and even if I'm taking classes, considering how

language acquisition works, considering the window for language acquisition, how old I am, the fact that I'm not speaking Korean every day, I don't have a lot of Korean friends, like all these important components to becoming relatively fluent in the language, I don't necessarily have them, even though I'm in the middle of Korea. I wonder if they really understand that.

Sun Ok, thirty-eight at the time of our second interview, raised the important issue of age. As various studies have shown (e.g., Deng & Zhou, 2016; Krashen et al., 1979), adults acquire second languages with more difficulty than children do. Considering that most of the participants in the current study were adults when they reunited, that they have limited time for language study due to work and other obligations or interests, and that they tend to lack everyday contexts for practicing Korean, it is understandable that most participants who had attempted to learn Korean felt discouraged by how challenging it was and how much time and work it required. These challenges cause many adoptees' language abilities to plateau. At the time of second interviews, Sun Ok was the only participant who was making deliberate attempts to learn Korean, and she recognized that when she returned to her adoptive country, much of the language that she had acquired would be lost quickly and easily.

In addition to time constraints and age, finances can pose a significant challenge to studying Korean language. Although some adoption agencies and NGOs such as G.O.A.'L. offer partial or full language scholarships to learn Korean, these scholarships are for intensive language study at universities in Seoul and do not cover housing or meals. This coursework, combined with speaking Korean every day in Korea, is likely the most efficient and effective path toward learning the language. However, this trajectory requires daily in-class time, usually four hours per day, in addition to homework, requiring a flexible or nonstandard work schedule. Adoptees must pay registration fees and the amount of the tuition not covered by scholarships, which are usually awarded to cover 30 to 50 percent of the tuition (InKAS, n.d.). For most adoptees living in Korea, this arrangement seems sustainable only for a limited amount of time. Language programs with more flexible schedules are available, but they typically require students to pay out of pocket.

Despite legitimate reasons for not learning Korean (or not learning much Korean), some participants expressed guilt for not speaking the language. Ashley, a physician in her early thirties and a mother of a young child, speaks enough Korean to have simple conversations with her birth family. Still, she lamented, "I wish my Korean was better. It's hard to keep up with that, but I could be better about it, definitely." Others discussed how one or more members of their birth family had expressed a desire that they learn Korean and became frustrated if they did not. On multiple occasions throughout the years, Mark's birth father pressured him to learn Korean. Mark described one of their last visits, saying,

> It was clear that he was frustrated, and he was like, "I'm too old to learn English. It's really up to you; you can still learn." And yeah, for a lot of Korean adoptees, it's like, you think of yourself as a relatively intelligent person (small laugh). You've been able to do well in school, learn languages in the past, and then with Korean, sometimes it's just like a wall that is so much harder than any other sort of academic pursuit that you've tried to do, or at least it feels that way, even if it's not right. It sometimes just doesn't click. Yeah, I felt really bad about it, and I felt mad about it for a long time, and I still feel bad about it.

Learning Korean can be viewed as a way to communicate and enact multiple layers of identity (Hecht, 1993): The *relational* layer as a member of one's birth family and the *personal* layer as a "real" Korean. Many adoptees experience feelings of inadequacy if they choose not to learn Korean or, for various reasons, cannot do so. Mark's reference to a "wall," or a mental block, that makes it difficult for him and others to learn Korean is not uncommon. Other Korean adoptees have also spoken about the difficulty of learning Korean because of the emotional weight it carries (Borshay Liem, 2000; Park Nelson, 2016). For many adoptees, the Korean language is both a vehicle for communicating with birth families *and* a way to access and enact a sense of Koreanness (Hoffman & Peña, 2013), giving it value and meaning but also imbuing it with a symbolic importance that may make it more difficult to learn. As Deann Borshay Liem (2000) articulated, "It's not just words and it's not just sounds or letters. I think learning the Korean language is about emotion and about memory" (26:14–26:40). Given its symbolic importance, as well as the popular and incorrect assumption that learning Korean will be easier for ethnic Koreans than non-Koreans (Ventureyra et al., 2004), many adoptees experience a heightened pressure to learn Korean that is, in all likelihood, counterproductive to the learning and acquisition of the language.

Mark was not alone in having a Korean father who didn't comprehend the difficulties of learning Korean. Eric's birth family assumed he would learn Korean and move to Korea. As an established actor in the United States, Eric spoke with me about how he would be unable to do the same type of work in Korea, but his father did not understand the difficulty of learning Korean or the difficulty of Eric establishing an acting career in Korea. He said,

I'm trying to explain what I do and that I can't really do that in Korea and I don't speak the language and everything. And they're like, "No, you'll learn, you'll learn." It's just assumed that you'll learn, you're the one that's gonna do the work, you know? My brother said that he was gonna learn English, but my father's never said that, you know (laughs).

Reunion asks a lot of adoptees: Most must search for birth family members, travel to Korea, manage cultural differences, and extend forgiveness to all parties involved in their relinquishment. On top of these things, they often feel pressure to learn Korean so that they can communicate directly with their Korean families. The fact that it is often assumed that they can and will do so with little difficulty seems to compound the discursive burden they experience.

Family Communication and Language Differences

Walls, Limits, and Misunderstandings: Language Differences as Barriers

All but one participant indicated that their birth parents either spoke no English or spoke only a limited number of practiced phrases, such as "I love you" or "I'm sorry." However, due to "English fever" in Korea,[3] many young people speak at least some English. As a result, participants' siblings tended to speak more English than parents did, and school-age nieces and nephews were reported to be learning English in school. Yet even though some birth family members may speak English (at varying levels), they conversed among themselves in Korean, leaving participants unable to understand the conversations happening around them. This inability and the fact that adoptees weren't able to express themselves inhibited communication. As Meagan explained,

> It was really *hard*, definitely on all trips, because I wanted so badly to talk to them. Not being able to just talk and say everything with the emotion that I was feeling. I did feel a little bit, you know, on the outside. It created this definite wall. . . . It was a huge barrier in getting close to them.

Notably, Meagan spoke of a wall between herself and her birth family, and Mark spoke of a wall between himself and the ability to learn Korean. Walls serve as a metaphor for obstacles, whether those obstacles are somehow within oneself or between people. Regardless, they inhibit individuals' abilities to express what they are thinking and feeling and limit their understanding of those around them.

Language differences also created an obstacle for participants to speak with their birth families about "deeper" topics. Participants, even those who were able to speak some Korean, described how limited they were in the breadth (number of topics) and depth (personal nature of topics) (Altman & Taylor, 1973) that they talked about with their birth families. Ashley spoke of her first reunion meeting, saying,

> We couldn't have the deep conversation that, you know, *they* were waiting for but also I was waiting for, so that was kind of awkward. It just kind of made the situation awkward because we could only do superficial things. We couldn't really have a deep conversation.

Jorgen also spoke of the superficial nature of his conversations with his mother's side of the family. In fact, their lack of shared language has led him to rent a room on his own while in Korea, rather than staying with his family. When I asked him about this choice, he said,

> It's mainly because of language actually. It's really (laughs), it's really quite boring, sitting for too many hours, just sitting in a room, of course, full of people that you like because they're your family. But if you don't understand what's going on (laughs), it can be quite boring. And then again, that's a limit. . . . So at some point, maybe after one or two hours, and you try to ask all the questions you could with your level of English or Korean, and then it's like, now we did all we could. . . . And I tried [staying with my birth family] so many times and for so many years and now I just realize that, yeah, it's fine. But I prefer, let's just meet and let's talk and ask each other what we want with the ability we have, to ask questions and understand answers. And then it's okay to say goodbye again after we had some good time together. Instead of, say, me having to sit there for that many hours, but also for their part, it's like, "Oh it's too sad he cannot understand anything" (laughs). So that's just something I realized. This is fine. You don't have to spend that many hours together because we don't really have the ability to really make the most out of that.

Jorgen's words and experiences highlight some of the choices available to adoptees in reunion and also the changing nature of how participants enact reunion relationships over time. After many years, he elected to not stay with his birth family during his visits to Korea, which allowed him to enjoy the limited amounts of time they spent together but not be immersed in hours of Korean conversation he could not understand. Relatedly, he believed that limiting their time together freed his birth family from feeling bad for him. In his interview, Jorgen emphasized the importance of the relationship that they shared while at the same time stressing its limitations due to language. In some ways, these discursive struggles (Baxter, 2004), or apparent contradictions, of *importance and closeness* on one hand, and *superficiality and limits* on the other, reflect the complexity of relationships with birth families more generally. For many participants, relationships with birth parents were important and also limited. But the same is likely true for nearly all families and perhaps all relationships. Although Westerners tend to idealize family relationships characterized by openness and honesty (Baxter, 2011), family communication is generally characterized by an ongoing negotiation of individual and family-level needs for privacy (Petronio, 2010). Yet for adoptees and birth family members who have idealized expectations for their reunion or relationship, these limitations can feel disappointing.

For a few participants, language differences resulted in conflict or misunderstandings with birth family members. Most of these incidents were minor. Sylvia, however, experienced a very challenging conflict due to a blog post she had written about her experiences with her birth family before, during, and after their first meeting. She started the blog for her own expression and emotional processing before reunion but then decided to make it public in the hopes that her experiences could be helpful to other adoptees who wanted to search and/or reunite. However, after their first reunion meeting, her birth sister, who was able to read in English, read the blog unbeknownst to Sylvia and stopped responding to Sylvia's e-mails and messages. After several weeks of receiving no response, Sylvia learned that the blog had upset her sister. She recalled the aftermath, saying,

> And [the issues] were all things like mistranslated words like "crazy" or "shock" from culture shock. Or things like, they took that I thought my birth mom was cheap for ordering the cheapest thing on the menu. Or like, I don't like to be touched. Or like, the night that [my husband] got drunk from too much soju, they thought I was criticizing my birth father for drinking too much, which was not the case at *all*. . . . The first day when I found out that there was a problem, you know, I was like *really* emotional. I called [my birth parents] crying. And they knew I was crying. And I just said I'm sorry. And they understood that. And they told me, *"Ara seo,"* I understand, I know. And, like, "I love you."

And I found out from one of my cousins that after reading my blog that my birth parents were hurt, but my sister was furious. And so at that point, that was when I really started to apologize for it as much as I can and trying to explain every little thing.

Although Sylvia believed that the relationship had been repaired after these conversations, this misunderstanding resulted in negative fallout. She said,

Especially through this thing with the blog, I've *learned* that these people (pause) are not part of my life no matter what. I was really worried that I was gonna lose them. And I think that had I not been insistent on trying to fix things, I might have.

Sylvia's attempts to talk with her birth family, to explain, and to apologize are all examples of relational repair strategies (Dindia & Baxter, 1987), which are communicative acts aimed at restoring relationships after a real or perceived transgression. Interestingly, Sylvia and her birth family seem to believe that she is the only person "at fault" in this situation, when the main issue seems to be related to language and misinterpretation, a process involving both parties. Regardless, the task of relational repair—an additional discursive burden—was left to Sylvia, who was very fearful that her actions had resulted in irreparable damage that would result in her being abandoned again. Her reference to her birth family as "these people" conveys a sense of distance that lingered even after her parents accepted her multiple apologies.

Sylvia's family interactions surrounding her blog also highlight the inseparability of language and culture (Jiang, 2000). I speculate that part of Sylvia's family conflict was due to language misinterpretation, while another part was the shame her family may have felt at being described online in ways that they perceived as negative. In this way, cultural differences and language differences can layer on one another, or intersect with one another, in complicated ways that defy easy resolution or repair. Eric also shared one such example: In 2016, he was visiting his *eomeoni*, his birth mother, and his Korean friend, Sunah,[4] was interpreting for him as she had done often, since 2010. He had been giving her a little money during each visit to thank her for her time and help, and he was hoping that his *eomeoni* would do the same. In preparation for the visit, Eric had asked a different Korean friend to type a message in Korean on his phone, asking his *eomeoni* to help compensate Sunah, even if it was a small amount. While Sunah was in the restroom, Eric showed the message to his *eomeoni*. He described what happened next:

My mom completely misunderstands the message. She thinks that I've been lying to her, that I *can* speak and read and write Korean. She doesn't understand that I've had this translated (laughs) from a friend. And she basically thinks that I am asking her to pay my airfare back to the States. Not understanding how round-trip tickets work, et cetera.

Eric did not find out about this misunderstanding until two years later when Sunah told him about it. He went on, saying,

And finally, this light bulb goes off in Sunah's mind and she's like, "I think your mom is illiterate. I don't think she can read." (chuckles) Or she can read at such an elementary level, that that's why it got confused. . . . But now we're in this situation where (laughs) I know that she is illiterate, but I can never say anything about it. Like, I can't correct her on that. I'm sure it's just way too sensitive, you know, and after, I was like, "Well, we have to fix it" and Sunah's like, "No, you can't." Basically (laughs). But that was just like this total trip.

After some reflection, Eric understood his birth mother's illiteracy as a product of the aftermath of the Korean War, when many people, girls especially, were not educated or were removed from school before their education was complete (Choe, 2019). Although he wanted his *eomeoni* to know that he had not asked her for money and would never do so, he also realized that such a conversation would require them to address her illiteracy, which would cause her shame. Therefore, Eric had very little choice but to move forward despite this cultural and language misunderstanding remaining unresolved.

Learning "a Little Bit" of Korean

Although participants talked about the difficulty of learning Korean and their inability to discuss topics with their birth families beyond the superficial, they also indicated that learning even a small amount of Korean was helpful in communicating during reunion meetings. Meagan, who described her Korean as "very basic," took Korean at a university in the United States and at a university in Korea after her initial meeting with her birth family. She recalled,

The second and third [meetings], I had taken some language classes and so even when I was able to just say a *sentence* to them in Korean, they'd get so excited. And it also, in turn, made *them* want to be more open to try and speak English. And I can't even tell you how amazing it feels when you are able to say, like, "I love you," and they say, "I love you too." Or you know, "Where are you?" or something like that and you get that response back. And just those little things made me feel like, "Oh my gosh, we're having a real family conversation."

Jorgen, who also studied Korean in his adoptive country and in Korea for six months, spoke of how being able to speak very basic Korean made a difference because it allowed him to communicate directly with his birth mother. He stated,

Just that little bit. I know that, of course, has meant a huge deal because at least that has given me the ability to communicate and express mostly positive things, just being able to say, "I love you." Or "I really enjoyed the food. I want more of this, and no, I can't eat anything more. Now I want to go. I want to go there. I don't have time today. We can meet tomorrow." At least my level was at that point where I could say these things. So just being able to say these things made life and communication much more easy. If I couldn't say that, then I'd need a translator for everything.

Sun Ok, who was living in Korea at the time of her second interview, also spoke of the meaningfulness of learning Korean and speaking with her family. She recalled a recent moment with her birth sister and niece, saying,

Learning Korean has opened up doors in the sense that I can at least have these small conversations. I think out of all the visits I've had, the one most recently with my second sister has felt like the biggest win. It's felt like my Korean has paid off, because there was a time where my brother-in-law was not there [to interpret]. . . . That was just me and my niece and my sister, and we were walking around and we're still able to have really small conversations and I noticed that those conversations didn't always reflect all the grammar and all the stuff I knew, but I was still able to successfully communicate and that meant a lot. . . . [Learning Korean] has opened up a door to just have a little bit of communication with them. Just to kind of better understand how they think, how they move in the world, the communicative scripts that they use, the social scripts that they use.

All three of these participants spoke of the meaningfulness of being able to communicate directly with their birth family while also indicating that their conversations were limited. Participants thus spoke of communication and birth family relationships using the same language—meaningful but limited—reflecting the inseparability of communication and relationships. What is notable, however, is the investment necessary to reach this basic level. These participants had spent many hours, in and out of the classroom, learning and studying the Korean language. While they were glad they had done so, they remained within the constraints of simple expressions when interacting with their birth families.

Participants also spoke of the helpfulness of translation apps, which helped fill in the gap between their language ability and what they wanted to convey or understand. Participants described typing messages on their phones in English into the translation app and then showing their birth family members the translation, and then vice versa. However, some participants, like Eric, learned that one of their birth family members was illiterate, making this type of exchange more challenging. Translation apps also tend to require users to simplify the messages they want to translate, both in structure and in content, as mistranslations and misinterpretations become increasingly likely with messages that are not literal or concise. The challenge, then, is that thoughts and emotions about birth family members and adoption are far from simple or concise, making translation apps inadequate for the deeper discussions that adoptees may wish to have, particularly if they don't see their birth families regularly. For these conversations, participants tended to rely on interpreters, who were helpful but also, at times, added complexity to interactions.

The Invaluable and Complicated Work of Interpreters

All participants relied on interpreters at some point during their interactions with their birth family and spoke of interpreters as essential. Interpreters included adoption agency staff, acquaintances or friends of participants, volunteers from adoptee-support organizations, and birth family members. Often, participants described the involvement of various interpreters over the years depending on who was available. Importantly, adoptees often have limited choices in who interprets for them. During first meetings at the adoption agency, reunion participants often must rely on the social worker who is in the office that day, and in subsequent meetings, they may call on a friend who is local, if they have one, or a volunteer from an adoptee organization. Adoptees who have no connections in Korea will be more reliant on adoption agency workers or volunteers from organizations, whom they do not know and whose perspectives and practices may vary widely.

Interpreters were relied on to facilitate communication during in-person meetings and to translate correspondence (i.e., e-mails and letters). As some participants' ability to speak and understand Korean grew over the years and as translation apps became more common, some became more comfortable communicating with their birth family without interpreters. Still, nearly all participants indicated that if they were to have an in-depth conversation with their birth families, they needed an interpreter. One exception was Mee Joo, who had lived in Korea for over a decade, speaks Korean, and is married to a Korean adoptee who also speaks Korean. However, early in her interactions with her birth family, she, too, used interpreters.

Naturally, each interpreter varies in their English proficiency (or Korean proficiency in the case of an interpreter whose first language is English), their interpretation skills and experience, their knowledge about transnational Korean adoption, their ability to provide cultural context for participants, their ability to maintain impartiality, their familiarity with the adoptee, and more. As a result, participants' experiences with interpreters varied depending on who was interpreting for them. Regardless, the work of translation and interpretation[5] is challenging; it is not a linear process of hearing a word or phrase in one language and selecting the exact corresponding word or phrase in the other, because, frequently, there are no exact corresponding words or phrases. As someone whose Korean language abilities are very basic, I gain insight into the process of translation and interpretation from bilingual Korean adoption scholar Hosu Kim (2016), who conducts research on Korean birth mothers in Korean but writes and publishes on this topic in English. She describes her own process of translating and interpreting as aiming to "express the intent of the original" and acknowledges that a "transparent transfer of meaning from one language to another" (p. 21) is impossible. Yet given the positionalities of the people involved in reunion and the sensitivity of the topics discussed, the work of translation and interpretation during reunion meetings is both difficult and vital. Participants conveyed the stakes of this work as they spoke about the challenges of communicating through interpreters.

Issues of Accuracy and Completeness
Although participants expressed that they needed and appreciated the work of interpreters, sometimes issues arose concerning the accuracy and completeness of their interpretations. Eric's first meeting with his *hyeong*, his older brother, took place at his adoption agency and was video-recorded. He recalled his frustration with the agency social worker's interpretations, saying,

I felt like the most frustrating thing was that at the first meeting with my brother, you can see it on the video. He'll be sitting there. I'll ask him a question, and he's doing his best to explain it, in Korean, of course. But I'll just be sitting there listening for six minutes while he's talking and, you know, the translator's taking it all in. But then the translation is like less than a minute. Like, I *know* that's not everything he said. The translator is so biased in many ways in terms of the translation that she's giving, and that was what was most frustrating was knowing that, as nice as she's being, that I'm not getting the full story from him.

In all likelihood, most people who interpret for reunions have not received training as interpreters.[6] Rather, they are called on because they speak both Korean and English. The lack of skill and/or impartiality by some interpreters, then, can feel frustrating for adoptees like Eric, who feel that they are missing important parts of long-awaited conversations. Similarly, Hanne recalled that during her first meeting, her birth mother and the interpreter would talk "a lot" with one another, without this information being interpreted for Hanne. Although Hanne expressed that she appreciated how the interpreter provided Korean context for her mother's messages, she also wondered whether she was missing something by not having all conversations interpreted.

Nikki experienced challenges when she asked a nonadopted Korean acquaintance to translate letters between herself and her birth mother. But, unlike Hanne, she did not want further explanations of her mother's messages, nor did she want this person's advice on what to write. She recalled,

I don't know if she was trying to protect me, because sometimes she would say, "In Korean culture, this is very common" and then she would want to tell me how to write things. So, like, "My honorable mother" (typing motions) or something like that. And I was trying to tell her, like, "She's not my mother, she's my *birth* mother," so it was difficult for me because then I think she would sometimes translate my written letters back in a different way. So, then, I just kinda transitioned out and just removed myself and kinda just stopped talking about it with her . . . I don't exactly know how she would paraphrase or summarize things for me, because she would say things like "[Your birth mother] says this, and that's very common to have those feelings and how she's saying it." So she would always kind of have a secondary sentence after she read the first one. It was just very difficult to process the letter with somebody else when it's private, even though there wasn't really any private information in it. It was just a personal letter that at the time I was very attached to.

Nikki did not receive many letters from her birth mother, which perhaps made them feel more personal and private. As a result, her translator's input and advice seemed more intrusive than helpful. Although it may be possible for adoptees to communicate their expectations, feelings, or hopes to their interpreters, interpreters are often unpaid—volunteers, acquaintances, or friends—which creates a feeling of indebtedness on the part of the adoptee. The sense that interpreters are volunteers who are trying to help can make it difficult to request changes in how they are doing the work. Additionally, during a reunion meeting, adoptees tend to be processing a lot of information and experiencing many emotions, which may make it challenging to metacommunicate about the interpretation in the moment.

Christine spoke of the uncertainty involved in relying on an interpreter. Her main concerns with interpretation were about her own ability to express herself about difficult or personal topics related to adoption and how these topics were being relayed to her family. She spoke specifically of her responses to her birth parents' guilt over her relinquishment. She said,

> I can barely verbalize how I feel in my *own* language . . . and you got a translator there who's supposed to, like, translate for you. I don't know what they're saying. I don't know how accurately that information is being transmitted. I don't know if what I'm saying is going to be culturally, like, accepted or understood or processed and you have so much pressure to convince everyone else that they didn't do anything wrong.

Christine's words reveal the difficulty and pressure adoptees may experience working with an interpreter during reunion. They have to manage uncertainty about the interpretation of their and their birth family's words on multiple levels: Denotative (literal meanings of words), connotative (contextual and emotional meanings), and cultural (appropriateness of the topics and wordings based on Korean cultural rules and norms). This uncertainty can contribute to heightened feelings of pressure, nervousness, and anxiety, which were common. At the same time, Christine expressed a desire to protect her Korean family's face, or public image (Brown & Levinson, 1987). In addition, reunion meetings are often infrequent, which adds to feelings of urgency. As Christine explained,

It's been hard because you have such complicated feelings. And complicated things that you want to ask. And you want to say them in the right way. Like, obviously you have to trust your translator to do it for you. But it just sucks that, like, you don't know if they're going to be able to capture the same sentimental feelings that you have or the same words that you want to. Cuz I feel like when you go into a situation like that, you want to use the right words cuz these opportunities don't arise very often. So it really did make it difficult to just accept the fact that I'm *never* going to be able to say *exactly* what I want to say to my birth family. Cuz they won't be *my* words. Like every word in English has a different meaning. It might mean the same thing, but it has different, you know, weight. And it's hard to realize that you're not going to be able to fully communicate the weight of your sentiments to somebody that means so much to you.

Christine's words convey the profound challenges of communicating across languages during reunion. As words are translated from one language to another, meaning can shift due to differing cultural and linguistic associations (Jiang, 2000). Adoptees who do not speak Korean are unable to ascertain whether their meanings are being adequately expressed to their birth family, and vice versa. Therefore, in most cases, adoptees have no option other than to try to trust their interpreters and to accept the inevitability of a gap between what they intended to express to their birth family and the meaning that their family received based on the interpretation.

Participants tended to speak most favorably of interpreters whom they felt they could trust based on having a history with them. Usually, these interpreters were birth family members who they had built a relationship with over the years, someone who had interpreted for them on multiple occasions, or a Korean friend outside the family. For example, Catherine, who was proficient in Korean, asked a close friend to accompany her to a recent family dinner so that she could talk about some of the "hard stuff." Catherine knew her friend from their time in college when he was a Korean international student studying in the United States. She spoke of how she appreciated having him interpret, saying,

And I think the biggest difference for me that felt like such a gift was that I could bring one of my close friends who's, like, heard me through the years. And, you know, he didn't know everything obviously . . . but I think he knew me well enough, that having a *friend* there was actually the biggest piece for me, because it's like, with those emotional things it's hard enough to say it in English and trust your translator, because there's *soooo* much nuance in Korean, of how you say things and what you say. And so even to be able to understand what he's saying in Korean, and be like, "Shoot, I should have been able to say that, but like, I couldn't find the words," and letting him do that, but also trusting him in that way, I think that was the biggest difference for me.

For some participants, trust was built through experience with one's interpreter over multiple meetings. Those who had positive experiences with particular interpreters tended to call on them to interpret again. Participants who had friends who spoke English and Korean had built a foundation of trust before the reunion meeting, which led to a belief that family messages were being conveyed and interpreted accurately in both directions. In other words, a participant's relationship with the interpreter can be an important part of the reunion itself.

Interpreters as Outsiders

At times, participants or members of their birth family felt uncomfortable due to the presence of an interpreter. Cat expressed that she felt uncomfortable communicating through an interpreter because she felt that she had to "simplify" what she wanted to express to her mother and twin sister. "It did affect the intimacy of the reunion," she said. This lack of intimacy, in some ways, was unavoidable, given that Cat spoke virtually no Korean and her birth family didn't speak English. Although complex messages may have required simplification, they would not have been conveyed at all without an interpreter present. Similarly, Meagan, who spoke a basic level of Korean, talked about how she would like to ask her birth family some questions about what it was like when Meagan contacted them the first time; however, she expressed that she would rather not use an interpreter for this conversation. "That's something I would love to hear from them directly, rather than through a translator, because I don't think you can be quite as open, or you can be, but it's different," she explained. In both Cat's and Meagan's experiences, interpreters were described as both facilitating and hindering openness and communication, another discursive struggle found in reunion.

Jorgen experienced an unexpected reaction from his Korean family when he brought a nonfamily interpreter to one of their meetings, after they had been in reunion for over fifteen years. In the past, Jorgen's cousin had interpreted during reunion meetings, but during a recent visit, Jorgen brought along an interpreter from an adoptee organization. He described,

So I brought [the interpreter] and then they were kind of a little bit offended. . . . It was like, "Why did you bring in a translator? Cause you usually don't bring a translator." But my idea was, "Okay, so now we, both sides, can say whatever we want and then she can translate." But that was something, I don't know if it was cultural, it was a surprise, something where it was not really seen as a positive thing, from *their* side.

He speculated that their preference for Jorgen's cousin to interpret was because they have a history with him, and it feels more "natural" to them. However, having a family member interpret had both benefits and drawbacks for participants.

Family Members as Interpreters
After their initial meetings with their birth families, most participants relied on a family member for interpretation, such as a sibling, in-law, or cousin who spoke English and Korean. Depending on this family member's English language proficiency, participants also supplemented interpretations with translation apps. Having a family member interpret was helpful in that there was someone present and available when needed, and participants had a family member to communicate with directly in English. At the same time, it was challenging when family interpreters were reluctant or seemed biased in their interpretations.

Some participants described that they had younger siblings in their birth family who interpreted with some resistance. Early in her relationship with her birth family, before she spoke conversational Korean, Ashley relied on her younger sister to interpret during meetings with their parents. However, Ashley stated that her sister didn't always want to be interpreting and also that her sister protested some of Ashley's questions about her family history and her relinquishment. Ashley recalled,

[My sister was] like, "Why do you keep asking [our mom] all these difficult questions?" It's like, "Well, I want to know." She's like, "You already *asked* that question," but it didn't really get answered fully.

Ashley's younger sister appeared to be trying to protect their mother and didn't understand Ashley's desire to learn more about the past. As someone who grew up with their mother and was only getting to know Ashley at this point, her sister's protectiveness makes sense but also served as a barrier to Ashley getting answers and information from their parents.

Sun Ok spoke of differences in how her brother-in-law (her older sister's husband) and her younger brother interpreted between herself, her mother, and her sister. Whereas her brother-in-law worked in a position that required him to have fluency in English, her younger brother, a young adult, had learned English in school and was less proficient. Based on her interactions with her younger brother, Sun Ok was unsure about how he felt about her and also speculated that it was "stressful" for him to have to interpret. But when her brother-in-law was unavailable, Sun Ok's younger brother stepped in. Sun Ok was also taking Korean language courses at this time, and her younger brother would also, occasionally, translate Sun Ok's Korean into Korean that their mother could understand. Sun Ok expressed that she felt her brother-in-law had lost his "autonomy" in family interactions because he had to interpret for her, and that she was unsure about how her younger brother felt toward her more generally. Some of these dynamics contributed to Sun Ok feeling like an "obligation" to her birth family, but as she learned more Korean, she was able to rely less on others' interpretations. Still, she reflected, "Korean's just a hard language. So, it's always going to be somewhat limited and I've really kind of just come to accept that. And what I can do, I can do, and I'll be good with that."

Minsun, whose birth mother died in 2017, relied on her maternal aunt to translate during her most recent visit to Korea in 2019. However, she realized that her aunt's English was not as good as Minsun thought it was initially and that her aunt was translating an estimated 10 percent of what was being said in Korean. For her final family dinner of the trip, then, Minsun invited a Korean adoptee friend who had been living in Korea and spoke Korean. With his interpretation, she was even able to understand "the gossip in the corners" and ask some difficult questions that she felt her aunt had been evading.

Birth family members who translate may find themselves in a difficult position. Although their ability to communicate in two languages, albeit at varying levels, may facilitate communication during reunion, they may also feel pulled in multiple directions. Information that the birth family may wish to withhold or protect may be the same information that the adoptee is seeking. Related, cultural differences likely shade how they view adoptees' messages and questions, which may impact their interpretations. At the same time, their ability to make meaning in two languages may also contribute to a deeper understanding of all family members present.

Transcending Language Differences

Although language differences posed continual challenges for participants and their birth families, especially when they wanted to communicate about personal or complicated topics, some participants emphasized that they still felt close and/or comfortable with members of their birth family despite not sharing a language. Specifically, participants described how they were able to communicate with members of their birth family using nonverbal cues and translation apps.

Nonverbal communication was important in helping adoptees and birth families communicate across language differences. The term *body language* is a common misnomer for nonverbal communication, which does not comprise a discrete language and includes more than body movements. Nonverbal codes include any or all of the following:

- Facial expressions, such as smiling or frowning
- Head and body movements, such as gestures and posture
- Eye behavior, such as eye contact and eye rolling
- Touch behaviors, such as hugging and holding hands
- Physical characteristics, including clothing, grooming, and alterations such as piercing or tattoos
- Smell
- Physical space, including personal distance when interacting, as well as environment (e.g., how a home or room are decorated and maintained)
- Paralinguistic features such as voice volume, pitch, and rate
- Use of time, such as being late, not spending time together, or not responding quickly (Knapp et al., 2014)

Nonverbal communication is particularly important for conveying what communication scholars have called *relational messages*, which indicate how one person feels about the other person and their relationship (Burgoon et al., 1984). Liking and status, for example, are relational messages and tend to be communicated nonverbally. A genuine smile may indicate happiness to see the other person, indicating value for the person and the relationship. Whereas verbal messages (i.e., spoken words) are deliberate and conscious, nonverbal messages tend to be less controlled and less conscious. Of course, nearly all nonverbal communication is highly contextual and culturally specific. Yet as participants navigated language differences with their birth families, they often spoke of relying on nonverbal cues, along with translation apps, to convey and/or interpret meaning, particularly about the relationship. Alexander provided an example from a recent visit to see his birth mother, saying,

Mostly when you're walking around Seoul, it's just sort of hand gestures. Are you hungry? Just little things like that, but mostly the last few times, it's been really easy to just use an app to talk into and then navigate with them.

Throughout the interview, Alexander described how he felt close with his birth mother and described her as supportive. He also noted that when they are apart, she responds quickly to his texts. Often without realizing it, communicators use time as a nonverbal message (e.g., response time, being late/early, spending time with someone), so it makes sense that Alexander interprets her quick response time as a positive relational message.

Eric also described feeling very close to his older brother despite the language difference. Eric has traveled to Korea to see his brother about every other year since 2010, and even though his brother is very busy with multiple jobs, he always spends as much time with Eric as he can and also finds fun things for them to do together. He spoke of their interactions at this point, saying,

> We don't actually really need translators that often. I mean, of course, there's very specific things and there's always gonna be, like, those confusions of, like, "Oh, I thought you meant that we were going there" and then we end up somewhere completely different (laughs). But you know, my brother and I are close enough that, you know, just hanging out, it's not uncomfortable *at all*. And, you know, he speaks a little more English than I do Korean. We both speak each other's language terribly, but he's slightly less terrible at it. But the apps have gotten a lot better. . . . So when there's specifics that we need, we'll just, like, sit around the dinner table and we'll have the translator on.

When Eric and his brother are apart, they text one another via KakaoTalk, the most popular messaging and video-calling app in Korea (Lebow, 2021). Eric expressed that he can sense his brother's and sister-in-law's happiness when he contacts them, saying, "They're *so* excited to hear from me and I can tell that through the emojis." Here, Eric is referencing the various stickers and moving emojis that KakaoTalk users can purchase to personalize or enhance their messages. These can be particularly useful when there are language differences because emojis serve as nonverbal messages to communicate emotion when texting (Erle et al., 2021). Their text exchanges and in-person interactions led Eric to summarize their relationship in this way:

> I feel like he's on board. He's invested in me, you know. I can feel that through the language barrier. And it's not a simplistic, like, I pity you for being sent abroad and so I feel obligated. It's like, no, he actually

likes spending time with me, and I like spending time with him. And that just means the *world*.

Despite language differences, Eric and his brother convey liking, a relational message, to one another. Meagan also spoke of how, despite language differences, she felt close with her birth family. She spoke of an interaction about five years ago when she was going to meet her father and uncle at the train station before she left Korea. She felt nervous, as neither her father nor uncle speak English, and Meagan's Korean is limited. She described what happened when it was time for her to board her train, saying,

> We went to the train when it was time to leave and he came down to the track with me and he was, like, trying to show me and I showed him my ticket and he tried to take me to the wrong one and I was try-ing to say no, and I didn't have a choice, so I was just like yelling at him in Korean and I was just like, *"Appa,*[7] *appa*, No, it's this one, this one!" you know, like yelling the number and I remember feeling like, "Oh. Well, this feels like a very like father-daughter thing to be like yelling at him and being like, 'You're at the wrong one, it's right here!'"

At the time of our second interview, Meagan's father had dementia and was living in a care facility. She recalled her most recent visit to see him and re-flected on how she felt about their relationship, even though they do not com-municate using words, saying,

> When I saw him last time at the hospital, you know, he's definitely aged, but I mean he still knew who I was, and he just sits and he just holds my hand, you know, the very Korean way where they hold your hand and they just like (pats the top of her hand repeatedly with the other hand) pat you the whole time. . . . I feel like he sort of just looks at me, and again, we don't, we don't really speak very much, but he just sort of looks at me and I feel like he's just sort of like, "Okay, I think she's healthy, I think she's good." . . . I'm like, I should have learned more Korean, I should have, I should have. But for what I have, like even finding him or him finding me and the way that it worked out, I just feel so lucky . . . I will take this. This is greater than anything I could have ever hoped for.

Clearly, these interactions evoke guilt that Meagan "should have" learned more Korean, a sentiment she expresses three times, a clear discursive burden. However, her description highlights the vital role of nonverbal communication in expressing care and affection, both of which are relational messages. Later, Meagan described how rituals with her older brother and older sisters also contribute to her feeling like a member of the family. One particularly important ritual, which they have performed since her first reunion meeting, is visiting their mother's grave. She described a recent visit, saying,

> One thing we always do, is that they will always take me to our mom's grave. . . . We drive up there and they bring a big blanket and her favorite snacks and we do the traditional, you know, bowing. And then when I was there last time, it was just me and my brother and my sisters and we just sat there and we just chatted. It was *so fun* because it felt so natural and it felt completely unforced and just like sitting there and it wasn't this huge, sad thing, you know, it was more of like, "We're coming here, this is our tradition that we do, and now we just get to sit here and we get to hang out just without the kids, without a translator." Technology does help us a lot when we don't know the word or something, but I *love* doing that, I love doing it. It just makes me feel *part* of, like, "We are, like, family," you know.

In this description, Meagan implies that not having an interpreter helped to create a "natural" feeling among her and her siblings. Between her siblings' basic English, her basic Korean, and the translation apps, they are able to enjoy a family ritual that holds meaning and comfort and gives her a sense of belonging in the family.

Conclusion

Understandably, language played a significant role in interviewees' communication with their Korean families. Although birth family relationships provided participants with an impetus for learning Korean, they also made the task more daunting and emotion laden. In her second interview, Sun Ok spoke of taking her midterm language exam at a Korean university. This exam involved a written component and a "speaking interview" with her Korean language professor. Sun Ok recalled the exam in light of her identity as an adoptee in reunion, saying,

> I struggled a lot with learning the language during our midterm and final speaking interviews and I think some of it had to do with the fact that I realized that if I *was* successful in it, I would *actually have to talk*

to my family. And that would be a whole new level of vulnerability. That would be a whole new level of connection that that would open. So, I think that was psychologically and subconsciously there, or is one of the reasons why I struggled. But I think also, you know, aside from all the baggage we have as adoptees, I think that when I did these [speaking] interviews, I don't like being judged for being Korean or not being Korean or whatever, and I'd literally have a person sitting in front of me whose sole job right now was to judge me on my Korean speaking skills. (laughs)

Transnational Korean adoptees have reported learning Korean to reclaim their Korean culture, a process that has been called *reculturation* (Baden et al., 2012). For adoptees like Sun Ok, attempting to learn Korean is about identity and relationships. And although Korean language skills can provide adoptees with an avenue toward reclaiming their ethnicity and communicating with their families, the magnitude of the challenge can be intimidating and discouraging, leaving them with the sense that there will forever be a gap between how they look and who they are, as well as a limitation in their ability to express their thoughts and feelings to their birth families. Perhaps an acceptance of this gap is, ironically, necessary for sustaining these relationships. It is an acknowledgment that the relationships that could have been, can never be, and yet there is still room for meaningful connection.

Across participants' experiences, it appears that learning some Korean is helpful, but not necessary in creating meaningful relationships with birth families. For most adoptees, reaching a conversant level of Korean language proficiency takes a large investment of time and, often, money. Then, retaining one's level of Korean when not living in Korea takes a great deal of commitment. As most transnational Korean adoptees live outside Korea and do not use the Korean language in their careers or daily lives, for many, the motivation to study Korean is low but the demands of daily life are high. Those who choose to study Korean would be wise to have measured expectations for what they will be able to accomplish with the time and resources that are available to them.

As those who were relinquished, raised abroad, and returning to their birth family, transnational adoptees have the right to know what is being communicated during their reunion meetings. If they are unable to ascertain this information directly—and most are not—they must be able to trust their interpreters. For most adoptees, reunion meetings are rare, which heightens the desire and need for moments of shared meaning and understanding. Adoption agencies that facilitate reunions should more comprehensively train workers and volunteers to offer competent, empathetic, and culturally sensitive interpretations and translations. When possible, these agencies should also work with birth family member interpreters so they are aware of adoptees' perspectives on interpretation. Adoptees themselves should feel empowered to express when interpretation or translation work is not meeting their needs, although doing so can create discomfort. This potential negotiation serves as an additional discursive burden for transnational adoptees, and yet it may increase the likelihood that they leave their reunion meetings feeling that messages and meanings were exchanged fully and accurately.

5

Adoptees In-Between

Communicating Family with Birth Parents and Adoptive Parents

Fargo, North Dakota, early 1980s

Sunday school and church punctuated every week of my childhood. I didn't mind; I liked getting dressed up, playing hide-and-seek in the church with my friends, and seeing the smiling old people who sometimes gave me a quarter or a butterscotch hard candy.

Our Sunday school teachers varied, but the routine for us little kids was always the same: A story, an activity or worksheet, a song, and sometimes, doughnut holes. But one Sunday morning was special: Our teacher told us she had a surprise for each of us. I reached into the paper bag she was holding and pulled out a small, hot-pink pom-pom character the size of a ping-pong ball. Its googly eyes bounced around when I shook it. Attached near its feet was a ribbon of paper that read, "You are a chosen child." I ran to show it to my parents afterward, mostly excited about the color. Although I suspect they understood the biblical message implied by the words on the paper—that through Christ, people are God's chosen ones (Galatians 4:4-7)—they spoke of it as a reference to adoption. "That's right! You *are* a chosen child! We chose you!" my mom said, her mouth stretched wide into her beautiful smile. My dad nodded in agreement. This was the story I inferred my entire childhood: That not only did my parents choose to adopt from Korea, they chose *me*, specifically.

My mom, my American mom, died in 2003 after many years of illness. She was diagnosed with multiple sclerosis when I was twelve, and, due to a variety of conditions, her health worsened with each passing year. She was in and out of the hospital often. Once, when I was a preteen and my dad was frustrated at me for sulking about something small, he said to me, "How your body feels on a bad day is how your mom's feels on a good day, so stop complaining." When I was sixteen and she was forty-eight, she had her first stroke, which paralyzed the left side of her body. Despite countless hours of physical and occupational therapy, she never approached full recovery.

Yet her core disposition never changed: She seemed to like and befriend everyone she met, yet she also was a master at maintaining connections with friends she'd had for decades. She had an unfailing amount of optimism and good humor; the only time I heard her complain about her health was when she was on her literal deathbed, in hospice. "I feel like shit," she said. She was a mother who made cookies on every first day of school, who had the "Always Teen" pack of pads ready when I got my first period, and who made sure I attended Korean adoptee camp in high school and went to Korea with other adoptees after college. She loved me and told me so, each day.

And yet love is never perfect. When, as a child, I told her that some kid had made fun of my hair or the shape of my eyes, she responded with a bewildered sadness. "But your eyes are beautiful, and your hair is beautiful," she would say, as if she couldn't comprehend an alternative appraisal. Later, in my high school years, when someone called our house and said, "You're not her fucking mother" and then hung up, she burst into tears telling me what had happened. We hugged each other, but there was no further conversation. Soon after, we had caller ID installed.

I understand now that, combined with my adoption trauma, my mom's health left me in a state of constant high alert, ever watchful of her condition and in constant fear of her dying. I kept my struggles to myself and strived, in all things, to be perfect. I interpreted the Bible verse Matthew 5:48 to the letter: "Be perfect, therefore, as your heavenly Father is perfect." More than that, I didn't want to disappoint or hurt my mom, and I knew, after seeing her have a stroke, that any conversation could be our last. When my Korean family contacted me in 2001, I didn't even consider telling her.

My dad, my American dad, stood at six feet, four inches and served in the medical unit for two wars: Vietnam and Desert Storm. He was, like many men in his demographic, blunt in expressing his opinions and unapologetic in his actions. He saw life in black-and-white. As a nurse anesthetist, he woke every weekday at 5:15 a.m., often not getting home until after dinnertime, and yet, on the weekends, he regularly took me out on solo trips to grab breakfast or go to the movies. He seemed to have all the answers. Yet if I told him someone mimicked karate moves at me or directed the singsong chant "Chinese, Japanese, dirty knees, look at these" at me, he would respond, "Well, they're ignorant" and then look at me with a small shrug, as if there was nothing further to say or discuss. These conversations taught me from an early age that racism—not that my parents or I would have used that term for what I was experiencing at the time—was something I had to bear alone.

Based on my dad's initial reaction to my birth family's outreach, I didn't tell him when my Korean brother and I started e-mailing in 2007. I didn't share with him the latest pictures I had received of my three-year-old Korean nephew, even though I looked at them daily. I didn't share news about the DNA test that confirmed that I was the "offspring" of my *eomma*. I didn't know how to initiate these conversations, and I knew I couldn't explain things to him that I didn't even fully understand yet. I planned to have these conversations with him eventually, but, as it turned out, we ran out of time. He died in 2008 in a motorcycle accident.

Adoptees, myself included, protect their adoptive parents for many reasons.[1] And although Americans tend to idealize family communication as being open, intimate, and egalitarian (Caughlin, 2003), people in close relationships, including families, often avoid communicating about certain topics. They do so for various reasons: To protect the relationship because the topic is perceived as socially inappropriate, to protect themselves, and/or because one's family member is expected to be unresponsive (Docan-Morgan, 2010; Golish & Caughlin, 2002; Guerrero & Afifi, 1995). Certainly, topics such as race, one's birth family, and ambiguous loss can be viewed as inappropriate and threatening to adoptive family identity and to family members' relationships with one another. Adoptive parents who ascribe to the narrative that the adoption was a "happy ending" or who see the birth family as a threat may struggle with conversations surrounding the loss and pain that are also inherent parts of adoption.

Of course, there is a fine line between topic avoidance that may be helpful (e.g., avoiding talking about controversial topics at holiday gatherings) and that which is problematic. For example, when adoptees believe they have to protect their relationship with their adoptive parents and themselves by not talking about race, culture, difference, or their birth family, they may be slowed in their attempts to develop their adoptive identity, the sense of who they are as an adopted person (Dunbar & Grotevant, 2004) and have lower self-esteem (Brodzinsky, 2006). This topic avoidance may also be related to a lack of closeness and/or satisfaction within the parent-child relationship (e.g., Dailey & Palomares, 2004). In other words, topic avoidance about adoption-related topics, including the birth family, may be detrimental to the adoptee and their relationship with their adoptive parents.

Because my adoptive parents had so firmly established my identity as their daughter and had not encouraged conversation about my birth family or Korean identity, I concluded that these topics were unimportant and, essentially, irrelevant to my daily life. What is more, in the 1980s and 1990s, a color-blind approach to race dominated public and private spaces, which eclipsed conversations about my racial difference and wiped away any possibility that I, as an Asian American (a label I didn't avow until adulthood) had experienced racism. Looking back, and, as an imperfect parent myself, I believe that my parents did their best and were managing significant life events (e.g., my dad's military deployment, my mom's chronic illness), the scale and implications of which I couldn't comprehend fully as a child or adolescent. Still, I wish they would have done more. What a gift they would have given me, to bring my birth parents into conversations, to talk about race, to connect my story to the story of other Asian Americans throughout history, to learn Korean recipes, to ask more questions rather than provide their answers, to create space for ambiguous loss (Powell & Afifi, 2005). Had they done these things, perhaps I wouldn't have waited so long to meet my Korean family, and perhaps my relationship with my Korean family could have been a point of connection that would have brought my adoptive parents and me closer to one another and helped me to grow closer to knowing and accepting myself sooner.

This chapter examines how Korean adoptees talk about maintaining relationships with birth families and adoptive families, and the role of adoptive family members during reunion meetings. Participants' words and stories reflect the ways in which dominant cultural discourse about family can constrain communication with both adoptive parents and birth parents. In particular, messages about exclusive belonging and the discourse of mutual care provide an explanation for some participants feeling the need to protect their adoptive parents' feelings before and during reunion meetings. This protection, while understandable, can limit communication with birth families and, therefore, constrict adoptees' ability to learn about their origins.

Adoptive Family Identity: Strong but Questioned

As described in Chapter 1, transnational Korean adoptions helped shift the dominant paradigm of adoption from one of secrecy to one of visibility. However, the visibility and increased openness about adoption, both within and outside the family, did not remove the stigma for those most affected. Whereas adoptees have reported being stigmatized by people outside the family who question their place in the adoptive family and/or their lack of known biological ties (Docan-Morgan, 2011; March, 1995), adoptive parents have spoken about the stigma of assumed infertility and the implication that adoption is "second best" to having children through birth (Daniluk & Hurtig-Mitchell, 2003). Birth parents are often the most stigmatized group, rendered invisible or stereotyped in one-dimensional ways as poor, single, and unfit as parents (Coleman & Garratt, 2016; Wiley & Baden, 2005).

Traditionally, among members of the adoption triad, adoptive parents have exerted and been accorded the most power. This power is wielded economically and also communicatively as "the discursive capacity to define social reality" (Baxter, 2011, p. 124). Stated differently, adoptive parents have long held the most power because their words and perspectives have typically been viewed as both true and correct. For the past several decades, adoptive parents, along with adoption professionals, have shaped public and private communication in ways that challenge the stigma surrounding adoption and strengthen adoptive family identity. Because adoptive families are formed through "law and language" (Galvin, 2006), they rely on communication, rather than biogenetic ties, to constitute their identity as a family and legitimize themselves to outsiders (Galvin, 2006). A discussion of how adoptive parents use communication to create and maintain adoptive family identity provides context for understanding communication surrounding birth families and reunion. Writing of adoptees, Sara Dorow (2006) observes, "The child is many things but cannot be all of them—she must be made to belong to her adoptive family, despite and because of difference" (p. 114). The following discursive strategies are used to make an adoptee "belong to" an adoptive family.

Naming

One of the first communicative things that adoptive parents do to include their adopted child as a member of their family is to change the child's name. Sometimes the process of renaming a child occurs communicatively before it occurs legally. For example, upon receiving a referral (photo, background, and medical information about a specific adoptable child), prospective adoptive parents may begin referring to the child by a new first name, even though the adoption process is still far from complete, the child's legal name has not changed, and they have not met the child yet. Like all parents, prospective adoptive parents invest a significant amount of thought into what they will name their child-to-be. However, unlike all parents, they must change the child's existing name. The child's preadoption name may have been given by the birth parents or by employees of the child's orphanage or adoption agency, but, regardless, this name almost certainly reflects the child's birth culture. Adoptive parents must make the decision about whether to integrate this piece of the child's identity into their new name.

In a study of naming practices for transnationally adopted Chinese or Vietnamese children, communication scholar Elizabeth Suter (2012) found that adoptive parents tended to choose one of four naming options: Integrating the birth culture name as the middle name (Mary WangXiaoHong Smith), altering the birth culture name (Mary Xiao Smith), creating a new name based on the birth culture (Mary Mei Smith), or excluding the birth culture name (Mary Sue Smith) (p. 216). Adoptive parents based these choices on wanting to preserve their child's ethnic identity, to create a sense of adoptive family identity, to create an individual identity for the child, and for practical reasons such as pronounceability in the receiving country's language. Regardless, adoptive parents choose names that help solidify their child's identity both in the adoptive family and in the adoptive country.

Narratives and Discussions

Adoptive parents who tell their child's adoption story or "entrance story" tell and retell the story of how their family was formed through adoption. These stories, which vary in nuance and detail, may involve the adoptive parents' decision to adopt, information about the birth mother and the child's birth country, and/or the first time the adoptive parent(s) met the child (Marko Harrigan, 2010). These stories are told with the intention to provide the child with a coherent sense of their history, to affirm the child's belonging in the family, and to express the family's commitment to the child. Contemporary adoptive parents report telling these narratives in an ongoing, developmental, and interactive manner that engages the adopted child and attempts to normalize adoption talk (Marko Harrigan, 2010).

One powerful component of these stories is the discourse of the *forever family*. The *forever family* has become ubiquitous in adoption, appearing in the names and mission statements of adoption agencies, on photo frames, in children's books, as social media hashtags, and more. Drawing on the language of fairy tales, adoptive parents can even purchase coordinating T-shirts demonstrating their pride as an adoptive family, with "Family Ever After" emblazoned on the parents' shirts and "Wanted, Chosen, Loved, Adopted" on the adoptee's shirt or onesie. Adoptive parents who apply the label *forever family* to themselves legitimize their identity as a family by suggesting the permanency of their familial relationship.[2] This label also expresses the adoptive parents' commitment to their child, providing reassurance that adoptees may need or want in order to feel secure. Importantly, language of the *forever family* creates a discursive tension with the discourse of the *real* or *natural* family, which presumes the preeminence and permanence of biogenetic relations over other types of family bonds, including adoption (Baxter & Braithwaite, 2010). Held up against one another, the discourse of the *forever family* suggests that the birth family is not forever, and the discourse of the *real* family suggests that the adoptive family is less than real.

Two additional discourses reflected in adoptive parents' narratives include *destiny* and *mutual care*. The discourse of destiny suggests that fate or God's plan brought the adopted child to the adoptive parents (Krusiewicz & Wood, 2001). More specifically, the discourse of destiny suggests "the inevitability and rightness of the children's entrance into their adoptive families—the conviction that this particular child was supposed to join this particular family" (Krusiewicz & Wood, 2001, p. 793). In other words, the message is that the adoptive family was "meant to be." Underlying this discourse, however, is the implication that the adoptee was not meant to remain with their birth family.

In addition, adoptive families, and many families that fall outside of the biogenetic, nuclear form, invoke what Baxter and Braithwaite (2010) call the *discourse of mutual care*, which suggests that relational history, day-to-day communication, and emotional closeness—not biogenetic bonds—are the ultimate criteria for defining family. A popular children's book, *And That's Why She's My Mama* (Nazario, 2018), exemplifies this discourse, depicting mothers engaging in various tasks with their children, who do not resemble them physically. The mothers perform duties such as helping their child brush their teeth, assisting with homework, and taking care of them when they are sick. The book concludes, "So even though we may look different, she loves me every day, and that's why she's my mama, in every single way."[3] These types of books help to maintain the discourse of mutual care, affirming that parent-child relationships are built from communication, not blood.

The Ritual of Adoption Day

The discourse of the *forever family*, which appears on both the cultural level and in daily interactions, aligns with the family ritual of Adoption Day (a.k.a., the more problematically named "Gotcha" Day[4]), where many adoptive families recognize the day that the parents met and/or brought their adopted child home.

Adoptive families who celebrate Adoption Day may give gifts to their adopted child, eat a special meal together, and/or review their child's adoption file or videos from the day they met. Similar to the discourse of the *forever family*, celebrations of Adoption Day can create and strengthen a sense of adoptive family identity and reaffirm an adoptee's place in the family in positive ways. For some adoptees, this annual ritual is meaningful and enjoyable (McKee, 2019), whereas others have reported that it stirs emotions of grief or loss (Choi Robinson, 2022).

The Contradictions of Family

Adoptees as Forever In-Between

To be clear, it is necessary for adoptive parents to use communication to create a sense of adoptive family identity and to cultivate their children's adoptive identity. In the absence of biogenetic ties, communication is particularly needed to constitute and maintain family relationships. Yet adoptive parents, in their desire to create a cohesive adoptive family identity, may overlook or undervalue their child's origins, either intentionally or unintentionally. The challenge is that adoption, and transnational adoption in particular, situates adoptees as forever in-between. They lack a fixed position and what Barbara Yngvesson (2005) has called an "exclusive belonging" in either family or either country. Adoptive parents can too easily gloss over the reality that their child is adopted, almost as if being adopted were an issue or a personal fault. In sharp contrast, reunions draw attention to the enduring ties between adoptees and their birth family and country. For adoptive families who do not have open communication surrounding birth families, reunion may threaten to undo all of the discursive labor that the family has invested in making an adopted child a legitimate member of the family. Yet, as Barbara Yngvesson (2005) expressed so beautifully, adoptees "came from someone, and from somewhere, and bear the traces of that elsewhere just as they bear the traces of the pull or desire that links them to their adoptive parents and adoptive country" (p. 43).

By the time an adoptee reunites, they have been renamed and, in nearly all circumstances, received the message that their adoption was the best and only option for all people involved. The discourses of the *forever family, destiny,* and *mutual care* build and uphold adoptive family identity in both private and public spaces. At the same time, the discourse of the *real* or *natural* family centers biogenetically related family members and implies that adoptive families are counterfeits. Overall, the dominant discourse of family is one of contradiction and irony. Adoptive parents are somehow "not real" but "forever," and birth parents are the "real parents" but deemed extraneous or unfit. Understandably, adoptees who reunite can find it difficult to navigate relationships with multiple families. Indeed, research has found that adoptees in reunion can find it challenging to see themselves as members of two families simultaneously (Colaner et al., 2014).

Adoptees: In Reunion but Still "Loyal"

In addition to messages inside the family that help create a sense of adoptive identity and adoptive family identity, adoptees have also reported receiving messages that they should be grateful to be adopted. Combined, this discursive context (i.e., the "already-spokens") (Baxter, 2011) can cultivate a bifurcated perspective on family: Adoptees are *either* grateful and loyal to their adoptive parents, *or* they decide to search for their birth parents. As adoptees and postadoption professionals Steve Kalb and Angela Tucker (2019) articulated, "The love adoptees have for their parents and their instinct to protect them emotionally tends to prevent honest conversation about the challenges they face as adoptees" (p. 2). Therefore, some adoptees may forgo searching, reuniting, and/or conversations about birth families—all of which contribute to their own identity development—for the sake of their adoptive parents.

Those who proceed with search and reunion can find themselves positioned to express their loyalty and love to their adoptive parents, affirming one parent in order to search for another. Such reassurances signify allegiance to the nuclear family form, in which individuals have only one legitimate mother or father. For example, a transnational Korean adoptee in Palmer's (2010) study indicated that, upon finding his birth mother, he told his adoptive mother that she did not have to worry, saying, "You're the only mother I've ever had and you're the only mother I will ever have in my life" (p. 130). Although reassurance is a common relational maintenance strategy (Canary & Stafford, 1992), it is notable that adoptees feel a particular obligation or need to maintain their relationship with their adoptive parents in preparation for reunion. In this way, reassurance becomes a discursive burden, an additional item on adoptees' communication "to-do" list surrounding reunion. The emotional and communicative spotlight is turned on the adoptive parents' feelings, rather than on the adopted person's experience.

Adoptive Parents: Supportive but Anxious

Although adoptions, in general, have become increasingly open and contemporary adoptive parents are encouraged to engage in dialogue about their child's origins, many adoptive parents' responses to reunion can be complicated or contradictory. For example, nearly all adoptive parent participants in a study by Petta and Steed (2005) viewed search and reunion to be important processes for their adopted children, yet they also experienced fear of losing their child and felt they had to reevaluate their role and entitlement as parents. Importantly, the study's only parent of a transnational adoptee spoke of particularly intense feelings related to her child's safety in his birth country of Vietnam, fear of losing her child, and her lack of control in the reunion. Sociologist Leslie Wang and colleagues (2015) found similar sentiments among parents of transnationally adopted Chinese children during first meetings with birth parents. Although these parents supported and facilitated their children's reunions, they experienced difficulty during the reunion meetings due to a loss of control and the realization that they would need to "share" their child with the birth parents (p. 57). The perceived loss of control described by transnationally adoptive parents, in particular, may be especially salient due to their status as outsiders in their child's birth country and birth family.

In addition, due to the closed nature of transnational adoptions, adoptive parents may be surprised by the prospect of reunion. The unanticipated entrance of the biological parents can cause some adoptive parents to feel threatened that they will lose their child or that their relationship with the child will change in unwanted ways (Dorow, 2006), even though adoptees who search tend to do so to learn more about themselves, not to replace their adoptive parents (Park Nelson, 2016). Adoptive parents may also assume wrongly "that all blood kin have an innate desire to have access to their birth children in ways that would interfere with the adoptive family's life" (Brian, 2012, p. 121). However, as discussed in previous chapters, Korean birth parents tend to express gratitude toward adoptive parents and encourage adoptees to respect them.

Reunion may rouse intense emotions in even the most supportive and open adoptive parents, and adoptees can likely sense unspoken insecurities or fears. Yet even in the absence of these feelings, adoptees have been steeped in the discourse of the *forever family*, the discourse of *mutual* care, and the narrative that their adoption was a happy ending, which may lead them to feel that they need to justify or explain their reasons for reuniting, particularly if the topics surrounding adoption and one's birth family have been avoided, either intentionally or unintentionally.

Next, I detail participants' descriptions of their communication with their adoptive families before, during, and after reunion. I begin by discussing the various ways that adoptive parents communicate support for reunion; however, this support does not always meet adoptees' wants or needs. I then discuss the tensions present when adoptive parents accompany adoptees to reunions, which often results in adoptees needing to reassure them, to hold back when interacting with birth parents, and/or to bear witness to their birth family's shame. Finally, I draw attention to ways in which communicative openness—open, direct, and nondefensive communication within the adoptive family (Brodzinsky, 2006)—surrounding birth families and reunion can provide an opportunity for relational growth. What will be most evident is that the cultural and day-to-day discourse of adoption—in particular, the discourse of mutual care and the perceived rightness of the nuclear family form—constrains adoptees during the rare times they are with their birth families.

Support from Adoptive Parents

To varying extents, nearly all participants described their adoptive parents' role or responses surrounding reunion as "supportive." Support was enacted in a variety of ways, depending on the adoptee's age and the extent of communicative openness in the family. Supportive behaviors included initiating or facilitating the search and initial meeting, attending the initial reunion meeting(s), planning the trip to Korea, paying for travel to the reunion, open conversations with participants about reunion and the birth family, and/or displaying an active and ongoing interest in discussing the reunion or birth family.

Ongoing Emotional Support

Some participants, particularly those who met their birth parents when they were children or teenagers, indicated that their adoptive parents provided all of the above forms of support and also, from a very young age, cultivated communicative openness about topics related to adoption and the birth family. These parents provided opportunities for learning about Korean culture through camps or language lessons, nurtured curiosity about birth parents and Korea, and made space for adoption-related talk. Predictably, participants whose adoptive parents created this type of communicative environment tended to describe their parents and their relationship with them in positive ways using words such as *close*.

Catherine, who met her birth family when she was ten, recalled how her adoptive parents completed all of the paperwork for the search, then paid for the search, for multiple trips to travel to Korea to meet with her birth family, and for years of Korean language classes so that she could communicate directly with her birth family. More recently, her adoptive mom helped Catherine pick out gifts for her young nephew in Korea. Catherine described her relationships with both adoptive parents as "very close" and indicated that she can talk with them about anything related to her adoption and birth family relationships. She acknowledged that although she did not realize how much work and money her parents invested when she was younger, she appreciates their support deeply now. Catherine described their ongoing support, saying,

> They're behind me one hundred. They're behind me one hundred per-cent no matter what I do. . . . Financially they've paid so much, but it's a lot more than that. It's knowing that they're behind me one hun-dred percent. . . . You know, not just like, "Okay here's the money," but they're *proud* of how much I want to learn about my culture.

Participants whose adoptive parents did not attend their reunion meetings spoke about the importance of their adoptive parents' support before the re-union and their active, ongoing interest afterward. Eric described his adoptive parents as "rapt" when he talks about his birth family. He stated that they sent gifts for him to take to his birth family, that they ask about his birth family regularly, and that his adoptive mother makes an effort to pronounce his Ko-rean brother's name correctly. He viewed their ongoing interest and engage-ment as an expression of genuine care.

Support during Initial Meetings

Sylvia spoke positively of her adoptive parents' support during her reunion, which occurred in the city where she and her adoptive family all lived. She described how her adoptive parents hosted Thanksgiving dinner for the entire family, including Sylvia's birth family, were welcoming and warm toward Syl-via's birth family, listened and provided emotional support to Sylvia when she was struggling during the reunion, and were "on call" to take care of Sylvia's children the entire time her birth parents were in town. Reflecting on her adop-tive parents' support, she stated that her search and reunion experience made her "more appreciative of [my adoptive parents] because they've been so sup-portive." Overall, Sylvia's adoptive mother, in particular, showed her support for the reunion in tangible ways that were responsive to Sylvia's needs during the reunion.

Sylvia is an exception in that most transnational adoptees must travel to their birth country, which involves financing the trip, navigating in an unfa-miliar country, and being away from one's place of comfort and familiarity. Participants spoke of the importance of having the support of family members or friends during initial meetings in Korea for both practical and emotional reasons. This support involved taking pictures, getting coffee, taking notes during meetings with birth family members, and/or listening and providing perspective on the meetings. Participants who attended initial meetings without a support person spoke of daily calls to family members or friends who were at home and appreciated the ability to be honest about what they were experiencing, with someone who knew them well.

"Support"

Several participants indicated that their adoptive parents were supportive of their reunion but only on a superficial level or in ways that were unhelpful. Ji Kyoung recalled that although she told her adoptive family about her initial reunion beforehand, they did not express any emotions, either positive or negative, and, more troubling to her, they have not shown any subsequent interest in discussing her reunion with her. They respond politely if Ji Kyoung tells them about a visit to Korea or if she talks about her birth family, but they do not ask any questions or demonstrate any meaningful engagement. She stated that their response "clarified" to her that their relationship is "challenged and troubled." She elaborated, saying, "I think that the way they reacted just made it more clear what I actually already knew, that it's not like a family I feel is really interested in me at all. It's actually very sad."

Cat, who met her birth family in the United States in a different state than where she lived, recalled a similar cursory reaction from her adoptive parents when she told them about her upcoming reunion. She said that although they said that they were happy for her, "it wasn't a big deal to them," even when Cat sent them a photo of her twin sister for the first time. They also refused to attend the reunion when Cat asked if they would come to support her. Then, when Cat's birth mother called Cat's adoptive parents during their initial meeting to thank them for raising Cat, the conversation did not go well. Cat described how her adoptive mom started joking about how Cat "used to be sweet but now is not" and then started talking about how Cat's father fought in the Korean War, which made Cat feel uneasy. Soon, Cat felt that she had to intervene; she recalled, "I got on the phone and I go, 'Mom, we gotta go!' (laughs) cuz she was offending them." Both Ji Kyoung and Cat described their relationships with their adoptive parents as distant or strained before their reunion, and their communication surrounding reunion exemplified this lack of closeness.

Sometimes, adoptive parent support was complicated. Christine first met her birth family at the age of nine, accompanied by her adoptive parents. Now a thirty-year-old adult, she described a recent incident where she had to negotiate the presence of her adoptive parents in a reunion meeting. In 2016, her adoptive parents had planned a family trip to Korea to attend the wedding of a family friend, but conflict arose when Christine said she wanted to meet her birth family by herself during the trip. She recalled,

> I really wanted to be with [my birth family] by myself. My [adoptive] mom was not having that. My mom was very like, "That story is also my story and our stories as your adoptive parents, and so if you wanna go to Korea and you wanna see your birth family, you have to include us in that meeting somehow." Which I am still emotionally grappling with. I have a lot of, kind of, resentment towards that, because I felt like she was using my connection with my birth parents as a sort of manipulative, maneuvering, way of like, "If you wanna go to Korea and do this, you have to (trails off). If you want to see them, you have to take us," whatever. We did work out some sort of compromise, though, where like, you know, we would have dinner all of us together and then after that, I went off separately with [my birth family] and my friend who was there translating for me, and was able to spend time with *just them* and myself, and my parents went and did something else.

Still, Christine described her relationship with her adoptive mom as very close and credits her for ensuring that Christine cultivated and maintained a connection to Korea and her Korean heritage growing up. Yet, over time, Christine has realized that despite this closeness, she and her mom have fundamentally different experiences and perspectives. She said,

> My mom knows me better than anybody else probably, but there are still going to be barriers that we're just not gonna be able to cross together. And I think that sometimes that's really painful for me to, like, realize, but also, like, it's just fact.

She also indicated that over the past two years, she has "made" her mom sit and listen to her talk about adoption "for hours, multiple times" and that her mom's perception of adoption has "probably changed a lot" since their trip in 2016. However, she spoke of emotional residue from the compromise, saying, "I'm still currently at this day and age struggling with having given in to that. I mean, it alleviated a huge argument, and it allowed me to go to Korea, because they were paying for the trip." She concluded that, in the future, she will not allow this situation to repeat itself. She stated,

> I will not make those compromises again. I *don't* think that I have it in me to continue to make compromises when it comes to my adop-

tion. I'm not doing that anymore. And I'm also not going to let myself be in a financial situation where I can't leverage that on my own. So if that means, I don't go to Korea for the next five, ten years again, I'm not going until I can pay my own ticket. My own place. My own food. The whole kit and kaboodle, because I am not going to (trails off). I haven't had agency in *anything* regarding my adoption, so to ask me to do that again, to give up, you know, my right to ask for things, or my right to need things, it's not flying anymore.

Christine's words reveal that she is claiming agency to enact her relationship with her birth family on her own terms. This development, which seems healthy, especially for a thirty-year-old, enables her to navigate a relationship with her birth family that is, for the first time, independent of her adoptive parents. Her story draws attention to the way in which adoptive parents can exert power within adoptees' relationships with their birth families. As adoptees move from childhood to adolescence to adulthood, adoptive parents may need to renegotiate their role and communication in reunion, even if they had been instrumental—like Christine's adoptive mother had been—in facilitating the initial meeting.

Reassurance: Maintaining Relationships with Adoptive Parents

Throughout various stages of reunion, participants who recalled reassuring their adoptive parents told them that they valued the relationship and would not leave them in favor of their birth parents. These reassurances included statements telling adoptive parents that they are the "real" parents and reaffirming their love for them and their commitment to the adoptive family. In a very clear example, Sylvia, whose adoptive mother started crying upon learning of Sylvia's birth family search, spoke of offering extensive reassurances—sending cards, writing blog posts—to all members of her adoptive family. In the weeks leading up to her birth parents' first visit, she stated,

I mean that was the biggest thing, that I was just worried about hurting [my adoptive parents] and (pause) for the next few weeks I just was trying to *really, really* reassure them that, you know, no matter what, they're my *parents* and that nothing changes between *us*. And like (pause), that it, just that it didn't have to do with them and that it wasn't anything they *didn't* give me because I've *always* known that they loved me and they've *always* treated me like I was their biological child so it wasn't like (trails off). Yeah, I was just really feeling like I needed to reassure them as much as possible. I was just really worried about how they were gonna (pause) *feel* about everything.

During this time, Sylvia also made multiple efforts to reassure her five non-adopted brothers of how much she valued their relationship despite her plans to reunite. She spoke of this time, saying,

I felt for, like, the next several weeks that I needed to reassure every-one in my family that they were still my family and that nothing had changed. And nothing changed about how I feel about them or how I see myself in my family and that no, no matter what, they are my siblings. Like I have always been really intentional about when I refer to *my family*. Like my adoptive family, I don't call them my adoptive family, ever. They're my *family* and it's like they are the norm, and the abnormal is my birth family. So, you know, I sent cards and talked to different members of the family just telling them how thankful I was to *be* in the family I'm in and how they've affected who I *am*. . . . There was a [blog] entry that I wrote about each of my brothers and how they affected who I am today and the personality I have. And the interests that I have and stuff. And I know that at least three of the men in my family cried when they read it (laughs). My other two brothers, the *two* middle ones, they *actually* had a really difficult time with [the reunion]. And I'm not exactly sure why, because I think they understood what was happening but *didn't*, kinda. Like, it just was kinda traumatic for them because (pause) you know, they don't see me as being adopted, so it was a reminder to them that I *wasn't* initially theirs. So yeah, it was hard for them especially, I think . . . I found out in a roundabout way that [they] were having a hard time. They didn't want to add stress for me by telling me that, and, you know, that reminded me how much they love me.

Because Sylvia's adoptive mother reacted with tears to the news of Sylvia's birth search, Sylvia felt a strong need to reassure her adoptive family repeatedly and in multiple ways. Her inference that her adoptive brothers found it "traumatic" to think of Sylvia as not "theirs" suggests a preexisting lack of communicative openness surrounding Sylvia's birth family and expresses the belief in her exclusive belonging (Yngvesson, 2002) to the adoptive family. The adoptive, nuclear family identity had been built to be watertight, and Sylvia's impending reunion was seen as a threat to its structure. After her initial meeting, Sylvia affirmed the nuclear adoptive family structure and spoke of her adoptive family as her "real" family. In addition, she spoke of how she valued her relationship with her birth sister more than her birth parents. In explaining why, she reasoned, "I never had a sister, so she's kinda filling a hole, whereas I *have* parents." For Sylvia, steeped in the discourse of mutual care and the nuclear family ideal, there was no room for additional parents.

Some participants spoke of reassuring adoptive parents preemptively. When asked about their adoptive family's communication surrounding reunion, these participants started by describing a general communicative openness in their adoptive families when it came to talking about adoption and Korea, and, often, birth parents as well. These participants described their communication about these topics with words such as "open" and "comfortable." The precedence of openness allowed participants to share their feelings with their adoptive parents in light of reunion, yet they still felt a need to offer reassurance. For example, when Ashley was eighteen, she returned to Korea with her adoptive family for the first time, but before the trip, she reassured her adoptive parents. She recalled,

> I was just kind of like, "Oh this is cool but it's not really something that I'm, you know, *seeking* or anything," but I just told them, "You always know, like, you're my *real* family" and stuff, and I think they really appreciated that, but I think that's it, we didn't really have a, like, sit-down conversation.

When I asked her why she chose to reassure them, she said,

> So they won't, wouldn't feel, you know, insecure about it in any way, or feel like I was, kind of like, "Oh hey, here's my birth family, you know, bye," or stuff like that. So, you know, your real family's the people that *raised* you and taught you values and were there for you, so I just wanted them to know that.

Ashley's words clearly reflect the discourse of mutual care and the adoptive family as the *real* family, even though she reported that her adoptive parents had always been very encouraging of her relationship with her birth parents from a very young age. This finding suggests that there were likely other, powerful discourses circulating around her suggesting that she needed to be aware of her adoptive parents' feelings and preserve her relationship with them in light of reunion.

Similarly, Nikki recalled a conversation with her adoptive parents after her reunion meeting, saying,

> On my side I would say, you know, "This doesn't affect how I think about *you* guys. You know you're always gonna be my parents, you're always gonna be my mom and dad. This person is just, you know, a woman who, who *birthed* me." (Laughs) . . . But yeah, we've always had open communication, my parents and I. So I've always felt comfortable, and they always know that I care about them, that I love them. But I think it's also good that I *said* that. I think that it's always good to hear it and reinforce that.

Nikki's reassurance also resists the discourse of the "real" family, where she minimizes the role of her birth mother in her life. Although she believes that her adoptive parents already knew how she felt about them and their relationship, the physical presence of her birth mother evoked a desire to reinforce her relationship with them.

Similarly, although Mee Joo's parents responded supportively to her search and reunion, she reassured them afterward, explaining,

> Although they hadn't made any indication that they were seeking any kind of reassurance or feeling *threatened* in any sort of way, I would also have to say that after I met my birth family and after I had spent time with them, after several months, that I was more vocal about reassuring my parents even for my own side because I think at that point, from my perspective and most adoptees that I've met and have discussed this with, have said or have expressed that there's always kind of this wondering, this lingering thought in your mind about our so-called, quote unquote, so-called *real parents* and the notion that, yes, despite whatever kind of relationship we might have with our adoptive family, they're not necessarily what society would call or what we in our own minds would call our real parents. And so it became evidently more *clear* to me as time progressed that I felt more confident in not just saying but also *sincerely* believing that they were my real parents because they were the ones that raised me.

Mee Joo's words reflect knowledge of the discourse of the *real* family and its persistence in her mind and in the minds of other adoptees. She also invokes the discourse of mutual care; she believes her adoptive parents to be her *real* parents because they raised her, a belief that was cemented after her initial meetings with her birth family and that she wanted to further reinforce by articulating it to her adoptive parents.

Eric, who was twenty-nine at the time of his first reunion meeting and whose adoptive parents were very supportive of his reunion, also chose to reassure his adoptive parents. He based his choice on knowledge of other adoptees' experiences, an example of an "already-spoken" discourse influencing family communication. He recalled,

> I think that I really *did* assure them that, I think I said something to the effect of, "I just want you to know, you know, I've read about other instances where this has happened and it's really caused a rift between the adoptee and adoptive family, and I just want you guys to know that you're *still* my parents and I *still* love you." . . . I think they didn't really know how to take that and just kind of answered sarcastically by saying, "*Awwww*" (Laughs). Or something like that. Not what I was expecting at all. And so, you know, it kinda made me a little self-conscious that I was, like, being *too* cautious for them, when actually they're pretty emotionally resilient people evidently (laughs).

Overall, participants' reassurances suggest that they were anticipating their adoptive parents feeling threatened or hurt by reunion, but in most cases, adoptive parents did not express these emotions. Rather, their adoptive parents expressed high supportiveness of their reunions. These interactions lay bare the ways in which family communication exists within a context that is contradictory and complex: Although participants didn't receive parental messages prompting reassurance and although they didn't seek to "replace" their adoptive parents, they based their communication on preexisting cultural discourses of exclusive belonging and mutual care.

"Holding Back" to Protect Adoptive Parents

Participants also reported that they "held back" expressing emotion when talking about their birth family with their adoptive family, or that they withheld affection or curiosity when interacting with their birth family in the presence of their adoptive parent(s). These participants held back to protect the feelings of their adoptive family. Olivia, who was thirty-two at the time of her first and only reunion and thirty-five at the time of her first and only interview, recalled her adoptive parents being very enthusiastic and supportive surrounding her reunion. Specifically, she recalled her adoptive mother's response to the news of her upcoming reunion, quoting her as saying, "Oh my god, Olivia, that is great. You *have* to meet them! Take lots of pictures, take a video." Although she didn't recall reassuring her adoptive parents, she spoke of holding back, saying,

> I think I'm just too old for them to think that, you know, one parent is going to replace another parent. But it did cross my mind at times, that. (pause) Emotionally maybe I held back a little because I didn't want to disrespect *my* parents here. And I wanted them to know that *they're* my parents. They're the ones who raised me. But I don't think I needed to say that because still today, my parents, my mom and my dad, they both treat me like their own.

Like Mee Joo, Olivia affirms the discourse of *mutual care* and defines parents as those who "raised" her, similar to adoptee participants in a study by Anzur and Myers (2020). Olivia's words also reinscribe a belief in the nuclear family composition, suggesting that she can have only one set of parents. Although she resisted the idea that her adoptive parents would have felt apprehensive about losing her to the birth parents, she was still compelled to hold back in order to communicate that their role as her parents was secure.

Ashley also spoke of holding back when talking about her birth family with her adoptive parents. Although her adoptive parents had been very encouraging about her reunion throughout her life, she stated that she has to "dilute" her descriptions when talking about her birth family with her adoptive mom especially, even though she described her relationship with both mothers as close. She explained,

> [My adoptive mom] is, like, great, but I know she, like, kinda gets a little jealous of me and my birth mom's relationship because we are close, so I'm just like, "Oh, my birth mom's driving me crazy." Like, I can't tell her, "Oh, we, like, totally had a lot of fun." You know, I can tell that stuff, but, like, not too much. And she's a great person, I just feel like it kinda makes her sad a little bit, that we're so close.

When she reflected on this discursive burden, needing to hold back to protect her adoptive parents, Ashley stated that it didn't feel onerous and focused instead on the good fortune of having two families. She said,

> And I don't mind doing that between the birth family and the adopted family, because, I mean, I'm really fortunate so I can't complain. You know, it's just a natural thing, I think, to have to do, maybe, and I'm

just happy to, like, have the opportunity to have two families, and some people only have one family, so I really can't complain or it's not *that* much of a burden. You know, it's juggling things a little bit, or people's emotions, it's fine. That's life, with any relationship.

Ashley was able to maintain close relationships with both sets of parents, perhaps due, in part, to her ability to accommodate her communication. For participants like Ashley, holding back during discussions about birth families seemed to have very little impact on relationships with adoptive parents. However, holding back during reunion meetings may have different stakes.

Participants whose adoptive parents attended reunion meetings with them spoke of holding back affection toward, or interest in, their birth family, to protect their adoptive parent. Still, these participants were thankful that their adoptive parents were there. Mark, who was fourteen at the time of his first meeting and twenty-three at the time of his first interview, stated the following:

I was glad that [my adoptive parents] were there because, you know, for me it was like the meeting of two parts of my identity, two parts of where I came from and I wanted both of them to know the other. . . . But also it probably made me a little bit more reluctant to ask personal questions about, you know, my birth parents' background.

Meagan was twenty years old at the time of her initial reunion, and her adoptive mother accompanied her. Even though she described her relationship with her adoptive mother as very close and her mother's interactions with her birth family as extremely positive, she described reassurance *and* holding back very clearly, stating,

I think I held back at certain times because I didn't want [my adoptive mom] to feel like I was maybe connecting with them *more*. You know, I was *very* aware of her feelings, and after each meeting, you know, I would tell her, "You know that, like, I love you. And I'm not going anywhere, and you are my *real* mom, you know?" And, you know, she'd say, "Oh I know that. I know that. I know that, you know. No, you're mine (laughs). You're not anyone else's baby." But I think that it made *me* feel better saying that. Even if she already knew that. I didn't doubt for a second that she would ever really question, like, my loyalty or who I consider my family.

Meagan also stated that she always ensured that she sat next to her adoptive mother during dinners with her birth family. Further, she mentioned that she "held back" asking questions about her deceased birth mother due to an awareness of her adoptive mom's feelings. She stated, "I'm not sure exactly what questions that I held back on, but I do remember, you know, leaving and not being . . . not feeling like I knew *that* much about her. Or about, you know, her death and stuff like that." Although Meagan seemed to find her adoptive mom's expressions of "You're mine" and "not anyone else's" reassuring, such statements are a clear articulation of a belief in Meagan's exclusive belonging—in the adoptive family. Over time and during subsequent visits with only her birth family, Meagan has been able to gain more information about her birth mother, but not all adoptees are able to return to their birth country with regularity.

Despite holding back during her initial reunion, Meagan discussed how very thankful she was for her adoptive mom's presence, practical assistance, and emotional support. Indeed, Meagan and her adoptive mom visited her birth family again several years later, and Meagan spoke of the fond relationship between her mom and her birth family. In other visits, Meagan brought her adoptive sisters, sister-in-law, and adoptive dad. She explained, "These are the people that have made me who I am and I just wanted them to meet so badly because I love them both so much." In the future, she hopes to bring other members of her adoptive family and stepfamily to meet her Korean family.

Given the large investment involved in orchestrating these reunions and the fact that such meetings can only happen rarely due to time, distance, and resources, adoptees should be able to express themselves freely and ask questions of their birth family during face-to-face meetings. In attempting to preserve the adoptive family relationship and protect adoptive parents' feelings, adoptees may be forgoing potentially meaningful interactions with their birth family or not gaining desired information. In other words, the discursive burden to protect adoptive parents can compromise adoptees' communication with the birth family. Perhaps instead, adoptive parents should enact reassurance—expressing that they will not feel hurt or threatened by reunion and encouraging adoptees to communicate with their birth parents as if they were not there. In reunion, the focus should remain on the adopted person and their birth family, and adoptive parents can use their discursive power to maintain this focus.

Birth Parents Meeting Adoptive Parents: Gratitude and Shame

Participants often recalled that their birth parents expressed gratitude toward their adoptive parents, whether indirectly, by telling the adoptee to pass along messages of deep thanks, or directly, when they met the adoptive parents face-to-face. Adoptive parents also expressed gratitude to birth parents for "allow-ing" them to raise their child. Birth parents' gratitude seemed to stem from their belief that the adoptive parents fulfilled a responsibility or duty that they themselves should have done. In adoption, birth parents are typically framed as the givers, the adoptive parents as the grateful receivers, and the child as a gift that was freely given (Yngvesson, 2002). Yet various scholars have point-ed out that often, birth mothers' relinquishment often results from gendered economic and social constraints (Dorow, 2006; Kim, 2016; Yngvesson, 2002), calling one to question whether the birth mothers would have made a differ-ent choice if they had more resources or support. In addition, the "gift" is not received freely; rather, adoptive parents pay agency fees, legal fees, and travel costs, and offer gifts to caretakers and donations to the orphanage in order to receive the "gift child" (Yngvesson, 2002). There exists between birth parents and adoptive parents an inherent power differential, one that led the former set of parents to *not* raise the child and the latter to raise the child. Whereas adoptive parents are often viewed as noble for taking in a parentless child, birth parents tend to be seen as pitiable and incapable. Some participants described the inequality between the two sets of parents as palpable during reunion meet-ings where both sets of parents were present. As a result, several participants described how their birth families seemed much more comfortable during meet-ings without the adoptive parents. In 2011, during her first interview, Cath-erine speculated on how her Korean birth father feels in the presence of her adoptive parents, saying,

> And so, for *him*, he's, like, you know, *man* of the house. But then once he has my [adoptive] parents in his house, he has two people to whom he owes everything. You know, like, "You raised my daughter" and I think *not* having that power kinda made him uncomfortable. And so, I mean, that's the only thing *I've* really concluded from it.

As Catherine has gotten older and traveled to Korea alone, she has noticed that interactions with her birth parents are more comfortable when her adoptive parents aren't present. In her second interview, she expressed similar thoughts about why her birth parents feel uneasy around her adoptive parents, saying,

> I think it takes a huge piece of *guilt*, I would guess, guilt and shame out of it. Like, obviously there's still guilt and shame; it's still a broken family in some ways, but there's not, like, guilt staring them in the face, you know, of "You took on the burden I was supposed to have, of par-enting this child."

Although Catherine and others articulated that their adoption relieved their birth parents of some burdens and some shame, reunion meetings also draw ambiguous loss into sharp focus. Participants spoke of how reunion meetings caused them to reflect on what they had lost by being adopted abroad and what their lives would have been had they stayed in Korea with their families. Naturally, then, reunion must also cause birth parents to reflect on the ways in which they lost their child. Birth parents can never regain childhood years with their daughter or son, nor will they ever have the same type of bond with their child—now an adult—that they would have had otherwise and that their child may have now with their adoptive parents. Ashley recalled a moment when her birth father's grief and sense of loss overtook him. Her birth parents had flown to the United States for her wedding, and during the reception, the first dance was the traditional Father-Daughter Dance, in which the father of the bride and the bride dance together, alone, usually to a sentimental song about a father-daughter relationship. This common American wedding ritual can evoke tears or poignant emotions for any attendee, but for Ashley's birth father, it evoked an intense response, which she learned about later. She told me,

> [My birth father] ended up, like, walking out afterwards and was like, hysterically crying. And then my [adoptive] dad had to go and comfort him. And there was this whole thing. Because I still think he feels really guilty and stuff so that was a big step for them. And my birth mom was crying and they ended up like, I think, having a good time in the long run, but it was really emotionally exhausting.

Although guilt was likely a partial explanation for Ashley's birth father's response, I suggest that ambiguous loss also played a role. In this moment, her birth father saw Ashley, his daughter, during a major life milestone, literally in the arms of her adoptive father. This visual must have compelled him to see how he has been supplanted in his role as her primary father, a role he can never regain.

Christine, who, like Catherine, had her first reunion as a child accompanied by her adoptive parents, expressed an evolution in her understanding of her birth parents' perspective as she has gotten older, which has made her more uncomfortable having her adoptive parents attend her reunion meetings. After her most recent reunion meeting, which her adoptive mom insisted on attending, she described being struck by the contrast between her two sets of parents. She contrasted her adoptive parents with her birth parents, respectively, saying,

And, you know, I'm so hyperaware of how uncomfortable the reality of that situation really is for my birth family, you know. What it did, I think, for me, in that meeting, really *physically* showed me the different stories in the space. That was the story of "This is so amazing. I'm so grateful to your family for giving us the opportunity to raise you as a daughter and *we* have a wonderful family now" and blah, blah, blah, blah, blah. And on the opposite side of the room, then having to look at the people that (pause), you know, that is not their fault, but it's pain, there's so much *pain* across that table, you know, and me, being in the middle.

In addition to feeling caught between these two stories and feeling guilty for being "the cause" of her birth parents' pain, Christine described the impact of her adoptive parents' unwelcome presence during her time with her birth family, saying,

That's one of my big reasons for why I didn't really *wanna* do the whole adoptive family, birth family get-together, because I'm so much more aware now of, like, how awkward that is and how painful that must be, you know, for my birth family's side, and I just didn't want to have to feel like I had to pander to *either* side to feel comfortable and, you know, there are lots of questions that I have for my family that I don't need everybody else to know, like, they're very *personal* questions and they're gonna be questions that I'm sure are really *hard* for them to answer, you know, emotionally and all that stuff. I'm just *so much* more aware now of, like, the awkwardness and the sort of pain that's associated with adoption than I was when I was a teenager . . . I feel like there are so many questions that I have from my birth family that I am worried will make my adoptive family feel bad, or, like, whatever, where I didn't wanna *shame* them in front of my adoptive parents by *asking* them certain questions. So, like, when they're all in the space together, I feel very limited by what I can express and what I can ask and what I can feel. And I don't want to. You know? Like, I wanna feel comfortable, getting information, what I need right now.

David L. Eng (2003) observed that transnational adoption is "largely devoid of emotional agency for the adoptee" (p. 22). Christine's words reveal her desire for emotional agency during her reunion meetings and the ways in which her adoptive parents' presence diminishes this agency because she is focused on their feelings. In addition, birth parents also lack emotional agency in the presence of adoptive parents; their feelings of indebtedness and their relative lack of power compared with adoptive parents may prevent them from communicating in ways they would have otherwise. As adoptees' developmental needs change throughout long-term relationships with birth families, adoptive parents will need to reevaluate their roles and presence and to discuss these topics with adoptees.

Reunion as a Natural Step

Although most participants reported either reassurance and/or holding back, a few participants recalled doing neither. They described their adoptive parents as viewing reunion as a "natural" and expected step in self-knowledge and identity and, therefore, not a threat to the adoptive family. For example, Sun Ok stated that because her adoptive mother was interested in her own genealogy, she had assumed that Sun Ok would also eventually seek out information on her birth parents. Therefore, Sun Ok stated that she did not feel a need to offer any reassurance to her adoptive parents.

Other participants who did not recall reassuring or holding back had either reunited as minors and/or reported a high level of openness about adoption and the birth family while growing up. These participants described their discussions with their adoptive parents about their birth parents with words such as "natural." Hanne, a Danish Korean adoptee, recalled, "My Danish mother was very open about things. And had always been very open about the adoption. So we talked a lot—a lot about it. And it was very natural." Isabel, whose parents were very open in talking with her about her birth parents, foster parents, and adoption throughout her childhood, stated,

> We just kind of, I don't know, had a natural understanding that, you know, we were kind of meant to be together and the [reunion] situation happened as it did and we just hoped we would find some answers, no matter what, in the end.

Isabel draws on the discourse of destiny in articulating that she and her adoptive parents were "meant" to be together, yet she described a high level of communicative openness within her adoptive family. Thus, the discourses that affirm adoptive family identity are not mutually exclusive of conversations about reunion or birth families. Isabel's use of the plural pronoun "we" in referring to a "natural" understanding and hopes for the reunion suggests a shared perspective on birth family and reunion, which could only be achieved and known through ongoing, open communication within the adoptive family.

For these participants, previous open conversations about birth families and adoption created a communicative context in which search and reunion were unsurprising and/or viewed as natural. As Baxter (2011) wrote, "The relational meaning system—what kind of relationship the parties regard themselves as having—is *always an inheritance from past interactions that serve as a backdrop for current interactions*" (p. 51, italics added). Thus, adoptive families' "relational meaning system" surrounding reunion is in constant creation from the moment the adoptee and adoptive parents meet one another, long before a search has been initiated or a reunion meeting has been planned. Not all adoptees will want to discuss adoption topics or search and reunite, but adoptive parents have a responsibility for creating a "backdrop" that welcomes such conversations. If adoptive parents do so, search and/or reunion will not come as a surprise. When openness about adoption and birth families is normalized within families, adoptees appear to feel less of a need to reassure their adoptive parents or hold back in their presence. In this way, adoptive parents can lighten adoptees' discursive burden.

Reunion as a Relational Turning Point

Overall, participants who indicated that their adoptive parents facilitated communicative openness throughout their childhood described their relationships with them as close or very close. These participants indicated that because their relationship with their adoptive parents was already close, reunion either did not change their relationship or it drew them closer. Other participants, whose adoptive parents were not particularly open and who did not convey significant interest in the adoptee's reunion experience or birth family, expressed that, following reunion, their relationship with their adoptive parents remained unchanged or became more distant. For some, however, reunion provided an opportunity for a new level of openness and for relational growth. Jorgen described changes in his relationship with his adoptive parents throughout his years in reunion. He described,

> In the beginning I would actually be very enthusiastic and so I wanted to share with them my joy and so I told them everything that happened and that I was feeling very good about this reunion. And so in the beginning they were kind of reserved. They would, you know, express that they were happy on my behalf, but I could feel that they had some reservations. So then we got into some discussions about what it meant to me and how I felt about them. And then I reassured them that it didn't mean that I wanted to replace them, and then after that, they

could actually really partake in my joy and they were very happy for me. And *then* that led to some, like, groundbreaking developments in my relationship with my parents especially, because up until that point we had had some unresolved conflicts, and this became a topic where we could meet and they could sympathize with me and it was just a positive thing we could share together, my reunion with my birth family. And that was the stepping stone for beginning to talk about other serious topics that we needed to discuss. So after that I actually became closer with my parents. I think that's the greatest gift I actually got out of it, that I got a closer bond with my adoptive parents.

Communication scholars would say that reunion served as a *relational turning point*, "an event or occurrence that is associated with change in a relationship" (Baxter & Bullis, 1986, p. 470) for Jorgen and his adoptive parents. Relational turning points can have positive or negative impacts on relationship closeness, and reunions do not always serve as relational turning points for adoptees and their adoptive parents. Yet Jorgen's reunion and the ensuing conversations he had with his adoptive parents allowed for the creation of a closer bond, even as he was engaged in the process of deepening his relationship with his birth family. His story draws attention to the possibilities that reunion offers for adoptive parents to show support in new ways and suggests that it may never be too late to cultivate communicative openness.

Similarly, Alexander, who reunited for the first time at age sixteen and who had traveled back to Korea with his adoptive mother multiple times, spoke of how reunion has strengthened their relationship. In his first interview, which took place when he was eighteen, he mentioned that the fact that he is a teenager made his relationship with his adoptive parents challenging at times. However, his adoptive mother's willingness to facilitate his initial reunion and their multiple trips to visit his birth mom in Korea together over the years have helped them forge a close relationship. In his second interview, he said,

My adoptive family and I didn't always agree on everything. So going back to Korea each time, it feels like a little bit more relief on me, so I got a little bit happier, so it's a little easier to navigate my relationship with my adoptive family. . . . It was really nice to never feel also from my adopted family that I was going to abandon them and that my feelings would change. They just know that it's a different part of me and they respect that. I love that about them because that's a feeling that I had when I originally wanted to go through with the reunion, was feeling like, my relationship with them would change in some way and then it *did* but it was not the way that I was expecting. I was expecting it to be sort of more negative or just difficult to talk about with them, but they've been really open with me, so I hope that I can bring back my adoptive family a little bit each time I go.

Adoptees commonly fear that reunion may have a negative impact on their relationship with their adoptive parents, even when adoptive parents do not communicate feelings of being threatened (Powell & Afifi, 2005). In all likelihood, the already-spoken discourses of the *forever family* and of *mutual care* contribute to adoptees' perception that reunion will jeopardize their relationship with their adoptive parents, but when adoptive parents offer supportive communication surrounding reunion while respecting adoptees' boundaries, reunion carries the possibility of strengthening their relationships.

Conclusion

Given the cultural and day-to-day discourse surrounding adoption (e.g., forever family, naming, rituals), adoptees in reunion often feel a need to protect their adoptive parents. Although some would argue that transnational adoption has allowed for the formation of new types of kinship, in many ways, Korean transnational adoption has been only a slight variation on the nuclear, biogenetically related family form (Eng, 2003): One mother, one father, and their child(ren). Language surrounding adoption, which emphasizes the singularity of the parent-child relationship (i.e., exclusive belonging), the preeminence of the adoptive family (i.e., the discourse of *mutual care*), and the destiny of the adopted child's place within the adoptive family, creates a context in which adoptive parents can be threatened by the presence of birth parents and where adoptees who choose to search and reunite can be deemed disloyal to their adoptive parents. At the same time, adoptees, particularly visible (i.e., transracial) adoptees, receive messages from outsiders that question their belonging in their adoptive families and suggest that their "real" parents are their birth parents. In other words, the already-spokens create a contradictory context in which adoptees in reunion can find it challenging to navigate relationships with multiple sets of parents.

Within this swirl of contradictory messages, adoptive parents must work to undo messages about exclusive belonging and narrate their child's story in ways that include accurate, known information about the birth family, even when information is limited (Marko Harrigan, 2010). At the same time, these parents must communicate in ways that build adoptive family identity wherein a child feels secure enough to explore, ask questions, and feel a range of emotions about adoption. Research suggests that open communication about adoption results in adoptees feeling more secure in their adoptive families, experiencing less ambiguous loss about their origins, and having higher self-esteem (Brodzinsky, 2006; Colaner et al., 2018; Powell & Afifi, 2005). When there are multiple adoptees within the same adoptive family, adoptive parents must be prepared to tailor their communication based on individual differences and experiences, as most participants with siblings who were also Korean adopted mentioned how their interest in adoption and reunion differed from that of their sibling(s).

When a transnational adoptee approaches reunion or is maintaining a relationship with their birth family, their needs and desires for support will vary according to their age, development, past experiences, and individual characteristics. However, one observation remained clear across all interviews: Adoptees want adoptive parents to communicate support for reunion and interest in birth families. This support may be emotional (e.g., listening, verbal or nonverbal expressions of support, refraining from unsolicited advice) or instrumental (e.g., driving to the airport, taking notes, getting coffee), but because adoptive parents and birth parent relationships are often framed as mutually exclusive, support must be offered proactively and communicated clearly. Ideally, adoptees and their birth parents can communicate openly and directly about this support, with the adoptive parent asking what the adoptee needs and, when possible, providing it or finding someone who can. And although adoptees tend to reassure adoptive parents during reunion, reassurance should also flow from adoptive parents to their adopted child, with expressions that the adoptive parents support the reunion and are open to discussions about it, before, during, and after.

Participants reiterated the idea that adoptees undertake birth family search and reunion to know themselves more; they are not trying to replace their adoptive family. In other words, participants viewed search and reunions as a part of their own adoptive identity work (Horstman et al., 2016). Although participants in the current study said that they felt guilty when members of their adoptive family expressed emotions such as sadness surrounding the reunion, they also wanted to maintain open communication and to know what their adoptive parents were thinking and feeling. If these types of conversations have not been normalized before the reunion, perhaps the reunion can serve as a turning point for increased closeness, depending on the adoptive parents' willingness and communicative abilities.

As the people who had no agency or voice in the adoption process, adoptees should be the subjects of their own adoption and reunion stories. They must be empowered to communicate in ways that feel most natural and authentic to them; if they have questions for their birth family or want to express immediacy or affection toward them (or not), these are their decisions to make. This freedom will allow them to focus on their own identity, their birth family, and their reunion, rather than on their relationship with their adoptive family, which, ideally, would be resilient and steadfast, even in the midst of change.

6

Long-Term Relationships
with Birth Families

Communicating across Space, Time, and Difference

Fall 2017

We are at the house of my *keun oppa*, my oldest older brother. A decade ago, he left Seoul for a small town in the center of the country. Here, he and his wife can have a house and a garden for his vegetables, and his dog can play outside all day. My siblings are preparing for dinner while my kids play with their cousins. I watch as *keun oppa* sets two cinder blocks upright against a slope in his yard. He lays a smooth flat stone across the top of the blocks and makes adjustments until it sits level. My *jageun oppa* assists him, pausing to tell me what they are doing: Building a grill. Once the structure is complete, *keun oppa* stokes a fire between the cinder blocks, heating the flat surface. His wife emerges from the house, carrying white trays of *samgyeopsal*—sliced pork belly—a small pair of tongs, and kitchen scissors. *Eonni* follows, holding bowls of vegetables—curly leaf lettuce still wet from being washed and slender, bright green peppers. I help them make more trips, and soon the picnic table is set with *banchan*—kimchi and other various small side dishes eaten communally—and *ssamjang*—a spicy/savory paste for lettuce wraps—a jar with metal chopsticks and spoons, and covered aluminum bowls of warm rice. Soon, *keun oppa* and his wife begin to cook. She pinches a small piece of pork fat with tongs, gliding it across the hot grill top; the fat sizzles and melts, greasing the surface. Squatting, *keun oppa* takes the tongs and lays long strips of the meat flat on the grill. Daylight is turning to dusk, but I can see the meat browning at the edges as he turns and presses it until it turns golden. *Jageun oppa* squats by the grill as well, removing the cooked meat and using kitchen scissors to snip it into bite-size rectangles that fall into a shallow dish. He stands, motions us to the table, and we begin to eat. The flavors are contrast upon contrast—rich, fatty meat and delicate lettuce; warm rice and cold, spicy peppers that snap in my teeth. The table goes silent except for the smacking of lips savoring each bite.

After dinner, in the cool dark, everyone is in the house but my siblings and me. The fire is out, but its smell still perfumes the air. We sit at the table, sipping Cass beer out of cans. I can discern the shape of my siblings' bodies, but not their expressions; in the same way, I can hear their voices and their friendly, easy tones with one another, but I don't know what they are saying beyond an occasional word. I am overflowing: With the food of my birth country and my family. With love for the people at this table. With awe and gratitude that this moment is happening. With grief for knowing that long ago, I lost—and was lost to—my Korean family in a way that can never be fully regained. With guilt for feeling sadness about my adoption, which has, in some ways, made my life easier than theirs.

For me, a long-term relationship with my Korean family means to be able to sit with all of these emotions and contradictions, as well as a persistent unknowing. I love my Korean family and think about them multiple times each day, and I've told them this; yet I will never know with certainty if they understand what they mean to me. I know that they love me, but I still worry that I might, unknowingly, offend and alienate them. I dislike uncertainty, but to be in reunion, I must accept it. Yet, perhaps uncertainty—not knowing the future of our relationship—also leaves room for hope and the possibility of good moments that I am unable to anticipate, like the night at my *keun oppa's* house. When I was sitting at his outdoor table with my siblings, I thought to myself, "Remember this." I often visit this memory, not knowing if we will re-create it. In the meantime, whenever we text, I include the same message, one of the only ones I know how to type without having to check it in a translating app: " 보고 싶어요." *I miss you.* Or, more literally, *I want to see you.*

In the summer of 2020, during the height of the COVID-19 pandemic, I began second interviews with the adoptee participants I had spoken with ten years before. Having spent many hours reading, analyzing, and writing about the reunion stories they shared in their first interviews, I felt deep gratitude that they were willing to open up to me once again. They updated me on the changes and developments in their lives and relationships since our previous interview. All spoke of significant life events such as changing jobs, moving, finishing degrees, marriage, and/or becoming a parent, and they spoke of similar changes in the lives of their siblings in Korea. Two interviewees had returned from Korea after years of living there; one had moved to Korea recently. Another had moved to a different East Asian country and returned to the United States. Several had lost loved ones, including birth parents and adoptive parents. Some had visited Korea regularly, while an equal number had not returned since we last spoke. With the exception of one participant, Olivia, who indicated that she and her birth family had lost touch, all participants indicated that there had been at least some contact between themselves and their birth family since our last interview.

This chapter explores the nature of long-term relationships between transnational Korean adoptees and their birth families and the communication that maintains or changes these relationships. In many ways, the odds are stacked against transnational adoptees and birth families who wish to remain in contact over time. There are the undeniable realities of geographical distance, different time zones, the expense and time of travel, and challenges due to cultural and language differences. In addition, uncertainty and continual ambiguity often characterize these relationships, planting questions just below the surface: What *are* we to one another? Are we perceiving this relationship or conversation the same way? Am I acting the way I should be? and more. Participants described the challenges of long-term reunion relationships as well as the reasons they continue to maintain them.

Although each reunion story is unique, I describe some of the particularities of communication and circumstance that make some participants' relationships with birth families seem more rewarding and enjoyable than others, or that enable family members to move past moments of hurt and frustration. At the same time, I wish to underscore that these descriptions of interactions and relationships are subjective and dynamic: The meanings that participants have ascribed to their exchanges with their birth family members may be different than the meanings ascribed by the birth family, and all parties' perceptions of their relationship are likely to change due to time, experience, and circumstance. Perhaps the dynamism of relationships has helped participants to be steadfast and hopeful in times of struggle or conflict.

Changes in Families and Perspectives

Situational and Technological Changes

In addition to changes in their personal or professional lives since our last interview, participants mentioned changes in their birth families and the means by which they communicate with them. Participants spoke of how the death or illness of a birth parent, marriage of siblings, and/or the birth and growing up of nieces and nephews led to changes in their communication with them. Those whose siblings, nieces, and nephews had been children during earlier meetings had grown into teenagers navigating Korea's competitive education system, young men preparing for or returning from Korea's mandatory eighteen-month military service, or young adults working jobs in a country with one of the longest workweeks of all Organization for Economic Cooperation and Development (OECD) countries.[1] These changes necessitated shifts in interactions as well. Some participants' siblings who had been able to meet at restaurants or go out drinking during previous visits had gotten married and had children, which limited their availability and flexibility. Participants spoke of how their siblings' work schedules limited their spare time, which explained delays in communication while apart. Multiple interviewees expressed uncertainty as to whether a parent was even alive presently, as long lapses in communication were common and some birth parents did not use mobile phones or other technology such as e-mail.

Relatedly, since the first interviews a decade ago, technology has developed in ways that have eased communication between participants and their birth families. Smartphones have given people continual and unlimited access to communicating internationally. From 2011 to 2021, U.S. smartphone ownership increased from 35 percent to 85percent (Pew Research Center, 2021); in Korea, the respective numbers are 21.6 percent to 91 percent (Statista, 2022). Smartphone penetration in Scandinavian countries is even higher, at 92 percent in 2019 (Malmlund et al., 2019). Almost simultaneously, social media sites such as Facebook and Instagram, both of which launched in 2010, as well as the Korean messaging app KakaoTalk, which was also launched in 2010, has made connecting via text and video chat free (as long as the user has a smartphone, mobile number, and data or Wi-Fi) and convenient. Participants spoke of texting photos back and forth with their birth family or communicating via direct message, often with the help of translating apps. Most participants described using social media and KakaoTalk in tandem with apps such as Google Translate or Naver Papago. Participants often received text messages from a Korean relative, in Korean, and then used an app to translate the message into English. Then, to reply, participants performed the sequence in reverse, typing a message in English, using an app to translate it into Korean, and sending the Korean message to their Korean relative. Participants did, however, indicate that sometimes the translations from Korean into English were slightly confusing or unclear and that they had to type their message in a simplified form to minimize mistranslations, but overall, this technology allowed more frequent and more informal communication between participants and their birth families.

Some participants, however, described how their birth parents' lack of technology use made communication difficult. For example, Hanne encountered an array of challenges in maintaining a relationship with her birth mother since the first and only time they met, in 2009. Because her birth mother did not use a smartphone or have Internet access, their only method of communication was handwritten letters that were translated by either Hanne's adoption agency or one of her friends in her adoptive country. This process made communication slow and infrequent. In addition, her Korean mother experienced socioeconomic struggles and moved many times, leaving Hanne reliant on her adoption agency to find out her mother's updated contact information. At the time of our second interview, Hanne hadn't heard from her birth mother in several years, and because her mother had disclosed that she had a chronic illness in the past, Hanne wasn't certain whether or not her mother was still alive.

In contrast, Alexander reported a close relationship with his birth mother and discussed their reliance on technology. He had traveled to Korea approximately every other year since his initial meeting, and he and his mother use KakaoTalk along with translating apps to maintain their relationship when apart. Alexander estimated that he and his Korean mother communicate with each other about every other month, sometimes just exchanging pictures of flowers. He described how, despite her busy work schedule, they remain in regular contact, saying,

> We've just become a lot closer with the communication. It definitely helps with the apps. I know the time difference is a little bit hard to get in contact, but I know that if I send a message, she'll respond to it as quickly as possible.

Alexander attributes their closer relationship in part to technology, making particular mention of the promptness of his mother's responses. This interpretation of short response times has been found in past nonverbal communication research on texting, where long response times may be perceived as uneasy silences, and short response times can be interpreted as signs of thoughtfulness, eagerness, or closeness (Döring & Pöschl, 2017). Thus, although technology facilitates communication, relational meanings can often be found beyond the words that are exchanged.

Translation apps allowed participants to communicate directly with members of their birth family through texts rather than relying on an adoption agency worker or other interpreter as intermediaries. In addition, when participants were physically together with their birth family without an interpreter, they tended to use these apps when they or someone in their Korean family couldn't convey a message in a way that was understandable to the other person.

Participants also mentioned communicating with their birth families through social media, such as Instagram or Facebook, much more than in their previous interviews. Although younger members (e.g., siblings) of birth families were more likely to use social media than older members, there were exceptions. Sylvia spoke of how she and her birth father communicate via Instagram direct message and how he recently started following her fourteen-year-old daughter and direct messaging her, which Sylvia appreciated. She expressed that she feels closer to her birth father than her birth mother because he is "making an effort" in their relationship. This example is notable because it was the outreach to her daughter, not just herself, that Sylvia viewed as meaningful. Other participants spoke of how it was nice to be able to simply see photos of their birth families on social media and "like" one another's posts. These minimal means of communication provided a sense of connection and acknowledgment, which can help maintain relationships over time (Butler & Matook, 2015).

Changes in Perspective

Perspectives on Birth Family

Importantly, participants talked about changes within themselves, how time and growing up have given them maturity and perspective to see their birth family and their relationship in a more empathetic and nuanced way. When I spoke with Jorgen in 2011, he told me, "I'm not part of [my birth family] and I don't know that I will ever be." In the decade between our two interviews, Jorgen went to Korea approximately every other year and spent time with his birth family during each trip. During his second interview, nearly twenty years after his initial reunion, I read this quote back to him and asked him if he felt the same way about his place in his birth family. He replied,

> Yeah, it's definitely the same, I think. Hundred percent the same. But now I'm okay with it. I guess maybe at that point I wasn't that okay with it. But now I'm actually really okay with it. I guess it's just because I got older (laughs) and I got more wisdom, which is a good thing. Some people get wiser and I think I got a little bit wiser, I guess. And also, I don't have this demanding attitude of other people, of my family, not even my family in Denmark or my family in Korea. I have another philosophy now. Whereas, like, if I want something to happen, it's de-

pending on me. And it's more about what I can give others and what I'm able to receive if somebody wants to give me, but I'm really the one in charge of my own happiness. So I think that changed my perspective.

Jorgen described how, in the early days of his relationship, he used to spend more time with his birth mother and her side of the family, but in recent visits, he has chosen to spend less time with them and to stay at a hotel rather than with his birth family. His half-brothers on his mother's side have gotten married and have had children, so they often meet for a meal and to catch up, but he is "content" with these interactions. He described their time together, saying,

> Well, it's more like visiting, which *it is*, distant relatives which I don't really know that well. And yeah, we just talk about, "What are you doing? What am I doing?" So it's mostly more an exchange of some information. And of course, spending time and also enjoying each other's company and being happy to see each other because we have some connection. . . . But I think I have come to terms with our relationship. And also, I guess I have a more positive idea about what it is I got out of this. And I'm quite content with the interactions I had and I still have with my family. I'm not seeking another family. I'm not trying to make them repair something that maybe was broken inside of me.

Jorgen's words convey a change in his expectations and evaluations of the relationship. He views his birth family as "distant relatives" with whom he has a meaningful connection, and he feels content with this level of closeness. This acceptance and understanding, however, took him many years and a great deal of self-reflection to achieve.

Nikki also described changes in herself since her one and only reunion meeting with her birth mother in 2009. Since then, Nikki's birth mother has either not responded to the e-mails Nikki sent through her Korean adoption agency social worker, or she has sent very brief responses with no follow-up questions for Nikki. She also "refused" Nikki's requests for her personal e-mail address or updated photos of Nikki's half-siblings, who do not know that their mother has a child who was relinquished for adoption. Nikki stated that making peace with her mother's lack of engagement in the relationship has been "very difficult," but she described how her perspective has changed over time, stating, "So, I think it's evolved that way, where it's *not* the center of my life. It's an added benefit when I get [a response] back. It doesn't drive me in the same way it used to drive me." When I asked her what contributed to this change, she replied,

I think when I realized after a couple of years that it took her longer and she was no longer writing me back. First I had to remove myself and process it myself and then later on, kind of put it more reflective as to her perspective on what she was feeling, not so much about me. Because I think, we do that for *all* relationships or should, you know, where we think about how *we* feel, but then also say, "Well, how is it towards the other person," and then we get more of a better connection and relationship with the other. So, I think it took me many years to kind of get out of my *own* selfishness and me-me-me and why-why-why types of things and to really look at it from her perspective and say there's probably a lot of other things going on in her life, emotionally, physically, who knows? And so, I think taking the focus away from myself.

Like Alexander, Nikki interpreted her birth mother's response times as a relational message, but in her case, a long response time was viewed as a lack of interest in the relationship. In addition, Nikki had reflected extensively on what her mother's life might be like and how stressful it would be for her mother to keep Nikki a secret from her current husband and their children. Over time, Nikki came to believe that her mother's apparent lack of interest in their relationship stems from a need for secrecy and fear of being discovered as someone who relinquished a child. As much as Nikki had hoped for more of a connection and a relationship with her Korean mother, she also recognized that investing deeply in the relationship was causing her too much pain. She elaborated, "I think, for me, it's what's *healthiest*, to give myself that rationale and that story. Because it just, it feels right when I analyze it, but it also feels right emotionally, you know, in how I process it all." Nikki's acceptance of her mother's actions did not mean that she lost hope, however. Nikki continues to send e-mails to her Korean mother one to two times per year, via her Korean social worker. Often, it is a photo and a very brief description, such as a photo of her son on his birthday with a caption several words long. These occasional outreach attempts have replaced Nikki's earlier and lengthier e-mails in which she would ask her mother questions about her life and their relationship. These brief e-mails allow Nikki to maintain a connection and preserve her hope of a stronger relationship without the large investment of time, emotion, or energy she used to expend.

Distinguishing between Cultural versus Personal
Many participants expressed an increased ability to understand their birth parents' behaviors as reflections of Korean culture rather than as reflections of themselves or their birth parents' feelings about them. Over time, they had

learned to situate their family's circumstances within a larger historical context of war, poverty, and the cultural oppression of women, as described in Chapter 1. Doing so enabled them to view potentially hurtful messages from their birth family as less personal. Research suggests that, in general, communicators vary in the extent to which they tend to take conflict personally, and that people who take conflict personally tend to experience hurt feelings as a result of others' messages and experience feelings of stress and/or discomfort (Curran & Arroyo, 2018; Hample & Dallinger, 1995). Nearly all interviewees spoke of experiencing hurt feelings and/or discomfort as a result of messages from their birth family. Over time and with considerable reflection on their own part, most participants learned to attribute their birth family's communication to Korean culture, which allowed them to understand their family's perspective better.

Catherine, who had been in reunion for twenty years, starting at the age of ten, described an evolution in how she sees her birth father, whose previous communication with her tended to be inflexible, critical, and hierarchical. She recalled an observation from her last visit, saying,

> My birth father's lost a bunch of his teeth, like, he's just this old man, just like, not in great health, and he's playing with some of his grandkids, like my sister's kids, and there was so much joy, actually, in his face. And I was just realizing, like, here's an old man who's sitting here, who did the best he could with his context and what he's learned of the world and what he knows. And this is all he could do. And not that there's not some sort of responsibility and that I wasn't affected, but like, from his perspective, that's just what his life has been, you know, and so I think, to be able to get to that point was pretty crazy and I didn't realize . . . I feel like having that perspective, then, his attitude, what he's saying, it's not so much about me, it's like this cultural difference, right, where that's just how he talks to all his daughters. (small laugh)

Catherine was not the only participant to discuss a shift in her ability to see her Korean family's communication as a reflection of culture and to take it less personally. Mee Joo spoke of a similar evolution over the seventeen years she has been in reunion, many of which she spent living in Korea. She shared stories of how it was very common for her birth family to either withhold seemingly important information from her, such as her father's cancer diagnosis and condition, or for her birth mother to treat her differently than she treated Mee Joo's older siblings. She also described her internal process of trying to understand their interactions in the context of Korean culture, saying,

Is it because I'm adopted? Is it because I don't understand, that they're not telling me? Like, is it a language thing, is it a cultural thing, is it? You know, it is trying to kind of almost go through this list of, like, moving it from, like, your heart space into your head space and back, and trying to contextualize it and understand it all. And realizing some of it is cultural, like some of what they're doing; not telling me things is cultural, I've learned, which has helped me to a certain extent, not take it quite so personally. It's not just me. It's not just because I'm adopted. This is just how Koreans are in their families. "What is the point?" is the mindset, like, "What is the point of bothering this person with that information, like we're the older ones. It's our responsibility, we'll take care of it." But you know, those are the things that make it really *hard*, because even then, it still takes so long to process it, to first understand that, okay, there *are* factors that are cultural about this and that, and then to accept it (small laugh) because I think especially coming from a Western mindset, some of this, just, like, doesn't make sense to me. And then to have to put it into like this context of, like, Korea and Korean culture and to understand it that way, it lessens it. . . . So those are challenges that, you know, to a certain extent, I would learn to live with over time, and to some extent, are comfortable, I have gotten comfortable with, but to another extent, I don't know if I'll ever really be comfortable with it.

Participants like Catherine and Mee Joo had to learn what it means to be a member of their specific Korean family, which was situated within the Korean cultural context. The family dynamics they and others experienced, such as criticism and secrecy, were based on traditional Korean cultural assumptions about family relationships. Because parents are assumed to know what is best for their children, the children are expected to respect their parents and to view their criticism as helpful. Similarly, from this cultural lens, secrecy is viewed as protective, whereby the older members of the family (parents and older siblings) shield younger members from worry or pain by not sharing certain information. Although criticism and secrecy are common in Western family communication as well, the challenge for participants was learning to see how these dynamics manifest in Korean culture and, consequently and ideally, to take them less personally. Whereas participants were raised with their adoptive families and had spent their lifetimes gaining an understanding and unspoken acceptance of their family's assumptions and behaviors, they had spent limited time with their birth families. As a result, it often took participants years to make sense of their birth family's communication and its cultural dimensions. As Mee Joo's words illustrate, a full and complete understanding may be unattainable. Although she had lived in Korea the longest of all participants and had the most experience with Korean culture, her words are rife with contradiction: Between the cultural and the personal, between the heart and the head, between the comfortable and uncomfortable. An acceptance of these unresolvable contradictions may be necessary for adoptees' long-term relationships with birth families.

The process of thinking from a cultural perspective and accepting unresolvable tensions required effort and self-reflection, but doing so seemed to help reduce the hurt participants felt. They talked about their own sensemaking processes, which were complex and metacognitive: Participants like Mee Joo had to put themselves in their birth family's metaphorical shoes, in a cultural context that they didn't fully understand, and, sometimes, imagine a developing but economically struggling Korea that is a stark contrast to the modern, wealthy Korea they experience today. They had to understand their own cultural assumptions as Westerners and distance themselves from their own ethnocentric bias that the way they have come to see the world is somehow "right." At the same time, participants were often navigating language differences, dealing with the logistics of travel/life in a foreign country, and/or processing their own grief related to adoption. Long-term relationships with birth families may offer opportunities for healing and reconnection, but these relationships demand a great deal from adoptees mentally, emotionally, and physically.

Mee Joo described how, when she was living in Korea, on the rare occasion that her birth mother would call her, she would ask Mee Joo "mundane" questions such as whether she was sleeping well or eating well. Over time, Mee Joo came to understand these conversations as situated in a historical and cultural context. She explained that it took her

a really long time, years, to really kind of accept that that was just *normal* and that it didn't necessarily have anything to do with them not having anything to say to me. Like, that was kind of like asking someone like, "How is the weather?" but it was just part of a cultural *thing*. And just, really again, getting to a place where I could understand it and then, not just understand that in my head . . . I don't know, this sounds a little cheesy, but accept it in my heart. And *feel* really comfortable with it. That that's just *totally normal*. And understand where that was coming from, you know. Even for example, in a historical context, where people would say ["Did you eat well?"], because in the Korean War, you just literally didn't know if someone had a meal. You wanted to check, to see that they actually, did they eat, did they eat well. So there's all these layers and all these nuances that I think you go through over time. And it's not just this learning all about it intellectually, but really *feeling* it, how it affects people and integrating it into your own life, to the point where you can say it and you can understand why you're saying it. Not just because it's something you learned in a book or you hear other people doing it, but because it's just natural to do.

This long process enabled Mee Joo and other adoptees to recalibrate their hopes and expectations for their relationships with members of their birth family and to shift away from Westernized idealizations of reunion to the work of building a relationship. This emotional and cognitive work was also necessary for participants to protect themselves from feeling hurt by their birth parents' messages. At the same time, this type of inner work is a choice. Jorgen articulated this perspective very clearly. After he told me that his birth mother has never told her current husband about Jorgen's existence, I asked him if it bothered him. He responded,

In the beginning, it did a lot. It's like, "Wow, why? It must mean something." I *could* make it mean something in my mind, that she didn't want to tell. But then over the years I've been thinking about it and just come to terms with that's the way they choose to live their life.

Jorgen's words reflect the complicated processes of attributions in communication, which refer to a communicator's subjective interpretation or assessment of another person's, or one's own, behavior (Manusov, 2018). Adoptees in reunion are likely to experience novel ways of interacting when communicating with their birth family and, as a result, will try to understand and provide explanations for what they experience. These explanations, or attributions, involve multiple dimensions, including responsibility (How much control or influence does the other person have over their behavior?), valence (To what extent is this behavior positive or negative?), consensus (Have other people experienced this behavior?), and distinctiveness (Do other people act this way?) (Manusov, 2018). As participants matured and learned more about the history of transnational Korean adoption, their own family's circumstances, and patterns in how Korean families interact, they were often able to attribute their family's messages to Korean culture and see their family's actions as a result of having a small repertoire of choices: Their birth parents only knew Korean culture and Korean families, and were, in some ways, constrained in their ability to act differently. Participants attempted to provide culturally based explanations of actions that they found hurtful or puzzling (e.g., criticism and secrecy) while still acknowledging the difficulty and pain that these interactions had caused them. Participants learned to accept the inherent tension between recognizing and validating their own experiences, emotions, and limitations while doing the same for members of their birth family. All of the participants discussed how it took years to really understand the cultural components of their birth family's communication and to not internalize messages or interactions that caused them hurt or confusion. This process is multilayered and challenging particularly because of the emotional investment involved in reunion. Participants expressed the desire for their birth families to like them, or they spoke of their own fear of rejection or abandonment by their birth families. They wanted to make these relationships work, which motivated them to want to understand their birth families while still minimizing their own frustration or hurt.

Ashley spoke of this evolution when she told me about how her birth parents and sister traveled to the United States for her wedding. Although they attended the wedding ceremony and reception, they did not attend the extra events in the days prior, where they would have had the opportunity to interact with members of Ashley's extended family who were excited to meet them. Ashley, however, spoke of how she understood that her birth parents likely experienced a lot of shame for not raising her and were also exhausted from the international travel and overwhelmed at being in an English-speaking context. She said, "I think ten years ago I would have been, like, 'Oh, what the heck, like, they're not open to meeting my family and stuff.' But now, I know it probably just, like, was a lot for them." Rather than taking her birth parents' behavior personally and feeling offended, Ashley was able to attribute their behaviors to culture, circumstance, and language.

Understanding Transnational Korean Adoption: Political and Personal

In second interviews, participants spoke increasingly of their awareness of the politics of transnational Korean adoption and the larger social, economic, and political forces that impacted the trajectory of their lives. Whether it was through interacting with other Korean adoptees online or in person, or reading about the topic, interviewees spoke of issues such as deception by orphanages and adoption agencies, ensuing trauma for birth families and adoptees, power discrepancies between women and men in Korea, and the lack of agency for single mothers in Korea. They observed the disjuncture among the ways transnational adoption is often framed as a happy ending for adoptees and their adoptive families, while birth families, who are usually omitted from adoption stories, often experience deep, lifelong loss. Christine, who was a few days away from turning thirty at the time of her second interview, articulated her change in perspective, saying,

> I feel like as I'm getting older, I'm feeling so much more connected to my birth parents' side of the story, because I'm realizing that I'm getting closer and closer to the age that my birth mother had *me*. And so, you know, when I was younger, so much of my perception of adoption was what my family *here* has always kind of promoted and spread: This idea of, like, "Adoption is amazing and it created a family and, you know, it's so great that we're all together and it's a beautiful thing." And it's not that it's *not* that, but there's also this other side to adoption that I am very strongly starting to be more aware of, which is, there's so much grief, there's so much loss, there's so much hardship, there's so much heartbreak. And, you know, at the same time it created a family, it also, like, tore a family apart.

In the years since our previous interview, Christine had returned to the United States from living abroad, had gotten married, and had graduated from college with a degree in anthropology. These life events, maturing from age twenty to thirty, and her propensity to reflect on her adoption and reunion all contributed to her increased empathy for her birth mother and the rest of her birth family.

Participants who had lived in Korea for extended periods (a year or more) were also likely to talk about how their experience of living in Korea impacted their opinions on transnational Korean adoption. Some mentioned interactions with Korean adoptees doing advocacy and activism work in Korea; others had been involved in this work themselves. Mark spoke of how living in Korea for a total of six years and interacting with his birth family shaped his view of the practice, saying,

> Even though I didn't necessarily go back [to Korea] with the intention of, you know, trying to understand, say, the neocolonial relationship between the U.S. and Korea, like, I didn't go back to research on *that*. I feel like I've lived it. I guess it's really weird to say, like, my (small laugh) political ideology is, like, the most rewarding thing about it, but it speaks to one's understanding of the forces that shape them and that shape the world. And that, I would say, is something that I feel I've gained from it, and I feel *lucky* to have gained that.

Today, there are an estimated three hundred to five hundred transnational Korean adoptees living in Korea (Jones, 2015), although there is a continuous flow of adoptees entering while others are leaving. Organizations for and by Korean adoptees host regular events where adoptees can connect with one another while learning more about the search and reunion experiences of other adoptees, current adoption law in Korea, advocacy for adoptee rights, and alliances between adoptees and single mothers in Korea. These experiences were instrumental in contextualizing several participants' relationships with their birth families, giving them more vantage points for viewing their own experiences and enabling them to see their birth families' communication as a function of culture and cultural constraints.

Lingering Questions

Participants tended to have one of three answers when I asked them during second interviews if they had any remaining questions for their birth families, addressing what has been called the "adoption information gap" (Wrobel & Grotevant, 2019). Most participants said that yes, they still had questions for their birth families and hoped for the opportunity to ask them at some point; others still had questions but emphasized the importance of "not pushing" for responses; and finally, a few participants either felt that their questions had been answered or had "made peace" with not knowing.

Eric, a professional actor, was among those who still have questions. He stated that he plans to continue asking them, in part for his older Korean brother, his *hyeong*, as they have grown close over the years. During his initial meeting and in subsequent visits to Korea, Eric has pieced together some of the reasons for his relinquishment, although his mother and father have provided different accounts: Whereas his father told him that he was working and drinking too much, his mother said that Eric was relinquished because his father was abusive and she was running from him constantly. His *hyeong* has a clearer memory, yet his story contains gaps: Not long after Eric was sent abroad for adoption, his *hyeong*, who was almost four years old at the time, was riding his bike, got in an accident, and couldn't find his way home. He was picked up by the police, but, as a young child, he was too scared to tell them where he lived. He ended up being taken to a Catholic workhouse with very difficult conditions for children, where he stayed until he graduated from high school. To his knowledge, their parents didn't look for him.

Because of the discrepancies between his father's and his mother's stories and because of the outlandish nature of his brother's experience, Eric still believes that he is missing key information. He said,

> I don't think that I'm ever gonna stop wanting to know the rest of those stories, you know. I'm always gonna try to fill things in, in terms of

hyeong's and my early life. Because the other thing about it is we weren't babies, you know. I was almost three and he was almost four, so like, we *had lives* in Korea. I had a life in Korea, and that's the thing, I'm not trying to fill in a *few months* before I was adopted, I'm trying to fill in a few *years* and it's disappointing. As much as I feel like I'm someone who, in my *career*, like, engages with story and narrative, it's so frustrating how hard it is to fill in those pieces, like, *impossible* in many ways. But I think I just keep trying, keep wanting to have that conversation that's going to make things *somewhat* clearer, find out even like, where I was born (chuckles), you know. Like I talk to different sides of the family and they're like, "Oh, yeah, you were born here," and then my mother would be like, "No, I think it was over here." Like, nobody actually knows, because, of course, Seoul looks completely different than it did in the eighties. (Pause.) Yeah. I'm still, I guess I'm still on the hunt.

Part of the reason Eric remains "on the hunt" for answers is that he wants to find answers for his *hyeong*. He continues, saying,

The other *main* question is, What happened to *hyeong*? Like, it's still not a satisfying answer about how he was, like, in this bus accident on his bike and got lost and taken to this, like, workhouse, and you know, I don't think those are lies. I think those things happened, but I think there's a whole other part of it that I'm not privy to. And that *hyeong* is also not privy to, you know. And (pause) that's *so* frustrating. When you're picturing this little kid, *hyeong*, and there's horrible things happening to him and there's nobody there to take care of or look for him. And that really still weighs heavy on him as well. I think, you know, I think there's a lot of missing pieces for him too. And, you know, I think in general, it comes down to, like, "Why didn't you guys just *care more*?" Basically. And that's why you can't get a satisfying answer. Because nobody can actually answer that question. They can say, "Oh, I was drunk," my father. My mother can say, "Oh, I was running from your father." They can't answer that kind of nebulous thing about like, "Why were you just not available when he needed you?"

When I asked him how he attempts to get answers to his questions, he responded,

I just ask. I pull out my notebook. So, I have notebooks of basically, like, the same story told in six different, confusing ways. But I'll say, like, to *eomeoni*, "Can you please tell me *again*, basically, the story of our lives *before* I was adopted?"

Eric stated that neither his birth mother's nor his birth father's memory is very good, making it difficult to elicit a cohesive or coherent narrative of the events that unfolded during that time almost forty years ago. Eric recognized that their lack of clear memory of the past may be attributable to trauma, which can inhibit the ability to articulate one's feelings or retell stories about profoundly painful experiences (Van Der Kolk, 1998). Eric expressed frustration that it has been so difficult to obtain information from his birth parents, and yet he is tenacious in his efforts to gain understanding, both for himself and his *hyeong*.

Christine recognized the tension between her continued desire for answers and the costs of making her birth parents revisit painful events from their past. She explained,

> I *have so many questions that I personally want to know the answers to* (frustrated voice) that I know are gonna be *so painfully hard* for my birth family to answer. And it stops me from asking the questions that I actually really *want to know*, like, "How long did you *wait* to decide this? How did that happen? Did you *cry*? Like, do you celebrate my birthday when I'm not there? . . . How many years did you celebrate my birthday or not celebrate? What do you *do* when January twelfth comes around?" . . . I have so many other questions that I don't know if I'm actually gonna get answers to. Do I have the right to those answers? I mean, a part of me says, *yeah*, and then a part of me is like, "Well, do you have a right to make somebody feel like shit for, like, answering questions that really have no, like, lasting" (trails off). I don't know, you know what I mean? Like, *I* want [answers] because everybody else I know has access to those answers and again, it comes down to, I gotta protect *them*. I gotta make sure that I'm not *causing* more pain from *my* pain because I don't want to be that person either.

Christine's words reflect her strong desire to ask questions of her birth family, and a simultaneous, contradicting urge to protect them from discussing painful topics related to the past. She questions whether or not she has "the right" to these answers when they come at the expense of her family's emotions. Her words, which express the tension between self and selflessness, illustrate that sometimes family members avoid certain topics to protect one another or protect the relationship (Guerrero & Afifi, 1995). Catherine, who has been in reunion for over twenty years, starting at the age of ten, expressed a similar goal of protecting her birth family from pain, saying,

> Like, I've noticed, I've struggled with mental health things and just, like, self-worth, self-esteem, depression, kinds of things through the years, like, rejection, abandonment, all those things, and they've asked, kind of, not point-blank questions, but, you know, questions about those kinds of things, and I don't wanna say I've lied, but I haven't painted the most honest picture. It'll be kind of like the candy-coated version of things (small laugh) and so, in seeing how I want to protect them from that, I'm *sure* they're doing that for me, too, in some ways.

Catherine continued, indicating that her remaining questions relate more to the present rather than the past, and that she has made peace with not having answers to all her questions. She said,

> I think the questions I have are almost just like *any* questions you have when you're in a relationship with someone. Like, "Is this really how you feel?" like, there's moments of that . . . I mean, I think overall, I don't need to *ask*. Like, I think ten years ago, I would have been, like, I need to ask them, "Why did you give me up? Give me an honest answer," but I don't need to know. Like I know enough about the situation to kind of put it together and that's all I need, kind of.

Other participants also indicated that their remaining questions focused on their birth family's lives and thoughts now, not on the details of their relinquishment. Isabel stated that she and her birth family had already done the "hard" talks during her previous visits, but a close look at her words reveals that she has some remaining adoption-related questions that may be sensitive or challenging to discuss. She had not been back to Korea to see them since 2007, but she hoped to visit them again soon. She stated,

> You always want to know more details about them, I think, as individuals and people and their backstories and you know, I'd just like to learn more about what their lives have been together and how they kind of traversed the whole adoption subject, I guess. Maybe more their thoughts and feelings on that in general and, you know, there's still a question of my younger brother who I'm pretty sure is adopted and whether he knows that he is or not. It was kind of, you know, conveyed that he did not know that. So that would, I'd like to see what that situation (laughs) is like, or what he knows. And doesn't know.

Due to the cultural value placed on shared blood lines in families, most Koreans have resisted domestic adoption, despite the government's attempts to promote the practice (Cachero, 2018). Those who do adopt domestically may keep their child's adoption a secret (Ministry of Health and Welfare, 2013), which explains why Isabel's brother may not know about his adoption.

Overall, participants acknowledged that there were still unknowns in their relationship with their birth families, whether about their place in their family's history and story or who their birth family members are today. Language differences and lack of time together make it difficult for these information gaps to be filled, and for some birth parents, the loss of their child and the circumstances surrounding this loss were traumatic, which may impact their recall abilities. For most participants, questions about the past persisted years after the initial reunion, which suggests that conversations about family history are very rarely one-time events but rather an ongoing dialogue. Because the process of forging adoptive identity can depend on adoptees' developmental stage and age (Wrobel & Grotevant, 2019), different questions are likely to emerge at different times. In addition, the way in which participants viewed information from their birth families also shifted over time, particularly as they came to understand Korean culture and history more deeply. Regardless, if adoptees and birth families are able to accept that the process of making meaning is without end, or "forever unfinalizable" (Baxter, 2011, p. 31), they may be able to communicate with more flexibility and tolerance for uncertainty.

Perceived Effort in Relationship Maintenance

From a communication perspective, relationships between all adult members of families are at least somewhat voluntary. Although the biological relation between family members is unalterable, the communication that constitutes the *relationship* itself can be suspended or stopped at any time. It is not uncommon to hear an American say, "I don't have a relationship with my father" or "I have a sister, but we don't really have a relationship," meaning that they do not communicate with one another or, at least, not in a way that the speaker finds meaningful or satisfying. In other words, from a Western perspective, a "relationship" necessitates communication between the people involved, even if the people are genetically related to one another. However, the communication (i.e., verbal and nonverbal messages) necessary to maintain these relationships and the criteria constituting satisfying relationships are highly subjective and cultural.

Relational maintenance refers to the efforts that people undertake to keep a relationship in existence or at its current level of closeness (Dindia, 2003).

For the most part, these behaviors have been studied in voluntary, non-familial relationships such as romantic relationships and friendships, but relational maintenance is also necessary among family members (Vogl-Bauer et al., 1999), such as young adults and their parents (Morr Serewicz et al., 2007) and adult siblings (Mikkelson et al., 2011). In American cultural contexts, prominent maintenance behaviors include positivity (being cheerful and positive), openness (self-disclosure about the relationship), assurances (showing love and commitment to the relationship), sharing tasks (helping equally with shared responsibilities), and social networks (including friends and other family members to help maintain the relationship) (Canary & Stafford, 1992). These maintenance strategies have been found to be important, as they are correlated with liking, commitment, and satisfaction in relationships (Stafford & Canary, 1991). Shared activities and rituals, such as family meals and/or vacations, can also help maintain family relationships, as they create collective memories that serve as a basis for family communication during and after. The popular American assumption that close relationships require "work" presumes the importance of relational maintenance. However, relational maintenance, both as a concept and a practice, is cultural. Over the years, a number of participants experienced differences in how they and their birth families maintained—or did not maintain—their relationship.

Cultural Differences in Relational Maintenance

Given that assumptions about self, other, and family relationships vary cross-culturally, it follows that relational maintenance would also vary across cultures. Research on relational maintenance has been conducted primarily in White, middle-class American contexts, where communicators default to the assumption that equity and social exchange characterize good relationships. From this cultural perspective, people in a relationship are expected to contribute equally to relational maintenance through investments such as time, effort, and resources, and both partners should benefit equally from the relationship (Dainton & Zelley, 2006). Indeed, the Western assumption that good relationships are horizontal (where partners perceive one another as equals) implies equity and social exchange in maintaining relationships. However, in cultures like Korea, where adherence to hierarchical, vertical relationships is valued, equity seems much less relevant and important (Yum & Canary, 2009). Differences in cultural assumptions about the nature of relationships lead naturally to differences in how people maintain these relationships.

Communication researchers Young Ok Yum and Daniel Canary (2003) explored several features of Korean culture that may help explain cultural differences in relational maintenance. These concepts are *eui-ri* (의리), *jeong*[2] (정), and *yon*[3] (연). In describing these concepts, I do not presume that all Koreans or all Westerners view or maintain relationships in the same way. Rather, these Korean cultural assumptions may provide a possible, or partial, explanation for some of the differences in how participants and their birth families maintained their relationships.

Eui-ri (의리) is a Korean concept denoting attachment and loyalty to one's relational partner. According to Yum and Canary, *eui-ri* "presumes a long-term, obligatory nature and asymmetrical reciprocity in interpersonal relationships" (2003, p. 282). Koreans who presume that relationships are long-term and obligatory "likely take for granted their partners' intention to stay in the relationship and pay relatively little attention to what their partners contribute to and what they receive in ongoing relationships" (p. 282). In contrast, Westerners tend to think of close, ongoing relationships as requiring mutual effort and investment, suggesting the importance of maintenance strategies and a balanced give-and-take from relational partners (i.e., equity). Based on these differing assumptions, Westerners are more prone than Koreans to think that a relationship needs to be maintained and to engage in a mental calculation of their relational maintenance efforts relative to those of their partner or family member.

Jeong (정) is a broad and somewhat ambiguous concept that has no direct translation into English. *Jeong* can be thought of as a feeling *within* one's heart and as a bond *between* people in a relationship. *Jeong* "requires a long history of interaction, mutual experiences, deeply rooted feelings, and mutual interdependence" (Yum & Canary, 2003, p. 283). Some of the feelings that *jeong* connotes include love, passion, and sympathy. At the same time, *jeong* is also thought to exist when the boundaries between self and other have dissipated, making the idea of exchange, or give-and-take, in a relationship irrelevant (Lee, 1994). Instead, there is an assumption and a shared understanding that the relationship will be ongoing (Chung & Cho, 2003). *Jeong* contrasts sharply with the value of equity underlying many Westerners' relationships; when *jeong* exists between people, maintenance efforts and individual benefits are considered irrelevant.

Yon (연) refers to the belief that forces beyond one's control determine a relationship's trajectory. According to Yum and Canary (2003), "Without *yon*, the relationship will fall apart no matter what relational maintenance strategy the partners enact, which will naturally discourage individuals from exerting conscious communicative efforts to maintain a relationship" (p. 284). This fatalistic belief implies that relational maintenance may be unnecessary in a relationship that is "meant to be" and useless in a relationship that is destined to fail.

As *eui-ri*, *jeong*, and *yon* are Korean cultural assumptions, birth families likely do not discuss them, just as Westerners do not discuss social exchange explicitly. Although these assumptions exist below consciousness, they help guide individuals' communication and serve as a basis for understanding—or misunderstanding—others.

Efforts to Keep in Touch

Taken together, *eui-ri*, *jeong*, and *yon* provide an explanation for why participants often felt that they had to initiate communication with their birth family and that their efforts were neither reciprocated nor balanced. Whether via texts, social media, e-mail, or video/phone calls, most participants expressed the idea that if communication were to occur, the discursive burden, or responsibility, was on them to initiate it. Notably, the frequency with which participants mentioned this observation reaffirms the idea that perceived equity in relationships is often important to Westerners. For example, Isabel observed,

> I've always had the impression from them that it's on me to reach out first, you know, they've never really reached out to me, and I, you know, it was explained that it was kinda more of a cultural thing. They won't really reach out unless there's some big *reason* to, or a death or something like that. So, you know, it kinda puts pressure on me to kinda be the one to reach out. And then if I don't, then I kinda start feeling a little guilty and feeling that I need to go [to Korea] . . . I've always told them, you know, please feel free to reach out to me (laughs). Not that they've ever taken me up on that offer. . . . Just having the pressure and that that's all on me to maintain that relationship. So it would be nice if they would get in touch with me every once in a while. . . . And it's also on top of your life and, you know, this part is definitely very *emotional* too, you know, you don't necessarily always want to go there (laughs) because when you do start thinking about those things or making efforts, you know, there's that emotion that's wrapped up in it too. It makes it a little bit more difficult.

Although Isabel's birth family does not initiate contact with her, she feels guilty if too much time passes without her going to Korea or getting in touch with them. She feels "pressure," a word she uses twice here, to maintain the relationship, a discursive burden. Although she attributes their lack of initiating contact to culture, she wishes this burden could be shared, especially given the emotional weight of adoption and reunion. When Christine was still in college, she articulated similar sentiments surrounding efforts to reach out to her birth family, saying,

> It's not that I'm, like, *reluctant* to talk to my birth family. It's just I know it's so much more work and it's really *exhausting* to delve back into those emotions and have to think about it. So a lot of times, it's just like, I just don't really want to have to deal with this right now. Like, I have homework to do. Like, I don't want to have to *really* put myself in that position again and force myself to think about it right now. You know, that's really hard. And I know a lot of people who may or may not have met their birth parents or don't understand adoption would be like, "Why would you not want to stay in contact with your birth family? Why would you not want to do that?" And it's not that I don't *want* to, it's just the process is so hard. And it's so exhausting. And it's just *emotionally* draining to reopen that, you know, that box. And be vulnerable to it. It's so hard.

Both Isabel and Christine spoke of how they felt fortunate to be in reunion when not all adoptees who want to reunite are able to do so. At the same time, this sense of good fortune created an additional discursive burden regarding maintaining the relationship with their birth families. Their words underscore that remaining in contact with their birth families requires emotional investment as well as an investment of time in the face of other life obligations. Birth families also have similar constraints, but perhaps they assume that maintaining contact in between visits is unnecessary due to *eui-ri*, *yon*, and *jeong*.

Eric expressed frustration and confusion over how some of his birth family members, his birth parents in particular, have never contacted him when he is in the United States. During his second interview, he articulated,

> The thing is that it's a one-way street. I am the one that is always reaching out to them. My brother contacts me through, like, Kakao and stuff, but for *all* the rest of my family, I'm the one that always has to initiate. I've never heard from them *once* while I've been in the States over these ten years and that's *so* frustrating. It's so frustrating to have had a good reunion where love is expressed and, you know, they're asking for forgiveness, and it's like, no matter if I forgave them or not, it's just like, "Oh, well, that's kind of the end of the conversation," you know.

Participants spoke of talking with nonadopted Korean friends or other Korean adoptees about their family's lack of relational maintenance and were told that it was common for older people, including parents, to not initiate communication unless there was a specific reason. However, Eric found this explanation insufficient, saying,

> I tell other people this and they're like, "Yeah, it's the culture, it's the culture." I'm like, "Yeah, and also this culture that you're talking about, has been, like, torn apart because of their actions and they still do nothing." My parents' generation has done nothing to, like, try to mend that rift, you know, other than taking me out to dinner, which is not the same thing.

In contrast to those who wished their birth families would initiate contact more, Ashley expressed that she didn't mind having the responsibility of reaching out. She stated,

> In Korean society, it seems like it's mostly the responsibility of the children to, you know, reach out. Like, there's an elderly lady that we ended up becoming friends with when I was living in another [U.S.] city, and usually I'm the one to reach out to *her* as well for communication. So it seems like maybe that's a traditional thing for Koreans? I don't know for sure if that's true; I just figured in general, that's the responsibility of, like, the younger party or the child.

It took years, however, for Ashley to accept what she perceived as the imbalance between her and her birth family's efforts in maintaining the relationship. She recalled,

> They were always like, "Oh, we're gonna come to America," blah, blah, and they never did. I knew they never would. And I was like, (sigh) "I always come. I always go to Korea. Why can't they come to America?" and then I realized maybe like, it was like they felt shameful to meet my American family as a whole.

Over time, Ashley arrived at a different attribution for her birth parents' communication. Rather than interpreting their behavior as a lack of effort, she came to understand their actions as cultural and situational, which made her feel more empathetic and less frustrated.

Articulating another perspective, Christine expressed that she was "thankful" that she was in charge of initiating contact because it allowed their communication to be based on her "emotional calendar" and when she was prepared in some way. This imbalance gave her a perceived sense of control. Indeed, hearing from a birth family member unexpectedly or too often may evoke emotions that an adopted person may not wish to experience at a given time. Minsun described how, shortly after her birth mother's death, her aunts (her mother's three sisters) kept sharing messages and photos of her mother (their sister) via a KakaoTalk group chat, but it felt like too much for her. She recalled,

> I got a little angry because they showed a lot of pictures with my birth mother, old pictures sometimes and family reunions and events in Korea and I'm just like, *"I'm not a part of it,"* and it is a bit traumatic in a way. . . . They wanted to shoot texts all the time and I was just like, "Stop (puts hands up). It's too much. This is painful for me." I just wrote it like that. And I think they respect it, but now they don't respond that often as well.

Minsun engaged in metacommunication—communication about communication—by telling her aunts how their texts made her feel and the changes that she needed. Although her words suggest that her aunts may be overcorrecting and not responding to her often now, metacommunication allowed her to express herself and gain some much-needed space. The varying experiences above highlight the subjectivity of the people involved in these relationships, demonstrating that the same message (lack of initiating contact or initiating contact) can be met with multiple interpretations and emotional responses. Although it can be uncomfortable for family members to speak directly about communicative intentions and interpretations, such conversations have the potential to clarify misinterpretations and help with current or future interactions.

Getting to Know Me

When speaking about people in their birth families whom they felt closest with, participants invoked language reflecting Western assumptions of social exchange and individualism. They described feeling closer to members of their birth family who demonstrated "effort" in maintaining their relationships, whether it was during time together in person or across distance. Some participants also spoke of feeling known as individuals for "who they are," as opposed to being known only as someone who fulfills a family role or obligation. Sun Ok, who was living in Korea at the time of her second interview, described how she felt closest to her birth mother because her birth mother texted her and spent time with her, even though their ability to communicate was limited by language differences. In the future, she hoped that her relationship with her older sister would deepen. She explained,

> Right now, I feel like the connection I have with my birth mother is familial, we are connected because we're blood related, versus . . . there's a different kind of relationship potential [with my sister] where it seems like she genuinely wants to know who I am. And get to know me.

Sylvia made a distinction between her birth mother and birth father in terms of their relational maintenance efforts and how she feels about her relationship with each of them. She said,

> [My birth father is] on Instagram and he'll try harder to use English words, even though he doesn't know them. It feels like he's trying harder, trying a little bit more to know me for who I *am*, whereas with [my birth mom], I feel a little bit more like she wants me to be someone I can never be. She wants me to be her daughter and that's just never going to happen . . . I just felt more like she was reuniting with her daughter, whereas I was meeting complete strangers. And I mean, looking at when you meet a complete stranger, it's so different than when you're meeting a long-lost kid. I mean, on one hand, it's nice because I feel like she loves me. But I also don't feel like she's really trying to get to know who I actually am.

Toward the end of her second interview, she summarized her relationship with both of her birth parents, saying,

> It feels like a loving relationship, but I don't think that any of us are really loving each other for who we actually are, because we don't really know each other. So I believe that they love me. And I love them, but it's not, it's not like a deeply connected (pause) kind of love.

Sylvia's words imply that, for her, a "deeply connected" love necessitates knowing one another as individuals, for who they "actually are." Based on the Korean cultural emphasis on bloodline and the Confucian importance given to family roles, her birth parents likely do feel a deep connection to her, despite not knowing her on a deep or personal level. They recognize her as their daughter, and, perhaps, this bond is experienced as a deep connection, but Sylvia finds it difficult to feel similarly without a sense of knowing one another as individuals.

Similarly, Ji Kyoung spoke of feeling closest to two of her older sisters, saying, "Those are the two that actually have shown the most interest in actually getting to know me and spend time with me." These participants' words are a clear reflection of Western individualism and the desire for their birth family members to know them beyond their role in the family. For many Koreans, especially those who grew up in Korea during the war and the country's recovery, one's family role and membership *are* one's identity, and conformity to social and group expectations is more important than individual characteristics or idiosyncrasies. Therefore, birth parents and other older Korean relatives may be unlikely to make an effort to get to know their reunited child's individual tastes, hobbies, interests, occupation, and personality. As *jeong* develops between persons, individual selves "become fused," making distinct characteristics fade in comparison to the interpersonal bond itself (Choi & Choi, 2001). In contrast, many Western interpersonal communication scholars have found that sharing personal information with another tends to be viewed as the primary means to deepen relationships (e.g., Altman & Taylor, 1973; Mongeau & Henningsen, 2008), and that asking the other person questions during conversations is perceived as showing interest and involvement (e.g., Spitzberg & Adams, n.d.). Sun Ok and Sylvia saw their roles as a Korean daughter as a very small part of who they "actually" are, making their relationships with their birth parents meaningful but not particularly close.

Mutual Effort

In contrast to participants who told me that they felt solely responsible for initiating contact with their birth families, others indicated a clear sense of mutual effort in maintaining the relationship. Usually, this mutual effort was between participants and members of their birth family other than a parent, suggesting a generational difference in relational maintenance among Koreans. Meagan discussed how her older sister tended to check in on her about once per month, saying, "[My sister] will send me kind of like little updates or just check in. Like, she knew I was moving back [to the United States] and so she checked in with me last week, just to see how I was." Notably, Meagan's sister, who is forty, is only three years older than Meagan, so perhaps the closeness in their ages explains, in part, why she checks in regularly. In addition, because younger generations tend to be more comfortable using technology such as smartphones than older generations, initiating contact is likely easier for them.

Jorgen described his close relationship with his cousin on his father's side and contrasted it with his half-brothers on his mother's side. He also discussed the importance of mutual effort in communication, particularly as it relates to his family members' attempts at speaking English and trying to understand one another. He stated,

> And actually I think my half-brothers on my mother's side, they are actually *very* well spoken in English. But they're still more hesitant to use the language. They have this perfectionism inhibition which most Koreans have, where my cousin, he doesn't care, he's just trying to explain something, then he makes up a new word, he puts two words together which doesn't make sense, but then suddenly it makes sense because I'm trying to understand what he's saying. And so there's willingness and desire to communicate and try to reach out with strange and difficult words, which he's doing and I'm doing, and I'm trying to explain and we both take time understanding each other. And then of course, when we spend more and more time together, we also get to understand each other's way of communicating even better. Even though maybe he doesn't have more words, we just have better communication because we're both trying and spent a lot of time doing it.

Catherine spoke of mutual effort in her relationship with her older sisters. Although she speaks Korean, during a recent visit to Korea, she had asked a friend to accompany her to her sister's house so that she could express some deeper thoughts about their relationship. She recalled,

> I think there were so many things I felt like I *had* to say, that I wanted to say in words that I had my friend come to say. And [my sisters were] like, "We see it! Like, we see your heart," and I think that felt really good. It just felt like, "Oh, this is the reassurance that we're on the same page." Like, they can see that *I'm* trying and I can see that *they're* trying and that's, like, so much of a relationship. And so I think it's just gotten to this point where, like, we both want it enough and, like, we understand life happens. So, it's just, it feels good, I think, to feel like you're at the same place. I think for so long, it was maybe hard to maintain or I didn't *want* to maintain it because I didn't have that peace with it.

Catherine's response reflects mutual effort from her and her sisters, including an understanding that "life happens," which may impact how frequently they communicate with one another. This assumption of the other person's good intentions was also evident in other participants' responses and was important in maintaining relationships. Isabel reflected on her relationship with her birth family, saying, "I think there's an assumption there between us that, you know, don't take everything literally (laughs) or be offended, or take out of context or something." The effort, then, was not just about initiating contact but also about trying to make positive attributions for one another's behavior, particularly when there was confusion or when there were lapses in communication. Sylvia said that after her most recent reunion meeting, her birth sister made an effort to help her understand why she might not communicate often. Sylvia recalled,

> When she was here, the last day, when I was taking them to the airport, she was apologizing and telling me how if I don't hear from her for a long time or things like that, not to take it personally. Because I know that for everyone in our generation in Korea, they're always working a lot. And she does, she works *a lot*. And she was telling me like the hours that she works and I mean, even her daughter spends most of the time with [our] parents. She was telling me, apologizing and telling me it doesn't mean that there's anything wrong. "It doesn't mean that I don't love you . . . it's just because I'm too busy." So, we don't actually communicate very much . . . [but] I definitely would have worried about why I wasn't hearing from her and things like that.

Because Sylvia's sister had previously stopped communicating with Sylvia due to anger about Sylvia's blog (see Chapter 2), she felt the need to explain the likelihood that she may not be in touch frequently. This metacommunication helped Sylvia to understand her sister and to not take future lapses in communication personally. As a whole, this example demonstrates how interactions can be best understood as situated between the past and the future (Baxter, 2004).

Avoidance as Relational Maintenance

In contrast to positive maintenance behaviors such as initiating contact and making an effort to get to know one another, some participants also spoke of how limiting their time with their birth family helped to maintain their relationship. Communication researchers have named this type of maintenance strategy *avoidance*, whereby partners either take time away from one another physically or refrain from talking about contentious topics (Dainton & Gross, 2008). Interviewees spoke of not staying with their birth parents while visiting Korea or spending less time with them than in the past. Sylvia, who experienced difficulties when her birth parents stayed with her in her home during their visit to the United States in 2009, spoke of how, when her parents returned for a second reunion meeting in 2016, they stayed at a nearby hotel and the visit was "much, *much* better." Sylvia also described how there is a limit to how much time she can spend with her birth parents until "enough is enough." When I asked her why she thinks she feels this way, she explained,

> I think it's the way Korean parents relate to their kids. Like, you know, I've struggled with weight my whole adult life and they have no problem mentioning it. But then also no problem stuffing food in my mouth. And so I think I don't really understand that balance, like, "Well, I'm not hungry. Stop trying to feed me." And that's just even just a small one. I think a lot of it, I mean, part of it's probably just me, because I'm a pretty introverted person. But certain people I need a break from sooner. So it might be a lot of the language. I mean, that might be the biggest thing. But then also feeling like, I wouldn't say that I'm *trying* to be what they want, but I also feel a little bit, I guess I feel a little bit like I can never *be* what they want. So it's just exhausting to try and (trails off). Like I said, I don't feel like I'm trying to, but I don't know, maybe I am a little bit and it just gets exhausting after a little while.

Sylvia attributed the exhaustion she experiences when with her birth parents to several factors: Her introverted personality, language differences, and cultural differences. In addition, her words reveal a struggle between "trying" to manage her impression for her birth parents and also not trying: accepting that perhaps, even if she did try, she might not be able to meet their hopes or expectations. Regardless, she expressed that time apart, even during their rare visits, allows her to enjoy the moments they are together.

Other participants spoke of how, when they are visiting Korea, they try to limit their time with their birth family. Minsun spoke of how she and her partner planned a four-day trip to the seaside with their children while in Korea because "it wouldn't be a vacation" if they spent all their time with her birth family. Other participants spoke of how they did not stay more than one night with their birth parents but had different reasons for doing so. Whereas Jorgen spoke of how the language differences make it "boring" to be with his birth mother and her side of the family for more than several hours, Eric described his interactions with his birth parents saying, "It's not enjoyable. It's really arduous," which has led him to see his birth parents for one meal or one overnight stay during his visits to Korea, which often last several weeks. He spends the remainder of his free time with his *hyeong*, his older brother. Catherine spoke of how, when she visits Korea, her older sisters always ensure that she stays with them and not their parents, who have made her uncomfortable in the past by commenting on her weight and pressuring her to get married. In addition, her sisters also attempt to keep Catherine from having to interact with their parents on her own.

Avoidance allowed participants to maintain their relationships with their birth parents while minimizing the discomfort associated with language and cultural differences and the often overwhelming or exhausting feelings associated with reunion. Although a few participants spoke of feeling guilty for claiming space or time away during reunion, or of members of their birth family not accepting their decision, avoidance was an effective maintenance strategy.

Kin-Keeping and Social Networks

Adoptees and birth families often need support in maintaining their relationship over time. This support manifested in two interrelated ways: Kin-keeping and social networks. Most participants indicated that there was one family member who served as their point of contact in the birth family. These individuals, none of whom were birth parents, can be thought of as *kin-keepers*, family members whose communication helps keep the family connected to one another. Kin-keepers in any family typically disseminate information among family members, facilitate family rituals, and maintain family relationships (Leach & Braithwaite, 1996). Participants living in a different country than their birth family end up relying on kin-keepers to respond to communication from the adoptee, share information about the family (e.g., updates on a parent's health), and coordinate plans when adoptees return to Korea. The birth family member with the strongest English-speaking abilities usually ended up being the kin-keeper, and often, this person was a sibling, a sibling's spouse, or a cousin. The kin-keeper linked the adoptee to the birth family as a whole, sharing information both ways.

Christine's description of her sister exemplifies the role of a kin-keeper. She stated,

> What I do know is that my birth sister just is the engine behind, like, whatever interaction I have with my birth family, it's all engineered by my birth sister. She is the one I have heard tells my birth father, my birth mother, "Christine's coming. We need to see her. This is what's happening. This is the day that she's here. This is where we're meeting. This is the time. This is the place. We need to do this. I need to do this." I don't know what my relationship would be like with my birth fam-

ily if she wasn't open to it, you know. I don't know if my birth parents would want to pursue a relationship with me or not. I find out news about my birth mom and dad through my birth sister, and I am able to ask her a lot of questions that my birth mom may not feel comfortable answering, or that may be too uncomfortable to ask her. And then she does investigating for me and she finds out. You know, so she is my *person* in my family.

Ji Kyoung spoke similarly of her older sister as a kin-keeper:

My youngest big sister, who also said she always thought so much of wanting to meet me because she was always the youngest one, and she always dreamt of having a sister calling her "*eonni*"[4] because she didn't get (small laugh) to experience that before now. So she has been, like, the big drive in the family for making everything, this reunion, happen and she's been a strong force in this whole kind of project.

Although Ji Kyoung had other birth siblings who spoke English, her youngest big sister relished the opportunity to be an *eonni* for the first time. Her enthusiasm to serve in this "big sister" role prompted her to help maintain the family's relationship with Ji Kyoung.

The role of kin-keeper, however valuable, was sometimes complicated. The kin-keeper in Minsun's family was her mother's youngest sister, but Minsun referred to this maternal aunt as a "gatekeeper," in part because her aunt would not let Minsun meet her half-sister, even after her birth mother's death in 2019. Sun Ok also mentioned that there was a possibility that her brother-in-law, her birth family's kin-keeper, might be gatekeeping for the family, but it did not bother her. She said,

It didn't make me angry at all to think that maybe he's not telling me everything or that he's watering down things, because he didn't ask to be put in this position either. And I am "grateful" (makes air quotes gesture) for anything he's willing to do. I mean, I don't want to be a burden to him either. He didn't ask, I mean, clearly my siblings did not ask to be put in this position either, but he *definitely* did not ask to be put in this position. He married my second sister before we were in reunion. So, I respect the fact that his autonomy, his ability to just navigate the space as himself, has kind of been taken away. But he also has said, "Oh, it's no problem. You know, we're family. Of course I would do this," you know, and so it's a familial obligation in some ways. I think overall, I've mostly just been grateful for the fact that he's done what he's done.

Kin-keeping in Mee Joo's family was complex as well. She described the role of her *jageun oppa* (the younger of her two older brothers) and her older sisters as kin-keepers, suggesting that there may be more than one per family. Her narrative also emphasizes that kin-keeping across cultures and over time is complex and dynamic:

> My *jageun oppa*, I think I was closer to him because he would just *tell* me *so* many things and he'd walk, he'd want to go on these long walks with me all the time where he would hold my hand, which (small laugh) always felt *really* awkward. And he would just talk and talk and talk and talk and talk. So I think in those cases, it's almost difficult to not feel close to someone when they're telling you so many intimate details about their life and about your family members' lives. But the thing that I think always made it a bit strange was that it's not like he was saying it to be closer to me. I think it was that he was saying it with the intent to, like, pass on this knowledge to me. So that, you know, it gives a bit of a different dynamic to the relationship. And he had always been clear from the beginning. And he reiterated through the years, like, "I hate our siblings and I hate you too, because now you're my sibling. And you know, I kind of hate everyone" (small laugh) so, you know, almost like, "Don't be offended. You're just part of the family. And this is how I feel about our family members." And so, yeah, definitely (small laugh) a different feeling than my sisters who are a bit more warm and welcoming (small laugh), but who hide things from me. You know, these are, like, the ironies of the dynamics, of personal relationships, family relationships and things. You know, they would *really*, my sisters would really make a *warm* effort to kind of get me involved and to see if I was doing okay and to take care of me and, you know, really take time to sit down and talk to me. And my sister in [Korean city] likes to criticize. She's very, very critical so, you know, when she's criticizing you (small laugh), you know you've kind of, in a way that's like, you're part of the family, I guess (small laugh). It makes you feel like someone cares about you, annoying as it may be. I think things like that, or making the effort to, you know, send me a message on my birthday or, you know, calling me to check up on me, things like that. Those are things that those two sisters would do.

In Mee Joo's description, her *jageun oppa* was open to sharing the family's history and expressing physical affection, yet, confusingly, he told Mee Joo he hated her. At the same time, her birth sisters were less open with important family information but displayed more positive relational maintenance behaviors, such as positivity (being kind and warm) and checking up on her. Regardless, these multiple points of contact within her birth family, although confusing, seemed to help Mee Joo understand her family more, even if she had to piece together its history and make sense of it over time.

Like Mee Joo, all participants who discussed having at least semiregular, ongoing contact with their birth family had, at some point, met (full or half) siblings, cousins, and/or aunts and uncles, in addition to birth parents. These additional contacts within the birth family provided a social network of support for maintaining the relationship. Similar to how romantic couples maintain their relationship by interacting with one another's families and/or having common friends (Stafford & Canary, 1991), adoptees' relationships with their Korean families seemed to be strengthened by involving multiple members of the birth family, as well as adoptive family members, and/or friends.

Adoptive parents often paid for trips to Korea and/or traveled with participants, as well as provided emotional support regarding reunion. Friends, both adopted and nonadopted, provided emotional support as well as informational support. Specifically, Korean adopted or nonadopted friends who were familiar with Korean culture because of their own reunion experience or because they grew up in Korea with their own Korean families were able to help participants understand birth parents' behavior from the perspective of Korean culture. Some friends also helped translate letters or e-mails, or served as interpreters during in-person meetings.

Taken together, although the prototypical birth family reunion story involves an adoptee and their birth parents, the long-term maintenance of birth family relationships rests, at least in part, on the support of a broad network, both in and outside of the birth family. This finding affirms past research suggesting the importance of embedding birth family relationships within a wider network of support (Modell, 1997).

Still "Family" after All These Years

Participants who described their relationships with their birth families or certain members of their birth families as close tended to use similar words to describe their time together and/or their relationship. The most common word was *comfortable* or synonyms such as *relaxed*, *natural*, *easy*, and *normal*, and these interactions were typically with birth siblings or cousins rather than sole-ly with birth parents. One situational context for these types of interactions was spending time together in the home of a birth family member, as opposed to meeting in a public place such as a restaurant. Meagan described how, over the years, she has become more comfortable with her birth family and how part of the reason for that is that they spend unstructured time together in her brother's home. She explained,

> We often go to my brother's house and we'll all just gather in, like, the living area and everyone just sits on the floor. There's kids' toys every-where, they'll bring out the fruit and whatever else. And that just feels, *that* feels like real family time, you know, we're in their house, it's com-fortable, and people just start doing what feels natural to them, like my-sister-in-law's making food in the kitchen, my brother is playing with the kids and doing funny things. And sometimes, like, at first I sort of feel like I'm watching it all, but it's also kind of taking it in and seeing like, "Oh, this is probably very much what it would be like if I had grown up here with them, or if I had lived here longer," and so it just sort of feels, it's like what I would be doing with my family here [in the United States]. And that's what I'm doing with *them*, and so I think that's where it feels like there's that level of comfort, like, "Oh I'm here now, like I've reached that level."

Participants like Meagan seemed most comfortable when interactions with their birth families were unstructured. Ji Kyoung also spoke of comfort and feeling relaxed when she is with her birth family. Of her second trip to visit them, she said,

> And my boyfriend said after that, that I am the most calm and relaxed when I'm in Korea with my family. So that was actually quite interest-ing and then again, I had the same experience as the first time, like all of my cells in my body felt like they could just (exhales, drops shoul-ders) relax. And I just felt safe and yeah and happ—(stops midword). Yeah, it really felt like this, into the cell level, I was home.

In contrast, Sun Ok, who was living in Korea before and during the lock-down and COVID-19 pandemic, described her typical interactions with her birth mother as very regimented. As a result, she questioned whether her moth-er only spent time with her out of a sense of obligation and wondered if she was a "burden" to her birth mother. She described,

I've just recently started to understand that [my birth mother's] actions and behaviors, while, to me, seem very regimented, for lack of a better word. Like, there's an order: Like, I come there or we meet up; we eat; if we're out . . . we might get a coffee or something; or if I'm there, we might take a walk or we might watch TV. We would have a coffee or grapes, you know, food there. She gives me food and/or money. And I know that's my cue to leave.

In trying to understand her birth mom's communication, Sun Ok sought the perspective of other Korean adoptees and also nonadopted Koreans, who told her that her birth mother's behavior sounded very "typical" of Korean moms. Still, Sun Ok compared her interactions with her Korean mother to interactions she has had in her adoptive family, saying, "When I think about family visits back home, you know, it didn't seem as regimented." Sun Ok's and Meagan's words suggest that an adoptee's history of interactions with their adoptive family is often the baseline for comparison with their birth family.

Participants spoke of other types of comfort as well, such as the feeling that they can express their opinions, even if they differed from those in their birth family, or comfort with novel ways of communicating. Catherine talked about how, during a recent visit to Korea, she wanted to get a modern *hanbok* (Korean traditional dress) and went shopping with her older sister, whose style differed from her own. She recalled,

I didn't agree with her, but it didn't make me uncomfortable. Her style was just that she was like, "Oh, like, let's make it really frilly with all these flowers and all this pink," and I was like, "Oh, yeah, no, thank you." But it wasn't, like, an uncomfortable thing for me. So, to be at a point where you can disagree and that's all it is, I think there's some relationship there.

Catherine also spoke of how she felt less comfortable with her birth parents than she did with her older sisters, and perhaps the ability to express disagreement has created, and continues to contribute to, these feelings of comfort.

Participants who had lived in Korea for extended amounts of time (a year or more) spoke of how, the longer they lived there, the less frequently they saw their birth families. Mee Joo cited this dynamic and perceived it as an index of increased comfort. She said,

I think just because the longer I was there, that was my life, and I think we were comfortable enough where it was more natural family dynamics in that you just didn't see or contact people as much, or even, you know, when my mom would call me, she'd be asking me, and I'd be more comfortable with it, like, did I eat well, you know, am I sleeping well or things that were pretty mundane.

Both Sun Ok and Mee Joo spoke of conversations with other adoptees and nonadoptees in Korea, where they found similarities in how Korean mothers communicate with their adult children. Through these conversations, they surmised that their birth mothers were treating them the same way they would treat them if they had grown up with them in Korea. This knowledge, that their families didn't seem to be extending "special" treatment to them, was comforting. Participants wanted, in many ways, to not be treated distinctly even though they were adopted.

Fun was another common word to describe positive moments with birth family members, particularly siblings and cousins. Jorgen described comfort and fun with his cousin on his paternal side, saying,

> I'm much closer to him in the sense it's much more relaxed when I'm around him and I always spend a lot of time with my cousin. We go out drinking, we play Saga⁵, we do all sorts of things. He's more like a friend to me or he *is* my family, but he's also a friend I just hang out with, just for fun when I'm there.

In contrast to his time with his cousin, Jorgen described his time with his birth mother and her side of the family as fairly regimented, following a script of dinner at a restaurant and then possibly an overnight stay. Similar to Catherine, he also mentioned the ability to express his opinions when with his cousin, saying,

> Whereas when I'm with my cousin, I just do whatever I want (laughs). And *he* can do whatever he wants and we're just like two friends. "You want to do this? No. This? Yes. Okay. Let's do this." So it's completely different.

Eric also described fun activities with his older brother, describing their times together,

> We just go out to eat and drink. And have fun and it's just always such a blast and he is always trying to think of things to do for me, you know, to take me to, and he doesn't live in Seoul, he lives in [Korean city],

which is not a small town by any means, but it's nowhere near the size of Seoul and so, you know, you are limited in the things that you can do in terms of novelty. But, like, the things that we've done over the years include archery, like, renting go-karts in the park, riding bikes, batting cages, movies. He took me to this crazy Korean carnival (laughs). One of the foods was called "The Narcotic Hot Dog" (laughing). I'll always remember that.

These rituals of drinking and doing activities together both reflected and reaffirmed a sense of relational closeness between participants and their family members. Not surprisingly, when people in a relationship have fun together, they tend to like one another more (Bell & Daly, 1984). Participants who were able to have fun with their birth relatives spoke positively of the relationship they shared and described feelings of closeness.

Finally, a few participants used words such as *love*, *support*, and *acceptance* in talking about their relationships with their birth families. When I asked Alexander why he maintained his relationship with his birth parents and went back to Korea regularly, he said,

> They've always been really supportive, so that was the main reason I've been going back is because they've just shown unconditional love and that's really all I wanted since I was a child, so it's really good to develop *new* relationships with parents that I *don't* know that well, versus my adoptive parents here.

A potential factor that may have complicated Alexander's relationship with his birth parents is his sexual orientation. South Korea ranks low among developed countries in terms of LGBTQ acceptance (Choo & Kang, 2021), and he worried initially that his birth parents might judge him for identifying as gay. Although his birth father expressed some concern after learning about Alexander's sexual orientation on Facebook, he has remained supportive. Alexander stated that he feels accepted by both of his birth parents and would feel comfortable bringing a romantic partner to meet them in the future.

Isabel also mentioned how her birth family's supportiveness and her realization of her good fortune in finding them both make her want to maintain their relationship. She also spoke of the challenge of keeping in contact given the busyness of daily life. She reflected,

> I think, you know, you can go through life every day and then you have to stop and think, like, "Oh, yeah, I have this whole other part

of my life and this whole other family and this whole other dynamic that not everybody has." And sometimes I think that can get pushed back a little bit and other priorities come forward. But you know, I just really want to maintain that relationship and feel lucky that I even found them. One of my best friends is an adoptee and, you know, she was abandoned without any records of her own. And just feeling fortunate to have had that contact, that we had a really good relationship and it's always been positive and supportive and not judgmental. And I would love to have them be more part of my life.

Importantly, Alexander's and Isabel's words suggest that the ability to initiate and maintain a relationship with one's birth family is reliant, in part, on luck. An adoptee's ability to find information on their birth family (which can vary based on the day and the person they speak with at their adoption agency, the agency's records, and the circumstances of their relinquishment), members of their birth family being alive and willing to meet, someone in the birth family having the motivation and ability to communicate using technology, and birth family members' willingness to accept their cultural and individual differences—all of these things are beyond adoptees' control. The things an adoptee has at least some agency over—their expectations; communication; their network of support; their own self-reflection; their knowledge of Korean history, language, and culture; and their knowledge of reunion relationships based on other adoptees' experiences—often take time and maturity to develop.

Given all of these variables, it is a small wonder that most participants have been able to sustain relationships over time. Yet I wish to emphasize that there is no imperative for adoptees to remain in relationships with their birth family or for their relationships to follow a particular trajectory or timeline. Just as each adoptee and each member of each birth family is unique, each reunion relationship is unique and continually unfolding. During his first interview, Mark was living in the United States in proximity to his paternal birth aunt and cousins and saw them regularly. However, at the time of the second interview, after Mark had lived in Korea for six years, he had lost touch with his aunt and cousins, who had moved around the United States. In his second interview, he stated that he felt closer to his half-sister than his birth parents or the other extended family members he had gotten to know over the years. He explained how he rarely saw his birth parents while he was living in Korea, and when he did contact them, they hadn't known he was still in the country. His relationships with his birth parents were challenging due to his mother's secrecy about Mark to her current family, and his birth father's insistence that

Mark learn to speak Korean. At the time of this second interview, Mark had been back in the United States for over a year and had not communicated with his birth parents to let them know that he had left Korea. Reflecting on his relationship with his birth family, he said,

> I still do feel close to [my half-sister] and I feel like, even though I *don't*, if I feel like it, I could text her at any time. I don't necessarily feel that way about, you know, a lot of my other family members at this point, but I don't feel like I'm *never* going to talk to them again, you know. I still feel like the door is open. It's just (chuckles), we're all in our separate rooms and no one is choosing to go into the other room, but I don't feel like that was a chapter in my life and it's now closed and I have what I wanted out of Korea and now I've moved on, which I think is how a lot of people might interpret it if I explained my circumstances.

At the same time, Mark expressed struggling with feelings of guilt over not being proactive in maintaining his relationships with his Korean parents and for not learning to speak Korean fluently as his birth father had requested many times. Speaking about challenges in his relationships with his Korean family, he was reflective, saying,

> I think it was those feelings of guilt and trying to, I guess, forgive myself or, you know, at least convince myself that I can forgive myself for not having this relationship, not having a stronger relationship and that it's okay to define it on your own terms and to have whatever extent of a relationship you *want* to have. Or feel like you *need* to have.

Participants often spoke of guilt when discussing long-term relationships with their birth families. While birth families tend to express feelings of guilt about an adoptee's relinquishment, adoptees articulated guilt for reasons such as not initiating contact more often, not visiting Korea more, or not learning more Korean. One participant, Christine, also spoke of feeling guilty for causing pain and shame to her birth parents, and others spoke about feeling guilt about how reunion has made their adoptive parents feel. These feelings, while understandable, seem like a heavy load for adoptees to bear in addition to the challenges of being in reunion; the stresses and obligations of daily life; and challenges to family, racial, and ethnic identity. My hope is that adoptees will be able to carve out a version of family that communicates the love, support, and connection they need, and that, when possible, they can acknowledge feelings of guilt and then let them go.

Looking Ahead: Hopes and Constraints

When asked about their hopes for the future of their relationships with their birth families, most participants focused on their relationships with their siblings and nieces and/or nephews. While these hopes stemmed in part from the simple fact that their birth parents were aging, ill, or deceased, some participants expressed directly that their relationship with their Korean sibling(s) was the most important relationship among those they had with their birth family and that they felt closest with one of their siblings or cousins. There were several reasons these relationships took precedence over relationships with birth parents: Siblings were viewed as not culpable for the adoptees' relinquishment; siblings tended to speak more English than birth parents; and siblings were more similar to participants in age and perspective, which made being with them easier and more enjoyable. Eric reflected on his relationship with his *hyeong*, his older brother, saying,

> We just have such a good time together. Every other family relationship is so fraught. And I'm sure that, you know, the longer that this relationship goes on, we're gonna have those hurdles to jump as well, but he's so easy to hang out with. And he wants to hang out with me (chuckles). I mean, you just can't overstate how much that makes a difference, you know. Like I said, I don't think I would have kept going back [to Korea] if I didn't feel that from him . . . I also just think that, I know that if I don't go back, that the stories are gonna stop and that that progress in getting reunited with him is going to stop and I'm not, I'm not ready for that. I want us to have this relationship for the rest of our lives.

Interviewees also spoke of how they hoped to build and maintain relationships with their nieces and nephews, the children of their birth siblings. However, there was also some uncertainty about how well these children understood the adoptee's place in the birth family and how they would react to knowing the family's history. Catherine spoke of how her Korean nieces and nephews have asked her questions about why she lives in America. She described her response, saying,

> I try to defer to my sisters or just not, like, directly answer, just kind of change the subject, which I think will only last for so long (laughs) with, like, inquisitive, young children. Like, sure, it works, but there's especially one nephew who's asked me I think five times now, at least. And so I know at least some of my sisters, they don't know how to an-

swer that and they've kind of said, "Oh, they're young. I don't think they need to know" and, you know, I'm totally fine with that. I'm not trying to interrupt anything. It's actually a privilege to even be able to spend time with them and I think it's just something that they're trying to work out probably too.

Mee Joo spoke of her nieces and nephews as well, but she also mentioned another common theme: Adoptees' desire to connect their own children to Korea and to their Korean family. She recalled,

My sisters had said to me a few years after we reunited, or maybe even within the first year or two, they really wanted me to talk and to get to know my nieces and nephews, because that was how I would get to know *them*. Like, my nieces and nephews as people but also get to know the family and to get close to them. And that's also something that I would like for *my* kids, is to get to know their Korean family. I don't want them to be this far away foreign concept. I want it to just be normal, that we go to Korea, that we see family, that they speak another language, that we do things differently there. And so those are things I hope for. But I think if I don't make a very concerted effort to do it, it could easily not happen.

Mee Joo's words suggest the importance of her building and maintaining relationships with her nieces and nephews, not just for herself but also for her children. In fact, all participants who were parents at the time of the second interview mentioned the importance of connecting their children to Korea and, if possible, to their Korean family. This finding corroborates research by Zhou et al. (2021), who found that, despite feeling inauthentic at times, Korean adoptees make efforts to socialize their children to their Korean ethnicity. Minsun spoke of her hopes for her toddler son, saying,

My boyfriend and I have talked a lot about how we hope that Korea will be a country to our son that he would like to explore. And maybe he could also meet the family as well and he could explore all the family too. And get closer to the culture. . . . So he will grow up and have continuous travels to Korea. So it won't be some odd Asian country to him. But he would feel that it would be *his* country as well.

Minsun had taken her son to Korea before he turned two years old so they could receive the airfare discount for young children. Participants like Minsun and others spoke of the financial costs of traveling to Korea, reflecting that the maintenance of these relationships requires very tangible resources, as most birth families are unable to travel internationally to visit the adoptee. In addition, some participants mentioned that in visiting Korea, they are forsaking travel to other countries they would like to visit. For example, Jorgen, who estimated that he had been to Korea approximately fifteen times since his initial reunion twenty years ago, stated that he would probably visit Korea less frequently in the coming years. When I asked him why, he said,

> I think both because I actually want to see more of other parts of the world. And (pause) I think that's the main reason actually, that I want to see other destinations. And at the same time, that might also mean something, that I don't feel the same need to go and reconnect with my Korean family that often, as I have been. I don't think that means they are less important to me, but (pause) more that I don't need so much affirmation. I don't feel like I *need* to have so much affirmation or *give* so much affirmation. I guess the facts will remain as long as we live that we are related and we will still be happy to meet even if it was ten years later and just have a nice talk and a nice meal like we have now.

Interestingly, Jorgen's response reflects *eui-ri* and *jeong*, assumptions that loyalty and warmth persist in close relationships, regardless of time and maintenance. As someone who has been in reunion as an adult for over two decades and experienced both highs and lows during his time in reunion, Jorgen has come to see his relationship with his birth family through the lens of Korean culture.

Family and Not Family

The stories of transnational Korean adoptees in reunion reaffirm the idea that relationships are constituted in communication, that family relationships are continually being redefined and renegotiated, and that adoptees' birth family relationships manifest a number of discursive struggles, or contradictions. Naturally, participants often differentiated among members of their birth family, feeling more of a sense of family, or closeness, with some people than others. Relationships that felt most family-like to participants had been maintained over time and had included multiple face-to-face meetings where birth family members had demonstrated what participants viewed as supportive communication or effort in the relationship. Regardless, participants' words revealed a discursive struggle demonstrating the challenge of fitting birth family relationships into existing categories of relationships. A number of participants spoke of how they viewed their birth family as family, but also, even after many years, as strangers or acquaintances. Meagan's words reflect the challenges of classifying her relationship with her birth family:

> It's almost like, even though I, like, love them all, and I feel, I *do* feel so much closer to them, there is still this sort of distance between, the space between us, that I feel like sometimes I'm like, we're family but we're strangers, or not strangers, but we're almost like acquaintances or like long-lost friends and I just don't know sometimes how to navigate that.

Ashley's words reveal a very similar dilemma. When I asked her why she maintained a relationship with her birth parents, she stumbled over her words uncharacteristically, replying,

> I mean, I feel, I don't know, I *want* to, honestly. . . . I mean, they're like a part of my life now *too*, . . . I don't know, like, not like a *mother* and *father per se*, but like, basically, like, a close auntie or uncle, but like birth parents or, I don't know how to categorize. Like, I wouldn't categorize them as, like, my *main*, like the main parental figures but, like, definitely, like, close. And I want to. So I do.

In addition to highlighting the challenge of categorizing these relationships, Ashley's words reflect their voluntary nature. She maintains relationships with her birth family because she *wants to*. Catherine's words reflect the same desire but a stronger feeling of family, particularly with her older sisters. When asked why she maintains these relationships, she said,

> I think it's worth it to me. It's worth it in a lot of ways. I think in a lot of ways, like, we're at the point where it *feels* like they're family in some ways. So, it's not an obligation or duty, because it's something I wanted. . . . But I think, just in general, it's my personality that I've always wanted to kinda keep in touch with different connections that I've made. And I think it's obviously deeper than that. Yeah, like, I want to (small laugh) is a big, big part, I guess. . . . It seems like it's been more mutual, the correspondence actually, in the last year, it hasn't been just me or just them. And yeah, I guess I don't know how to explain it, like, I think in some ways I didn't realize how much they just feel like family. Like it's one thing to call them family, but to *feel* like they're family, I think that's pretty huge.

When I asked Ji Kyoung why she maintained her relationship with her birth family, she responded, "Because they're my family (nodding). I think that there is a time where you can't choose not to have the family any longer." However, she recalled specific moments, relational turning points (Baxter & Bullis, 1986), where their relationship became solidified, such as when her birth mother needed money to help pay her mortgage and for Ji Kyoung's father's hospital bills; at that time, all of Ji Kyoung's siblings in Korea were contributing to help their mother. Although her family did not ask her to contribute, she felt compelled to do so as a member of the family. She recalled,

> At that time I thought, you can't be part of a family and then say you don't want to participate. Because it was like, "Should I send money to them?" And there are all these stories about "Oh don't send money to your family, because they will just exploit you, take advantage of you," blah blah blah blah. So actually I decided not to tell anyone, but I talked to my boyfriend about it, and he actually agreed with me, and said, "You can't just say you're part of the family and not help, of course." So I actually started sending money to help pay those bills, and I felt it was the only right thing to do and because I can't go back now and say, "No, I'm not interested in a relationship any longer." It's too late. (small laugh)

In another important moment, when Ji Kyoung's oldest sister died from cancer, Ji Kyoung flew to Korea immediately to be with the family. Even though it was a painful time, she spoke of it as meaningful for her relationship with them because she was asked to help with tasks related to the funeral and because she was able to be with her family at a crucial moment. This time together differed greatly from their typical visits, which usually involved vacations. She recalled,

> I was all of a sudden given a lot of tasks that need to be done, a lot of practical things like, "Okay, so like, Ji Kyoung, you go and buy the flowers on the way home and then, can you do this, and can you do this?" And I'm like, "Okay, I have no idea, but I will. I will do it," so that was really nice, to be trusted and regarded as a family member that also had a job to do. . . . So I got to see my family in totally different circumstances, because I'd only seen them when it was like a holiday time, and now, they were in crisis and being around there, that was actually a very, funny enough or ironically enough, a very good experience.

Participants who felt that they were part of their Korean families had spent time with them over many years and in a variety of contexts. Their interactions had been generally positive and supportive, although both Ashley and Catherine had reported challenges with their birth fathers' traditional expectations, particularly when they were younger. Over time, and as they grew up, they gained more empathy and understanding of their families and Korean culture and also developed chronotopic similarity (Baxter, 2004), or a shared relational history, which created a sense of family.

Other participants expressed more ambivalence toward their birth families, particularly if they had limited and/or negative interactions. Hanne and her birth mother met once, in 2009, but, at the time of her second interview, Hanne had not heard from her mother in several years, despite having sent letters to her address in Korea. Reflecting on the possibility that her birth mother may no longer be alive, she stated,

> You know, what happens will happen. I can't control it anyway and this may sound a little bit cynical, but she's not a part of my life in Denmark, so *if* she has actually died, or if something bad has happened to her or she *doesn't* want any contact with me, for example, it's not that I will be devastated. It's sad if it is like that, but still, I have my life in Denmark and I have a good life and I don't *need* her in my daily life. So it's kind of, there are two levels, you can say. One is, you know, well, this is your birth mother and you can't just ignore her, you want to see her again. You want your family, your children to meet her. And the other level is, Well, she's not a part of my life and she's never been, so *if* she has died, well, then she has died and that's sad. But my life is just continuing, like it has *always*.

Sylvia, whose blog resulted in significant conflict with her birth family after their first meeting in 2009, also expressed some mixed feelings about her relationship with her birth family. She reflected in her second interview, saying,

> When I first started, I would have thought that ten years down the road, it didn't matter if I had a relationship with them. But I think the idea of losing them early on, I mean, it's not that I don't value a relationship with them at all. And it's just that it's different. It's not the same as family, but I do value it. I *do* feel some kind of connection because of our biological connection. But it's definitely on a weird in-between level of not quite family, but still kind of? So I do care about maintaining that to some extent now.

Overall, participants' words reflect the lack of cultural models for adoptee and birth family kinship (Modell, 1997) and that presuming a particular type of relationship or a common label for these relationships may be unrealistic and engender disappointment. Furthermore, participants' words convey that their feelings about, and toward, their birth families change over time, based on their own and their birth family members' age, life stage, and individual circumstances, many of which are beyond one's control.

Conclusion

Transnational adoptees who are in reunion with their birth families face significant challenges and opportunities. Language differences interlock with cultural differences, both of which impact how family members and adoptees view the relationship and how, if at all, members think of relational maintenance. In addition, transnational adoptees who have remaining questions for their birth family may differ in how they grapple with uncertainty about the family and their place in it, just as birth family members may differ in their willingness and ability to answer adoptees' questions. If people in the birth mother's life, such as her current husband, nonadopted children (the adoptee's half-siblings), or the birth father, do not know about the adoptee, secrecy can complicate the logistics of meeting as well as the adoptee's sense of connectedness to the family.

At the same time, long-term reunions can present adoptees and birth family members with opportunities to create new and emergent relationships that develop and change over time. Adoption scholars such as Kristi Brian (2012) have pointed out that the adoptive family is often "wrongly viewed as a *substitute* for the biological reproduction of the nuclear family" (p. 121, italics original) rather than an alternative form of family. Similarly, given the complexities of transnational reunion relationships, common criteria for judging family closeness and intimacy, such as shared history, comfort, and interdependence, may not apply, especially initially. Even when the traditional nuclear family members are present—mother, father, and their biological offspring including the adoptee—comfort in relationships and interactions may take years to develop. Some adoptees may find that their interactions with their birth family members never feel comfortable or enjoyable, whether it is because of individual differences, limitations due to time and distance, culture, and/or language. Birth family relationships must inhabit their own space and be evaluated on their own terms by adoptees and birth families, and all parties may need to recalibrate their expectations and adjust their communication regularly. Flexibility on the part of *all* family members—not just the adopted person—may play a key role in maintaining these relationships.

Although "reunion" often implies the presence of birth parents, relationships with siblings or cousins were reported to be particularly meaningful and, often, less challenging than relationships with birth parents. Birth siblings, half-siblings, and cousins tended to have higher proficiency in English, more cultural flexibility, more perceived similarity due to age and interests, and less emotional baggage related to adoption compared with birth parents, making communication with them more enjoyable and less taxing emotionally. Sibling and cousin relationships tend to span the most years of any family relationship (Gilligan et al., 2020), and they often result in new relationships with in-laws, nieces and nephews, and additional cousins. Some adoptees may be able to take comfort, then, in knowing that if their relationships with birth parents or older members of their birth family are strained or uncomfortable, they may be able to communicate with birth siblings or cousins with more ease. As time passes, each person in the relationship will change, the context surrounding the relationship will change, and the communication that constitutes the relationship will change. Amid these changes, if two or more people—an adoptee and a member of their birth family—communicate with one another even sporadically or rarely, the relationship is being maintained and holds possibility and reasons to be hopeful.

7

Concluding Recommendations

When an adopted person chooses to reunite, they are stepping into a relationship that will involve many unknowns. The most obvious unknown is one's birth family—who they are, what they are like, and how they will communicate. Aside from the personalities, histories, and relationships within one's birth family, transnational adoptees are required, often for the first time, to engage deeply and personally with their birth culture. Even if an adoptee has been exposed to cultural *practices*, such as food, traditions (e.g., performing arts), and language, there is often little that one can do to prepare for cultural *assumptions* about family, relationships, gender, and identity and the way these assumptions are enacted in daily family communication. Because initial reunion meetings are, by definition, novel communicative contexts, how an adoptee will respond to reunion is unpredictable, which creates additional unknowns. Over time, inevitable individual, relational, and situational changes will occur, reshaping communication in ways that are difficult to anticipate at the start of the relationship.

Despite the various unknowns and unavoidable uncertainty, I offer some recommendations that may be helpful to transnational adoptees who are in reunion or anticipating reunion, and the people who want to support them throughout this process. These recommendations are based on the experiences and advice of the adoptees whose stories have given life to this book. Yet I offer these suggestions with a slight hesitancy, knowing that each reunion meeting is different and believing that, at heart, all adoptees have the capacity to know what is best for them and that difficult moments can present openings for learning about oneself and others. Therefore, these recommendations are not a safe-guard against feelings of confusion, frustration, or alienation throughout re-union; rather, they are intended to help transnational adoptees navigate these interactions with as much knowledge and support as possible. I hope that the wisdom of the participants in this book can provide guidance and perspective to other transnational adoptees at any stage of reunion as well as to adoptive parents hoping to provide support.

Recommendations for Transnational Adoptees in Reunion

Secure Support at All Stages of the Initial Reunion Meeting

All participants spoke of the importance of having support, particularly sur-rounding initial meetings with birth family members. *Social support* has been defined as "an individual's perceptions of general support or specific support-ive behaviors (available or enacted upon) from people in their social network, which enhances their functioning and/or may buffer them from adverse out-comes" (Malecki & Demaray, 2003, p. 2). This definition centers on the re-ceiver's perception, implying that the possibility (or likelihood) that what is offered as support may not actually be perceived as supportive. For example, although family members often dispense advice with good intentions, unso-licited advice is often viewed as unsupportive (Goldsmith, 2004). Social sup-port can be emotional (e.g., listening, empathizing), instrumental (e.g., complet-ing tasks, giving money), informational (e.g., providing information or advice), or appraisal (e.g., providing evaluation) (Malecki & Demaray, 2003). I like to envision adoptive parents, adoptive siblings, partners, friends, other adoptees, and therapists as creating a web, or safety net, of various types of support for adoptees before, during, and after reunion. This metaphor suggests that although one person can provide various types of support, adoptees should, ideally, be able to rely on different people for different types of support. However, because social support is subjective and individual, I recommend early and regular con-versations about the support needed and desired.

If possible, I recommend that a trusted family member, friend, or partner accompany adoptees to initial meetings with birth families. Although adop-tive parents' presence can create an inadvertent hyperawareness of their feelings and experiences, a high level of support and communicative openness between adoptees and their adoptive parents can mitigate this potential drawback, par-ticularly if there is a preexisting close relationship. Trusted friends, siblings, or partners can also provide meaningful in-person support. In addition to empathetic listening, support persons can provide instrumental support by taking pictures and video, writing down notes during conversations, getting food or drinks as needed, and helping adoptees remember details or information. Also, because most reunions of transnational adoptees take place in the birth country, a traveling companion can assist with logistics such as navigating transportation and coordinating day-to-day activities. Support persons can also make the reunion travel experience more enjoyable, as participants spoke of doing tourist activities together or sharing humorous experiences or memories. If an adoptee must attend an initial meeting by themselves, I recommend designating certain friends or family members as "on call" to provide support via phone or text.

In addition, conversations with adoptee friends or acquaintances can provide crucial information and validation, both before and after reunion meetings. Adoptees who do not have adoptee friends can also use online groups on Facebook or Korean adoptee subreddits on Reddit to seek information. Given the number of Korean adoptee online communities, adoptees can easily find someone who shares their experience and who can offer perspective or advice.

Practice Cautious Optimism

Nearly all participants spoke of the importance of adoptees being aware of their expectations for their initial meeting and for their relationship with their birth family more generally. They used phrases like "Don't get your hopes up" and "Guard your heart" to convey the importance of not creating fantasies or rigid expectations of the initial meeting or birth family. Interviewees advocated an "open mind" and a "cautious but optimistic" approach to reunion. This approach allows room for hope and positivity while balancing the likelihood that birth families may not live up to idealized expectations and that, regardless, language, culture, and distance will present challenges to the relationship.

Remember: Reunions Are Unpredictable

Related to their recommendation for cautious optimism, participants stressed the unpredictability of reunions and birth family relationships. Participants spoke of being surprised at their own emotional reaction to reunion meetings, before, during, or after. Sometimes, participants didn't even realize that they were stressed. Sylvia spoke of how, months after her first reunion meeting, she went to the doctor because her hair was falling out in large clumps. When her doctor asked her whether she had experienced stress recently, Sylvia traced her hair loss back to her reunion meeting. The emotion and uncertainty of reunion can trigger unanticipated reactions, both emotional and physical.

In addition, participants mentioned that it is difficult to know how or when relationships with birth families will change. Sometimes, changes can bring about more closeness; other times, they can create distance. Sometimes, changes are sudden and external, such as the birth of a child or the death of a parent, and other changes are gradual and internal, such as increasing emotional maturity from adolescence through young adulthood. Regardless, knowing that relationships with birth families are dynamic can help adoptees to enjoy positive experiences and know that negative interactions may be momentary or reframed later.

Take Time Apart, If Needed

Adoptees in reunion often want to avoid offending their birth families, which may result in a sense of obligation to please others and to tolerate discomfort. And while I encourage all people involved in reunion to be respectful and flexible where possible, I also believe that adoptees—who are often infantilized—have the right to a sense of agency in reunion. As Eric articulated, "If things happen in that relationship that *you* aren't happy with, don't be afraid to pull yourself out of the equation. Because that's your right as the person who was *relinquished.*" Sometimes, protecting oneself involves creating distance or space from the source of discomfort. Examples include taking time away from the birth family while in the birth country, staying somewhere other than the birth family's home while visiting, or taking a break from communicating with the birth family in general. An adoptee who initiates reunion is not obligated to enact a close, ongoing relationship with their birth parents if doing so causes too much pain, discomfort, mental health struggles, and/or other undesired outcomes.

About Korean Culture and Korean Language . . .

Because initial reunion meetings can create substantial stress for adoptees, I hesitate to suggest that adoptees should expend additional efforts to study Korean culture and/or Korean language beforehand. At the same time, some adoptees may find it helpful to reduce their uncertainty by reading online about specific topics such as Korean mealtime etiquette and Koreans' views on age and gender. Perhaps the most useful source of information is other Korean adoptees who have traveled to Korea and/or reunited, who are often very glad to share their experiences with fellow adoptees online. I recommend searching for information through groups on Facebook, such as Korean American Adoptees and Korean Adoptees Searching for their Birth Families, as well as Facebook discussion boards such as Korean Adoptees Traveling in Korea.

For initial meetings especially, birth families tend to be very understanding about adoptees not speaking Korean, and adoption agencies have staff members who can interpret. Nongovernmental organizations (NGOs) such as G.O.A.'L., InKAS (International Korean Adoptee Service Inc.), or KoRoot can also help adoptees find interpreters, and Facebook groups such as Adoptees Living in Korea can be a valuable resource. After initial meetings, birth families may hope that an adoptee will learn Korean and may encourage them to do so, but adoptees should avoid feeling deficient or guilty if they cannot (or do not want to) study or learn Korean. The number of transnational adoptees who speak their heritage language conversationally or proficiently is very small; language is simply one of the casualties of transnational adoption. Those who undertake Korean language study may find it meaningful to enact and reclaim their ethnic identity in this way. They may also find that knowing even a small amount of the language can ease communication with birth families. However, the process of "learning Korean" is, like family relationships, ongoing and never complete.

Use Social Media with Caution

Although perceptions of child relinquishment and transnational adoption are changing, I encourage adoptees to ask their birth family about social media before posting photos or other content online. As multiple participants' experiences demonstrate, many birth families, especially birth mothers, feel ashamed of their past and might be uncomfortable having any information online, even if they are not tagged in posts or photos. Direct conversations may help avoid conflict or misunderstandings surrounding social media, yet, when in doubt, adoptees and adoptive parents would be wise to avoid posting publicly without permission.

Intercultural Communication Recommendations

Practice Flexibility—With Boundaries

When interacting with one's birth family, it is important to practice *behavioral flexibility*, the ability to adapt one's behavior in unfamiliar ways (Matveev & Merz, 2014). During reunion meetings, transnational adoptees find themselves outside their comfort zone, either a little or a lot. Examples from participants include being encouraged to eat unfamiliar foods, to hold hands with a family member, or receiving a bra as a gift in front of the family. Adoptees, particularly those with limited experience traveling internationally, can remind themselves that these interactions and accommodations are temporary and an opportunity for growth and self-discovery.

At the same time, adoptees are also encouraged to set boundaries when necessary, with the understanding that Korean families may not understand these boundaries (G.O.A.'L., 2008). For example, two participants spoke of how their birth mothers are very religious and would like them to go to church with them when they visit, but they do not. Church attendance is not a compromise they are willing to make, even if their birth mother finds their refusal upsetting. For some adoptees, flexibility will come easily, and setting boundaries will be a challenge; for others, the opposite is true. I encourage self-reflection and conversations with trusted others about this topic in preparation for reunion. Self-knowledge and tentative plans for flexibility and/or boundaries can help decrease the sense of uncertainty.

Accept Ambiguity and Release Control

Communicators who can be at ease, even amid many unknowns, possess what is called a *tolerance for ambiguity* (Martin & Nakayama, 2022). Western, middle-class adults tend to exert a fair amount of control over their lives—where they go and when, whom they spend time with, what they eat. During reunion, however, adoptees may not know, minute to minute, what is happening, how someone is related to them, what people are talking about, or where they are headed next. In other words, reunion involves relinquishing control and the desire for control. Korean adoptee in reunion, adoption researcher, and adoption organizer Hollee McGinnis (2000) wrote that an important question for adoptees approaching reunion is "Are you ready not to be in control?" (para. 13). I recall many instances walking in Korea with one or more of my Korean siblings, and my young son or daughter would ask me questions like "Where are we going? Are we going to eat soon? What are we eating?" As a mother, it felt strange to not be in control, to not have answers, to answer "I don't know" to their questions, one after another. But I had to accept the ambiguity of not knowing in order to find out what was next, both in the moment and in the relationship. Adoptees approaching reunion may consider what their general tolerance for ambiguity is and, when possible, accept that ambiguity is normal and unavoidable during reunion.

Practice Nonjudgmentalism

Nonjudgmentalism has been defined as the ability to refrain from evaluating other cultures based on one's own cultural frame of reference (Martin & Nakayama, 2022), and it can be challenging to practice in unfamiliar and emotionally heightened circumstances. I suggest an awareness of the tendency to jump to judgment and a commitment to pausing and practicing nonjudgmentalism, particularly for those with limited intercultural experiences and relationships. Often, when participants evaluated their birth parents' behavior in the context of Korean culture and history—the parents' life story, the family's history, the history of Korea—they had more empathy for them. This increased empathy allowed them to view potentially offensive messages (e.g., birth parents giving too much advice, offering criticism) with less judgment and as less personally threatening or hurtful.

Take the Long View

Family relationships—reunion relationships included—are anything but static. Over time, individuals' lives and perspectives will change, which can cause family members to reevaluate how they communicate with one another and what they want the relationship to be. Particularly in moments of unease, conflict, or frustration, I encourage family members to take the long view, trusting that either the relationship or the situation will change, or that they themselves can make a change that enables them to feel supported and healthy—mentally and emotionally.

Consider Therapy

A qualified therapist (licensed psychologist, licensed professional counselor, social worker) may be able to help adoptees process search, reunion, and birth family relationships in an environment free from judgment, personal interest or investment, or expectations. Korean adoptee and licensed professional clinical counselor (LPCC) Nicole Sheppard shared with me some of her professional expertise as well as some of her perspective from living in Korea for eight years, six of which she served as Vice Secretary General for G.O.A.'L. (Sheppard, personal communication, May 27, 2022). Currently, she specializes in providing counseling to transracial adoptees, both domestic and transnational, and adoptees in reunion.

Because most adoptees meet their birth family in the hopes of understanding themselves more, reunions raise many fundamental questions about self and others, and these questions bear a great deal of emotional weight. Just a few questions may include:

- What does it mean to be a member of my birth family?
- What would my life have been, had I been able to stay in this family?

- I don't feel close to my birth family. Is there something wrong with me?
- I met my birth family but still don't feel complete. What now?
- After meeting my birth family, I feel less Korean than I've ever felt. But I've always thought of myself as Korean. Who am I?

A few related emotions adoptees may experience before, during, and/or after reunion meetings include:

- Grief over meeting one's birth family and realizing what was lost.
- Sadness or anger about learning the story of their relinquishment.
- Frustration at not being able to communicate with one's birth family directly.
- A sense of loss from unmet expectations.
- Feelings of distance from people who can't understand one's experience, such as one's partner/spouse, friends, adoptive or birth parents, children, or coworkers.
- Intense emotional reactions (e.g., suicidal thoughts, urges to self-harm).[1]

Writing for the Korean American Adoptee Adoptive Family Network (KAAN) Sheppard (2020) recommends that adoptees see therapists who are adoption-competent—trained in helping adoptees understand their current situation in the context of adoption-related factors. Specifically, she recommends that adoptees consult the Beyond Words Adoptee-Therapist Directory (https://www.growbeyondwords.com/adoptee-therapist-directory/) to find "licensed U.S. mental health professionals who identify as adoptees and work with adoptees/adoptive families in a variety of public and private settings" (Beyond Words, 2022). Mental health professionals who have completed the Training for Adoption Competency program can be found at https://adoptionsupport.org/member-types/adoption-competent-professionals/

If you have never been in therapy, consider talking with friends or family members about their experiences and what to look for in a counselor. Sheppard (personal communication, May 27, 2022) also recommends consulting a resource focused on "red flags" when looking for an adoption therapist (Randolph, 2014). Currently, a list of these red flags can be found online at https://brooke-randolph.com/blog/10_red_flags_when_choosing_an_adoption_therapist/ (Randolph, 2016). If you feel hesitant or stigmatized about accessing support for your mental health, try to remember that reunion is a significant life event, one that addresses who you are and how you fit into your families and the world. I recommend accessing all types of support—therapy especially—

to help you navigate your thoughts, emotions, and relationships with as much self-compassion, ease, and mindfulness as possible.

Recommendations for Adoptive Parents
of Transnational Adoptees in Reunion

Practice Ongoing Communicative Openness about Korea and the Birth Family

Participants who described their adoptive parents as being proactive in fostering open conversation about adoption-related topics while growing up tended to describe their relationships with them as close. In other words, they were raised in an environment of communicative openness. They described how, throughout their childhood, their adoptive parents encouraged them to learn about Korean culture, attend Korean culture camps, discuss their adoption, and talk about their birth families. These adoptive parents helped their children develop their adoptive identity and their Korean identity through open communication and connections with other Korean adoptees and Korean nationals. Communicative openness with parents allowed participants to feel that their adoption, birth family, and reunion were safe, regular topics.

However, adoptive parents who have not cultivated open conversations surrounding birth parents may find that reunion can provide an opportunity to demonstrate support and to engage in new conversations. Adoptive parents can choose to ask questions and listen, while respecting adoptees' boundaries and privacy. These acts can serve as a meaningful first step toward more open communication. Within the climate of communicative openness, participants offered several specific pieces of advice for adoptive parents.

Let the Adoptee Lead

Several participants expressed that it is important for parents to not "force" an adoptee to search and/or reunite. Participants also noted that, although they themselves chose to reunite, they have siblings who are also Korean and adopted who are not interested in search and/or reunion. Adoptive parents should strive to create an environment where questions and thoughts about search, reunion, and birth family are cultivated and welcomed but not forced. There should be no parental pressure or expectation to enact an adoptive identity a certain way (e.g., to search and reunite, to learn the heritage language) but rather an openness to the adoptee's needs and emotions and to accept inevitable changes as they come.

Remember: It's Not about You

Over and over, participants expressed that reunion is part of an adoptee's ongoing effort to learn about their own identity and history, not an attempt to replace the adoptive parents. At the same time, participants were sympathetic to the uneasy feelings that reunion may evoke for adoptive parents. Adoptive parents who are experiencing feelings of insecurity or fear of abandonment may consider seeking therapy for themselves. Regardless, the main focus of reunion must remain on the adopted person and not the adoptive parents' need for reassurance or validation, particularly surrounding initial meetings. By now, it should be clear that reunion places various discursive burdens on adoptees. Adoptive parents should aim to protect adoptees from feeling obligated to reassure them or to hold back affection or questions during reunion meetings. Adoptive parents may consider reassuring adoptees that they are there to support them, and will continue to be, at all stages of reunion. Overall, adoptees should be allowed to tune into their own emotions, experiences, and birth family relationships without worrying about their adoptive parents or their relationship with them.

Listen and Communicate Interest

Adoptive parents should offer emotional support before, during, and after reunion meetings. Often, adoptees wish to debrief after meetings with their birth family, and having these discussions, whether in person or over the phone, with members of their adoptive family can create or maintain feelings of closeness. Participants felt hurt when adoptive parents (and adoptive siblings) did not express interest in their reunion or birth family, before, during, and/or after meetings. Those whose adoptive parents were ambivalent about the reunion and/or appeared threatened by the birth family were less likely to describe their relationships with their adoptive parents as close, and were more likely to feel drawn to their birth families. In general, adoptive parents' disinterest and lack of engagement surrounding reunion reflected previous patterns of communication and also set a precedent for future interactions.

Although all messages are relationship- and context-specific, there are specific communication behaviors that adoptive parents can enact to support adoptees. Adoptive parents who would like to establish a more open, supportive relationship with an adoptee should communicate that hope and intention, but they should also be prepared for some resistance. Relational changes take intentionality, effort, and time. That said, here are some specific behaviors that may help adoptive parents communicate interest and cultivate open communication about birth families and reunion:

- If an adoptee tells you, an adoptive parent, that they are searching or reuniting, they may be apprehensive about your reaction. Assure them that you support their desire to explore their identity.
- When an adoptee tells you about searching or reuniting, ask them open-ended, follow-up questions during the conversation, such as "How are you feeling about this process?" or "What hopes do you have?"
- Ask the adoptee, "What can I do to support you in this process?" Remember what they say, and, if possible, do it. Write it down if necessary.
- Provide words of affirmation, written and/or spoken, to the adopted person. Meeting one's birth family takes courage.
- During conversations about birth family and reunion, give your full attention to the adopted person to communicate that you care and are interested.
- Remember when an adoptee is going to be speaking to or meeting someone from their birth family, and afterward, ask them how it went and how they are feeling. If they don't wish to talk about it at that time, let them know you are available to listen if they change their mind.
- If an adoptee tells you the name of their birth city or the names of members of their birth family, remember these names. Write them down if necessary.
- Send or bring culturally appropriate gifts to the birth family if possible.
- Depending on the situation and your circumstances, offer some type of financial support, as reunions are expensive for adoptees. Attach zero expectations to this support.
- If an adoptee has been in reunion with their birth family for a long time, ask about the birth family occasionally. Bring them into conversations, especially if it seems like the adoptee enjoys talking about them.
- Accept the possibility that an adoptee may not feel comfortable talking with you about their reunion or birth family. This may or may not change. Do not pressure adoptees to disclose certain information, and do not assume an invitation to reunion meetings. Instead, listen and take cues from the adopted person in your life about how to provide support in ways that are helpful.
- Remember that social support is based on the receiver's perception. Check in occasionally and ask whether you are providing the support an adoptee needs. Avoid taking feedback personally, and make adjustments when possible.

During Reunion: Provide Emotional and Instrumental Support

As mentioned previously, adoptive parents attending reunion should provide emotional support (listening, affirming) and instrumental support (taking notes, getting food/drinks, carrying gifts) during reunion meetings. I would also add that adoptive parents should, if possible and desired, allow time for the adoptee to be alone with their birth family. The amount of time will be dependent on the situation and the comfort of the adoptee, but given the frequency of adoptees reporting that they held back questions or affection toward their birth family because of the presence of their adoptive parents, time alone with the birth family may be an important part of reunion. This time may also allow the birth family to feel more comfortable and act in a more natural manner, which may help the adoptee to feel more at ease.

Conclusion

To be "in reunion" is to embrace contradiction and uncertainty. What has been unknown and in the shadows is brought into the light and examined, often in detail. This experience—the anticipation, the meeting, and the denouement—is often unpredictable on individual and relational levels. For some, this uncertainty continues even years after the initial meeting. Several participants who had been in reunion for decades described how they still feel nervous before they meet with their birth families. Some spoke of the persistent fear of rejection, always below the surface, as well as feelings of anxiousness or grief that come in unpredictable waves. Over time, birth families become more familiar and perhaps more familial, but even participants who described very close relationships with their birth families articulated the ongoing challenge of these relationships. Ji Kyoung, who described a very close relationship with her birth family, said,

> I get to actually feel how it feels to be part of a family, even though I do also have a lot of struggling with not always feeling part of the family, because of the language barrier, because of the lack of history together. I just came in, in the adult life, so we don't have so much history as they do and that's very clear sometimes. So it is also sometimes very painful because being reminded of that. Yeah, so it has two sides.

For most adoptees, reunion meetings are brief but intense, and then they are over, and life resumes its regular rhythms. There is no tangible or visible change to the adopted person or their daily life. And yet, reunion creates something new. Even if an adoptee meets their birth family one time only, this reunion now lives in her memory and in her photos, and allows a returning and retracing that, although it may be painful at times, becomes a part of her story. And if an adoptee and their birth family try to maintain a relationship as the years pass, they are building a new structure out of fragments left decades ago. Regardless of whether a reunion is a one-time event or an ongoing relationship spanning most of one's lifetime, it requires individuals to stretch their ideas about family and their ways of communicating with one another.

Throughout this book, I have demonstrated that reunion places a large discursive burden on transnational adoptees—to adapt to cultural differences, to consider or attempt learning their heritage language, to express forgiveness for the birth parents, to narrate a happy life story to birth parents, to reassure adoptive parents, to manage interactions between adoptive parents and birth parents, to engage in emotion work during reunion meetings, to ask questions of birth families in a respectful way, and to maintain relationships with their birth family over time. Because of this enormous responsibility, transnational adoptees need support and resources surrounding reunion that enable and empower them to build the identities and relationships that they find rewarding and, hopefully, healing.

Coda

Korean, Adopted, and Reunited during a Pandemic

After two years of living in Korea, my family and I returned to the United States in the summer of 2018. I remember saying goodbye to *eomma*, bending down to embrace her tiny frame. We waved goodbye in the rear window as the car pulled away from her apartment building. I prayed silently that I would get to see her again. I didn't. She died in November 2019. I received the news in an early-morning text from my niece's husband, whose English is better than he thinks it is. I squinted into the bright light of my phone and read the message over and over:

> I'm sorry to say that your mother passed away at 15:30 18 November local time. Your sister, brothers, and other relatives hold a funeral now. We will put true heart to carry out this. So don't worry and cry for this . . .

I sat in the dark, trying to determine what I would do next. Part of me was already on a plane to Seoul, yet I remained glued in place. I longed to be with my family in Korea, but I worried that my presence would be a nuisance instead of a comfort or support. I felt more confusion and uncertainty than grief, and questions tumbled over one another in my mind.

> Would they find it annoying to have to explain everything to me?
> Would they get tired of introducing me to extended family and friends
>   as the little sister who was sent to the U.S. for adoption as a baby?

Would I be able to withstand people's pitying looks after they find out
    who I am?
Would my siblings wish I hadn't come?
Why would I go when I won't really be able to help?
What if I offend someone at the funeral?
And also, what if I *don't* go?

In the end, I didn't leave for Korea. Instead, I planned to take my husband
and our children the coming summer so that we could all spend time with our
family and pay our respects then. But like millions of people around the world,
our plans for 2020 turned into cancellations as the scale and severity of the
COVID-19 pandemic crystallized in our minds and lives. Rather than packing
suitcases, we stocked up on masks and sanitizer; rather than planning travel,
we practiced staying in place and wondered whether we needed to wipe down
our groceries with disinfectant.

————————

I conducted second interviews with participants between August 2020 and
February 2022, and they spoke of how the pandemic had impacted their communication with their birth families. Many mentioned how it had served as an
impetus for contact. Adoptees had read or heard the news of the high numbers of COVID infections in Korea and had reached out to their birth families, or vice versa. Through text, call, or e-mail, they checked in on one another,
and birth parents expressed concern and gave advice, such as telling participants to not leave the house. Plans to meet in person were canceled or delayed.
Ji Kyoung had to cancel the plane tickets she had reserved to meet her birth
family in Alaska. Eric, who had established a routine of visiting his family in
Korea every even year since 2010, was uncertain whether he would be able to
make the trip in 2020, and if he did, he knew it would carry a risk. The pandemic highlighted a mutual concern and shared experience between adoptees
and their birth families while at the same time making it difficult to connect
in person.

    As if the health and economic impacts of the pandemic weren't enough,
the virus also led to spikes in anti-Asian violence, fueled by some U.S. leaders'
references to COVID-19 as the "China virus" and the "kung flu." An increase
in attacks—some of them fatal—on Asians and Asian Americans, as well as
the mass shooting of six Asian women at a spa in Atlanta, Georgia, in March
2021 have reminded many Asian adoptees of their racialized status and the
disconnect between their upbringing and how the world sees them (Mitchell,

2021). These incidents, combined with the brutal murder of George Floyd by law enforcement officers in May 2020, have drawn wide attention to issues of racism and justice, a topic that arose in some interviews. For example, upon hearing news of violence in the wake of George Floyd's murder, Catherine's brother-in-law in Korea called to check on her. When he learned that Catherine had been out volunteering in her community, he told her, "No, no, no, you need to stay home. Be safe; being safe is the priority! Once you're safe, you can do something maybe, but do it from your house." Catherine was among the participants who said that the pandemic and/or the anti-Asian violence had spurred more consistent communication with her birth family, even as plans to see one another in person were placed on hold. Throughout the pandemic and at times when a sense of normalcy seemed unattainable, messages between family members—and all loved ones—sustained relationships.

My biggest regret is not getting on a plane to Korea when I learned that *eomma* died, and not just because the pandemic delayed travel for over two years. I believe that showing up for my birth family, being there with them to respect our *eomma* and to say goodbye to her together would have outweighed any inconvenience my presence would have caused. They never expressed this sentiment; I just know. I wish I had a do-over. Yet I try to give myself the same understanding and compassion that I would give to other adoptees in reunion and to trust that, in families, there is room for mistakes and imperfection, apologies and grace.

The morning I received the news about *eomma*, I placed the framed photo of my Korean mother and father as a young couple on our table and lit a candle on each side. Seeing my makeshift altar, my eldest son found a banana and an apple and placed them in front of the frame, an offering to her. "Does she like wine, Mom?" he asked, remembering how, when we lived in Korea, on Chuseok and Seollal, my brother sprinkled our father's favorite alcohol on his grave, intoning, "Drink, drink," in Korean. I couldn't recall the words. "I don't know, honey," I answered, trying not to sound too sad.

Later, when I was alone in our house, I faced the photo and bowed two and a half times, trying to emulate what my brothers taught me when we visited our father's and grandparents' graves in the Korean countryside. My movements felt and, I'm certain, looked awkward, like an improvised, beginner's yoga. And yet it felt good to do something, even small, to honor *eomma*, the woman whose body I once inhabited, whose face shape I see and love every time I look at my eldest son.

My niece told me that *eomma* hoped to return as a bird in her next life. Maybe she perched on our windowsill, noticed me with my forehead touching the floor, and tilted her head curiously, wondering what I was doing. I like to picture her flying away, bemused at her Korean American daughter. Somehow, she would know deep in her airborne soul that I love her and that I tried. I suppose this captures a great deal of what it means to be family: We love, we try, and, sometimes, we hold on while letting go.

Appendix

Interview Guides

INITIAL INTERVIEW: 2010–2011

- How did your first meeting with your birth family come about?
- Why did you decide to reunite with your birth family?
- Now I would like to hear about your adoptive family and your interactions with them regarding your reunion:
  - How, if at all, did you talk about your birth family reunion with members of your adoptive family?
  - How, if at all, did members of your adoptive family express their feelings about your birth family reunion? What was their reaction? How would you describe your feelings during these conversations?
  - What specific messages, if any, did you wish to convey to your adoptive family about your reunion?
  - How, if at all, did these conversations affect your relationship with members of your adoptive family?
  - How, if at all, did your upcoming reunion impact how you felt about your adoptive family or your place in it?
  - What, if anything, stands out in your mind about the conversations you had with your adoptive family about your reunion?
- Now that we have talked about your interactions with your adoptive family before your reunion, I would like to hear a little about your relationship with your *birth* family before your reunion.
  - How connected did you feel with the members of your birth family before your reunion?
  - How did you perceive your place within your birth family before your reunion?
- Now I would like to talk about your actual reunion. Could you please walk me through the reunion?

- What is the thing you remember most about your reunion? Why?
- What role did language differences play in your reunion? How, if at all, did these differences impact your sense of belonging in the family?
- How, if at all, did the presence of a translator/interpreter impact your reunion?
- What role did cultural differences play in your reunion? How, if at all, did these differences impact your sense of belonging in the family?
- You state in your questionnaire that your adoptive family [insert participation here: *was present, was not present*] during your reunion. How did this participation, or lack thereof, affect your reunion?
- What, if any, messages did you want to convey to your birth family during the reunion?
- What specific messages do you believe your birth family wanted to convey to you during the reunion?
- Going into the reunion, were there topics or questions that you hoped would be addressed? What, if anything, do you wish had been discussed during the reunion that was not?
- How did you address, or refer to, members of your birth family before your reunion? (For instance . . .) Did the reunion change these terms of address? For instance. . . . If so, how?
- How did members of your birth family refer to you during your reunion? How did you feel about the way they addressed, or referred to, you?
- To what extent did you feel like you were "a part" of your birth family during your reunion? After your reunion?

• Finally, I would like to talk about how you felt about your reunion afterward, and how you feel about it today.
  - How would you describe your relationship with your birth family, or specific family members, today?
  - What, if any, ongoing contact do you have with members of your birth family?
  - What, if any, ongoing contact does your adoptive family have with your birth family? How do you feel about this contact?
  - How, if at all, do you think your reunion impacted your relationship with your adoptive family?
  - In our culture, we are often led to believe that people can only have one "real" family. Having reunited with your birth family and having grown up with your adoptive family, how do you respond to this notion?
  - How, if at all, has your communication with your birth family changed since your reunion?
  - How, if at all, has your communication with your adoptive family changed since your reunion?
  - As an adoptee, I have noticed that people outside of my family are often curious about whether I have reunited with my birth family. To what extent, or under what conditions, do you tend to talk about your reunion or your birth family with people outside of your family? To what extent, if at all, does this differ from how you talk about the reunion with your adoptive family or other people close to you?
  - What, if any, advice would you give to other adoptees hoping to establish contact/reunite with their birth families?

- What, if any, advice would you give to adoptive parents who have a child who would like to initiate contact with their birth family or who is going to reunite with his/her birth family?
- Is there anything else you would like to share with me today?

SECOND INTERVIEW: 2020–2022

- The last time we spoke about your birth family was in (year). Have you been in contact with them since then, and if so, how have you been in contact (visits, video calls, email, letters, etc.)?
- How many times have you seen them in person?
- How would you describe your relationship then and now?
- What do you think has contributed to the changes in your relationship?
- How have you navigated cultural differences in your relationship?
- How have you navigated language differences in your relationship?
- Maintaining these birth family relationships across time and distance can be challenging. Why do you continue to maintain these relationships?
- Are there members of your birth family that you feel closer to than others? If so, why? How would you describe these relationships?
- What have been the biggest challenges to your relationship?
- What have been the most rewarding parts of your relationship with your birth family?
- What, if anything, do you wish you would have known ten years ago about your birth family or your relationship with them?
- What is your adoptive family's relationship with your birth family?
- How, if at all, has your relationship with your birth family impacted your relationship with your adoptive family?
- Are there any events or interactions that stand out to you from the past ten years?
- If you had to speculate, what do you see in the future for your relationship with your Korean family?
- Is there anything else you would like to share with me today?

Notes

ACKNOWLEDGMENTS

1. Dass, R., & Bush, M. (2018). *Walking each other home: Conversations on loving and dying.* Sounds True.

INTRODUCTION

1. Other adoption scholars have conducted research in the areas of psychology, focusing on variables such as adoptive identity (Grotevant et al., 2000), ethnic identity (Lee et al., 2015), and cultural socialization (Kim et al., 2013).

2. Transracial adoption occurs when a child of one race is placed with parents of another race. In transracial adoptions, the most common placement is children of color (a.k.a. non-White) placed with White (a.k.a. Caucasian) adoptive parents. Transracial adoptions can be domestic or transnational.

3. I use the term *American Indian*, as indigenous people have expressed a preference for it over the widely used label *Native American* when specific tribal information is not used (Smithsonian Institution, 2022; Yellow Bird, 1999).

4. The majority of Korean adoptees who conduct birth family searches are unsuccessful in locating their birth family.

CHAPTER 1

1. Under U.S. immigration law, an orphan is a foreign-born child who: does not have any parents because of the death or disappearance of, abandonment or desertion by, or separation or loss from, both parents OR has a sole or surviving parent who is unable to care for the child, consistent with the local standards of the foreign sending country, and

who has, in writing, irrevocably released the child for emigration and adoption (U.S. Citizenship and Immigration Services, 2021).

2. Also known as a referral.

3. New American Standard Bible (n.d.).

4. The years following the Olympics saw a drastic decrease in the number of children sent from Korea, from 6,463 in 1988 to 2,962 in 1990 (Kim, 2007). These numbers plateaued around 2,000 per year for over a decade before a mostly steady decrease from 2004 to 2013 (U.S. Department of State, n.d.).

5. Examples of discontinuity include formally terminating the legal relationship between adoptee and adopter, or retaining the legal relationship but the adoptee being removed from the family home.

6. Only heterosexual couples are eligible to adopt from Korea, and Korea Adoption Services "often consider marital status as part of the totality of the PAP's home study" (U.S. Department of State, 2021).

7. An exception is the case of U.S. adoptions from the Republic of the Marshall Islands, which have been characterized by openness (Roby et al., 2005).

CHAPTER 2

1. *Jageun oppa* translated literally is little older brother to a sister.

2. Portions of this chapter previously appeared in the following two journal articles: Docan-Morgan, S. (2014). They were strangers who loved me: Discussions, narratives, and rituals during Korean adoptees' initial reunions with birth families, *Journal of Family Communication*, *14*(4), 352–373. https://doi.org/10.1080/15267431.2014.946033. Docan-Morgan, S. (2017). Korean adoptees' discursive construction of birth family and adoptive family identity through names and labels, *Communication Quarterly*, *65*(5), 523–548. https://doi.org/10.1080/01463373.2017.1299192. © 2017 Eastern Communication Association. Reprinted by permission of Taylor & Francis, http://www.tandfonline.com on behalf of Eastern Communication Association, www.ecasite.org.

3. No one in this study was adopted along with their biogenetically related sibling.

4. See the work of ethnographer of communication, Gerry Philipsen (1992) for more on how middle-class Americans define real "communication."

5. Brooks (2020) notes that although the nuclear family was a norm in the United States only from 1950 to 1965, it is often viewed as the gold standard of family forms.

6. Pseudonym.

CHAPTER 3

1. Portions of this chapter appeared in Docan-Morgan, S. (2016). Cultural differences and perceived belonging during Korean adoptees' reunions with birth families, *Adoption Quarterly*, *19*(2), 99–118. https://doi.org/10.1080/10926755.2015.1088109. Reprinted by permission of Taylor & Francis, http://www.tandfonline.com.

2. The term *culture* has numerous definitions, each of which is situated within specific historical, political, social, and cultural contexts (Sorrells, 2016).

3. A top university in Seoul.

4. One of the main holidays in Korea, a celebration of the fall harvest. *Chuseok* is celebrated with family and visits to family gravesites.

5. Nonadopted.

6. *Hyeong*(형): Korean term for older brother to a male. Can also refer to an older male with whom a younger male has a close relationship.

CHAPTER 4

1. For readability, I have chosen to write these Korean sentences using the Roman alphabet, even though it is impossible to capture proper pronunciation of Korean without using hangul.

2. See J. K. Park (2009) for background on "English fever" in South Korea, and S. W. Park (2009) for information on English in the context of American militarization of South Korea.

3. Over the past three decades, Korea has become increasingly consumed by "English fever," the intense importance placed on English-language learning reflected in national policies, the education system, and parents who have come to view English as a path to upward social mobility (J. K. Park, 2009). Since the 1990s, each subsequent generation has incurred more pressure and more opportunities to learn English, whether in public school, through private tutors, or at "cram schools" known as *hagwons* (J. K. Park, 2009).

4. Pseudonym.

5. In general, translation involves written text, and interpretation occurs in live time (Kent State University, n.d.).

6. Interpreter training programs in the United States require multiple language proficiency as a baseline, and then require coursework in topics such as ethics, note-taking, types of interpretation, and more, as well as internship requirements.

7. *Appa* (아빠): Korean word for "dad."

CHAPTER 5

1. Portions of this chapter appeared as Docan-Morgan, S. (2021). Discursive struggles in "real" families: Korean adoptees, adoptive parents, and birth family reunions, *Family Relations*, *71*(2), 542–560. Advance online publication. https://doi.org/10.1111/fare.12596. © 2021 National Council on Family Relations.

2. Contrary to popular belief, adoptions do not always remain permanent. Instances of legal or residential disruptions have been reported for both domestic and transnational adoptions (Festinger, 2014; Kim, 2021).

3. Nazario, 2018.

4. The term *gotcha* has been criticized for focusing only on the adoptive parents' gain, obscuring the adoptee's loss, and for its objectifying connotation (Riben, 2015).

CHAPTER 6

1. In 2018, South Korea changed its maximum workweek from sixty-eight hours to fifty-two hours (Wamsley, 2018), but, as of 2020, the country still had the fourth-longest workweek of OECD countries (OECD, 2022).

2. Also anglicized as *jung* or *cheong*.

3. Also anglicized as *yeon*.

4. Younger sister's term of address for older sister.
5. Multiplayer role-playing video game.

CHAPTER 7

1. If you are experiencing suicidal thoughts, seek help immediately:

   a. Call the National Suicide Prevention Lifeline 800-273-8255 (or simply dial 988), https://suicidepreventionlifeline.org/.
   b. Text HOME to 741741 to reach a volunteer crisis counselor.

References

Adams, T., Jones, S. H., & Ellis, C. (2015). *Autoethnography: Understanding qualitative research*. Oxford University Press.

Afifi, W. A., & Johnson, M. L. (2005). The nature and function of tie-signs. In V. Manusov (Ed.), *The sourcebook of nonverbal measures: Going beyond words* (pp. 189–198). Routledge.

AGCI (n.d.). *About AGCI*. All God's Children International. https://allgodschildren.org/about-agci/

Ahn, A. J., Kim, B. S. K., & Park, Y. S. (2008). Asian cultural values gap, cognitive flexibility, coping strategies, and parent-child conflicts among Korean Americans. *Cultural Diversity and Ethnic Minority Psychoflogy, 14*(4), 353–363. https://doi.org/10.1037/1099-9809.14.4.353

Altman, I., & Taylor, D. A. (1973). *Social penetration: The development of interpersonal relationships*. Holt, Rinehart, & Winston.

American Adoptions. (2015). *Legacy of an adopted child*. https://www.americanadoptions.com/blog/legacy-of-an-adopted-child-author-unknown/

Anzur, C. K., & Myers, S. A. (2020). "To meet her, that changed everything": Adult adoptees' discursive construction of the meaning of "parent" following birth parent contact. *Journal of Family Communication, 20*(1), 1–15. https://doi.org/10.1080/15267431.2019.1656633

Aunola, K., Nurmi, J. E., Onatsu-Arvilommi, T., & Pulkkinen, L. (1999). The role of parents' self-esteem, mastery-orientation and social background in their parenting styles. *Scandinavian Journal of Psychology, 40*(4), 307–317. https://doi.org/10.1111/1467-9450.404131

Babe, A. (2018, March 1). The stigma of being a single mother in South Korea. *Aljazeera*. https://www.aljazeera.com/features/2018/3/1/the-stigma-of-being-a-single-mother-in-south-korea

Babe, A. (2021, May 13). Korean adoptees felt isolated and alone for decades. Then Facebook brought them together. *Rest of World*. https://restofworld.org/2021/stranger-than-family/

Baden, A. (2016). "Do you know your real parents?" and other adoption microaggressions. *Adoption Quarterly, 19*(1), 1–25. https://doi.org/10.1080/10926755.2015.1026012

Baden, A. L., Treweeke, L. M., & Ahluwalia, M. K. (2012). Reclaiming culture: Re-culturation of transracial and international adoptees. *Journal of Counseling & Development, 90*(4), 387–399. https://doi.org/10.1002/j.1556-6676.2012.00049.x

Bae, S. (2018). Radical imagination and the solidarity movement between transnational Korean adoptees and unwed mothers in South Korea. *Adoption and Culture, 6*(2), 300–315. https://doi.org/10.26818/adoptionculture.6.2.0300

Baerger, D. R., & McAdams, D. P. (1999). Life story coherence and its relation to psychological well-being. *Narrative Inquiry, 9*(1), 69–96. https://doi.org/10.1075/ni.9.1.05bae

Bang, K. S., Chae, S. M., Hyun, M. S., Nam, H. K., Kim, J. S., & Park, K. H. (2012). The mediating effects of perceived parental teasing on relations of body mass index to depression and self-perception of physical appearance and global self-worth in children. *Journal of Advanced Nursing, 68*(12), 2646–2653. https://doi.org/10.1111/j.1365-2648.2012.05963.x

Baxter, L. A. (2004). Relationships as dialogues. *Personal Relationships, 11*, 1–22. https://doi: 10.1111/j.1475-6811.2004.00068.x

Baxter, L. A. (2011). *Voicing relationships: A dialogic perspective*. SAGE Publications.

Baxter, L. A., & Babbie, E. R. (2003). *The basics of communication research* (1st ed.). Thomson/Wadsworth.

Baxter, L. A., & Braithwaite, D. O. (2006). Rituals as communication constituting families. In L. H. Turner & R. West (Eds.), *The family communication sourcebook* (pp. 259–280). SAGE Publications.

Baxter, L. A., & Braithwaite, D. O. (2010). Relational dialectics theory, applied. In S. W. Smith & S. R. Wilson (Eds.), *New directions in interpersonal communication research* (pp. 63–81). SAGE Publications.

Baxter, L. A., & Bullis, C. (1986). Turning points in developing romantic relationships. *Human Communication Research, 12*(4), 469–493. https://doi.org/10.1111/j.1468-2958.1986.tb00088.x

Baxter, L. A., Norwood, K. M., Asbury, B., & Scharp, K. M. (2014). Narrating adoption: Resisting adoption as "second best" in online stories of domestic adoption told by adoptive parents. *Journal of Family Communication, 14*(3), 253–269. https://doi.org/10.1080/15267431.2014.908199

Bell, R. A., & Daly, J. A. (1984). The affinity-seeking function of communication. *Communication Monographs, 51*(2), 91–115. https://doi.org/10.1080/03637758409390188

Bergquist, K. J. S. (2006). From kim chee to moon cakes: Feeding Asian adoptees' imaginings of culture and self. *Food, Culture & Society, 9*(2), 141–154.

Beyond Words. (2022). *Adoptee-therapist directory*. Beyond Words Psychological Services. https://www.growbeyondwords.com/adoptee-therapist-directory/

Bonilla-Silva, E. (2003). *Racism without racists: Color-blind racism and the persistence of racial inequality in the United States*. Rowman & Littlefield Publishers.

Borshay Liem, D. (2000). *First Person Plural.* MU Films.

Bourke, B. (2014). Positionality: Reflecting on the research process. *The Qualitative Report, 19*(33), 1–9.

Braithwaite, D. O., Bach, B. W., Baxter, L. A., DiVerniero, R., Hammonds, J. R., Hosek, A. M., Willer, E. K., & Wolf, B. M. (2010). Constructing family: A typology of voluntary kin. *Journal of Social and Personal Relationships, 27*(3), 388–407. https://doi .org/10.1177/0265407510361615

Braithwaite, D. O., & Baxter, L. A. (2008). Introduction: Meta-theory and theory in interpersonal communication research. In L. A. Baxter & D. O. Braithwaite (Eds.), *Engaging theories in interpersonal communication: Multiple perspectives* (pp. 1–18). SAGE Publications.

Braithwaite, D. O., Suter, E. A., & Floyd, K. (2018). Introduction: The landscape of meta-theory and theory in family communication research. In *Engaging theories in family communication: Multiple perspectives* (2nd ed.) (pp. 1–16). SAGE Publications.

Brian, K. (2012). *Reframing transracial adoption: Adopted Koreans, White parents, and the politics of kinship.* Temple University Press.

Briggs, L. (2003). Mother, child, race, nation: The visual iconography of rescue and the politics of transnational and transracial adoption. *Gender & History, 15*(2), 179–200. https://doi.org/10.1111/1468-0424.00298

Briggs, L. (2012). *Somebody's children: The politics of transracial and transnational adoption.* Duke University Press.

Brodzinsky, D. M. (2006). Family structural openness and communication openness as predictors in the adjustment of adopted children. *Adoption Quarterly, 9*(4), 1–18. https://doi.org/10.1300/J145v09n04_01

Brodzinsky, D. M. (2011). Children's understanding of adoption: Developmental and clinical implications. *Professional Psychology: Research and Practice, 42*(2), 200–207. https://doi.org/10.1037/a0022415

Brodzinsky, D. M., & Pinderhughes, E. (2002). Parenting and child development in adoptive families. In M. H. Bornstein (Ed.), *Children and Parenting* (2nd ed., Vol. 1, pp. 279–311). Lawrence Erlbaum Associates, Publishers.

Brown, L., & Winter, B. (2019). Multimodal indexicality in Korean: "Doing deference" and "performing intimacy" through nonverbal behavior. *Journal of Politeness Research, 15*(1), 25–54. https://doi.org/10.1515/pr-2016-0042

Brown, P., & Levinson, S. C. (1987). *Politeness: Some universals in language usage.* Cambridge University Press.

Brown, T. W., & Roby, J. L. (2016). Exploitation of intercountry adoption: Toward common understanding and action. *Adoption Quarterly, 19*(2), 63–80. https://doi.org/10 .1080/10926755.2015.1088107

Burgoon, J. K., Buller, D. B., Hale, J. L., & de Turck, M. A. (1984). Relational messages associated with nonverbal behaviors. *Human Communication Research, 10*(3), 351–378. https://doi.org/10.1111/j.1468-2958.1984.tb00023.x

Burgoon, J. K., Manusov, V., & Guerrero, L. K. (2016). *Nonverbal communication.* Routledge.

Butler, B. S., & Matook, S. (2015). Social media and relationships. In P. H. Ang & R. Mansell (Eds.), *The International Encyclopedia of Digital Communication and Society* (1st ed., pp. 1–12). Wiley. https://doi.org/10.1002/9781118767771.wbiedcs097

Cachero, P. (2018, April). *Korean orphans languish in system as tradition, new laws make adoption difficult.* The Groundtruth Project. https://thegroundtruthproject.org/korean -orphans-languish-system-tradition-new-laws-make-adoption-difficult/

Cai, J., Kim, A. Y., & Lee, R. M. (2020). Psychological correlates of interest in genetic testing among Korean American adoptees and their parents. *Journal of Genetic Counseling, 29*(3), 460–470. https://doi.org/10.1002/jgc4.1237

Cameron School of Business. (n.d.). *Determining language proficiency.* University of North Carolina Wilmington. https://csb.uncw.edu/cen/docs/determining%20language %20proficiency.pdf

Campbell, L. H., Silverman, P. R., & Patti, P. B. (1991). Reunions between adoptees and birth parents: The adoptees' experience. *Social Work, 36*(4), 329–335. https://doi .org/10.1093/sw/36.4.329

Canary, D. J., & Stafford, L. (1992). Relational maintenance strategies and equity in marriage. *Communication Monographs, 59*(3), 243–267. https://doi.org/10.1080/0363 7759209376268

Caughlin, J. P. (2003). Family communication standards: What counts as excellent family communication and how are such standards associated with family satisfaction? *Human Communication Research, 29*(1), 5–40. https://doi.org/10.1111/j.1468-2958 .2003.tb00830.x

Chira, S. (1988, April 21). Seoul journal: Babies for export: And now the painful questions. *The New York Times.* https://www.nytimes.com/1988/04/21/world/seoul-jour nal-babies-for-export-and-now-the-painful-questions.html

Cho, G. M. (2021). *Tastes like war: A memoir.* Feminist Press.

Cho, J., & Trent, A. (2006). Validity in qualitative research revisited. *Qualitative Research, 6*(3), 319–340. https://doi.org/10.1177/1468794106065006

Choe, S. H. (2013, June 29). An adoptee returns to South Korea, and changes follow. *The New York Times.* https://www.nytimes.com/2013/06/29/world/asia/an-adoptee -returns-to-south-korea-and-changes-follow.html

Choe, S. H. (2019, May 1). Attending school with a South Korean 70-year-old. *The New York Times.* https://www.nytimes.com/2019/05/01/reader-center/south-korean-illit erate-grandmothers.html

Choi, S. C., & Choi, S. H. (2001). Cheong: The socioemotional grammar of Koreans. *International Journal of Group Tensions, 30*(1), 69–80.

Choi, Y., Kim, Y. S., Kim, S. Y., & Kim Park, I. (2013). Is Asian American parenting controlling and harsh? Empirical testing of relationships between Korean American and Western parenting measures. *Asian American Journal of Psychology, 14*(1), 19–29. https://dx.doi.org/10.1037%2Fa0031220

Choi Robinson, M. (2022, March 7). My adoption day is an anniversary of loss. *Intercountry Adoptee Voices.* https://intercountryadopteevoices.com/tag/expectations-of -gratitude-in-adoption/

Choo, S. B., & Kang, S. S. (2021, September 13). LGBTQ Koreans eager for anti-discrimination bill. *Time.* https://time.com/6094503/south-korea-lgbtq-discrimination/

Choy, C. C. (2013). *Global families: A History of Asian international adoption in America.* New York University Press.

Chu, M. (2017, December 5). Koreans still favor people with type O blood, dislike type AB: Survey. *Korea Biomedical Review.* http://www.koreabiomed.com/news/article View.html?idxno=2053

Chu, T. (2012). *Resilience*. Seventh Art Releasing.

Chudnovskaya, E., & O'Hara, L. L. S. (2022). Indulgence versus restraint: Exploration of a new cultural dimension in context. *Journal of Intercultural Communication, 22*(2), Article 2. https://doi.org/10.36923/jicc.v22i2.54

Chung, C. K., & Cho, S. (2003). *Significance of "jeong" in Korean culture and psychotherapy*. https://www.semanticscholar.org/paper/Significance-of-%E2%80%9CJeong%E2%80%9D-in-Korean-Culture-and-Chung-Cho/b492d8398d95aadefe1cf99f3782621cf6a55cb6

Chung, S., & An, H. (2014). Cultural issues of co-sleeping in Korea. *Sleep Medicine Research, 5*(2), 37–42.

Colaner, C. W., Halliwell, D., & Guignon, P. (2014). "What do you say to your mother when your mother's standing beside you?" Birth and adoptive family contributions to adoptive identity via relational identity and relational-relational identity gaps. *Journal of Family Communication, 81*(4), 469–494. https://doi.org/10.1080/03637751.2014.955808

Colaner, C. W., Horstman, H. K., & Rittenour, C. E. (2018). Negotiating adoptive and birth shared family identity: A social identity complexity approach. *Western Journal of Communication, 82*(4), 393–415. https://doi.org/10.1080/10570314.2017.1384564

Coleman, P. K., & Garratt, D. (2016). From birth mothers to first mothers: Toward a compassionate understanding of the life-long act of adoption placement. *Issues in Law & Medicine, 31*(2), 139–163.

Cox, S. S. (Ed.). (1999). *Voices from another place: A collection of works from a generation born in Korea and adopted to other countries*. Yeong & Yeong.

Creswell, J. (2003). *Research design: Qualitative, quantitative, and mixed methods approaches* (2nd ed.). SAGE Publications.

Crisp, H., & Gustafson, R. (Hosts). (2019–present). *Adopted Feels* [Audio podcast]. https://www.adoptedfeels.com/

Crisp, H., & Gustafson, R. (Hosts). (2022, April 3). Fact and fantasy in adoptee creative nonfiction: Jenny Heijun Wills on writing, consent, and self-preservation (No. 54). [Audio podcast episode]. In *Adopted Feels*. https://www.adoptedfeels.com/

Curran, T., & Arroyo, A. (2018). Emulating parental levels of taking conflict personally: Associations with behavioral and mental health outcomes in adult children. *Journal of Family Communication, 18*(3), 171–184. https://doi.org/10.1080/15267431.2018.1450254

Custer, C. (2013, July 25). Kidnapped and sold: Inside the dark world of child trafficking in China. *The Atlantic*. https://www.theatlantic.com/china/archive/2013/07/kidnapped-and-sold-inside-the-dark-world-of-child-trafficking-in-china/278107/

Dailey, R. M., & Palomares, N. A. (2004). Strategic topic avoidance: An investigation of topic avoidance frequency, strategies used, and relational correlates. *Communication Monographs, 71*(4), 471–496. https://doi.org/10.1080/0363452042000307443

Dainton, M., & Gross, J. (2008). The use of negative behaviors to maintain relationships. *Communication Research Reports, 25*(3), 179–191. https://doi.org/10.1080/08824090802237600

Dainton, M., & Zelley, E. D. (2006). Social exchange theories: Interdependence and equity. In *Engaging theories in family communication: Multiple perspectives* (pp. 243–259). SAGE Publications. https://doi.org/10.4135/9781452204420

Daniluk, J. C., & Hurtig-Mitchell, J. (2003). Themes of hope and healing: Infertile couples' experiences of adoption. *Journal of Counseling & Development, 81*(4), 389–399. https://doi.org/10.1002/j.1556-6678.2003.tb00265.x

Davis, T. L. (1995). Gender differences in masking negative emotions: Ability or motivation? *Developmental Psychology, 31*(4), 660–667. https://doi.org/10.1037/0012-1649.31.4.660

Deng, F., & Zou, Q. (2016). A study on whether the adults' second language acquisition is easy or not—From the perspective of children's native language acquisition. *Theory and Practice in Language Studies, 6*(4), 776. https://doi.org/10.17507/tpls.0604.15

Dindia, K. (2003). Definitions and perspectives on relational maintenance communication. In D. J. Canary & M. Dainton (Eds.), *Maintaining relationships through communication: Relational, contextual, and cultural variations* (pp. 1–28). Routledge.

Dindia, K., & Baxter, L. A. (1987). Strategies for maintaining and repairing marital relationships. *Journal of Social and Personal Relationships, 4*, 143–158.

DiVerniero, R. A. (2013). Children of divorce and their nonresidential parent's family: Examining perceptions of communication accommodation. *Journal of Family Communication, 13*(4), 301–320. https://doi.org/10.1080/15267431.2013.823429

Docan-Morgan, S. (2010). Korean adoptees' retrospective reports of intrusive interactions: Exploring boundary management in adoptive families. *Journal of Family Communication, 10*(3), 137–157. https://doi.org/10.1080/15267431003699603

Docan-Morgan, S. (2011). "They don't know what it's like to be in my shoes": Topic avoidance about race in transracially adoptive families. *Journal of Social and Personal Relationships, 28*(3), 336–355. https://doi.org/10.1177/0265407510382177

Docan-Morgan, S. J. (2014). "They were strangers who loved me": Discussions, narratives, and rituals during Korean adoptees' initial reunions with birth families. *Journal of Family Communication, 14*(4), 352–373. https://doi.org/10.1080/15267431.2014.946033 Reprinted by permission of Taylor & Francis, http://www.tandfonline.com

Docan-Morgan, S. (2016). Cultural differences and perceived belonging during Korean adoptees' reunions with birth families. *Adoption Quarterly, 19*(2), 99–118. https://doi.org/10.1080/10926755.2015.1088109 Reprinted by permission of Taylor & Francis, http://www.tandfonline.com

Docan-Morgan, S. (2017). Korean adoptees' discursive construction of birth family and adoptive family identity through names and labels. *Communication Quarterly, 65*(5), 523–548. https://doi.org/10.1080/01463373.2017.1299192 © Reprinted by permission of Taylor & Francis, http://www.tandfonline.com on behalf of Eastern Communication Association, www.ecasite.org

Docan-Morgan, S. (2019). Transnational Korean adoptees and the discursive burden of establishing individual and family identity. In E. J. Han, M. W. Han, & J. H. Lee (Eds.) *Korean diaspora across the world: Homeland in memory, imagination, and reality* (pp. 95–112). Lexington Books.

Docan-Morgan, S. (2022). Discursive struggles in "real" families: Korean adoptees, adoptive parents, and birth family reunions. *Family Relations, 71*(2), 542–560. https://doi.org/10.1111/fare.12596

Döring, N., & Pöschl, S. (2017). Nonverbal cues in mobile phone text messages: The effects of chronemics and proxemics. In R. Ling & S. W. Campbell (Eds.), *The Reconstruction of Space and Time* (1st ed., pp. 109–135). Routledge. https://doi.org/10.4324/9781315134499-6

Dorow, S. (1999). *I wish for you a beautiful life: Letters from the Korean birth mothers of Ae Ran Won to their children*. Yeong & Yeong.

Dorow, S. (2006). *Transnational adoption: A cultural economy of race, gender, and kinship*. New York University Press.

Du Bois, W. E. B. (1897, August 1). *Strivings of the negro people*. The Atlantic. https://www.theatlantic.com/magazine/archive/1897/08/strivings-of-the-negro-people/305446/

Dunbar, N., & Grotevant, H. D. (2004). Adoption narratives: The construction of adoptive identity during adolescence. In *Family stories and the life course: Across time and generations* (pp. 135–161). Lawrence Erlbaum Associates, Publishers.

Eng, D. L. (2003). Transnational adoption and queer diasporas. *Social Text, 21*(3), 1–37.

Epstein, S., & Joo, R. M. (2012). Multiple exposures: Korean bodies and the transnational imagination. *The Asia-Pacific Journal, 10*(33), 1–24. https://apjjf.org/site/make_pdf/3807

Erle, T. M., Schmid, K., Goslar, S. H., & Martin, J. D. (2021). Emojis as social information in digital communication. *Emotion*. https://doi.org/10.1037/emo0000992

Eun, K. S. (2007). *Family values in Korea: A comparative analysis*. In World Policy Forum Achieving Development without Losing Our Families. http://citeseerx.ist.psu.edu/viewdoc/download?doi=10.1.1.545.35&rep=rep1&type=pdf

Feigelman, W., & Silverman, A. R. (1984). The long-term effects of transracial adoption. *Social Service Review, 58*(4), 588–602. https://doi.org/10.1086/644240

Fessler, A. (2006). *The girls who went away: The hidden history of women who surrendered children for adoption in the decades before Roe v. Wade*. Penguin.

Festinger, T. (2014). Adoption disruption. In G. P. Mallon & P. McCartt Hess (Eds.), *Child welfare for the twenty-first century: A handbook of practices, policies, and programs* (2nd ed., pp. 437–454). Columbia University Press.

Foley, J. (2002). *Korea's divided families: Fifty years of separation*. Routledge.

Foreign Service Institute. (n.d.). *Foreign language training*. U.S. Department of State. https://www.state.gov/foreign-language-training/

Frederick, D. A., Kelly, M. C., Latner, J. D., Sandhu, G., & Tsong, Y. (2016). Body image and face image in Asian American and white women: Examining associations with surveillance, construal of self, perfectionism, and sociocultural pressures. *Body Image, 16*, 113–125. https://doi.org/10.1016/j.bodyim.2015.12.002

Futerman, S., & Miyamoto, R. (2015). *Twinsters*. Small Package Films.

Galvin, K. M. (2003). International and transracial adoption: A communication research agenda. *Journal of Family Communication, 3*, 237–253. https://doi.org/10.1207/S15327698JFC0304_5

Galvin, K. M. (2006). Diversity's impact on defining the family: Discourse-dependence and identity. In *The Family Communication Sourcebook* (pp. 3–20). SAGE Publications. https://doi.org/10.4135/9781452233024.n1

Galvin, K. M., & Braithwaite, D. O. (2014). Theory and research from the communication field: Discourses that constitute and reflect families. *Journal of Family Theory & Review, 6*(1), 97–111. https://doi.org/10.1111/jftr.12030

Galvin, K. M., Braithwaite, D. O., Schrodt, P., & Bylund, C. (2019). *Family communication: Cohesion and change* (10th ed.). Routledge.

Giles, H., & Powesland, P. F. (1975). *Speech style and social evaluation* (pp. viii, 218). Academic Press.

Gilligan, M., Stocker, C. M., & Jewsbury Conger, K. (2020). Sibling relationships in adulthood: Research findings and new frontiers. *Journal of Family Theory & Review*, *12*(3), 305–320. https://doi.org/10.1111/jftr.12385

Glionna, J. M. (2011, January 5). *A complex feeling tugs at Koreans*. Los Angeles Times. https://www.latimes.com/archives/la-xpm-2011-jan-05-la-fg-south-korea-han-2011 0105-story.html

G.O.A.'L. (Global Overseas Adoptees' Link) (Ed.). (2008). *Post reunion stories*. G.O.A.'L. (Global Overseas Adoptees' Link).

Goldsmith, D. J. (2004). *Communicating social support*. Cambridge University Press.

Goldsmith, D. J., McDermott, V. M., & Alexander, S. C. (2000). Helpful, supportive and sensitive: Measuring the evaluation of enacted social support in personal relationships. *Journal of Social and Personal Relationships*, *17*(3), 369–391. https://doi .org/10.1177/0265407500173004

Golish, T., & Caughlin, J. (2002). "I'd rather not talk about it": Adolescents' and young adults' use of topic avoidance in stepfamilies. *Journal of Applied Communication Research*, *30*(1), 78–106. https://doi.org/10.1080/00909880216574

Grotevant, H. D., Dunbar, N., Kohler, J. K., & Lash Esau, A. M. (2000). Adoptive identity: How contexts within and beyond the family shape developmental pathways. *Family Relations*, *49*(4), 379–387. https://doi.org/10.1111/j.1741-3729.2000.00379.x

Guerrero, L. K., & Afifi, W. A. (1995). Some things are better left unsaid: Topic avoidance in family relationships. *Communication Quarterly*, *43*(3), 276–296. https://doi .org/10.1080/01463379509369977

Hall, E. T. (1976). *Beyond culture*. Anchor Books.

Hample, D., & Dallinger, J. M. (1995). A Lewinian perspective on taking conflict personally: Revision, refinement, and validation of the instrument. *Communication Quarterly*, *43*(3), 297–319. https://doi.org/10.1080/01463379509369978

Han, K. K. (2007). The archaeology of the ethnically homogeneous nation-state and multiculturalism in Korea. *Korea Journal*, *47*(4), 8–32. https://doi.org/10.25024/KJ .2007.47.4.8

Han, Y. R., & Choi, H. Y. (2021). Risk factors affecting intimate partner violence occurrence in South Korea: Findings from the 2016 Domestic violence survey. *PLOS ONE*, *16*(3), e0247916. https://doi.org/10.1371/journal.pone.0247916

Harrigan, M. M., & Braithwaite, D. O. (2010). Discursive struggles in families formed through visible adoption: An exploration of dialectical unity. *Journal of Applied Communication Research*, *38*(2), 127–144. https://doi.org/10.1080/00909881003639536

Hecht, M. L. (1993). 2002—A research odyssey: Toward the development of a communication theory of identity. *Communication Monographs*, *60*(1), 76–82. https:// doi.org/10.1080/03637759309376297

Herman, E. (2012). *Matching*. The Adoption History Project. https://pages.uoregon.edu /adoption/topics/matching.html

Higgins, C., & Stoker, K. (2011). Language learning as a site for belonging: A narrative analysis of Korean adoptee-returnees. *International Journal of Bilingual Education and Bilingualism*, *14*(4), 399–412. https://doi.org/10.1080/13670050.2011.573064

Hochschild, A. R. (1979). Emotion work, feeling rules, and social structure. *American Journal of Sociology*, *85*(3), 551–575. https://doi.org/10.1086/227049

Hoffman, J., & Peña, E. V. (2013). Too Korean to be White and too White to be Korean: Ethnic identity development among transracial Korean American adoptees. *Jour-*

nal of Student Affairs Research and Practice, 50(2), 152–170. https://doi.org/10.1515/jsarp-2013-0012

Horstman, H. K., Colaner, C. W., & Rittenour, C. E. (2016). Contributing factors of adult adoptees' identity work and self-esteem: Family communication patterns and adoption-specific communication. *Journal of Family Communication, 16*(3), 263–276. https://doi.org/10.1080/15267431.2016.1181069

Hu, E. (2015, May 11). South Korea's single moms struggle to remove a social stigma. *NPR.* https://www.npr.org/sections/parallels/2015/05/11/405622494/south-koreas-single-moms-struggle-to-remove-a-social-stigma

Hübinette, T. (2003). The adopted Koreans of Sweden and the Korean adoption issue. *The Review of Korean Studies, 6*(1), 251–266.

Hübinette, T. (2004). Adopted Koreans and the development of identity in the "third space." *Adoption & Fostering, 28*(1), 16–24. https://doi.org/10.1177/030857590402800104

Hübinette, T. (2005). *Comforting an orphaned nation: Representations of international adoption and adopted Koreans in Korean popular culture.* http://urn.kb.se/resolve?urn=urn:nbn:se:su:diva-696

Hübinette, T. (2006). From orphan trains to babylifts: Colonial trafficking, empire building, and social engineering. In J. J. Trenka, J. C. Oparah, & S. Y. Shin (Eds.), *Outsiders within: Writing on transracial adoption* (pp. 139–149). South End Press.

Hübinette, T. (2007). Disembedded and free-floating bodies out of place and out of control: Examining the borderline existence of adopted Koreans. *Adoption and Culture, 1*(1), 129–162. https://www.jstor.org/stable/44755462

InKAS. (n.d.). *Language School.* International Korean Adoptee Service. http://www.inkas.org/en/service/scholarship/languageschool/

Jacobson, H. (2008). *Culture keeping: White mothers, international adoption, and the negotiation of family difference.* Vanderbilt University Press.

Jiang, W. (2000). The relationship between culture and language. *ELT Journal, 54*(4), 328–334. https://doi.org/10.1093/elt/54.4.328

Jones, M. (2015, January 14). Why a generation of adoptees is returning to South Korea. *The New York Times.* https://www.nytimes.com/2015/01/18/magazine/why-a-generation-of-adoptees-is-returning-to-south-korea.html

Jung, J., & Forbes, G. B. (2007). Body dissatisfaction and disordered eating among college women in China, South Korea, and the United States: Contrasting predictions from sociocultural and feminist theories. *Psychology of Women Quarterly, 31*(4), 381–393. https://doi.org/10.1111%2Fj.1471-6402.2007.00387.x

Kalb, S., & Tucker, A. (2019). How adoptees are shaping post-adoption services. *Rudd Adoption Research Program,* 1–6.

Kent State University. (n.d). *Translation vs. interpretation: How do they differ?* Institute for Applied Linguistics. https://www.kent.edu/appling/matranslationonline/blog/translationvsinterpretation

Kim, A. Y., Lee, J. S., & Lee, W. (2015). Examining Korean American parent-child relationships through bilingual language use. *Journal of Family Communication, 15*(3), 269–287. https://doi.org/10.1080/15267431.2015.1044089

Kim, D., Pan, Y., & Park, H. S. (1998). High-versus low-context culture: A comparison of Chinese, Korean, and American cultures. *Psychology & Marketing, 15*(6), 507–521. https://doi.org/10.1002/(SICI)1520-6793(199809)15:6<507::AID-MAR2>3.0.CO;2-A

Kim, D. S. (2007). A country divided: Contextualizing adoption from a Korean perspective. In K. J. S. Bergquist, M. E. Vonk, D. S. Kim, & M. D. Feit (Eds.), *International Korean adoption: A fifty-year history of policy and practice* (pp. 3–24). Routledge.

Kim, E. (2010). *Adopted territory: Transnational Korean adoptees and the politics of belonging.* Duke University Press.

Kim, H. (2016). *Birth mothers and transnational adoption practice in South Korea: Virtual mothering.* Palgrave Macmillan.

Kim, J. (2006–2022). *Harlow's Monkey.* https://harlows-monkey.com/

Kim, J. (2006). Scattered seeds: The Christian influence on Korean adoption. In J. J. Trenka, J. Chinyere Oparah, & S. Y. Shin (Eds.), *Outsiders within: Writing on transracial adoption* (pp. 151–162). South End Press.

Kim, J. (2009). An "orphan" with two mothers: Transnational and transracial adoption, the Cold War, and contemporary Asian American cultural politics. *American Quarterly, 61*(4), 855–880.

Kim, J. (2021). "Forever family is like a manufactured Hallmark idea": Adoption discontinuity experiences of intercountry adoptees. *Child Abuse & Neglect,* 105184. https://doi.org/10.1016/j.chiabu.2021.105184

Kim, S. H. (2003). Korean cultural codes and communication. *International Area Review, 6*(1), 93–114. https://doi.org/10.1177/223386590300600107

Kim, T. H., & Klug, F. (2019, November 9). AP Exclusive: Abusive South Korean facility exported children. *AP News.* https://apnews.com/article/adoption-asia-pacific-south-korea-international-news-busan-736590a2b96340c4aac66616d94eea33

Kimmel, R. (2021, July 3). How falsified adoption papers make it even more difficult to search for my origin. *Korea Times.* https://www.koreatimes.co.kr/www/opinion/2022/02/801_311436.html

Knapp, M. L., Hall, J. A., & Horgan, T. G. (2014). *Nonverbal communication in human interaction.* Wadsworth Cengage Learning.

Knapp, M. L., & Vangelisti, A. (2005). *Interpersonal communication and human relationships* (5th ed.). Allyn & Bacon.

Koenig Kellas, J., LeClair-Underberg, C., & Normand, E. L. (2008). Stepfamily address terms: "Sometimes they mean something and sometimes they don't." *Journal of Family Communication, 8*(4), 238–263. https://doi.org/10.1080/15267430802397153

Kohler, J. K., Grotevant, H. D., & McRoy, R. G. (2002). Adopted adolescents' preoccupation with adoption: The impact on adoptive family relationships. *Journal of Marriage and Family, 64*(1), 93–104. https://doi.org/10.1111/j.1741-3737.2002.00093.x

Koo, Y. (2019). "We deserve to be here": The development of adoption critiques by transnational Korean adoptees in Denmark. *Anthropology Matters, 19*(1). https://doi.org/10.22582/am.v19i1.508

Krashen, S. D., Long, M. A., & Scarcella, R. C. (1979). Age, rate and eventual attainment in second language acquisition. *TESOL Quarterly, 13*(4), 573–582. https://doi.org/10.2307/3586451

Kristensen, G. K., & Ravn, M. N. (2015). The voices heard and the voices silenced: Recruitment processes in qualitative interview studies. *Qualitative Research, 15*(6), 722–737. https://doi.org/10.1177/1468794114567496

Krusiewicz, E. S., & Wood, J. T. (2001). "He was our child from the moment we walked in that room": Entrance stories of adoptive parents. *Journal of Social and Personal Relationships, 18*(6), 785–803. https://doi.org/10.1177/0265407501186003

KUMFA. (2016). *Korean Unwed Mothers Families' Association*. https://kumfa.or.kr/

Kuper, A., Lingard, L., & Levinson, W. (2008). Critically appraising qualitative research. *BMJ, 337*, 687–692. https://doi.org/10.1136/bmj.a1035

Leach, M. S., & Braithwaite, D. O. (1996). A binding tie: Supportive communication of family kinkeepers. *Journal of Applied Communication Research, 24*(3), 200–216. https://doi.org/10.1080/00909889609365451

Lebow, S. (2021, May 13). *KakaoTalk is the most popular messaging app in South Korea by a massive margin*. Insider Intelligence. https://www.emarketer.com/content/ka kaotalk-most-popular-messaging-app-south-korea-by-a-massive-margin

Lee, H. W. (2018, March 1). The complex culture and history behind "K-beauty." *Nikkei Asia*. https://asia.nikkei.com/NAR/Articles/The-complex-culture-and-history -behind-K-beauty

Lee, J. P., Lee, R. M., Hu, A. W., & Kim, O. M. (2015). Ethnic identity as a moderator against discrimination for transracially and transnationally adopted Korean American adolescents. *Asian American Journal of Psychology, 6*(2), 154–163. https://doi.org /10.1037/a0038360

Lee, K. (2016–present). *Adapted*. [Audio podcast]. https://adaptedpodcast.com/

Lee, K. (2021). In search of identity—Kimura Byol (No. 3, Season 5) [Audio podcast episode]. In *Adapted*. https://adaptedpodcast.com/2021/11/15/season-5-episode-3-in -search-of-identity/

Lee, R. M. (2003). The transracial adoption paradox: History, research, and counseling implications of cultural socialization. *The Counseling Psychologist, 31*(6), 711–744. https://doi.org/10.1177%2F0011000003258087

Lee, S. M., Daniels, M. H., & Kissinger, D. B. (2006). Parental influences on adolescent adjustment: Parenting styles versus parenting practices. *The Family Journal, 14*(3), 253–259. https://doi.org/10.1177/1066480706287654

Lee, S. W. (1994). The cheong space: A zone of non-exchange in Korean human relationships. In *Psychology of the Korean people: Collectivism and individualism* (pp. 85–99). Dong-A Publishers.

Leeds-Hurwitz, W. (1990). Notes in the history of intercultural communication: The Foreign Service Institute and the mandate for intercultural training. *Quarterly Journal of Speech, 76*(3), 262–281. https://doi.org/10.1080/0033563900938 3919

Leeds-Hurwitz, W. (2006). Social theories: Social constructionism and symbolic interactionism. In D. O. Braithwaite & L. A. Baxter (Eds.), *Engaging theories in family communication: Multiple perspectives* (pp. 229–242). SAGE Publications.

Leeds-Hurwitz, W. (2010). Writing the history of intercultural communication. In T. K. Nakayama & R. T. Halualani (Eds.), *The handbook of critical intercultural communication* (pp. 17–33). Wiley-Blackwell.

Lenfield, S. L. (2018, April 23). Korean as a second language. *Catapult*. https://catapult .co/stories/adopted-korean-as-a-second-language

Lim, T. S., & Choi, S. H. (1996). Interpersonal relationships in Korea. In W. B. Gudykunst, S. Ting-Toomey, & T. Nishida (Eds.), *Communication in personal relationships across cultures* (pp. 122–136). SAGE Publications, Inc.

Lipitz, A. (2021). *Found*. Amanda Lipitz Productions.

Malecki, C. K., & Demaray, M. K. (2003). What type of support do they need? Investigating student adjustment as related to emotional, informational, appraisal, and instrumental support. *School Psychology Quarterly, 18*(3), 231–252. https://doi.org/10.1521/scpq.18.3.231.22576

Malmlund, J., Gullaksen, J., Behnk, F., & Jukka-Petteri, S. (2019). *Smartphone: The center of life. A study on Nordic mobile consumer behavior.* https://www2.deloitte.com/content/dam/Deloitte/se/Documents/technology-media-telecommunications/Global-Mobile-Consumer-Survey-2019-Nordic-Cut.pdf

Manning, J., & Kunkel, A. (2014). *Researching interpersonal relationships: Qualitative methods, studies, and analysis.* SAGE Publications. https://doi.org/10.4135/9781452270142

Manusov, V. (2018). Attribution theory: Who's at fault in families? In *Engaging theories in family communication: Multiple perspectives* (2nd ed., pp. 51–61). Routledge.

March, K. (1995). Perception of adoption as social stigma: Motivation for search and reunion. *Journal of Marriage and Family, 57*(3), 653–660. https://doi.org/10.2307/353920

March, K. (1997). The dilemma of adoption reunion: Establishing open communication between adoptees and their birth mothers. *Family Relations, 46*(2), 99–105. https://doi.org/10.2307/585033

March, K. (2000). Who do I look like? Gaining a sense of self-authenticity through the physical reflections of others. *Symbolic Interaction, 23*(4), 359–373. https://doi.org/10.1525/si.2000.23.4.359

Marko Harrigan, M. (2010). Exploring the narrative process: An analysis of the adoption stories mothers tell their internationally adopted children. *Journal of Family Communication, 10*(1), 24–39. https://doi.org/10.1080/15267430903385875

Martin, J. N., & Nakayama, T. K. (2022). *Intercultural communication in contexts* (8th ed.). McGraw-Hill Higher Education.

Martin, J. N., Nakayama, T. K., & Flores, L. A. (Eds.). (2002). *Readings in intercultural communication: Experiences and contexts.* McGraw-Hill.

Matveev, A. V., & Merz, M. Y. (2014). Intercultural competence assessment: What are its key dimensions across assessment tools? In L. T. B. Jackson, D. Meiring, F. J. R. Van de Vijver, E. S. Idemoudia, & W. K. Gabrenya Jr (Eds.), *Toward sustainable development through nurturing diversity: Proceedings from the 21st International Congress of the International Association for Cross-Cultural Psychology.* https://scholarworks.gvsu.edu/iaccp_papers/128/

McAdams, D. P. (2008). Personal narratives and the life story. In O. P. John, R. W. Robbins, & L. A. Pervin (Eds.), *Handbook of personality: Theory and research* (pp. 242–262). Guilford Press.

McDaniel, E., & Andersen, P. A. (1998). International patterns of interpersonal tactile communication: A field study. *Journal of Nonverbal Behavior, 22*(1), 59–75. https://doi.org/10.1023/A:1022952509743

McGinnis, H. A. (2000, February). Ten questions to ask yourself. *Hi Families.* https://www.motherschoice.org/app/uploads/2020/10/Ten-Questions-to-Ask-Yourself.pdf

McGinnis, H. A., Baden, A. L., Kim, A. Y., & Kim, J. (2019). Generational shifts: Adult adoptee scholars' perspective on future research and practice. *The future of adoption: Beyond safety to well-being,* 1–9. Rudd Adoption Research Program. http://www.umass.edu/ruddchair/sites/default/files/rudd.mcginnis.pdf

McGinnis, H. A., Livingston Smith, S., Ryan, S. D., & Howard, J. A. (2009). *Beyond culture camp: Promoting healthy identity in adoption.* Evan B. Donaldson Adoption Institute. https://affcny.org/wp-content/uploads/2009_11_BeyondCultureCamp.pdf

McKee, K. D. (2016). Monetary flows and the movements of children: The transnational adoption industrial complex. *Journal of Korean Studies, 21*(1), 137–178. https://doi.org/10.1353/jks.2016.0007

McKee, K. D. (2019). *Disrupting kinship: Transnational politics of Korean adoption in the United States*. University of Illinois Press.

Mikkelson, A. C., Myers, S. A., & Hannawa, A. F. (2011). The differential use of relational maintenance behaviors in adult sibling relationships. *Communication Studies, 62*(3), 258–271. https://doi.org/10.1080/10510974.2011.555490

Ministry of Health and Welfare. (2013). *History of Adoption in Korea*. Korea Adoption Services. https://kadoption.or.kr/en/info/info_history.jsp

Mitchell, R. (2021, April). *Asian adoptees neither here nor there on hate: Upbringings leave them feeling alienated from their heritage and families who have difficulty understanding reality of racism*. The Los Angeles Times. https://enewspaper.latimes.com/infinity/article_share.aspx?guid=a8f302d0-b685-4553-928b-1b65d5f50d45

Mitu, B. (2015). Confucianism and the contemporary Korean society. *Romanian Journal of Sociological Studies, 1*, 31–38.

Modell, J. (1997). "Where do we go next?" Long-term reunion relationships between adoptees and birth parents. *Marriage and Family Review, 25*(1–2), 43–66.

Mongeau, P. A., & Henningsen, M. L. M. (2008). Stage theories of relationship development: Charting the course of interpersonal communication. In L. A. Baxter & D. O. Braithwaite (Eds.), *Engaging theories in interpersonal communication: Multiple perspectives* (pp. 363–375). SAGE Publications.

Moon, K. H. S. (2015, June 29). The past and future of international adoption. *Brookings Institute*. https://www.brookings.edu/opinions/the-past-and-future-of-international-adoption/

Moriizumi, S. (2011). Exploring identity negotiations: An analysis of intercultural Japanese-U.S. American families living in the United States. *Journal of Family Communication, 11*(2), 85–104. https://doi.org/10.1080/15267431.2011.554359

Morr Serewicz, M. C., Dickson, F. C., Morrison, J. H. T. A., & Poole, L. L. (2007). Family privacy orientation, relational maintenance, and family satisfaction in young adults' family relationships. *Journal of Family Communication, 7*(2), 123–142. https://doi.org/10.1080/15267430701221578

Müller, U., & Perry, B. (2001). Adopted persons' search for and contact with their birth parents. *Adoption Quarterly, 4*(3), 5–37. https://doi.org/10.1300/J145v04n03_02

Myers, K. W. (2014). "Real" families: The violence of love in new media adoption discourse. *Critical Discourse Studies, 11*(2), 175–193. https://doi.org/10.1080/17405904.2013.852983

Myong, L., & Andersen, N. T. (2015). From immigration stop to intimizations of migration: Cross-reading the histories of domestic(ated) labor migration and trans-national adoption in Denmark 1973–2015. *RETFÆRD ÅRGANG, 38*, 62–79.

Nakayama, T. K., & Krizek, R. L. (1995). Whiteness: A strategic rhetoric. *Quarterly Journal of Speech, 81*(3), 291–309. https://doi.org/10.1080/00335639509384117

Nakayama, T. K., & Martin, J. N. (1998). *Whiteness: The communication of social identity*. SAGE Publications.

Nash, R. (2019). *Liberating scholarly writing: The power of personal narrative*. Information Age Publishing.

National Communication Association. (n.d.). *What is communication?* https://www.nat com.org/about-nca/what-communication

Nazario, T. (2020). *And that's why she's my mama.* Bowker.

Nelson, M. R., & Shavitt, S. (2002). Horizontal and vertical individualism and achievement values: A multimethod examination of Denmark and the United States. *Journal of Cross-Cultural Psychology, 33*, 439–458. https://doi.org/10.1177%2F002202 2102033005001

New American Standard Bible. Bible Hub. https://biblehub.com/nasb/ephesians/1-5.htm

Noh, J. W., Kwon, Y. D., Yang, Y., Cheon, J., & Kim, J. (2018). Relationship between body image and weight status in east Asian countries: Comparison between South Korea and Taiwan. *BMC Public Health, 18*, 814. https://doi.org/10.1186/s12889-018-5738-5

OECD. (2022). *Hours worked.* OECD Data. http://data.oecd.org/emp/hours-worked.htm

Oh, A. (2015). *To save the children of Korea: The Cold War origins of international adoption.* Stanford University Press.

O'Neill, D., McAuley, C., & Loughran, H. (2016). Post-adoption reunion sibling relationships: Factors facilitating and hindering the development of sensitive relationships following reunion in adulthood. *Child & Family Social Work, 21*(2), 218–227. https://doi.org/10.1111/cfs.12139

Ottaway, H. C. (2012). *Sibling connections: An exploration of adopted people's birth and adoptive sibling relationships across the life-span.* [Doctoral dissertation, University of East Anglia]. UEA Prints.

Palmer, J. D. (2010). *The dance of identities: Korean adoptees and their journey toward empowerment.* University of Hawaii Press. https://doi.org/10.1515/9780824860875

Park, H., & Raymo, J. M. (2013). Divorce in Korea: Trends and educational differentials. *Journal of Marriage and Family, 75*(1), 110–126. https://doi.org/10.1111/j.1741 -3737.2012.01024.x

Park, I. H., & Cho, L. J. (1995). Confucianism and the Korean family. *Journal of Comparative Family Studies, 26*(1), 117–134. https://doi.org/10.3138/jcfs.26.1.117

Park, J. K. (2009). "English fever" in South Korea: Its history and symptoms. *English Today, 25*(1), 50–57. https://doi.org/10.1017/S026607840900008X

Park, S. (2011). Korean multiculturalism and the marriage squeeze. *Contexts, 10*(3), 64–65. https://doi.org/10.1177/1536504211418459

Park, S. W. (2009). The present and future of Americanization in South Korea. *Journal of Futures Studies, 14*(1), 51–66.

Park Nelson, K. (2016). *Invisible Asians: Korean American adoptees, Asian American experiences, and racial exceptionalism.* Rutgers University Press.

Park Nelson, K. (2018). A decade of Korean adoption studies. *Adoption & Culture, 6*(2), 272–277. https://doi.org/10.1353/ado.2018.0025

Pate, S. (2014). *From orphan to adoptee: U.S. empire and genealogies of Korean adoption.* University of Minnesota Press.

Patton-Imani, S. (2000). *Birthmarks: Transracial adoption in contemporary America.* NYU Press.

Petronio, S. (2002). *Boundaries of privacy: Dialectics of disclosure.* SUNY Press.

Petronio, S. (2010). Communication privacy management theory: What do we know about family privacy regulation? *Journal of Family Theory & Review, 2*(3), 175–196. https://doi.org/10.1111/j.1756-2589.2010.00052.x

Petta, G. A., & Steed, L. G. (2005). The experience of adoptive parents in adoption re-union relationships: A qualitative study. *American Journal of Orthopsychiatry, 75*(2), 230–241. https://doi.org/10.1037/0002-9432.75.2.230

Pew Research Center. (2021, April 7). *Mobile fact sheet*. Pew Research Center. https://www.pewresearch.org/internet/fact-sheet/mobile/

Philipsen, G. (1992). *Speaking culturally: Explorations in social communication*. State University of New York Press.

Philipsen, G., & Huspek, M. (1985). A bibliography of sociolinguistic studies of personal address. *Anthropological Linguistics, 27*(1), 94–101.

Pietsch, B. (2020, November 23). Nice to meet you, Mom. Now let's go into quarantine. *The New York Times*. https://www.nytimes.com/2020/11/23/world/korean-adoptees -reunions.html

Ponting, S. (2022). Birth country travel and adoptee identity. *Annals of Tourism Research, 93*, 103354. https://doi.org/10.1016/j.annals.2022.103354

Powell, K. A., & Afifi, T. D. (2005). Uncertainty management and adoptees' ambiguous loss of their birth parents. *Journal of Social and Personal Relationships, 22*(1), 129–151. https://doi.org/10.1177/0265407505049325

Prébin, E. (2013). Meeting once more: The Korean side of transnational adoption. New York University Press.

Pyke, K. D., & Johnson, D. L. (2003). Asian American women and racialized femininities: "Doing" gender across cultural worlds. *Gender & Society, 17*(1), 33–53. https://doi.org/10.1177/0891243202238977

Quiroz, P. A. (2012). Cultural tourism in transnational adoption: "Staged authenticity" and its implications for adopted children. *Journal of Family Issues, 33*(4), 527–555. https://doi.org/10.1177/0192513X11418179

Ra, J. S., Cho, K. S., & Cho, Y. H. (2020). Gender differences regarding parental teasing of Korean children's weight and anti-fat attitudes. *Journal of Korean Public Health Nursing, 34*(2), 289–300. https://doi.org/10.5932/JKPHN.2020.34.2.289

Raleigh, E. (2018). *Selling transracial adoption: Families, markets, and the color line*. Temple University Press.

Randolph, B. (2014). Red flags that a potential therapist could do more harm than good. In L. Dennis (Ed.), *Adoption therapy: Perspectives from clients and clinicians on processing and healing post-adoption* (pp. 26–45). Entourage Publishing.

Randolph, B. (2016, January 5). 10 red flags when choosing an adoption therapist. *Brooke Randolph*. https://brooke-randolph.com/blog/10_red_flags_when_choosing_an_adoption_therapist/

Rankin, J., & Bishoff, T. (Eds.). (1997). *Seeds from a silent tree: An anthology by Korean adoptees*. Pandal Press.

Riben, M. (2015, May 6). The insensitivity of adoption day celebrations. *Huffington Post*. https://www.huffpost.com/entry/the-insensitivity-of-adoption-day-celebrations_b _7207100

Roby, J. L., & Matsumura, S. (2002). If I give you my child, aren't we family? A study of birthmothers participating in Marshall Islands-U.S. adoption. *Adoption Quarterly, 5*(4), 7–31. https://doi.org/10.1300/J145v05n04_02

Roby, J. L., Wyatt, J., & Pettys, G. (2005). Openness in International Adoptions. *Adoption Quarterly, 8*(3), 47–71. https://doi.org/10.1300/J145v08n03_03

Schein, E. H. (1984). Coming to a new awareness of organizational culture. *Edgar H. Sloan Management Review, 25*(2), 3–16.

Schuster Institute for Investigative Journalism. (2008–2014). *Fraud and corruption in international adoptions.* https://www.brandeis.edu/investigate/adoption/index.html

Scull, S. (2019, June 10). "We had a connection." *Creston News.* https://www.creston news.com/2019/06/10/we-had-a-connection/asgui6s/

Sheppard, N. (2020, September 10). *It's OK to not be OK: Navigating the stressors of 2020 as a community of adoptees.* KAAN. https://www.wearekaan.org/post/its-ok-to-not -be-ok

Shorrock, T. (2019, December 2). Welcome to the monkey house: Confronting the ugly legacy of military prostitution in South Korea. *The New Republic.* https://newrepub lic.com/article/155707/united-states-military-prostitution-south-korea-monkey-house

Shvedsky, L. (2020, March 23). In 1983, a Korean TV station ran a live show reuniting families separated by war. It became a 138-day marathon of hope. *Upworthy.* https:// www.upworthy.com/korea-family-reunions-1983-video

Silverman, P. R., Campbell, L., & Patti, P. (1994). Reunions between adoptees and birth parents: The adoptive parents' view. *Social Work, 39*(5), 542–549. https://academic .oup.com/sw/article-abstract/39/5/542/1892299

Simon, R. J., & Altstein, H. (1996). The case for transracial adoption. *Children and Youth Services Review, 18*(1), 5–22. https://doi.org/10.1016/0190-7409(95)00051-8

Simon, R. J., Altstein, H., & Melli, M. S. (1994). *The Case for Transracial Adoption.* American University Press.

Sjöblom, L. W. R. (2019). *Palimpsest: Documents from a Korean adoption.* Drawn and Quarterly.

Smithsonian Institution. (2022). *Native Knowledge 360° | Frequently Asked Questions.* Native Knowledge 360. https://americanindian.si.edu/nk360/faq/did-you-know

Smolin, D. (2005). *Child laundering: How the intercountry adoption system legitimizes and incentivizes the practices of buying, trafficking, kidnapping, and stealing children.* Berkeley Electronic Press. https://law.bepress.com/expresso/eps/749/

Soliz, J., & Colaner, C. W. (2018). Communication accommodation theory and communication theory of identity: Theories of communication and identity. In D. O. Braithwaite, E. A. Suter, & K. Floyd (Eds.), *Engaging theories in family communication: Multiple perspectives* (2nd ed., pp. 75–86). Routledge.

Sorrells, K. (2016). *Intercultural communication: Globalization and social justice* (2nd ed.). SAGE Publications.

Spitzberg, B. H., & Adams III, T. W. (n.d.). *The conversational skills rating scale: An instructional assessment of interpersonal competence.* National Communication Association: Diagnostic Series. https://www.natcom.org/sites/default/files/pages/Basic_Course _and_Gen_Ed_Conversational_Skills_Rating_Scale.pdf

Srivastava, P., & Hopwood, N. (2009). A practical iterative framework for qualitative data analysis. *International Journal of Qualitative Methods, 8*(1), 76–84. https://doi .org/10.1177/160940690900800107

Stafford, L., & Canary, D. J. (1991). Maintenance strategies and romantic relationship type, gender and relational characteristics. *Journal of Social and Personal Relationships, 8*(2), 217–242. https://doi.org/10.1177/0265407591082004

Statista (2022). *Ownership rate of smartphones in South Korea from 2011 to 2021.* Media. https://www.statista.com/statistics/777726/south-korea-smartphone-ownership/

Statistics Korea. (n.d.). *International migration statistics*. (n.d.). http://kostat.go.kr/por tal/eng/pressReleases/8/5/index.board

Sung, M., & Lee, J. (2013). Adult sibling and sibling-in-law relationships in South Korea: Continuity and change of Confucian family norms. *Journal of Comparative Family Studies, 44*(5), 571–587. https://doi.org/10.3138/jcfs.44.5.571

Suter, E. A. (2012). Negotiating identity and pragmatism: Parental treatment of international adoptees' birth culture names. *Journal of Family Communication, 12*(3), 209–226. https://doi.org/10.1080/15267431.2012.686940

Suter, E. A. (2016). Introduction: Critical approaches to family communication research: Representation, critique, and praxis. *Journal of Family Communication, 16*(1), 1–8. https://doi.org/10.1080/15267431.2015.1111219

Suter, E. A., & Ballard, R. L. (2009). "How much did you pay for her?": Decision-making criteria underlying adoptive parents' responses to inappropriate remarks. *Journal of Family Communication, 9*(2), 107–125. https://doi.org/10.1080/1526743090277 3253

Suter, E. A., Daas, K. L., & Bergen, K. M. (2008). Negotiating lesbian family identity via symbols and rituals. *Journal of Family Issues, 29*(1), 26–47. https://doi.org/10.1177 /0192513X07305752

Suter, E., & Seurer, L. (2018). Relational dialectics theory: Realizing the dialogic potential of family communication. In *Engaging theories in family communication: Multiple perspectives* (2nd ed., pp. 244–254). SAGE Publications.

Takaki, R. (1998). *Strangers from a different shore: A history of Asian Americans*. Back Bay Books: Little, Brown.

Talhelm, T., Oishi, S., & Zhang, X. (2019). Who smiles while alone? Rates of smiling lower in China than U.S. *Emotion, 19*(4), 741–745.

Tannenbaum, M. (2005). Viewing family relations through a linguistic lens: Symbolic aspects of language maintenance in immigrant families. *Journal of Family Communication, 5*(3), 229–252. https://doi.org/10.1207/s15327698jfc0503_4

Tracy, S. J. (2020). *Qualitative research methods: Collecting evidence, crafting analysis, communicating impact* (2nd ed.). Wiley.

Trenka, J. J. (2003). *The language of blood*. Graywolf Press.

Trenka, J. J., Chinyere Oparah, J., & Shin, S. Y. (Eds.). (2006). *Outsiders Within: Writing on Transracial Adoption*. South End Press.

Triandis, H. C., & Gelfand, M. J. (1998). Converging measurement of horizontal and vertical individualism and collectivism. *Journal of Personality and Social Psychology, 74*(1), 118–128. https://doi.org/10.1037/0022-3514.74.1.118

Trinder, E., Feast, J., & Howe, D. (2004). *The adoption reunion handbook*. John Wiley & Sons.

Tuan, M. (1998). *Forever foreigners or honorary Whites?: The Asian ethnic experience today*. Rutgers University Press.

23andMe. (2018, October 1). 23andme connects brothers. *23andMe Blog*. https://blog .23andme.com/ancestry-reports/23andme-connects-brothers/

23andMe. (2019, July 31). Seoul sisters and brothers. *23andMe Blog*. https://blog.23and me.com/23andme-customer-stories/seoul-sisters-and-brothers/

23andMe. (2020, September 25). Helping other Korean adoptees find their story. *23and Me Blog*. https://blog.23andme.com/23andme-customer-stories/korean-adoptee-helps -others/

U.S. Citizenship and Immigration Services. (2021, September). *Orphan Process.* https://www.uscis.gov/adoption/immigration-through-adoption/orphan-process

U.S. Department of State. (2021). *Country information—South Korea.* https://travel.state.gov/content/travel/en/Intercountry-Adoption/Intercountry-Adoption-Country-Information/KoreaRepublicof.html

U.S. Department of State. (n.d.). Adoption statistics. Travel.State.Gov. https://travel.state.gov/content/travel/en/Intercountry-Adoption/adopt_ref/adoption-statistics-esri.html?wcmmode=disabled

Van Der Kolk, B. A. (1998). Trauma and memory. *Psychiatry and Clinical Neurosciences, 52*(S1), S52–S64. https://doi.org/10.1046/j.1440-1819.1998.0520s5S97.x

Ventureyra, V. A. G., Pallier, C., & Yoo, H. Y. (2004). The loss of first language phonetic perception in adopted Koreans. *Journal of Neurolinguistics, 17*(1), 79–91. https://doi.org/10.1016/S0911-6044(03)00053-8

Vogl-Bauer, S., Kalbfleisch, P. J., & Beatty, M. J. (1999). Perceived equity, satisfaction, and relational maintenance strategies in parent–adolescent dyads. *Journal of Youth and Adolescence, 28*(1), 27–49. https://doi.org/10.1023/A:1021668424027

Volkman, T. A. (2005). Introduction. In T. A. Volkman (Ed.), *Cultures of transnational adoption* (pp. 1–22). Duke University Press.

Wamsley, L. (2018, March 1). South Korea shortens "inhumanely long" workweek. *NPR.* https://www.npr.org/sections/thetwo-way/2018/03/01/589895641/south-korea-shortens-inhumanely-long-work-week

Wang, L. K., Ponte, I. C., & Ollen, E. W. (2015). Letting her go: Western adoptive families' search and reunion with Chinese birth parents. *Adoption Quarterly, 18*(1), 45–66. https://doi.org/10.1080/10926755.2014.945703

Weaver, G. R. (1986). Understanding and coping with cross-cultural adjustment stress. In R. M. Paige (Ed), *Cross-cultural orientation. New conceptualizations and applications.* University Press of America.

Werman, M., & Yuen, L. (2013). A new magazine hopes to spark frank talk about race and identity in adoption. *The World from PRX.* https://theworld.org/stories/2013-08-15/new-magazine-hopes-spark-frank-talk-about-race-and-identity-adoption

Wiley, M. O., & Baden, A. L. (2005). Birth parents in adoption: Research, practice, and counseling psychology. *The Counseling Psychologist, 33*(1), 13–50. https://doi.org/10.1177/0011000004265961

Wolin, S. J., & Bennett, L. A. (1984). Family rituals. *Family Process, 23*(3), 401–420. https://doi.org/10.1111/j.1545-5300.1984.00401.x

Womble Edwards, C. (2019). Overcoming imposter syndrome and stereotype threat: Reconceptualizing the definition of a scholar: *Taboo: The Journal of Culture and Education, 18*(1), 18–34.

Wrobel, G. M., & Grotevant, H. D. (2019). Minding the (information) gap: What do emerging adult adoptees want to know about their birth parents? *Adoption Quarterly, 22*(1), 29–52. https://doi.org/10.1080/10926755.2018.1488332

Wrobel, G. M., Grotevant, H. D., Samek, D. R., & Von Korff, L. (2013). Adoptees' curiosity and information-seeking about birth parents in emerging adulthood: Context, motivation, and behavior. *International Journal of Behavioral Development, 37*(5), 441–450. https://doi.org/10.1177%2F0165025413486420

Yellow Bird, M. (1999). What we want to be called: Indigenous peoples' perspectives on racial and ethnic identity labels. *American Indian Quarterly, 23*(2), 1–21. https://doi.org/10.2307/1185964

Yngvesson, B. (2002). Placing the "gift child" in transnational adoption. *Law & Society Review, 36*(2), 227–256. https://doi.org/10.2307/1512176

Yngvesson, B. (2005). Going "home": Adoption, loss of bearings, and the mythology of roots. In T. A. Volkman (Ed.), *Cultures of transnational adoption*. Duke University Press.

Yum, Y. O., & Canary, D. J. (2003). Maintaining relationships in Korea and the United States: Features of Korean culture that affect relational maintenance beliefs and behaviors. In D. J. Canary & M. Dainton (Eds.), *Maintaining relationships through communication: Relational, contextual, and cultural variations* (pp. 277–296). Lawrence Erlbaum Associates.

Yum, Y. O., & Canary, D. J. (2009). Cultural differences in equity theory predictions of relational maintenance strategies. *Human Communication Research, 35*(3), 384–406. https://doi.org/10.1111/j.1468-2958.2009.01356.x

Zhang, Y. B., & Giles, H. (2017). Communication accommodation theory. In Y. Y. Kim (Ed.), *The international encyclopedia of intercultural communication* (pp. 95–108). Wiley. https://doi.org/10.1002/9781118783665

Zhou, X., Kim, J., Lee, H., & Lee, R. M. (2021). Korean adoptees as parents: Intergenerationality of ethnic, racial, and adoption socialization. *Family Relations, 70*(2), 637–652. https://doi.org/10.1111/fare.12439

Index

Sara Docan-Morgan is Professor of Communication Studies at the University of Wisconsin–La Crosse.